LARRY IN WONDERLAND

Other *Pearls Before Swine* Collections

When Pigs Fly
50,000,000 Pearls Fans Can't Be Wrong
The Saturday Evening Pearls
Macho Macho Animals
The Sopratos
Da Brudderhood of Zeeba Zeeba Eata
The Ratvolution Will Not Be Televised
Nighthogs
This Little Piggy Stayed Home
BLTs Taste So Darn Good

Treasuries

Pearls Blows Up
Pearls Sells Out
The Crass Menagerie
Lions and Tigers and Crocs, Oh My!
Sgt. Piggy's Lonely Hearts Club Comic

Gift Book

Da Crockydile Book o' Frendsheep

A *Pearls Before Swine* Collection

by Stephan Pastis

Andrews McMeel
Publishing, LLC
Kansas City • Sydney • London

Pearls Before Swine is distributed internationally by Universal Uclick.

Larry in Wonderland copyright © 2011 by Stephan Pastis. All rights reserved. Printed in the United States of America. No part of this book may be used or reproduced in any manner whatsoever without written permission except in the case of reprints in the context of reviews.

Andrews McMeel Publishing, LLC
an Andrews McMeel Universal company
1130 Walnut Street, Kansas City, Missouri 64106

www.andrewsmcmeel.com

11 12 13 14 15 RR2 10 9 8 7 6 5 4 3 2 1

ISBN: 978-1-4494-0817-6

Library of Congress Control Number: 2011921392

Pearls Before Swine can be viewed on the Internet at
www.comics.com/pearls_before_swine

These strips appeared in newspapers from August 23, 2009, to May 23, 2010.

─── **ATTENTION: SCHOOLS AND BUSINESSES** ───

Andrews McMeel books are available at quantity discounts with bulk purchase for educational, business, or sales promotional use. For information, please e-mail the Andrews McMeel Publishing Special Sales Department:
specialsales@amuniversal.com

To myself, because I've never seen anyone vain enough to do that before.

INTRODUCTION

If you write a syndicated comic strip, you really need to stay away from the "Letters to the Editor" section.

I don't know much about the section, but from the little I've been able to glean, it appears to be a place of much badness. A place where angry octogenarians go to be humorless.

Think of it this way. If the newspaper was a neighborhood, the "Letters to the Editor" section would be the old guy standing on his front porch yelling, "Hey, you stupid kids, get off of my lawn!"

And apparently, I'm on a lot of people's lawns . . .

Whittier Daily News (Whittier, California), April 16, 2008

Pearls Before Swine (has) a daily message of killing and violence. Reading the rest of the *Whittier Daily News* shows me we have plenty of killing and violence in the San Gabriel Valley. It doesn't need to be taught in our comic strips. And please don't tell me, "If you don't like it, don't read it!" My concern is for the morals of our society in general, children in particular, not just my own.

If you want your newspaper to be looked upon as an educational tool, you must accept the responsibility of uplifting society, not bringing it down to gutter level.

Other than that, the *Whittier Daily News* is a good newspaper and I enjoy reading it daily.

—(Name Deleted)
Whittier, California

Macon Telegraph, January 7, 2007

What idea or thought caused you to put *Pearls Before Swine* in (the newspaper)?

—(Name Deleted)

Kansas City Star (Kansas City, Missouri), August 18, 2005

As for *Pearls Before Swine*, there are no pearls, and we are not swine. Please do not feed us this garbage.

—(Name Deleted)
Lee's Summit, Missouri

Courier–Journal (Louisville, Kentucky), March 22, 2008

The *Courier-Journal* is messing with the comics again. This time it's serious; you've moved the comic strips around on the page! It's too bad that *Pearls Before Swine* is at the top of the page. I can't believe anyone actually reads that piece of imbecilic garbage.

—(Name Deleted)
Brandenburg, Kentucky

Daily News (Longview, Washington), January 17, 2008

I would like you to reconsider getting rid of *For Better or For Worse* in the comics. The old ones have got to be funnier than about half of the strips you run. As for *Beetle Bailey*, how funny is Sarge beating up Beetle over and over, or Beetle not working, or the men lusting over women?

As for *Pearls Before Swine*, I don't even know what to say.

—(Name Deleted)
Rainier, Washington

But sometimes the letters to the editor are entertaining. Like this next one, where the last sentence seems to be thrown in as an afterthought.

Register–Guard (Eugene, Oregon), June 25, 2006

A good comic has clever ideas and is artistically drawn. *Pearls Before Swine* fails miserably in both requirements. I may dislike *Mallard Fillmore*, but at least the author can draw artistically. *Pearls* is idiotic in its content and is drawn at the level of a 6-year-old child. There have been instances when it is denigrating to women.

—(Name Deleted)
Springfield, Oregon

Then there are times where it's not just my general imbecilic nature that offends them, but my specific imbecilic nature. As in a particular strip.

Like this one:

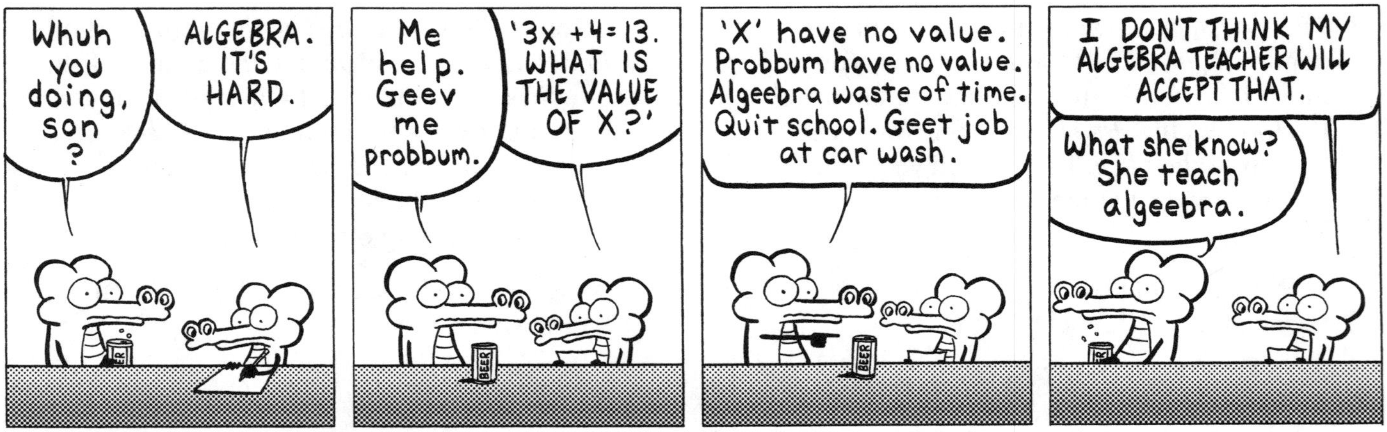

Whuh you doing, son?
ALGEBRA. IT'S HARD.
Me help. Geev me probbum.
'3x + 4 = 13. WHAT IS THE VALUE OF X?'
'X' have no value. Probbum have no value. Algeebra waste of time. Quit school. Geet job at car wash.
I DON'T THINK MY ALGEBRA TEACHER WILL ACCEPT THAT.
What she know? She teach algeebra.

Which didn't seem to please this fellow:

News–Press (Fort Myers, Florida), June 6, 2008

The fight is catching on to drop *Pearls Before Swine*, but writers do not get the nub of reasoning why it has no business in our paper. The reality is that it teaches young people, those who are learning proper English for the first time, and those whose parents speak street trash, that it's OK to say, and I quote from a recent strip: "Algeebra waste of time. Quit school. Geet job at car wash." Do our teachers not have enough to do that they have to combat this trash and prove it wrong to these kids? A couple hundred e-mails from teachers, principals, and yes, even Dr. Browder, would quickly bring the *News-Press* to its senses. I have sent in my vote, attended your meetings, and sent examples of this garbage, along with examples of a super replacement (*The Wizard of Id*) to no avail—as yet.

—(Name Deleted)
Fort Myers, Florida

Then there's this strip:

WHAT HAPPENED TO OUR STUPID GARDEN SHED? IT LOOKS LIKE IT EXPLODED.
I THINK IT WAS THOSE BUNNIES YOU TRIED TO POISON...YOU KNOW, THE ONES WHO ATE YOUR GARDEN?
WHAT MAKES YOU THINK A BUNCH OF STUPID BUNNIES COULD POSSIBLY BLOW UP OUR GARDEN SHED?
THE VIDEOTAPE THEY SENT.
GREETINGS, GREAT SATAN.

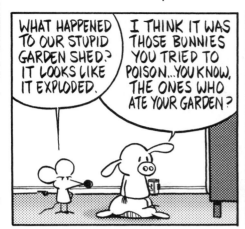

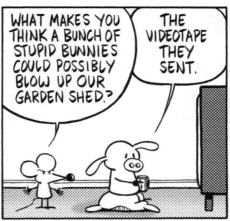

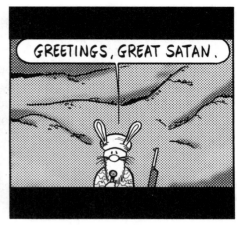

Which was not a fan favorite with this woman:

Appeal–Democrat (Marysville, California), February 24, 2008

I enjoy your paper every day. On Feb. 2, as I sat at home reading the newspaper, I read the comics and I came to the cartoon *Pearls Before Swine*. I could not believe what I was reading. It talked about a garden shed that had blown up because a rabbit had eaten the swine's garden. The last frame shows the rabbit in a video calling on Satan as if trying to get his help. Two times during the day I overheard someone mentioning this comic with disbelief.

—(Name Deleted)
Live Oak, California

And then there's this strip:

HEY, JOHNNY MALLARD... HOW ARE THINGS?
GOOD, PIG... I SAW THE CUTEST LITTLE DUCK AT THE POND TODAY, BUT I DIDN'T HAVE THE COURAGE TO TALK TO HER.
HEY... YOU KNOW WHAT THEY SAY... YOU ONLY LIVE ONCE! SEIZE THE DAY!
YOU'RE RIGHT! SHE'S SO PRETTY AND QUIET AND DEMURE... THANKS, PIG!... I'LL DO IT!
...GOT HIM.
SCORE ONE FOR THE DECOY.

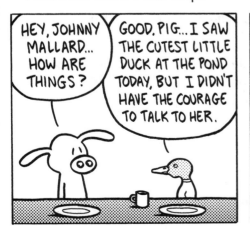

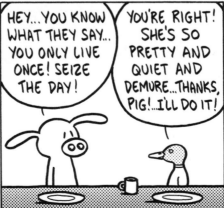

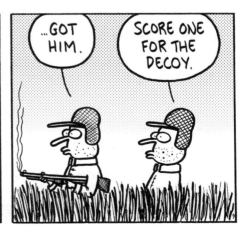

Which did not win me many points with this woman:

Press Democrat (Santa Rosa, California), February 16, 2008

I had to write about the *Pearls Before Swine* comic that appeared on Feb. 5. I fail to see what was funny about this "comic," where the pig tells the duck, "You only live once! Seize the day!" after the duck tells him he doesn't have the courage to approach the cute little duck at the pond. The duck then approaches the cute little duck and is blown away by the duck hunters. I suppose kids will be sad that the duck was killed, but maybe someone will say, "Awesome, they got him!" Is the latter reaction the kind of mentality this comic wants to appeal to. . . . You only live once, so seize the day and then get killed?

—(Name Deleted)
Healdsburg, California

But I don't want you to think *Pearls* is without its supporters. It has them. As you can see here:

Standard–Examiner (Ogden, Utah), July 25, 2010

Valdes E-Mails Letter to Paper

OGDEN—As Jeremy Valdes faces the death penalty in a double homicide, he recently e-mailed a letter to the *Standard-Examiner*, much to the surprise of lawyers on both sides of the case.

Commenting on a June 25 hearing on a motion to suppress his apparent confession to the murders, Valdes comments on a police officer cousin's testimony against him, calling another officer apparently drunk on the stand, and attacks, mildly, the credibility of his co-defendant Miranda Statler. She is the main witness against him and is already serving a potential 20-year prison term for her guilty pleas in the murder case.

Valdes also faults the *Standard-Examiner*'s coverage, and concludes by casting votes for cartoons under consideration by the paper.

"While I have you here, my friends and I would like to request that you bring back the comics, *Pearls Before Swine* and *Garfield*. Thank you."

And if that's not the greatest letter to the editor ever printed, I don't know what is.

Now if you'll excuse me, I have more lawns to stand on.

Stephan Pastis
August 2011

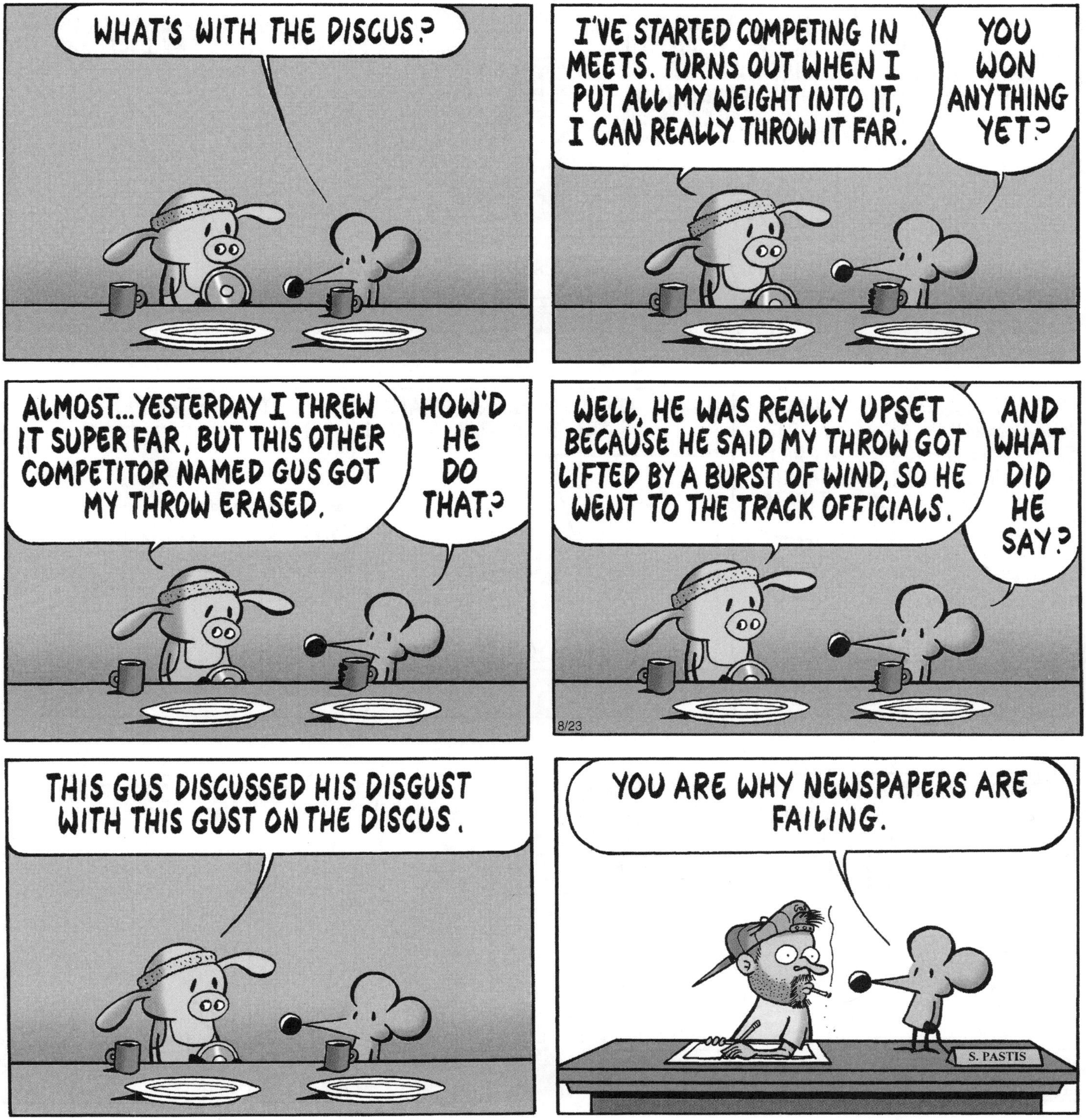
WHAT'S WITH THE DISCUS?
I'VE STARTED COMPETING IN MEETS. TURNS OUT WHEN I PUT ALL MY WEIGHT INTO IT, I CAN REALLY THROW IT FAR.
YOU WON ANYTHING YET?
ALMOST...YESTERDAY I THREW IT SUPER FAR, BUT THIS OTHER COMPETITOR NAMED GUS GOT MY THROW ERASED.
HOW'D HE DO THAT?
WELL, HE WAS REALLY UPSET BECAUSE HE SAID MY THROW GOT LIFTED BY A BURST OF WIND, SO HE WENT TO THE TRACK OFFICIALS.
AND WHAT DID HE SAY?
8/23
THIS GUS DISCUSSED HIS DISGUST WITH THIS GUST ON THE DISCUS.
YOU ARE WHY NEWSPAPERS ARE FAILING.
S. PASTIS

EXCUSE ME, BUT I'D LIKE TO PICK UP MY SHIRT PLEASE....

DRY CLEANING

OH NO...THERE'S A BIG RIP IN IT, JUST LIKE WITH THE SHIRT I GAVE YOU LAST WEEK.

DRY CLEANING

Arrrgh.

BLACKBEARD'S DRY CLEANING

PIRATES MAKE LOUSY DRY CLEANERS.

DUDE, THERE'S TOO MUCH STARCH IN MY SHIRT. TAKE IT BACK TO THE DRY CLEANER AND COMPLAIN.

I DON'T WANT TO. MY DRY CLEANER'S A PIRATE.

DUDE. IT'S A COMPLAINT. WHAT'S THE BIG DEAL?

IT'S A BIG DEAL.

KBEARD'S DRY CLEANING

OPEN

YE SAME DAY SERVICE

LISTEN, BLACKBEARD, I NEED TO PICK UP MY SUIT EVEN THOUGH YOU HAVEN'T CLEANED IT YET. IT WAS REALLY EXPENSIVE, AND NO OFFENSE, BUT I'D HATE FOR ANYTHING TO HAPPEN TO IT.

RD'S DRY CLEANING

ARRRR

YOU HAVE MY SUIT BUT YOU'RE NOT GONNA TELL ME WHERE IT IS? THEN HOW AM I SUPPOSED TO FIND IT?

D'S DRY CLEANING

ARRRR

Ye MAP

RD'S CLEANING

LONG STORY.

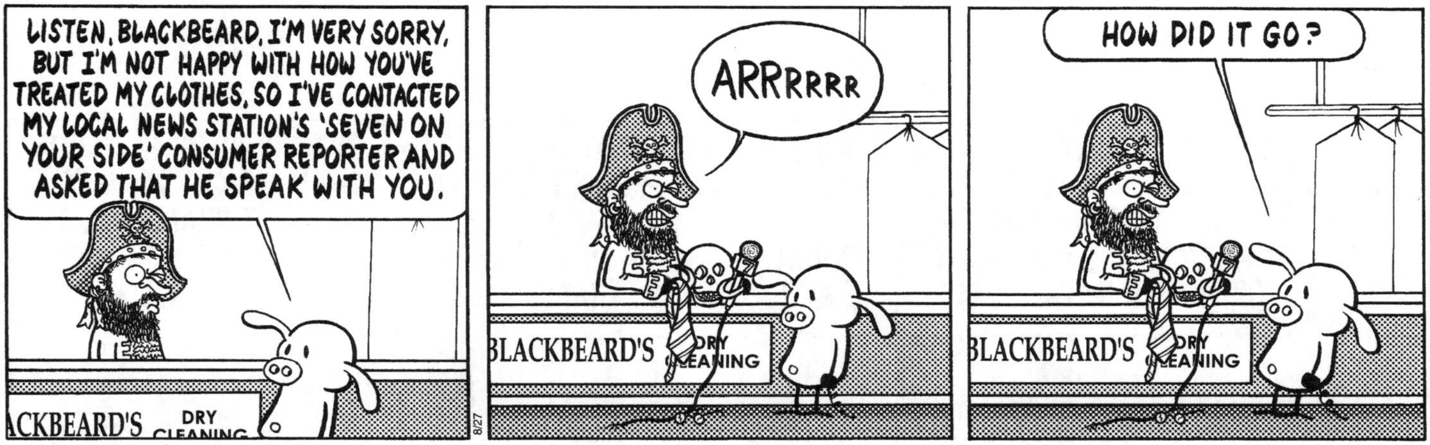
LISTEN, BLACKBEARD, I'M VERY SORRY, BUT I'M NOT HAPPY WITH HOW YOU'VE TREATED MY CLOTHES, SO I'VE CONTACTED MY LOCAL NEWS STATION'S 'SEVEN ON YOUR SIDE' CONSUMER REPORTER AND ASKED THAT HE SPEAK WITH YOU.
ACKBEARD'S DRY CLEANING
8/27
ARRRRRR
BLACKBEARD'S DRY CLEANING
HOW DID IT GO?
BLACKBEARD'S DRY CLEANING

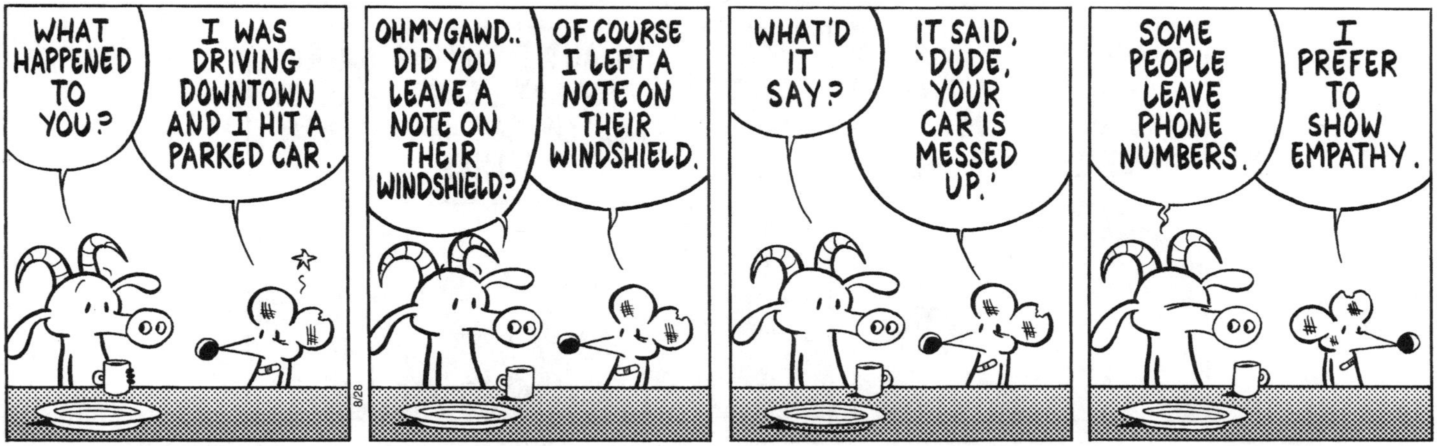
WHAT HAPPENED TO YOU?
I WAS DRIVING DOWNTOWN AND I HIT A PARKED CAR.
8/28
OHMYGAWD.. DID YOU LEAVE A NOTE ON THEIR WINDSHIELD?
OF COURSE I LEFT A NOTE ON THEIR WINDSHIELD.
WHAT'D IT SAY?
IT SAID, 'DUDE, YOUR CAR IS MESSED UP.'
SOME PEOPLE LEAVE PHONE NUMBERS.
I PREFER TO SHOW EMPATHY.

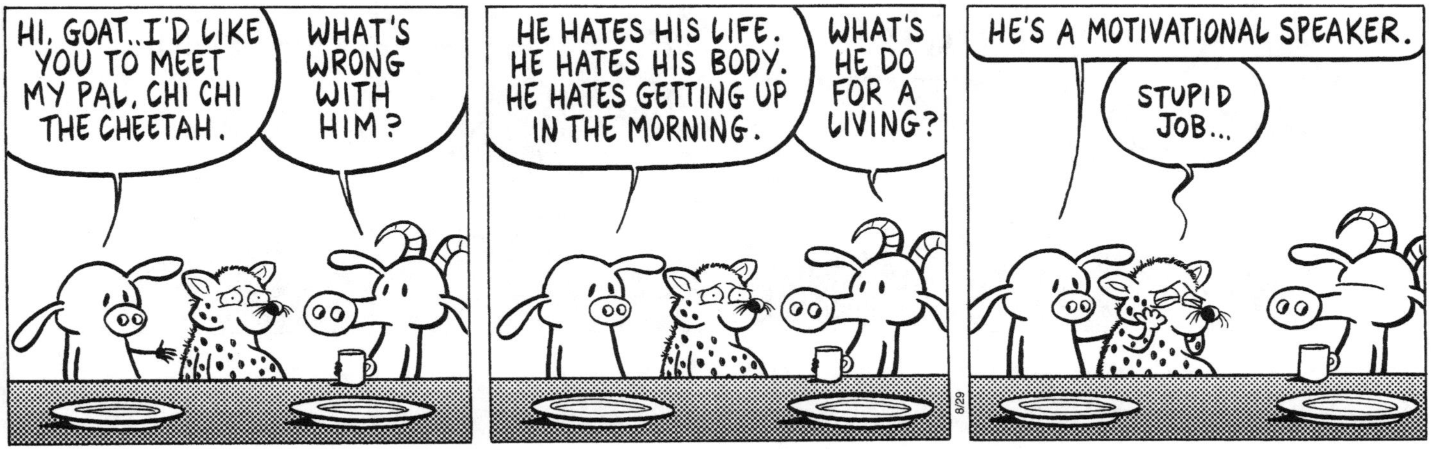
HI, GOAT..I'D LIKE YOU TO MEET MY PAL, CHI CHI THE CHEETAH.
WHAT'S WRONG WITH HIM?
HE HATES HIS LIFE. HE HATES HIS BODY. HE HATES GETTING UP IN THE MORNING.
WHAT'S HE DO FOR A LIVING?
8/29
HE'S A MOTIVATIONAL SPEAKER.
STUPID JOB...

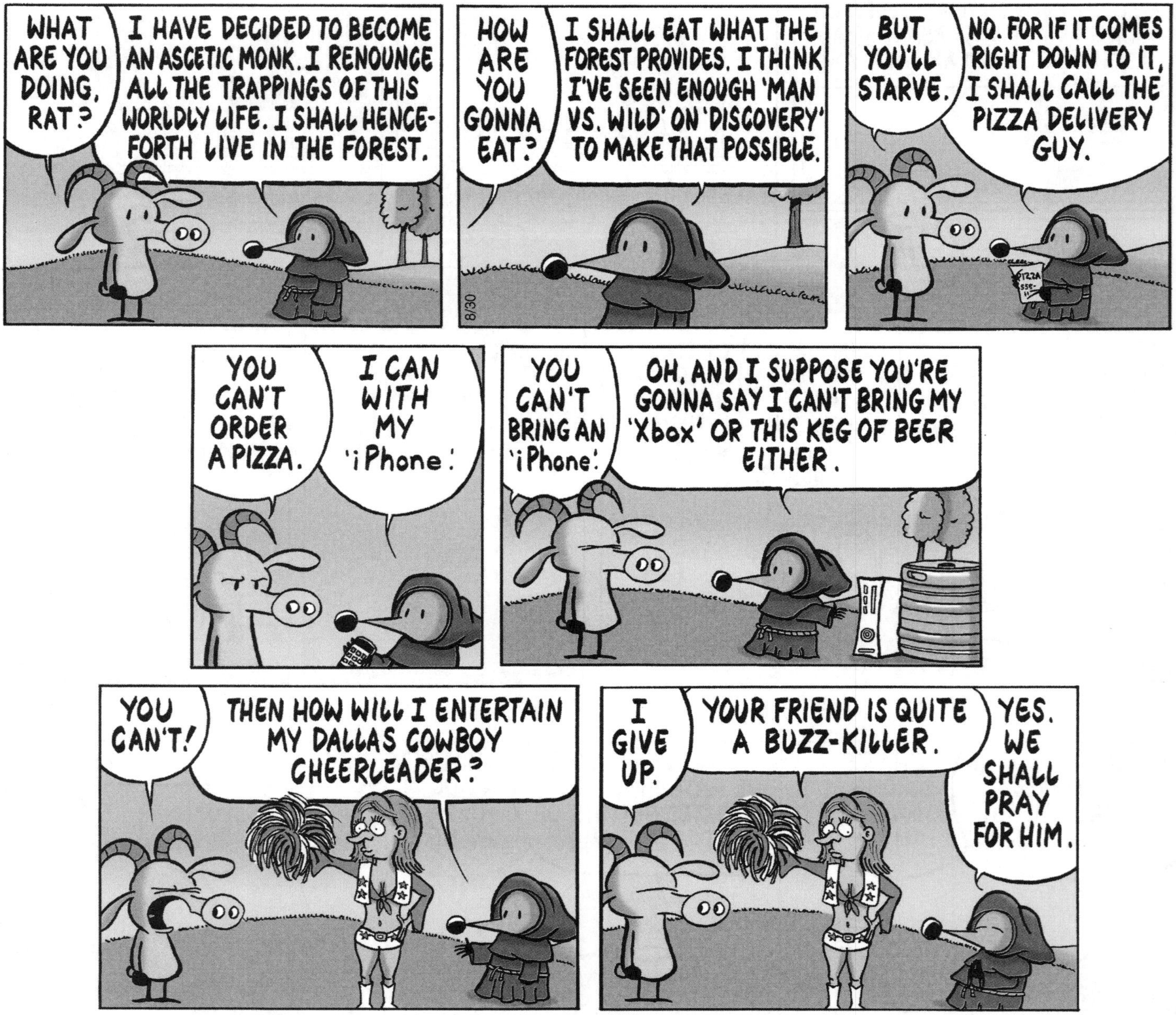
WHAT ARE YOU DOING, RAT?
I HAVE DECIDED TO BECOME AN ASCETIC MONK. I RENOUNCE ALL THE TRAPPINGS OF THIS WORLDLY LIFE. I SHALL HENCEFORTH LIVE IN THE FOREST.
HOW ARE YOU GONNA EAT?
I SHALL EAT WHAT THE FOREST PROVIDES. I THINK I'VE SEEN ENOUGH 'MAN VS. WILD' ON 'DISCOVERY' TO MAKE THAT POSSIBLE.
8/30
BUT YOU'LL STARVE.
NO. FOR IF IT COMES RIGHT DOWN TO IT, I SHALL CALL THE PIZZA DELIVERY GUY.
YOU CAN'T ORDER A PIZZA.
I CAN WITH MY 'iPhone.'
YOU CAN'T BRING AN 'iPhone.'
OH, AND I SUPPOSE YOU'RE GONNA SAY I CAN'T BRING MY 'Xbox' OR THIS KEG OF BEER EITHER.
YOU CAN'T!
THEN HOW WILL I ENTERTAIN MY DALLAS COWBOY CHEERLEADER?
I GIVE UP.
YOUR FRIEND IS QUITE A BUZZ-KILLER.
YES. WE SHALL PRAY FOR HIM.

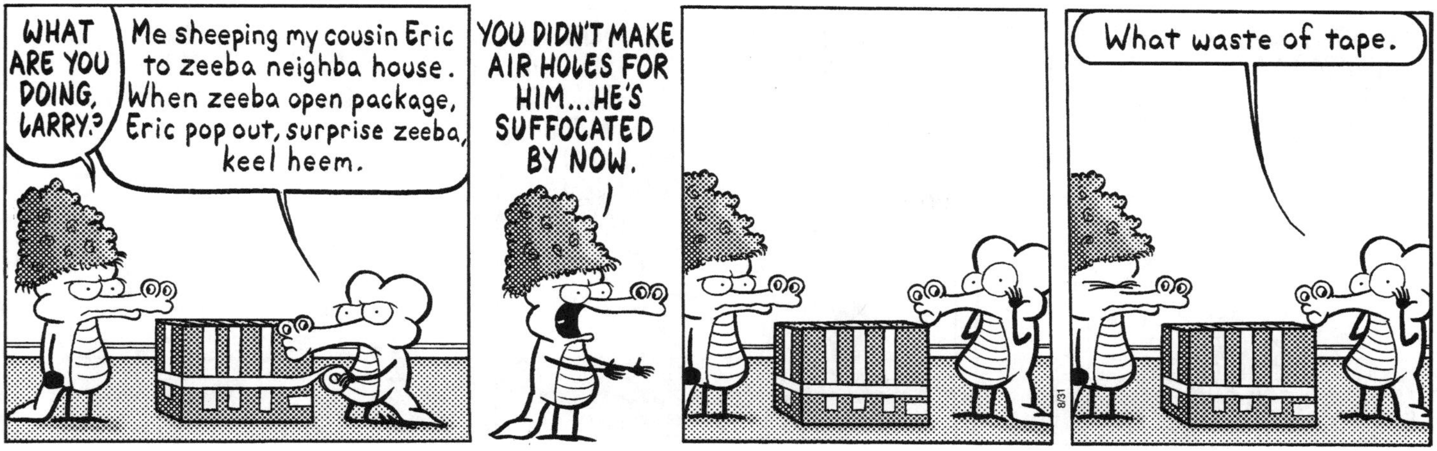

WHAT ARE YOU DOING, LARRY?
Me sheeping my cousin Eric to zeeba neighba house. When zeeba open package, Eric pop out, surprise zeeba, keel heem.
YOU DIDN'T MAKE AIR HOLES FOR HIM... HE'S SUFFOCATED BY NOW.
What waste of tape.
8/31

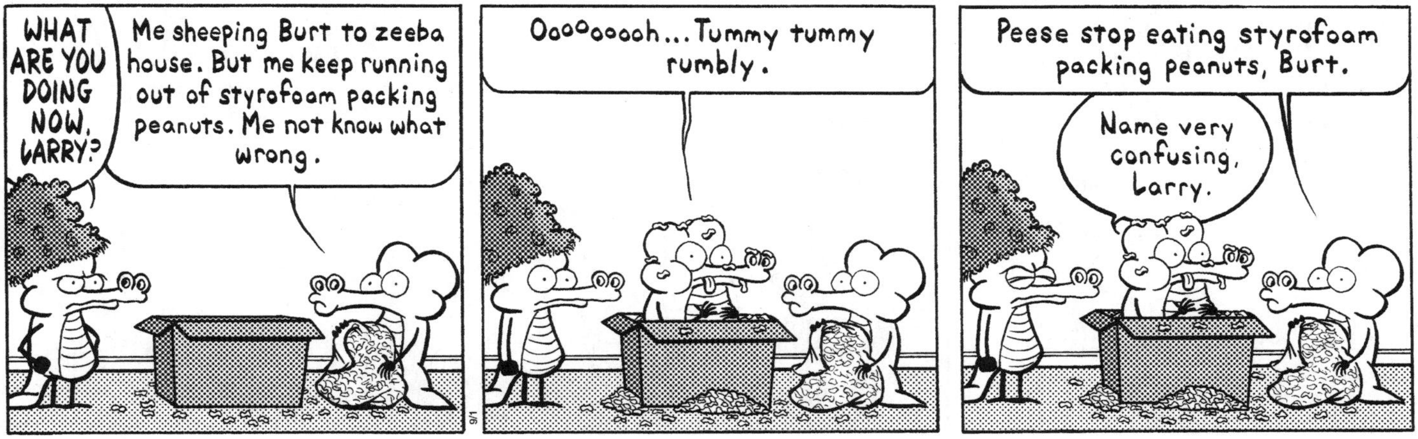

WHAT ARE YOU DOING NOW, LARRY?
Me sheeping Burt to zeeba house. But me keep running out of styrofoam packing peanuts. Me not know what wrong.
9/1
Oooooooh... Tummy tummy rumbly.
Peese stop eating styrofoam packing peanuts, Burt.
Name very confusing, Larry.

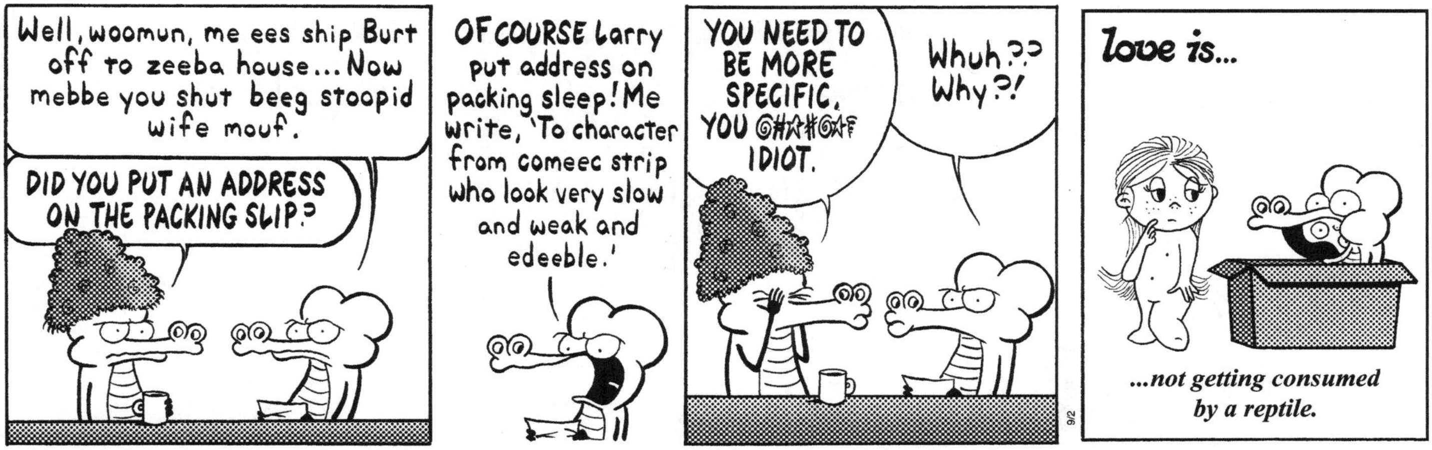

Well, woomun, me ees ship Burt off to zeeba house... Now mebbe you shut beeg stoopid wife mouf.
DID YOU PUT AN ADDRESS ON THE PACKING SLIP?
OF COURSE Larry put address on packing sleep! Me write, 'To character from comeec strip who look very slow and weak and edeeble.'
YOU NEED TO BE MORE SPECIFIC, YOU @#*#@*! IDIOT.
Whuh?? Why?!
9/2
love is...
...not getting consumed by a reptile.

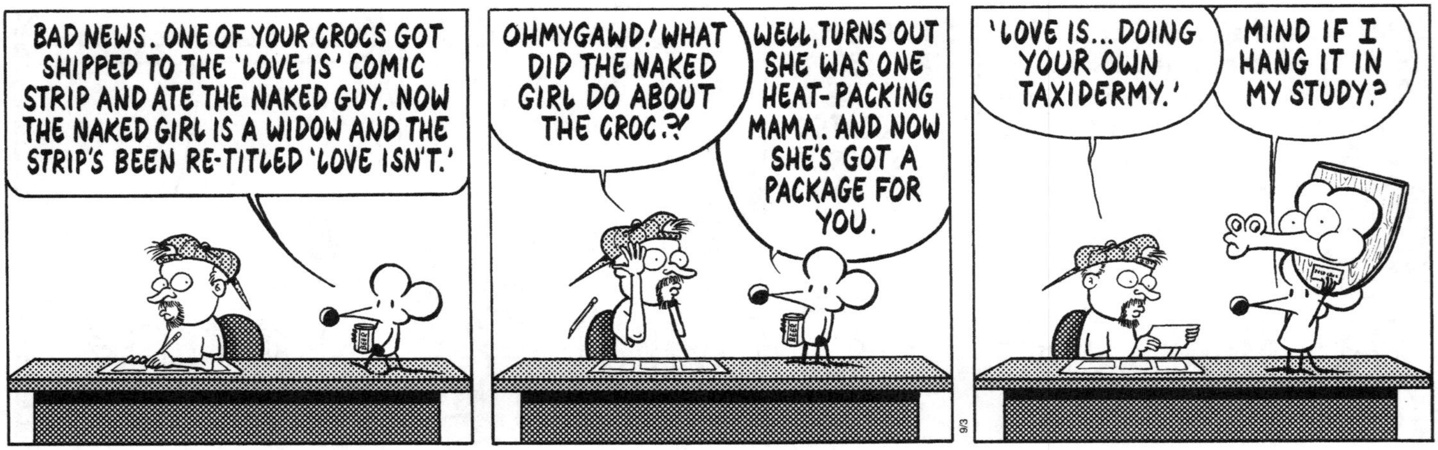
BAD NEWS. ONE OF YOUR CROCS GOT SHIPPED TO THE 'LOVE IS' COMIC STRIP AND ATE THE NAKED GUY. NOW THE NAKED GIRL IS A WIDOW AND THE STRIP'S BEEN RE-TITLED 'LOVE ISN'T.'
OHMYGAWD! WHAT DID THE NAKED GIRL DO ABOUT THE CROC?!
WELL, TURNS OUT SHE WAS ONE HEAT-PACKING MAMA. AND NOW SHE'S GOT A PACKAGE FOR YOU.
'LOVE IS... DOING YOUR OWN TAXIDERMY.'
MIND IF I HANG IT IN MY STUDY?
9/3

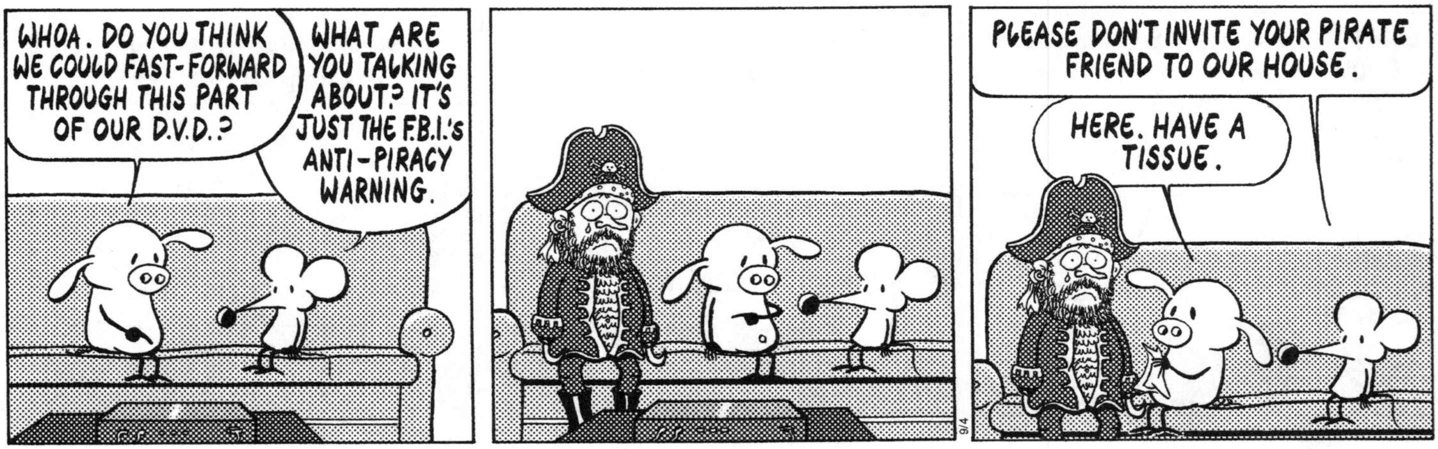
WHOA. DO YOU THINK WE COULD FAST-FORWARD THROUGH THIS PART OF OUR D.V.D.?
WHAT ARE YOU TALKING ABOUT? IT'S JUST THE F.B.I.'s ANTI-PIRACY WARNING.
PLEASE DON'T INVITE YOUR PIRATE FRIEND TO OUR HOUSE.
HERE. HAVE A TISSUE.
9/4

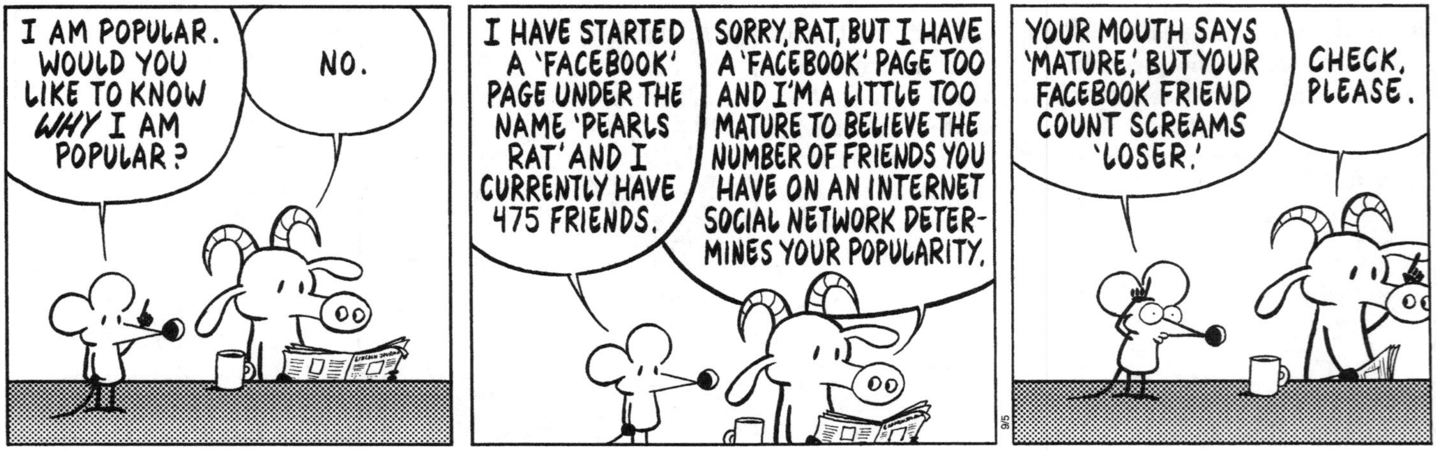
I AM POPULAR. WOULD YOU LIKE TO KNOW WHY I AM POPULAR?
NO.
I HAVE STARTED A 'FACEBOOK' PAGE UNDER THE NAME 'PEARLS RAT' AND I CURRENTLY HAVE 475 FRIENDS.
SORRY, RAT, BUT I HAVE A 'FACEBOOK' PAGE TOO AND I'M A LITTLE TOO MATURE TO BELIEVE THE NUMBER OF FRIENDS YOU HAVE ON AN INTERNET SOCIAL NETWORK DETERMINES YOUR POPULARITY.
YOUR MOUTH SAYS 'MATURE,' BUT YOUR FACEBOOK FRIEND COUNT SCREAMS 'LOSER.'
CHECK, PLEASE.
9/5

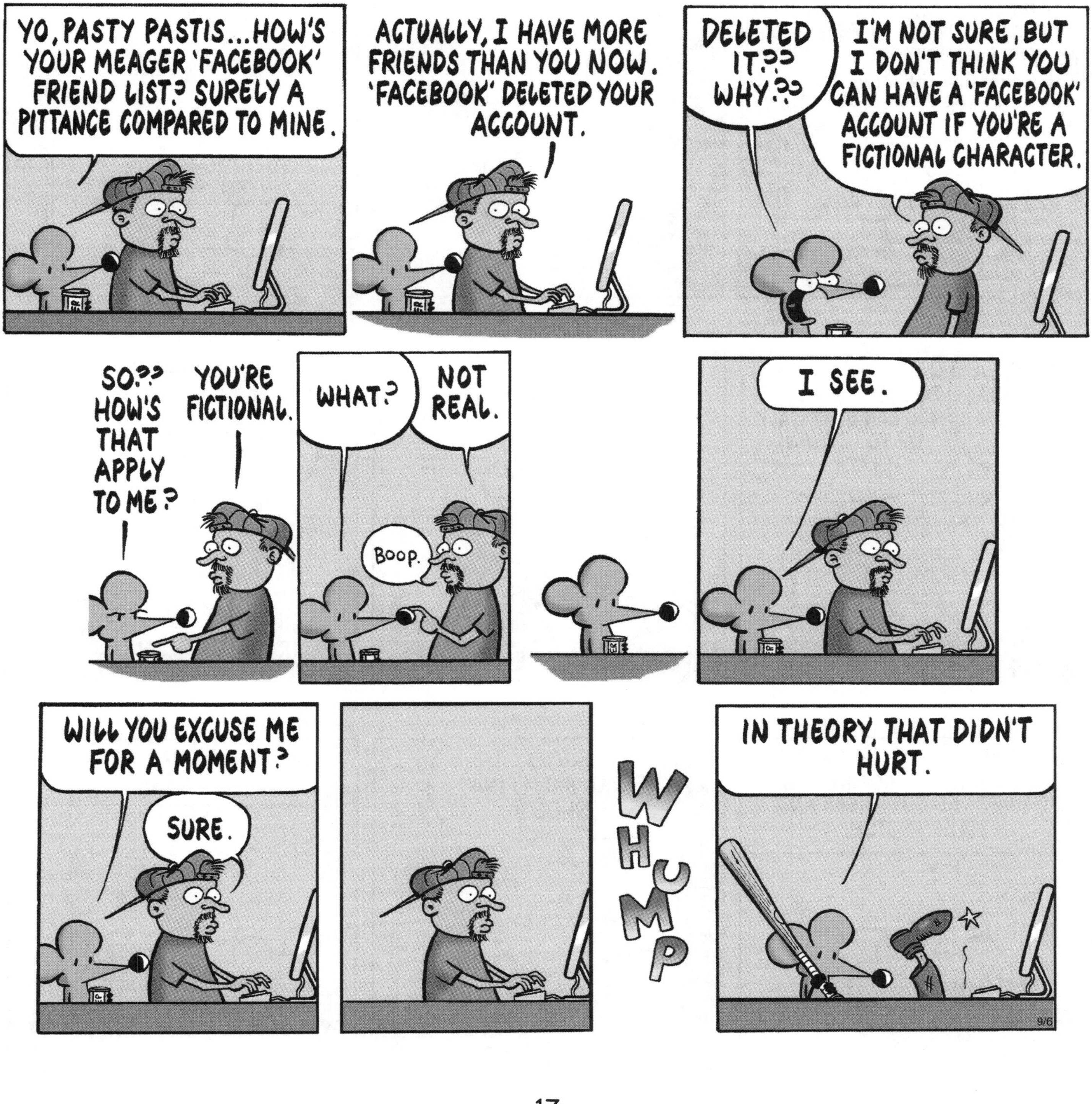
YO, PASTY PASTIS...HOW'S YOUR MEAGER 'FACEBOOK' FRIEND LIST? SURELY A PITTANCE COMPARED TO MINE.
ACTUALLY, I HAVE MORE FRIENDS THAN YOU NOW. 'FACEBOOK' DELETED YOUR ACCOUNT.
DELETED IT?? WHY??
I'M NOT SURE, BUT I DON'T THINK YOU CAN HAVE A 'FACEBOOK' ACCOUNT IF YOU'RE A FICTIONAL CHARACTER.
SO?? HOW'S THAT APPLY TO ME?
YOU'RE FICTIONAL.
WHAT?
NOT REAL.
BOOP.
I SEE.
WILL YOU EXCUSE ME FOR A MOMENT?
SURE.
WHUMP
IN THEORY, THAT DIDN'T HURT.
9/6

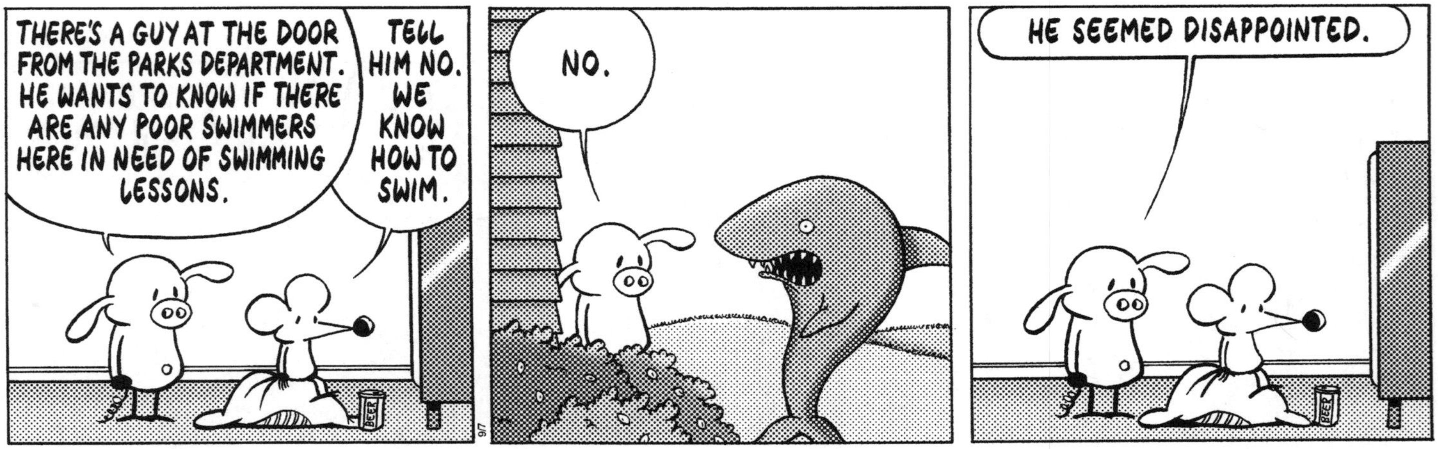
THERE'S A GUY AT THE DOOR FROM THE PARKS DEPARTMENT. HE WANTS TO KNOW IF THERE ARE ANY POOR SWIMMERS HERE IN NEED OF SWIMMING LESSONS.
TELL HIM NO. WE KNOW HOW TO SWIM.
BEER
9/7
NO.
HE SEEMED DISAPPOINTED.
BEER

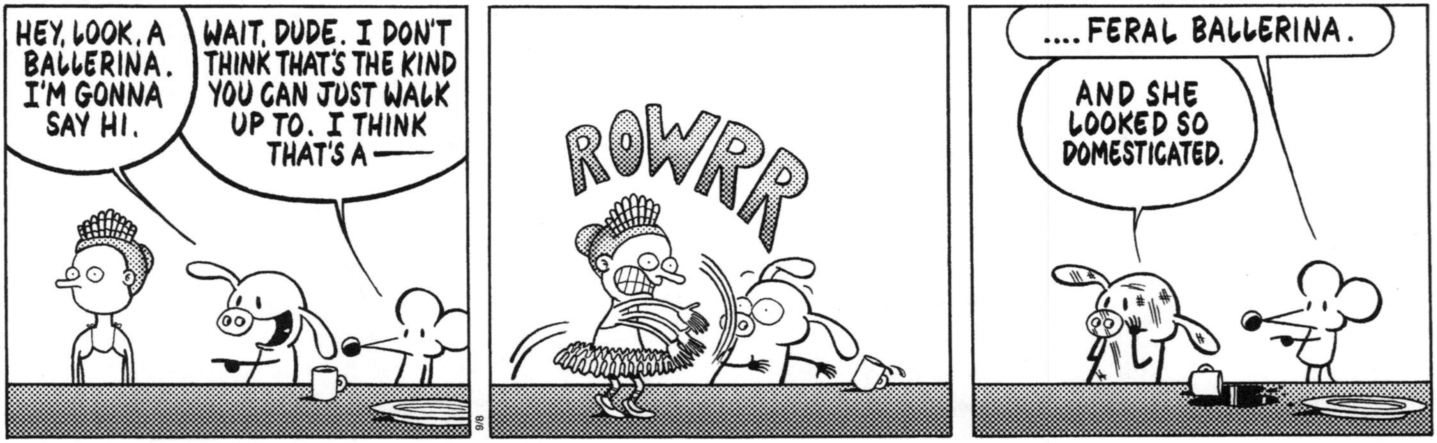
HEY, LOOK. A BALLERINA. I'M GONNA SAY HI.
WAIT, DUDE. I DON'T THINK THAT'S THE KIND YOU CAN JUST WALK UP TO. I THINK THAT'S A ——
9/8
ROWRR
.... FERAL BALLERINA.
AND SHE LOOKED SO DOMESTICATED.

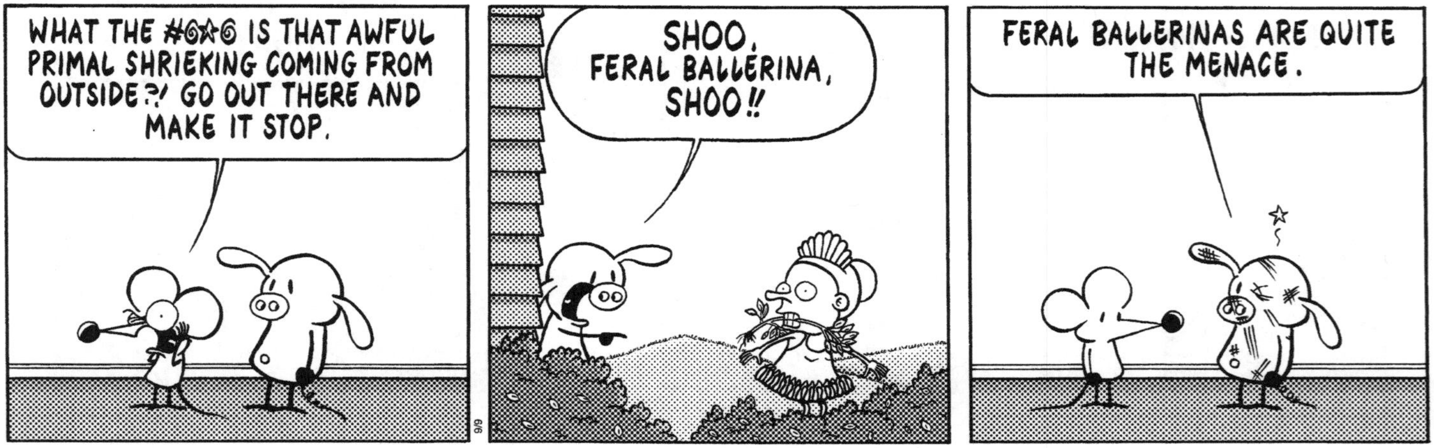
WHAT THE #@☆@ IS THAT AWFUL PRIMAL SHRIEKING COMING FROM OUTSIDE?! GO OUT THERE AND MAKE IT STOP.
9/9
SHOO, FERAL BALLERINA, SHOO!!
FERAL BALLERINAS ARE QUITE THE MENACE.

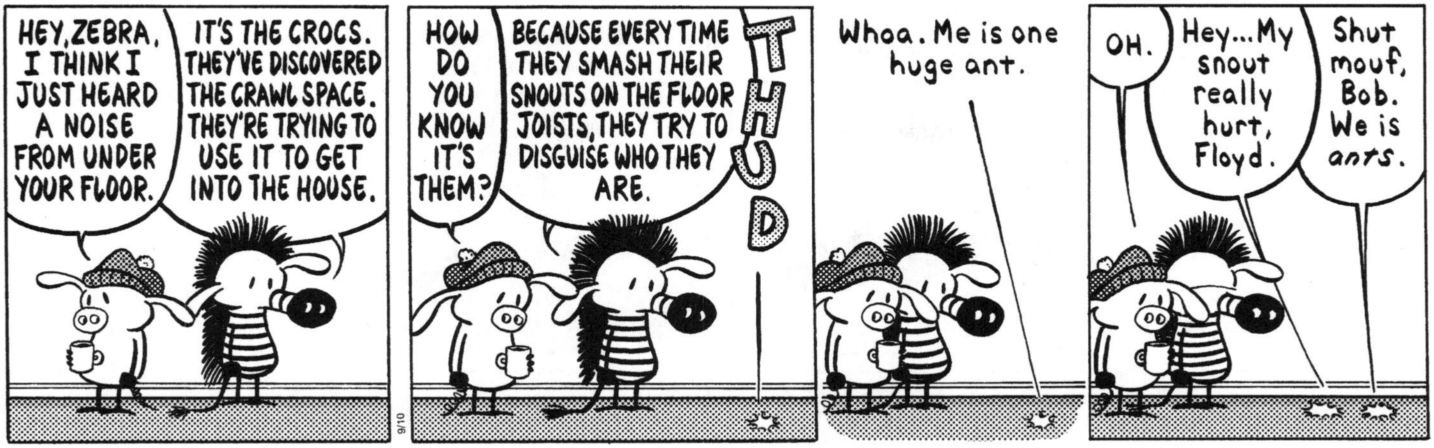
HEY, ZEBRA, I THINK I JUST HEARD A NOISE FROM UNDER YOUR FLOOR.
IT'S THE CROCS. THEY'VE DISCOVERED THE CRAWL SPACE. THEY'RE TRYING TO USE IT TO GET INTO THE HOUSE.
9/10
HOW DO YOU KNOW IT'S THEM?
BECAUSE EVERY TIME THEY SMASH THEIR SNOUTS ON THE FLOOR JOISTS, THEY TRY TO DISGUISE WHO THEY ARE.
THUD
Whoa. Me is one huge ant.
OH.
Hey...My snout really hurt, Floyd.
Shut mouf, Bob. We is *ants*.

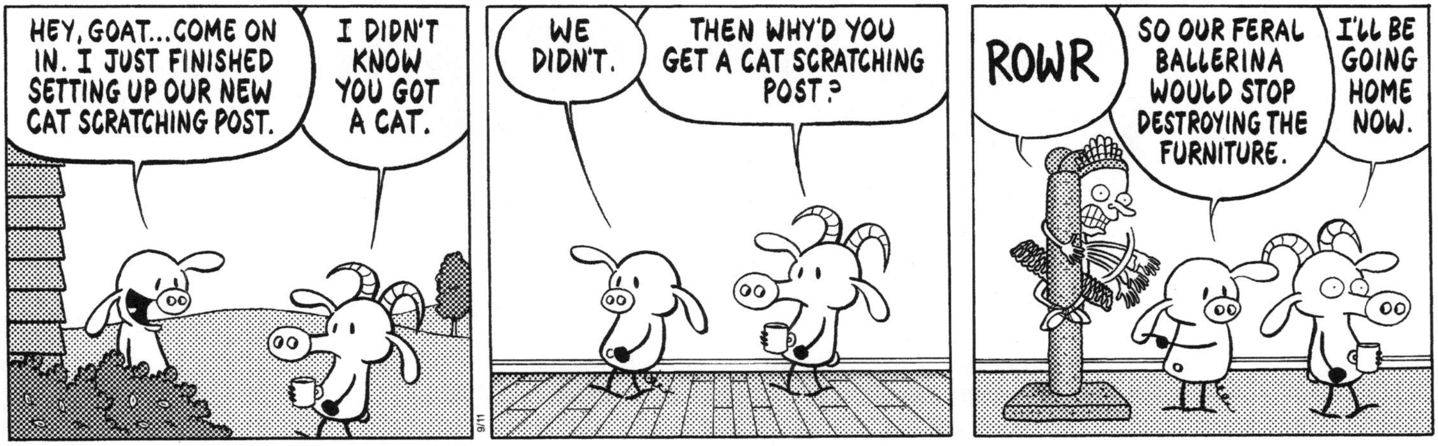
HEY, GOAT...COME ON IN. I JUST FINISHED SETTING UP OUR NEW CAT SCRATCHING POST.
I DIDN'T KNOW YOU GOT A CAT.
9/11
WE DIDN'T.
THEN WHY'D YOU GET A CAT SCRATCHING POST?
ROWR
SO OUR FERAL BALLERINA WOULD STOP DESTROYING THE FURNITURE.
I'LL BE GOING HOME NOW.

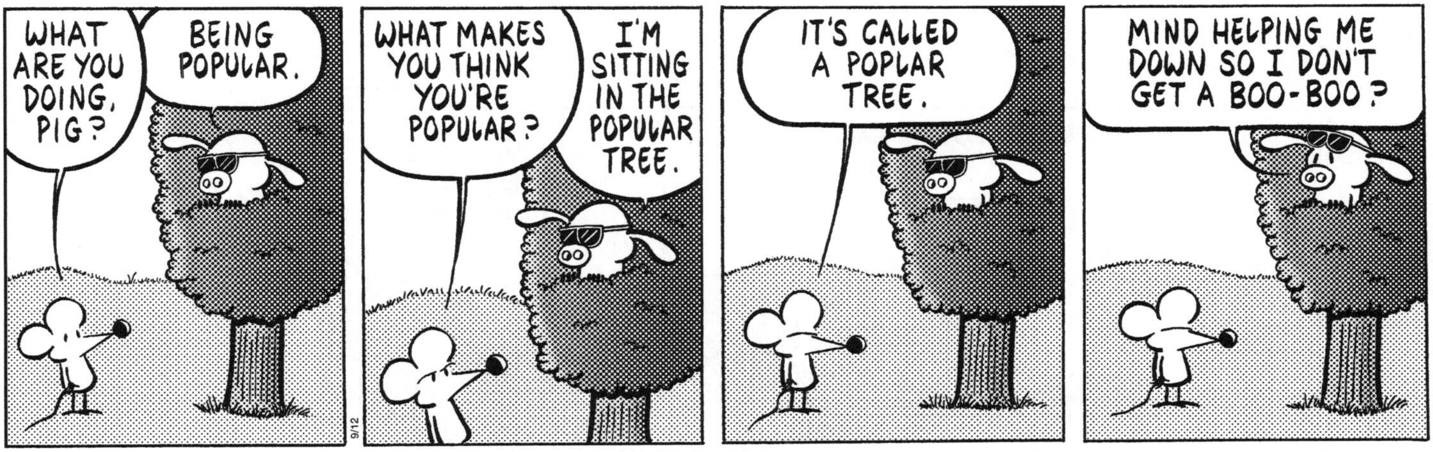
WHAT ARE YOU DOING, PIG?
BEING POPULAR.
9/12
WHAT MAKES YOU THINK YOU'RE POPULAR?
I'M SITTING IN THE POPULAR TREE.
IT'S CALLED A POPLAR TREE.
MIND HELPING ME DOWN SO I DON'T GET A BOO-BOO?

Elly Elephant
wanted
romance.

She wanted a knight.
She wanted brave.
She wanted bold.

She wanted Cary Grant.
She wanted held hands.
She wanted Central Park
in the rain.

She wanted intelligence.
She wanted depth.
She wanted books read together
with tea by the fire.

9/13

She wanted passion
and surprise.
Tuxedos
and bow ties.
Truth and
not the lies.
Hellos and
not goodbyes.

One embrace that
never dies.
To the tune of
heartfelt sighs.
All lost in
deep brown eyes.
Uninterrupted
by the cries...

of

"OPEN YOUR #%&$#%# EYES,
REF!"

Elly Elephant settled
for chocolate and
a romance novel.

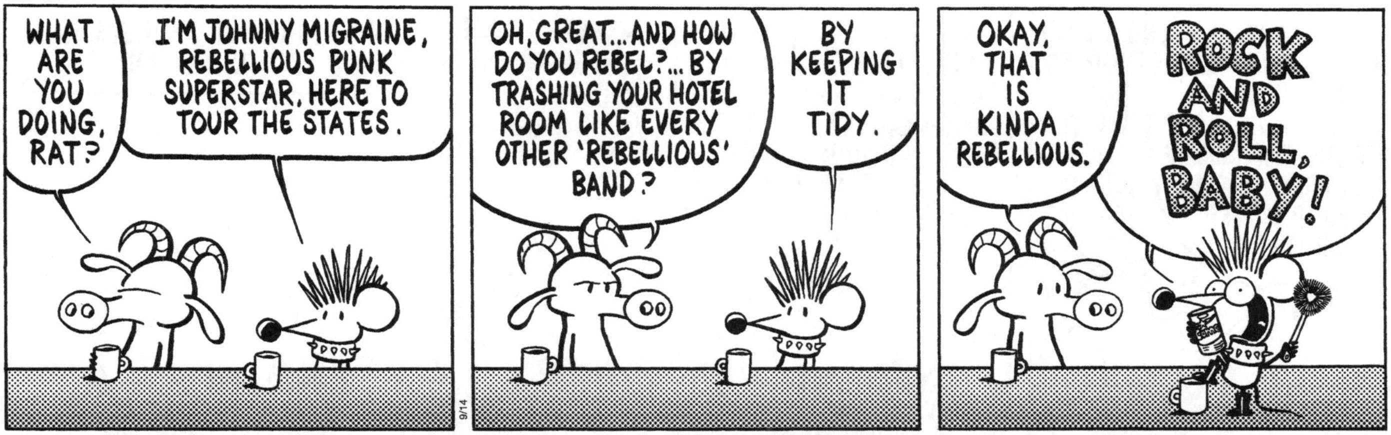
WHAT ARE YOU DOING, RAT?
I'M JOHNNY MIGRAINE, REBELLIOUS PUNK SUPERSTAR, HERE TO TOUR THE STATES.
9/14
OH, GREAT... AND HOW DO YOU REBEL?... BY TRASHING YOUR HOTEL ROOM LIKE EVERY OTHER 'REBELLIOUS' BAND?
BY KEEPING IT TIDY.
OKAY, THAT IS KINDA REBELLIOUS.
ROCK AND ROLL, BABY!

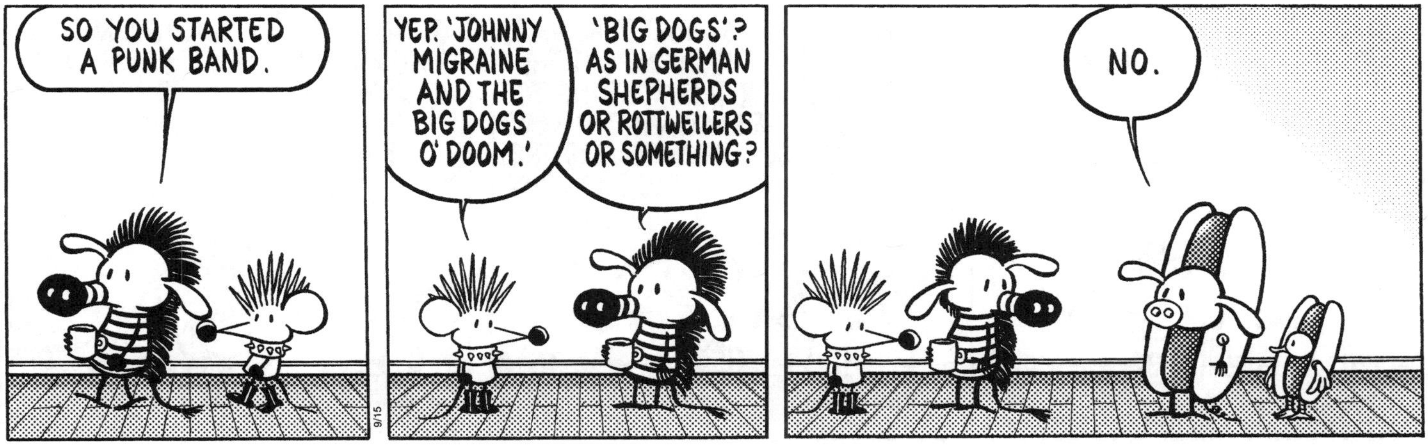
SO YOU STARTED A PUNK BAND.
9/15
YEP. 'JOHNNY MIGRAINE AND THE BIG DOGS O' DOOM.'
'BIG DOGS'? AS IN GERMAN SHEPHERDS OR ROTTWEILERS OR SOMETHING?
NO.

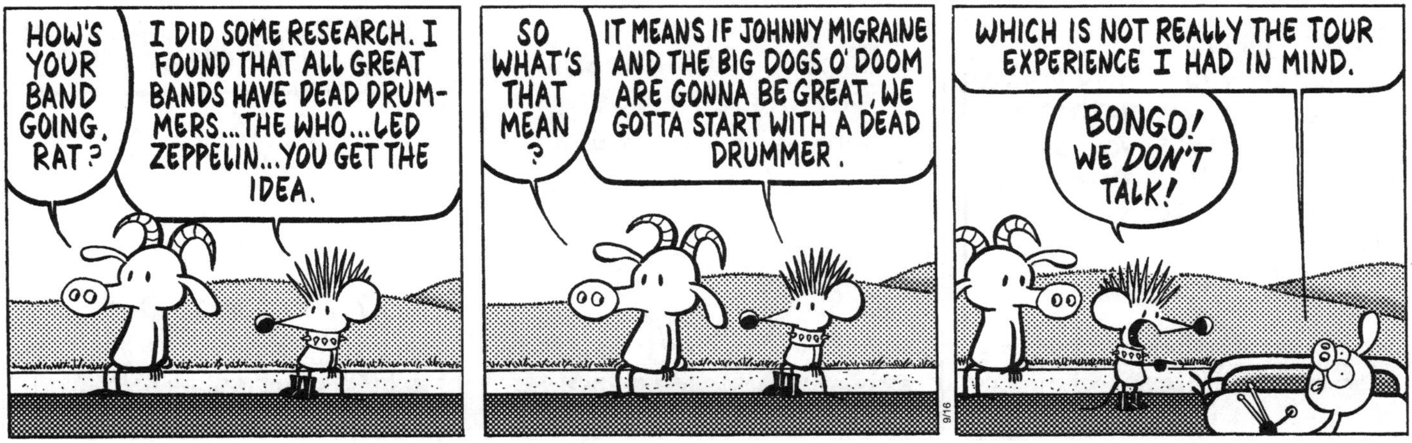
HOW'S YOUR BAND GOING, RAT?
I DID SOME RESEARCH. I FOUND THAT ALL GREAT BANDS HAVE DEAD DRUMMERS... THE WHO... LED ZEPPELIN... YOU GET THE IDEA.
SO WHAT'S THAT MEAN?
IT MEANS IF JOHNNY MIGRAINE AND THE BIG DOGS O' DOOM ARE GONNA BE GREAT, WE GOTTA START WITH A DEAD DRUMMER.
9/16
WHICH IS NOT REALLY THE TOUR EXPERIENCE I HAD IN MIND.
BONGO! WE *DON'T* TALK!

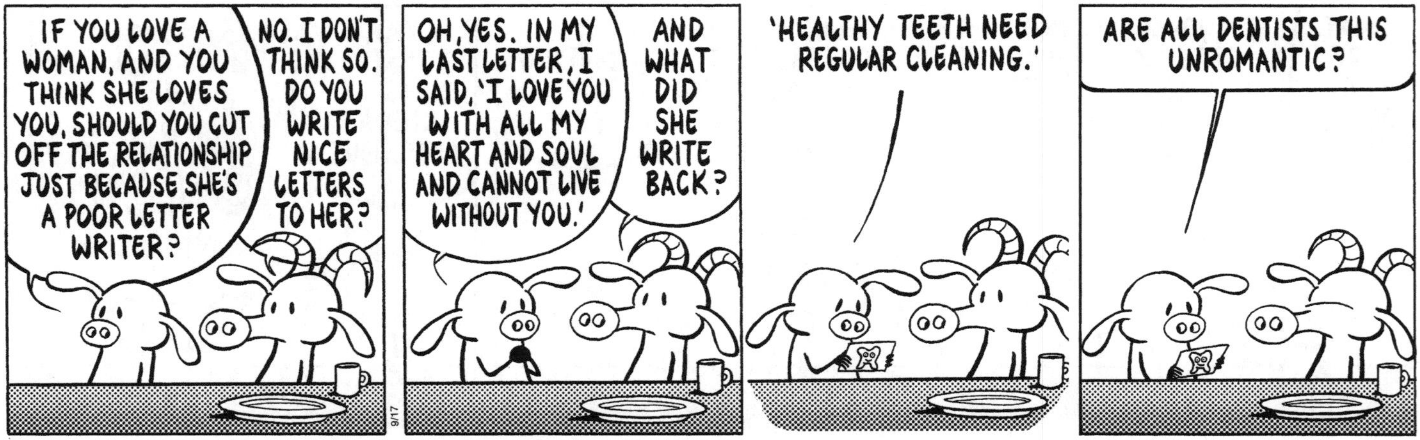
IF YOU LOVE A WOMAN, AND YOU THINK SHE LOVES YOU, SHOULD YOU CUT OFF THE RELATIONSHIP JUST BECAUSE SHE'S A POOR LETTER WRITER?
NO. I DON'T THINK SO. DO YOU WRITE NICE LETTERS TO HER?
OH, YES. IN MY LAST LETTER, I SAID, 'I LOVE YOU WITH ALL MY HEART AND SOUL AND CANNOT LIVE WITHOUT YOU.'
AND WHAT DID SHE WRITE BACK?
'HEALTHY TEETH NEED REGULAR CLEANING.'
ARE ALL DENTISTS THIS UNROMANTIC?
9/17

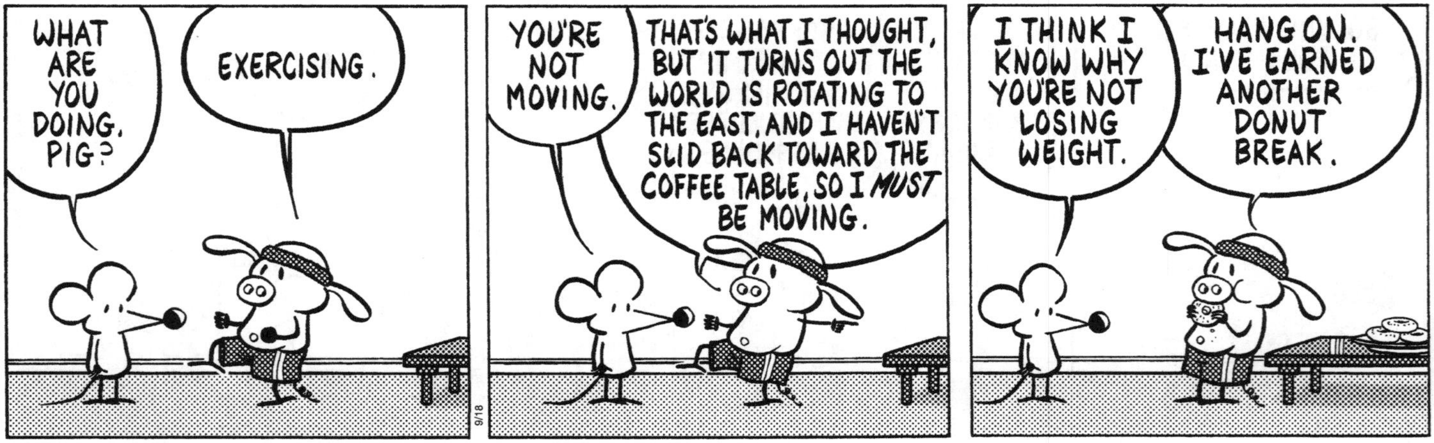
WHAT ARE YOU DOING, PIG?
EXERCISING.
YOU'RE NOT MOVING.
THAT'S WHAT I THOUGHT, BUT IT TURNS OUT THE WORLD IS ROTATING TO THE EAST, AND I HAVEN'T SLID BACK TOWARD THE COFFEE TABLE, SO I MUST BE MOVING.
I THINK I KNOW WHY YOU'RE NOT LOSING WEIGHT.
HANG ON. I'VE EARNED ANOTHER DONUT BREAK.
9/18

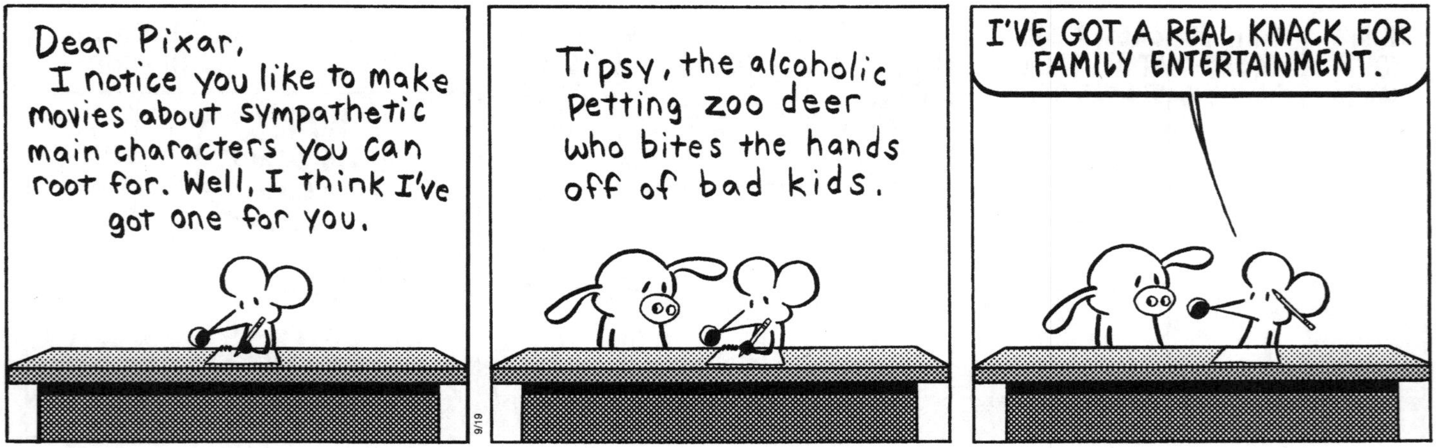
Dear Pixar,
I notice you like to make movies about sympathetic main characters you can root for. Well, I think I've got one for you.
Tipsy, the alcoholic petting zoo deer who bites the hands off of bad kids.
I'VE GOT A REAL KNACK FOR FAMILY ENTERTAINMENT.
9/19

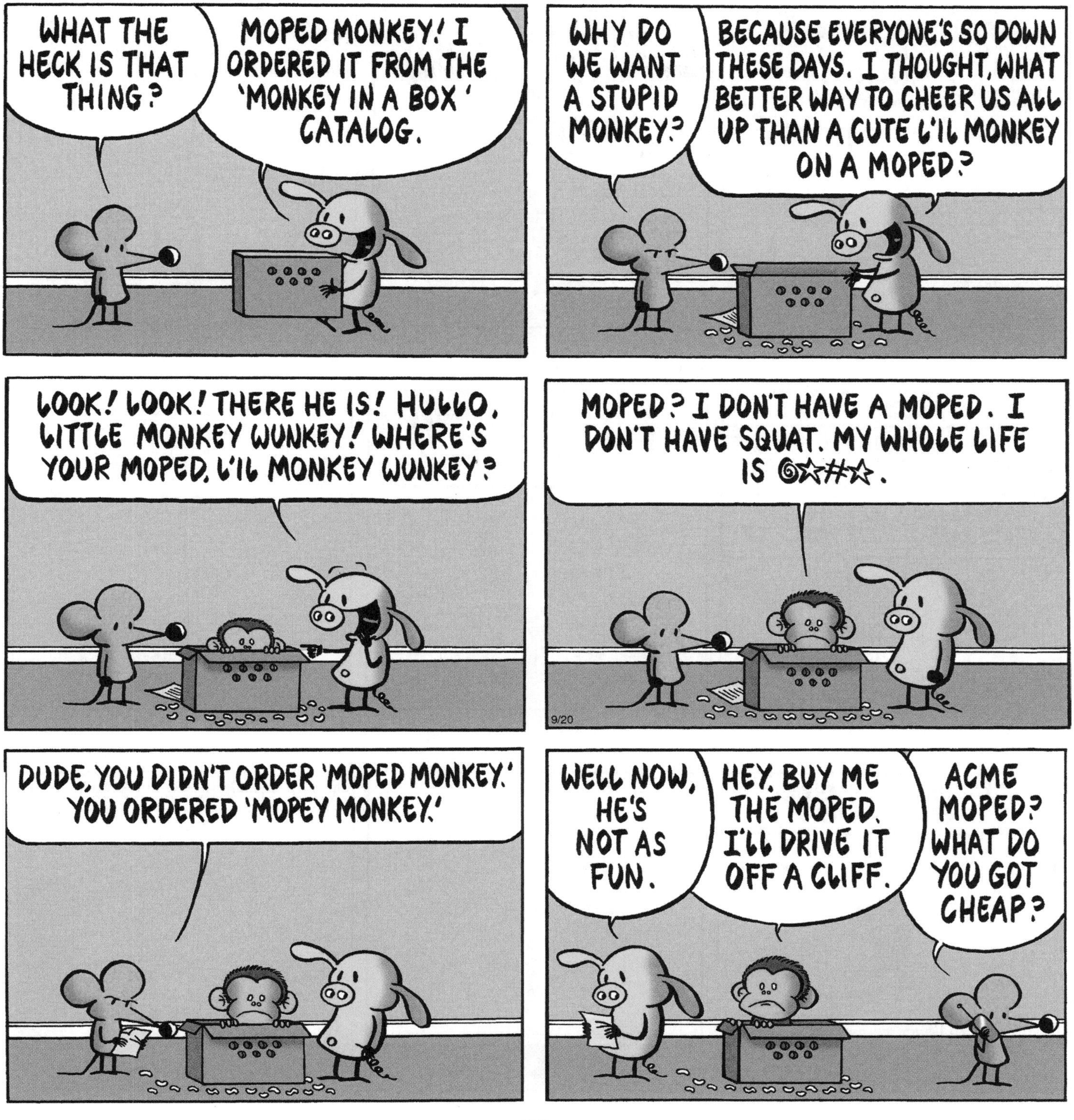
WHAT THE HECK IS THAT THING?
MOPED MONKEY! I ORDERED IT FROM THE 'MONKEY IN A BOX' CATALOG.
WHY DO WE WANT A STUPID MONKEY?
BECAUSE EVERYONE'S SO DOWN THESE DAYS. I THOUGHT, WHAT BETTER WAY TO CHEER US ALL UP THAN A CUTE L'IL MONKEY ON A MOPED?
LOOK! LOOK! THERE HE IS! HULLO, LITTLE MONKEY WUNKEY! WHERE'S YOUR MOPED, L'IL MONKEY WUNKEY?
MOPED? I DON'T HAVE A MOPED. I DON'T HAVE SQUAT. MY WHOLE LIFE IS @☆#☆.
9/20
DUDE, YOU DIDN'T ORDER 'MOPED MONKEY.' YOU ORDERED 'MOPEY MONKEY.'
WELL NOW, HE'S NOT AS FUN.
HEY, BUY ME THE MOPED. I'LL DRIVE IT OFF A CLIFF.
ACME MOPED? WHAT DO YOU GOT CHEAP?

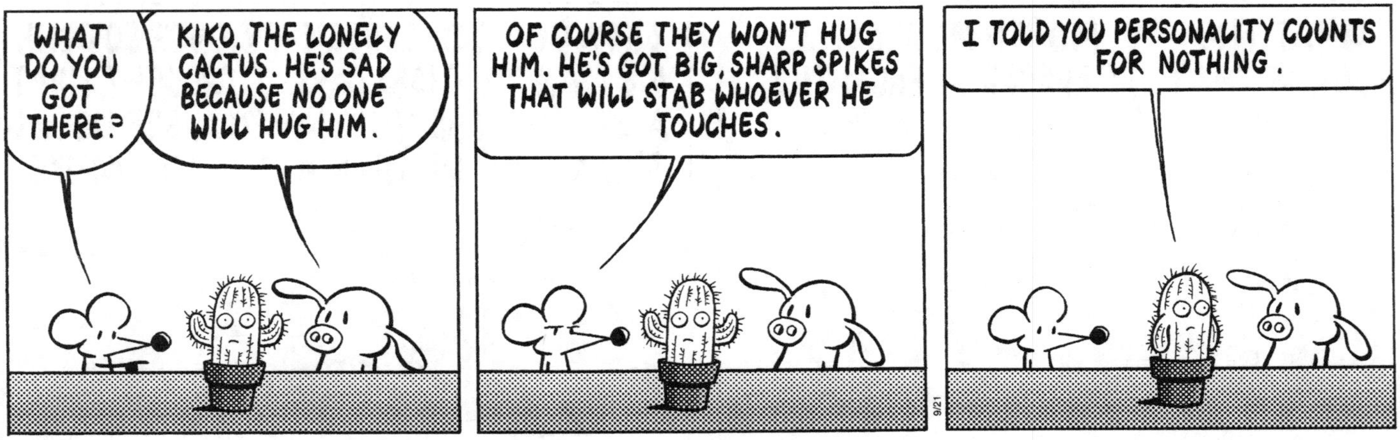
WHAT DO YOU GOT THERE?
KIKO, THE LONELY CACTUS. HE'S SAD BECAUSE NO ONE WILL HUG HIM.
OF COURSE THEY WON'T HUG HIM. HE'S GOT BIG, SHARP SPIKES THAT WILL STAB WHOEVER HE TOUCHES.
I TOLD YOU PERSONALITY COUNTS FOR NOTHING.

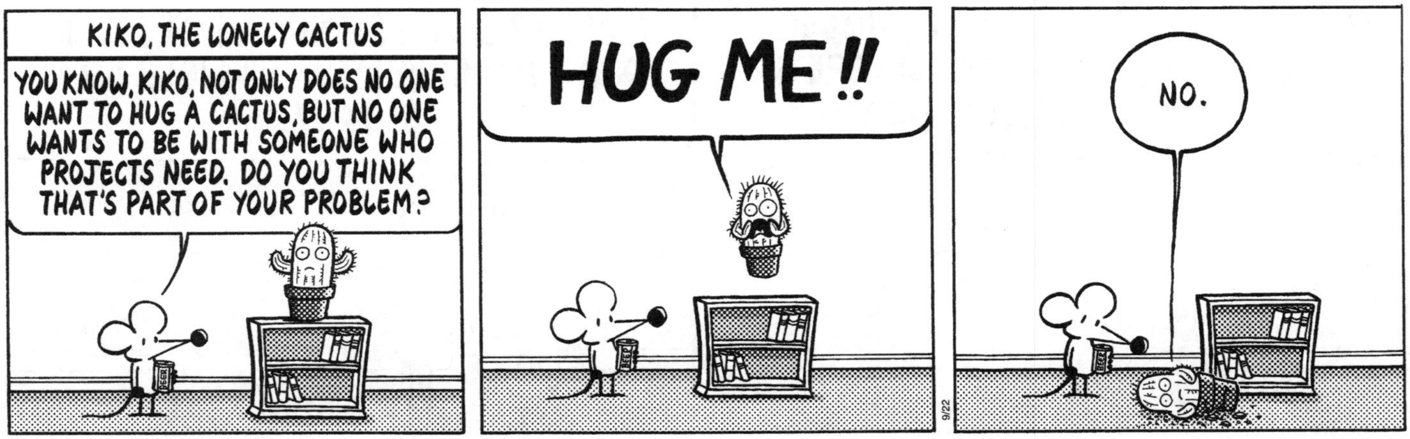
KIKO, THE LONELY CACTUS
YOU KNOW, KIKO, NOT ONLY DOES NO ONE WANT TO HUG A CACTUS, BUT NO ONE WANTS TO BE WITH SOMEONE WHO PROJECTS NEED. DO YOU THINK THAT'S PART OF YOUR PROBLEM?
HUG ME!!
NO.

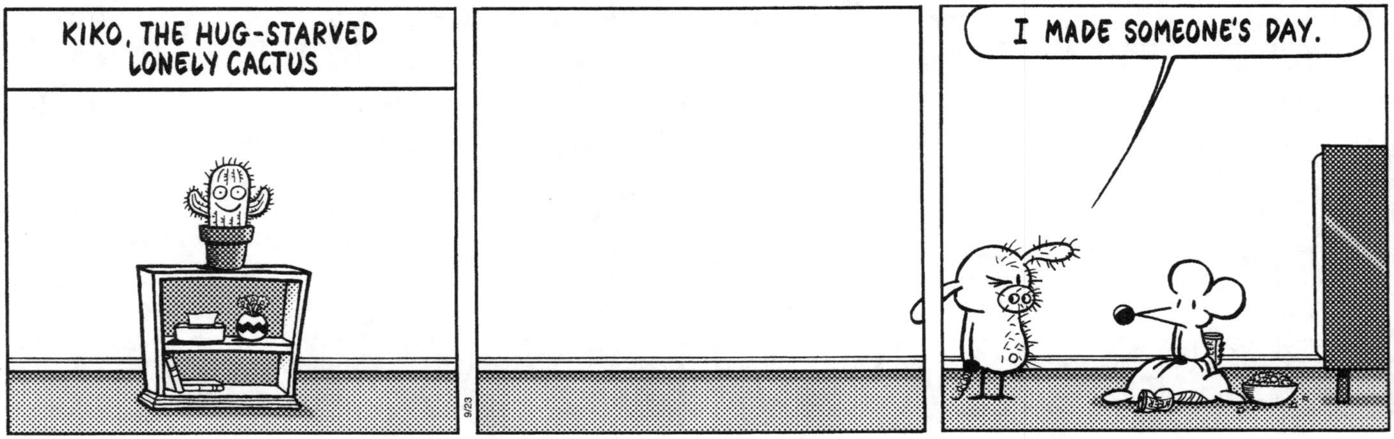
KIKO, THE HUG-STARVED LONELY CACTUS
I MADE SOMEONE'S DAY.

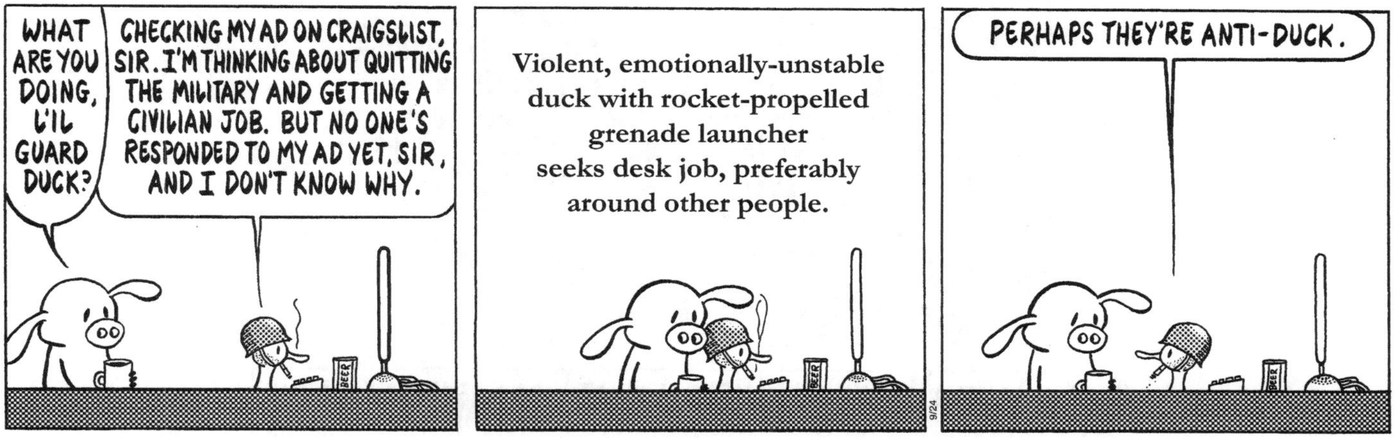
WHAT ARE YOU DOING, L'IL GUARD DUCK?
CHECKING MY AD ON CRAIGSLIST, SIR. I'M THINKING ABOUT QUITTING THE MILITARY AND GETTING A CIVILIAN JOB. BUT NO ONE'S RESPONDED TO MY AD YET, SIR, AND I DON'T KNOW WHY.
Violent, emotionally-unstable duck with rocket-propelled grenade launcher seeks desk job, preferably around other people.
PERHAPS THEY'RE ANTI-DUCK.

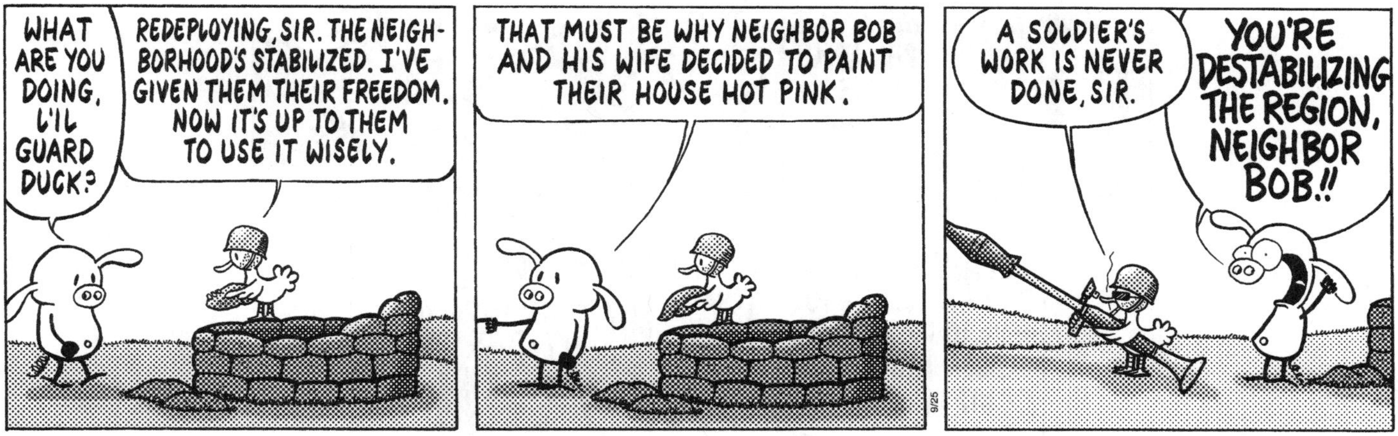
WHAT ARE YOU DOING, L'IL GUARD DUCK?
REDEPLOYING, SIR. THE NEIGHBORHOOD'S STABILIZED. I'VE GIVEN THEM THEIR FREEDOM. NOW IT'S UP TO THEM TO USE IT WISELY.
THAT MUST BE WHY NEIGHBOR BOB AND HIS WIFE DECIDED TO PAINT THEIR HOUSE HOT PINK.
A SOLDIER'S WORK IS NEVER DONE, SIR.
YOU'RE DESTABILIZING THE REGION, NEIGHBOR BOB!!

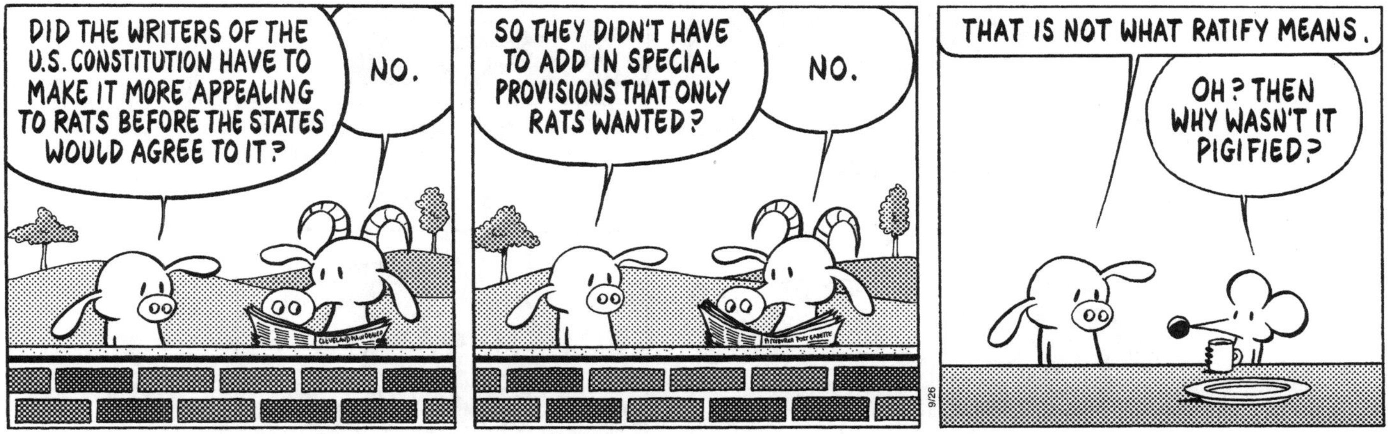
DID THE WRITERS OF THE U.S. CONSTITUTION HAVE TO MAKE IT MORE APPEALING TO RATS BEFORE THE STATES WOULD AGREE TO IT?
NO.
SO THEY DIDN'T HAVE TO ADD IN SPECIAL PROVISIONS THAT ONLY RATS WANTED?
NO.
THAT IS NOT WHAT RATIFY MEANS.
OH? THEN WHY WASN'T IT PIGIFIED?

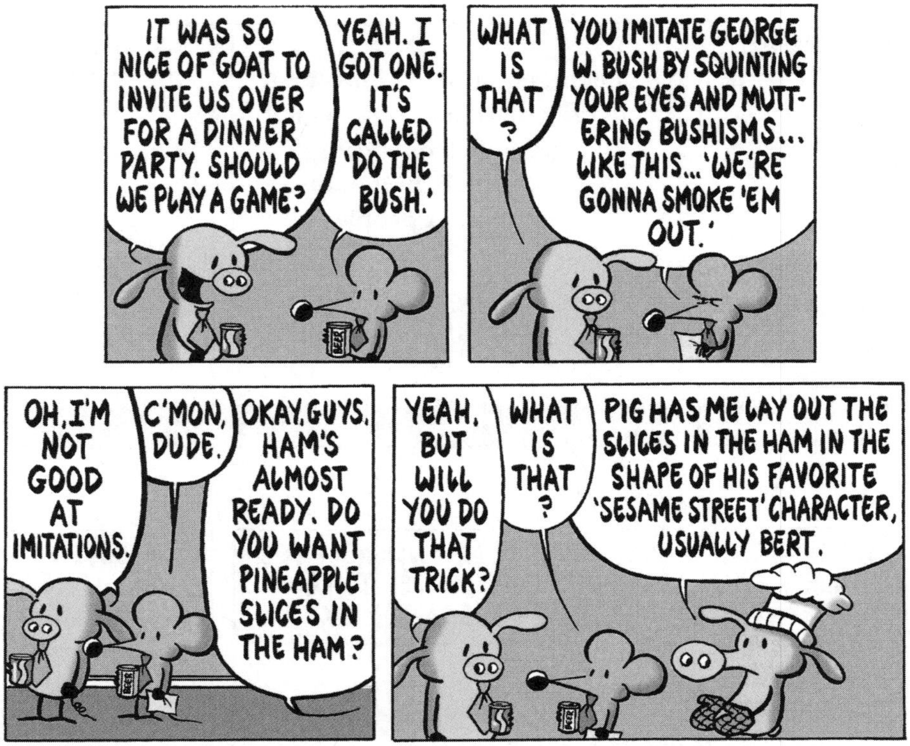
IT WAS SO NICE OF GOAT TO INVITE US OVER FOR A DINNER PARTY. SHOULD WE PLAY A GAME?
YEAH. I GOT ONE. IT'S CALLED 'DO THE BUSH.'
WHAT IS THAT?
YOU IMITATE GEORGE W. BUSH BY SQUINTING YOUR EYES AND MUTT-ERING BUSHISMS... LIKE THIS... 'WE'RE GONNA SMOKE 'EM OUT.'
OH, I'M NOT GOOD AT IMITATIONS.
C'MON, DUDE.
OKAY, GUYS. HAM'S ALMOST READY. DO YOU WANT PINEAPPLE SLICES IN THE HAM?
YEAH, BUT WILL YOU DO THAT TRICK?
WHAT IS THAT?
PIG HAS ME LAY OUT THE SLICES IN THE HAM IN THE SHAPE OF HIS FAVORITE 'SESAME STREET' CHARACTER, USUALLY BERT.
BEER

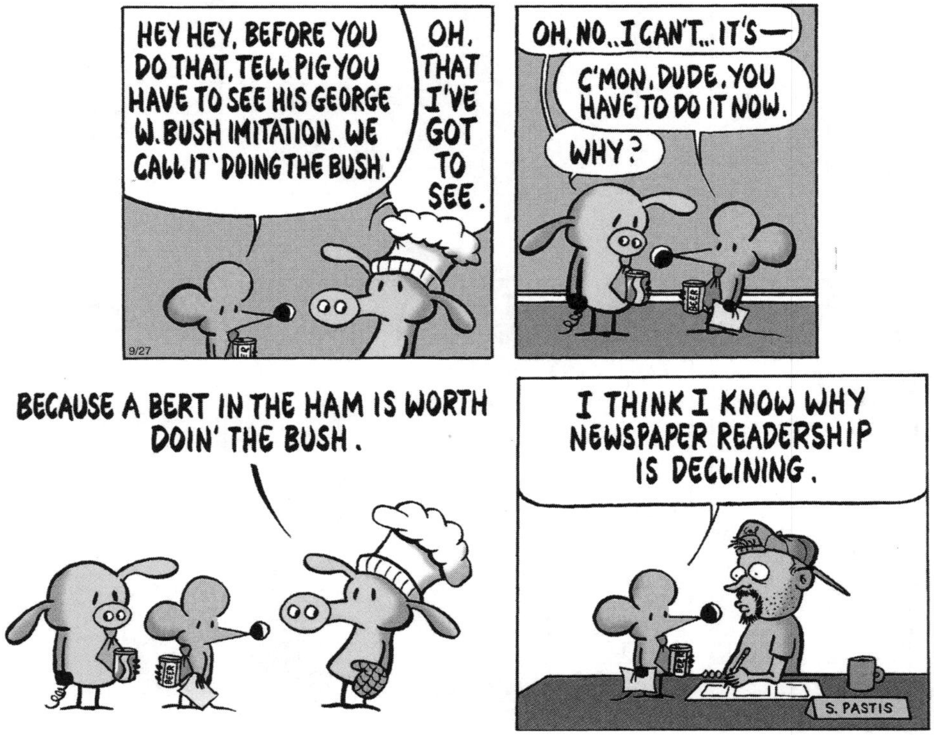
HEY HEY, BEFORE YOU DO THAT, TELL PIG YOU HAVE TO SEE HIS GEORGE W. BUSH IMITATION. WE CALL IT 'DOING THE BUSH.'
OH. THAT I'VE GOT TO SEE.
9/27
OH, NO.. I CAN'T... IT'S—
C'MON, DUDE, YOU HAVE TO DO IT NOW.
WHY?
BECAUSE A BERT IN THE HAM IS WORTH DOIN' THE BUSH.
I THINK I KNOW WHY NEWSPAPER READERSHIP IS DECLINING.
S. PASTIS
BEER

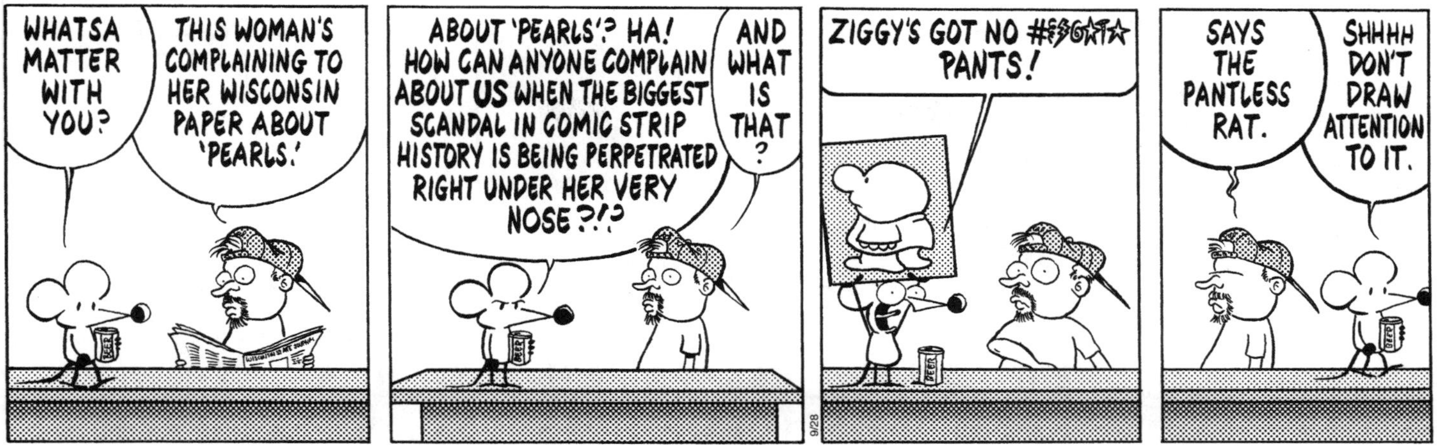
WHATSA MATTER WITH YOU?
THIS WOMAN'S COMPLAINING TO HER WISCONSIN PAPER ABOUT 'PEARLS.'
ABOUT 'PEARLS'? HA! HOW CAN ANYONE COMPLAIN ABOUT US WHEN THE BIGGEST SCANDAL IN COMIC STRIP HISTORY IS BEING PERPETRATED RIGHT UNDER HER VERY NOSE?!?
AND WHAT IS THAT?
ZIGGY'S GOT NO #$%&☆ PANTS!
SAYS THE PANTLESS RAT.
SHHHH DON'T DRAW ATTENTION TO IT.
BEER
9/28

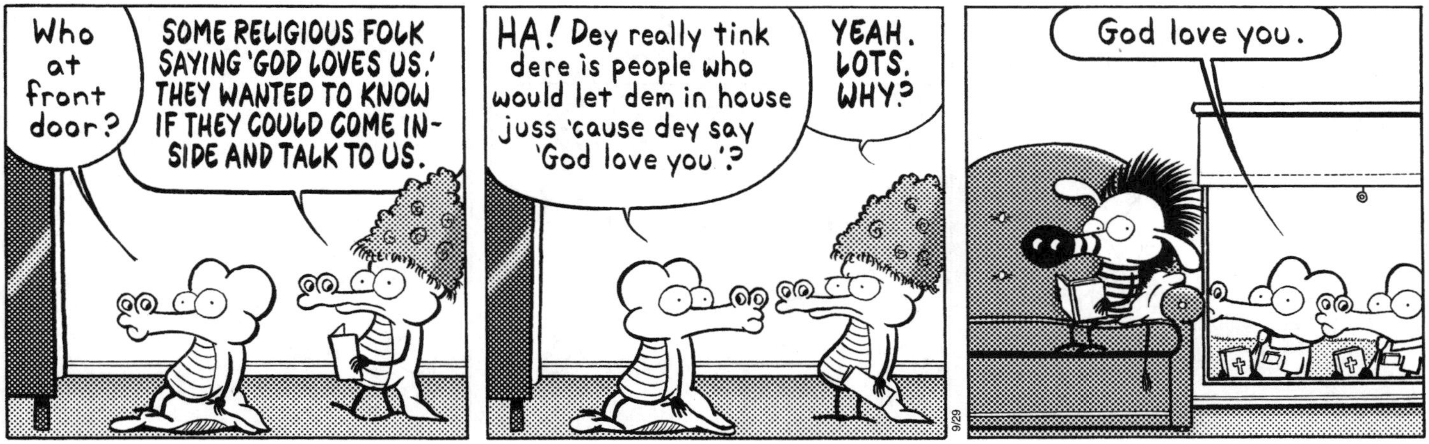
Who at front door?
SOME RELIGIOUS FOLK SAYING 'GOD LOVES US.' THEY WANTED TO KNOW IF THEY COULD COME INSIDE AND TALK TO US.
HA! Dey really tink dere is people who would let dem in house juss 'cause dey say 'God love you'?
YEAH. LOTS. WHY?
God love you.
9/29

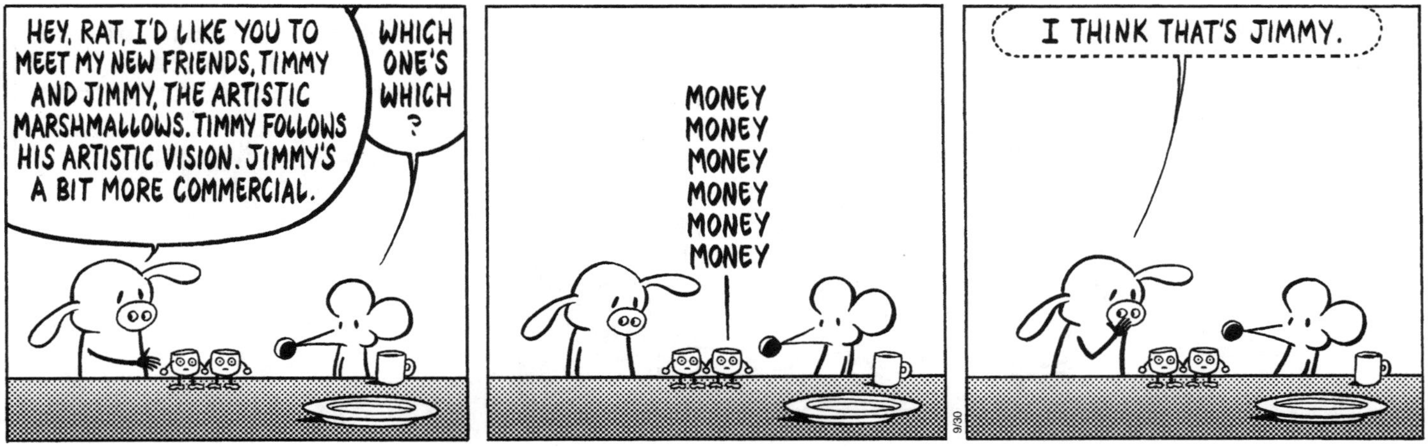
HEY, RAT, I'D LIKE YOU TO MEET MY NEW FRIENDS, TIMMY AND JIMMY, THE ARTISTIC MARSHMALLOWS. TIMMY FOLLOWS HIS ARTISTIC VISION. JIMMY'S A BIT MORE COMMERCIAL.
WHICH ONE'S WHICH?
MONEY MONEY MONEY MONEY MONEY MONEY
I THINK THAT'S JIMMY.
9/30

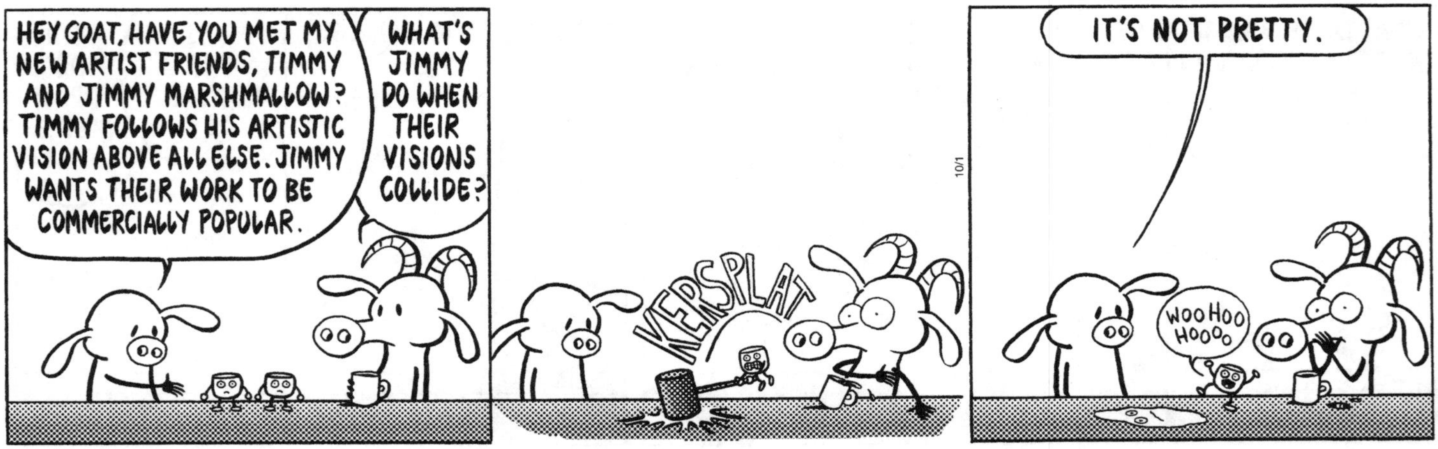
HEY GOAT, HAVE YOU MET MY NEW ARTIST FRIENDS, TIMMY AND JIMMY MARSHMALLOW? TIMMY FOLLOWS HIS ARTISTIC VISION ABOVE ALL ELSE. JIMMY WANTS THEIR WORK TO BE COMMERCIALLY POPULAR.
WHAT'S JIMMY DO WHEN THEIR VISIONS COLLIDE?
KERSPLAT
IT'S NOT PRETTY.
WOO HOO HOOOO
10/1

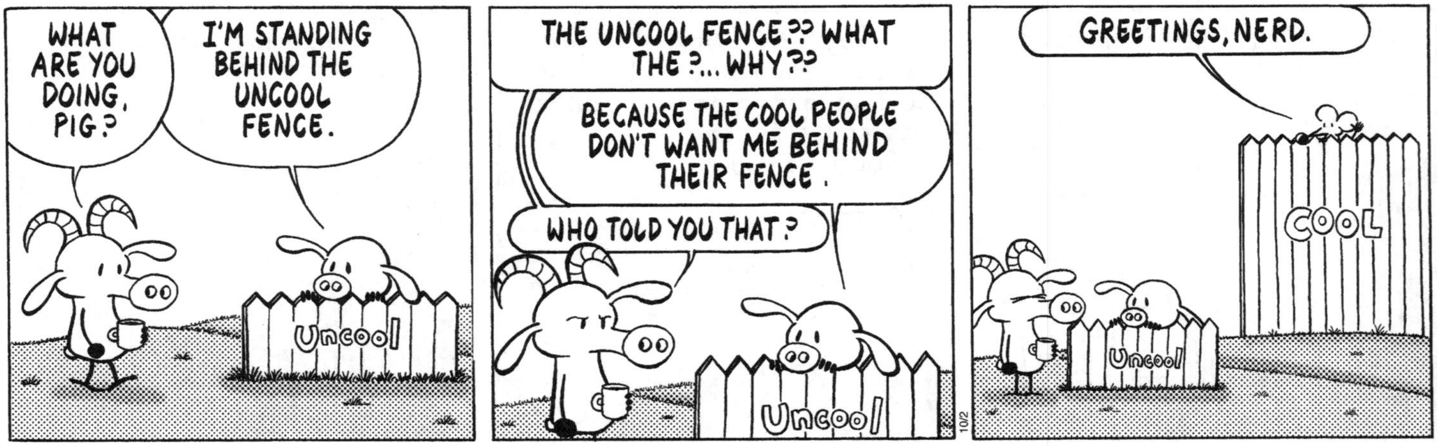
WHAT ARE YOU DOING, PIG?
I'M STANDING BEHIND THE UNCOOL FENCE.
Uncool
THE UNCOOL FENCE?? WHAT THE?... WHY??
BECAUSE THE COOL PEOPLE DON'T WANT ME BEHIND THEIR FENCE.
WHO TOLD YOU THAT?
Uncool
GREETINGS, NERD.
COOL
Uncool
10/2

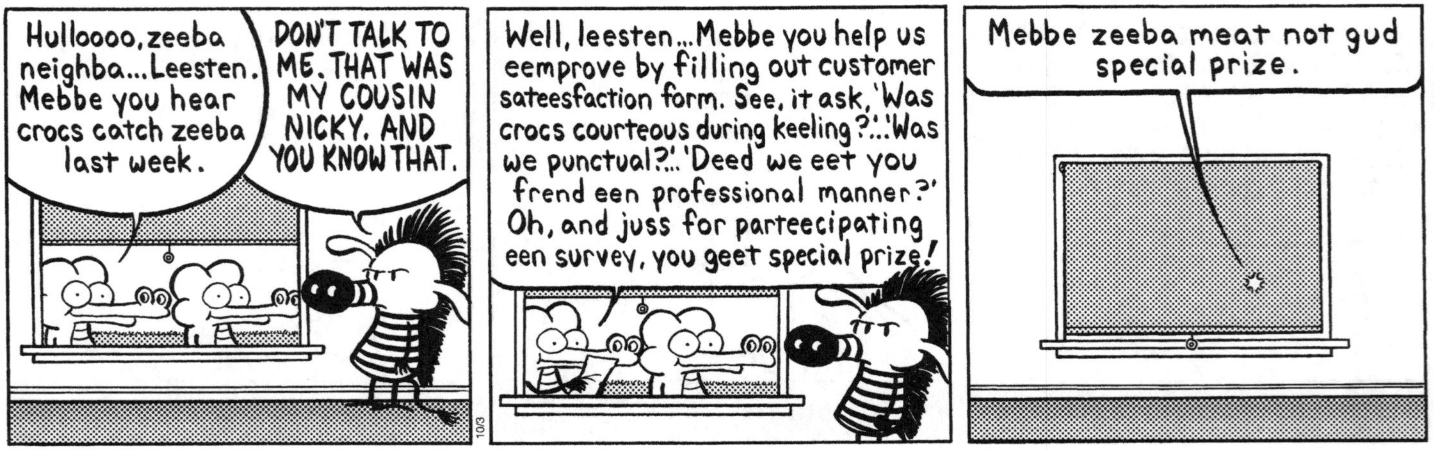
Hulloooo, zeeba neighba... Leesten. Mebbe you hear crocs catch zeeba last week.
DON'T TALK TO ME. THAT WAS MY COUSIN NICKY. AND YOU KNOW THAT.
Well, leesten... Mebbe you help us eemprove by filling out customer sateesfaction form. See, it ask, 'Was crocs courteous during keeling?'... 'Was we punctual?'... 'Deed we eet you frend een professional manner?' Oh, and juss for parteecipating een survey, you geet special prize!
Mebbe zeeba meat not gud special prize.
10/3

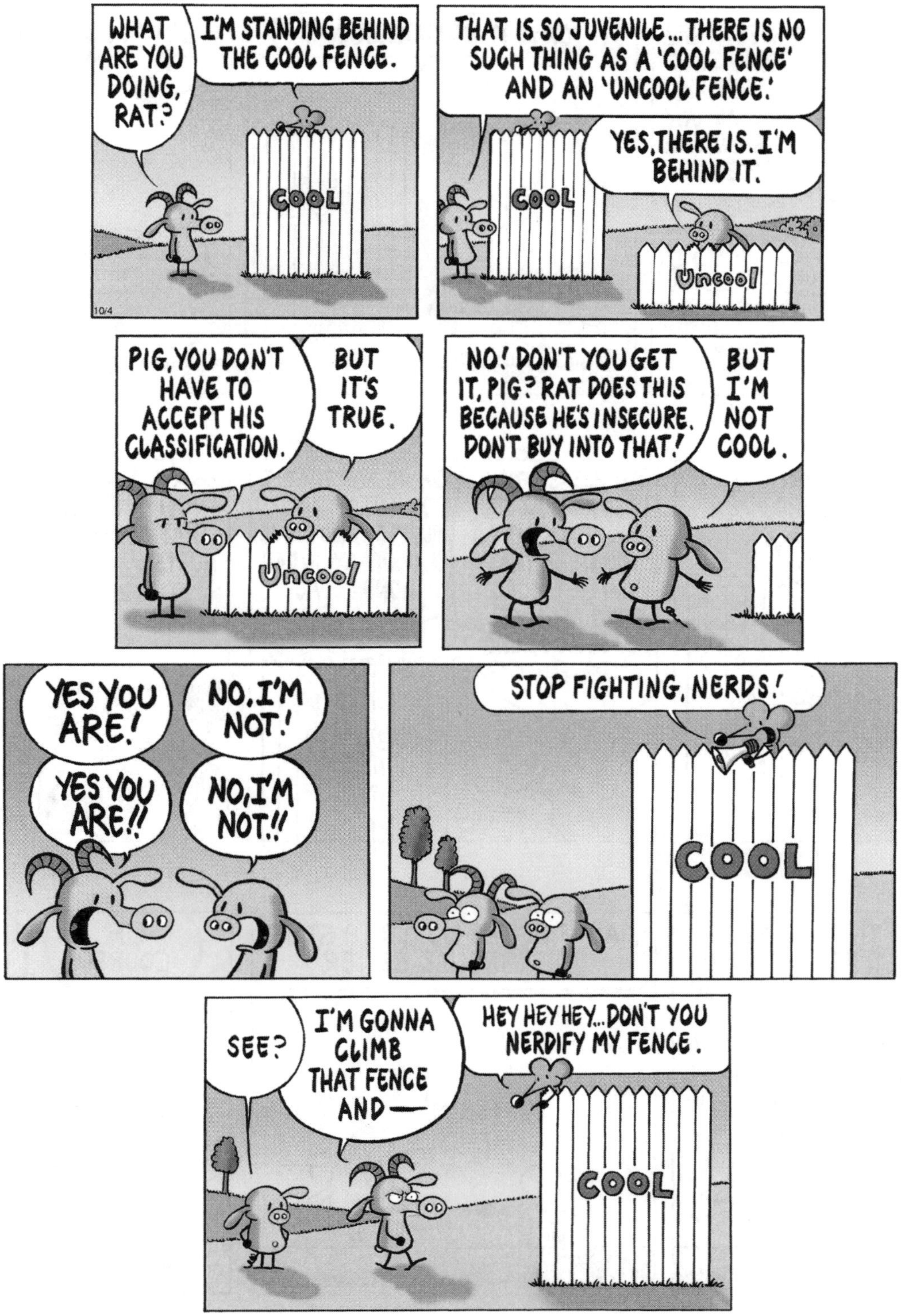
10/4
WHAT ARE YOU DOING, RAT?
I'M STANDING BEHIND THE COOL FENCE.
COOL
THAT IS SO JUVENILE... THERE IS NO SUCH THING AS A 'COOL FENCE' AND AN 'UNCOOL FENCE.'
YES, THERE IS. I'M BEHIND IT.
COOL
Uncool
PIG, YOU DON'T HAVE TO ACCEPT HIS CLASSIFICATION.
BUT IT'S TRUE.
Uncool
NO! DON'T YOU GET IT, PIG? RAT DOES THIS BECAUSE HE'S INSECURE. DON'T BUY INTO THAT!
BUT I'M NOT COOL.
YES YOU ARE!
NO, I'M NOT!
YES YOU ARE!!
NO, I'M NOT!!
STOP FIGHTING, NERDS!
COOL
SEE?
I'M GONNA CLIMB THAT FENCE AND—
HEY HEY HEY... DON'T YOU NERDIFY MY FENCE.
COOL

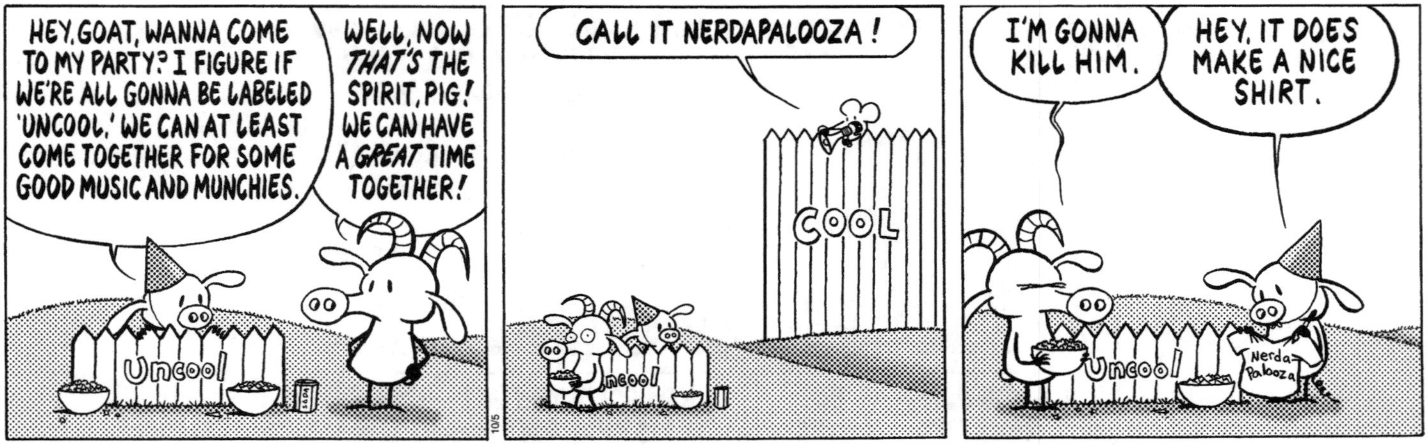
HEY, GOAT, WANNA COME TO MY PARTY? I FIGURE IF WE'RE ALL GONNA BE LABELED 'UNCOOL,' WE CAN AT LEAST COME TOGETHER FOR SOME GOOD MUSIC AND MUNCHIES.
WELL, NOW *THAT'S* THE SPIRIT, PIG! WE CAN HAVE A *GREAT* TIME TOGETHER!
Uncool
10/5
CALL IT NERDAPALOOZA!
COOL
Uncool
I'M GONNA KILL HIM.
HEY, IT DOES MAKE A NICE SHIRT.
Uncool
Nerda-Palooza

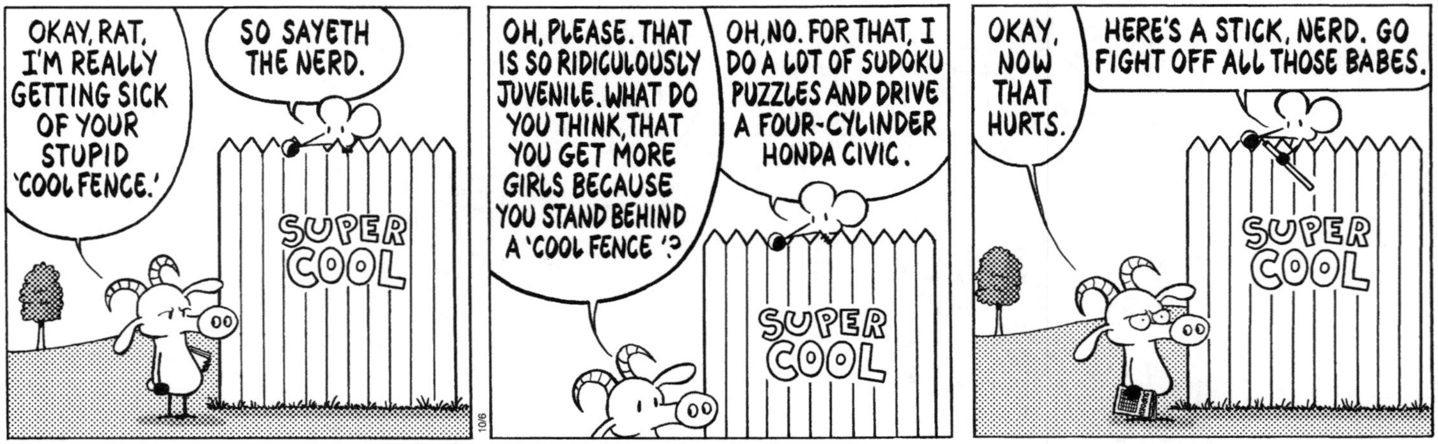
OKAY, RAT, I'M REALLY GETTING SICK OF YOUR STUPID 'COOL FENCE.'
SO SAYETH THE NERD.
SUPER COOL
10/6
OH, PLEASE. THAT IS SO RIDICULOUSLY JUVENILE. WHAT DO YOU THINK, THAT YOU GET MORE GIRLS BECAUSE YOU STAND BEHIND A 'COOL FENCE'?
OH, NO. FOR THAT, I DO A LOT OF SUDOKU PUZZLES AND DRIVE A FOUR-CYLINDER HONDA CIVIC.
SUPER COOL
OKAY, NOW THAT HURTS.
HERE'S A STICK, NERD. GO FIGHT OFF ALL THOSE BABES.
SUPER COOL

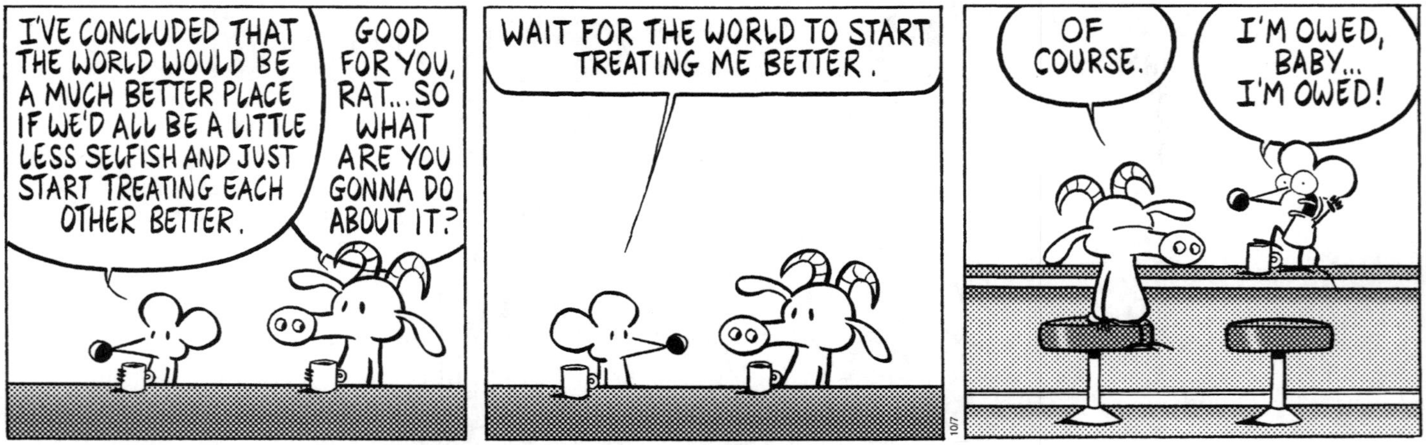
I'VE CONCLUDED THAT THE WORLD WOULD BE A MUCH BETTER PLACE IF WE'D ALL BE A LITTLE LESS SELFISH AND JUST START TREATING EACH OTHER BETTER.
GOOD FOR YOU, RAT... SO WHAT ARE YOU GONNA DO ABOUT IT?
WAIT FOR THE WORLD TO START TREATING ME BETTER.
10/7
OF COURSE.
I'M OWED, BABY... I'M OWED!

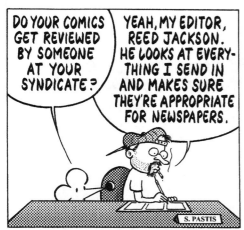

Panel 1: DO YOUR COMICS GET REVIEWED BY SOMEONE AT YOUR SYNDICATE? / YEAH, MY EDITOR, REED JACKSON. HE LOOKS AT EVERYTHING I SEND IN AND MAKES SURE THEY'RE APPROPRIATE FOR NEWSPAPERS.

S. PASTIS

Panel 2: SO, IN THEORY, IF THERE WERE NO REED, ONE COULD DO WHATEVER ONE WANTED IN THIS COMIC? / I GUESS SO. WHY?

S. PASTIS   10/8

Panel 3: AND WHACK HIM GOOD. EDITORS HAVE HARD HEADS.

HIT MEN Inc.

Panel 4: RAT'S SCHEME TO TAKE OUT THE 'PEARLS BEFORE SWINE' EDITOR / HELLO? / HELLO, SIR... IT'S ME, GUARD DUCK.. LISTEN, OUR PLAN HIT A LITTLE SNAG...

10/9

Panel 5: WHAT KIND OF SNAG? / WELL, SIR, WE GOT TO THE OFFICE OF YOUR 'UNITED FEATURE SYNDICATE,' AND WE LOOKED AROUND FOR YOUR EDITOR, BUT... WELL... I THINK WE PUMMELED THE WRONG GUY.

Panel 6: WHO THE 6#☆6 DID YOU PUMMEL ?!?

Panel 7: YOU TELL HIM.

STORY UPDATE

Rat sent Guard Duck and Mr. Snuffles to the United Feature Syndicate office in New York to take out Reed Jackson, the editor of "Pearls Before Swine." But due to an unfortunate case of mistaken identity, Mr. Snuffles and Guard Duck killed Dilbert.

Panel 8: ALRIGHT, YOU IDIOTS, SINCE YOU'RE THE ONES THAT TOOK OUT DILBERT, YOU'RE GONNA BE THE ONES TO BREAK THE NEWS TO THE OTHER DILBERT CHARACTERS. / HOW DO WE DO THAT?

10/10

Panel 9: I DON'T KNOW. JUST GET 'EM ALL TOGETHER IN A CONFERENCE ROOM, TELL THEM DILBERT'S PASSED AWAY, AND DEAL WITH THEIR REACTION. / BUT WHAT WILL THEY SAY?

Panel 10: DOES THIS MEAN WE CAN LEAVE EARLY?

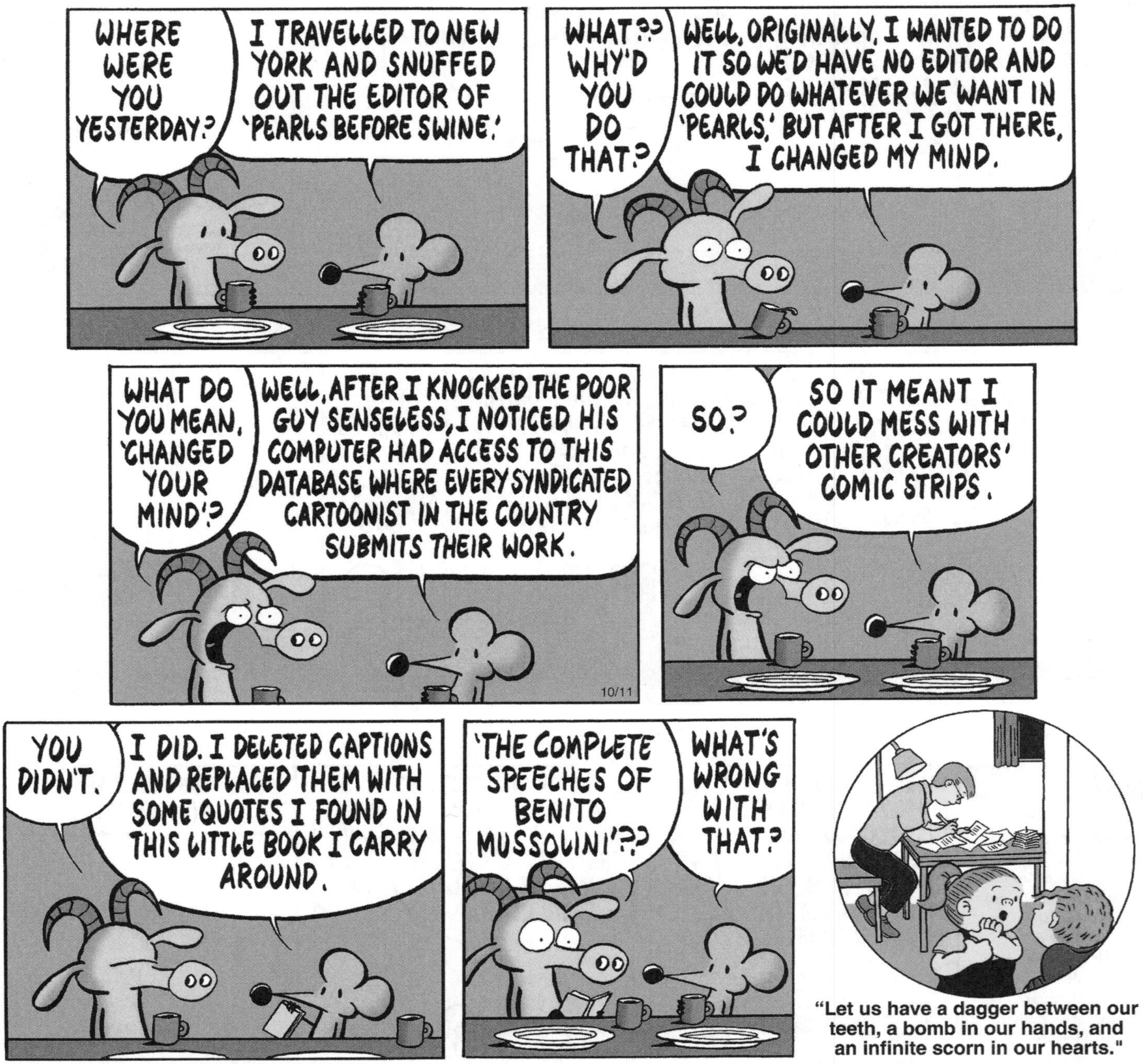
WHERE WERE YOU YESTERDAY?
I TRAVELLED TO NEW YORK AND SNUFFED OUT THE EDITOR OF 'PEARLS BEFORE SWINE.'
WHAT?? WHY'D YOU DO THAT?
WELL, ORIGINALLY, I WANTED TO DO IT SO WE'D HAVE NO EDITOR AND COULD DO WHATEVER WE WANT IN 'PEARLS,' BUT AFTER I GOT THERE, I CHANGED MY MIND.
WHAT DO YOU MEAN, 'CHANGED YOUR MIND'?
WELL, AFTER I KNOCKED THE POOR GUY SENSELESS, I NOTICED HIS COMPUTER HAD ACCESS TO THIS DATABASE WHERE EVERY SYNDICATED CARTOONIST IN THE COUNTRY SUBMITS THEIR WORK.
10/11
SO?
SO IT MEANT I COULD MESS WITH OTHER CREATORS' COMIC STRIPS.
YOU DIDN'T.
I DID. I DELETED CAPTIONS AND REPLACED THEM WITH SOME QUOTES I FOUND IN THIS LITTLE BOOK I CARRY AROUND.
'THE COMPLETE SPEECHES OF BENITO MUSSOLINI'??
WHAT'S WRONG WITH THAT?
"Let us have a dagger between our teeth, a bomb in our hands, and an infinite scorn in our hearts."

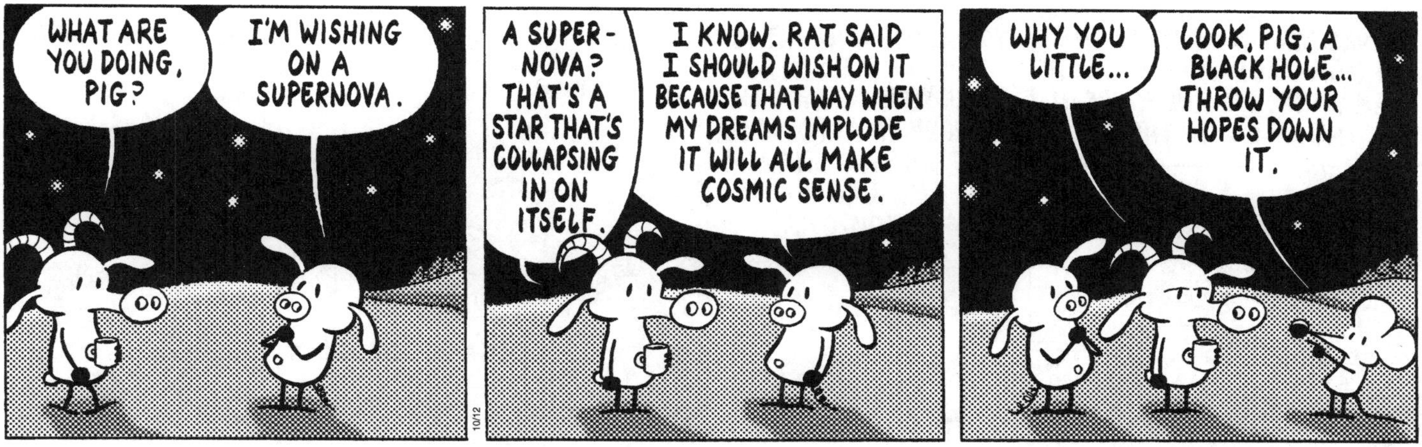
WHAT ARE YOU DOING, PIG?
I'M WISHING ON A SUPERNOVA.
A SUPER-NOVA? THAT'S A STAR THAT'S COLLAPSING IN ON ITSELF.
I KNOW. RAT SAID I SHOULD WISH ON IT BECAUSE THAT WAY WHEN MY DREAMS IMPLODE IT WILL ALL MAKE COSMIC SENSE.
10/12
WHY YOU LITTLE...
LOOK, PIG, A BLACK HOLE... THROW YOUR HOPES DOWN IT.

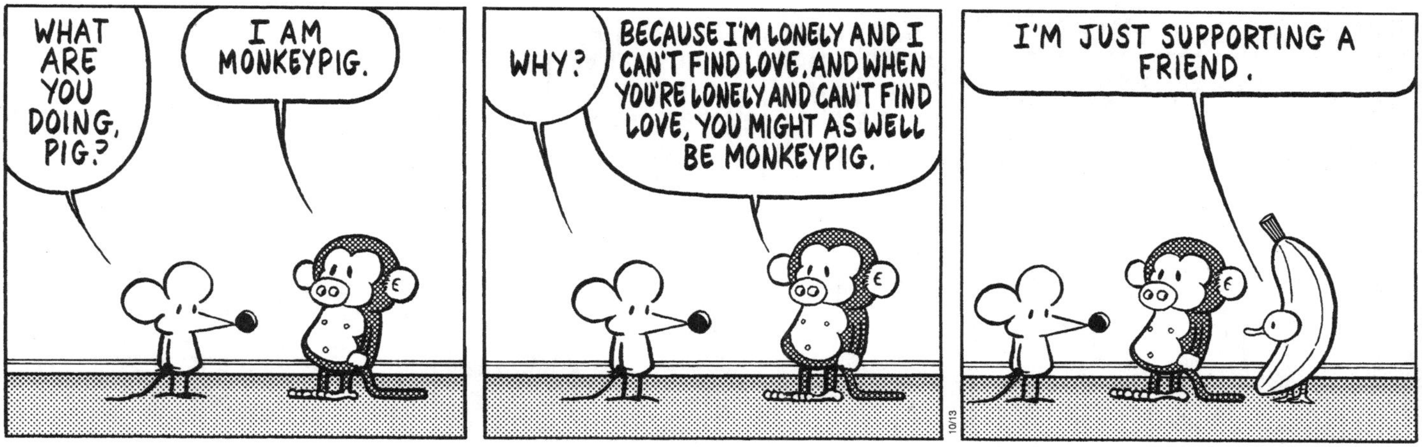
WHAT ARE YOU DOING, PIG?
I AM MONKEYPIG.
WHY?
BECAUSE I'M LONELY AND I CAN'T FIND LOVE, AND WHEN YOU'RE LONELY AND CAN'T FIND LOVE, YOU MIGHT AS WELL BE MONKEYPIG.
10/13
I'M JUST SUPPORTING A FRIEND.

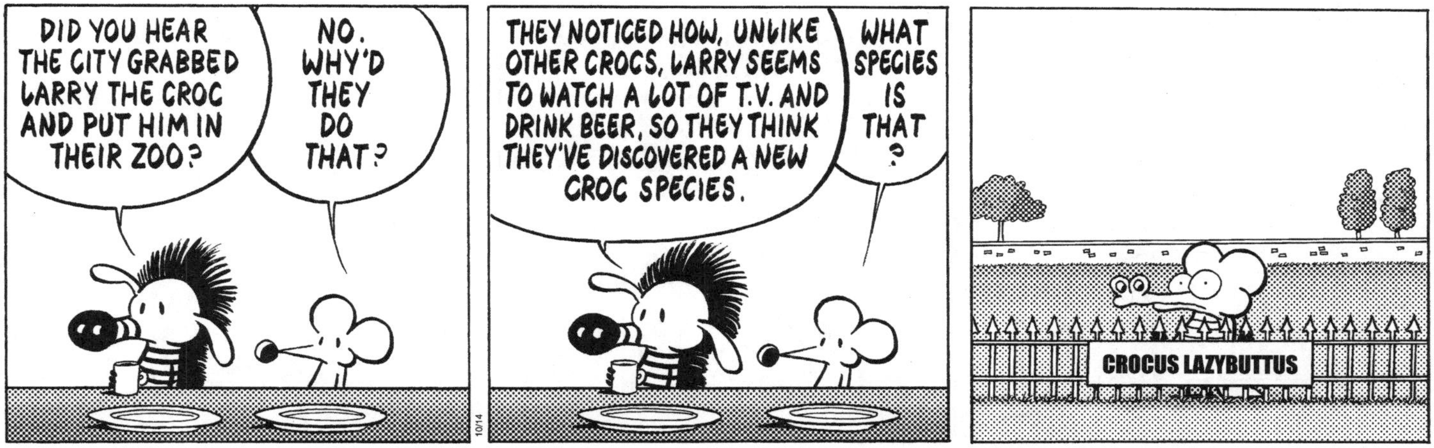
DID YOU HEAR THE CITY GRABBED LARRY THE CROC AND PUT HIM IN THEIR ZOO?
NO. WHY'D THEY DO THAT?
10/14
THEY NOTICED HOW, UNLIKE OTHER CROCS, LARRY SEEMS TO WATCH A LOT OF T.V. AND DRINK BEER, SO THEY THINK THEY'VE DISCOVERED A NEW CROC SPECIES.
WHAT SPECIES IS THAT?
CROCUS LAZYBUTTUS

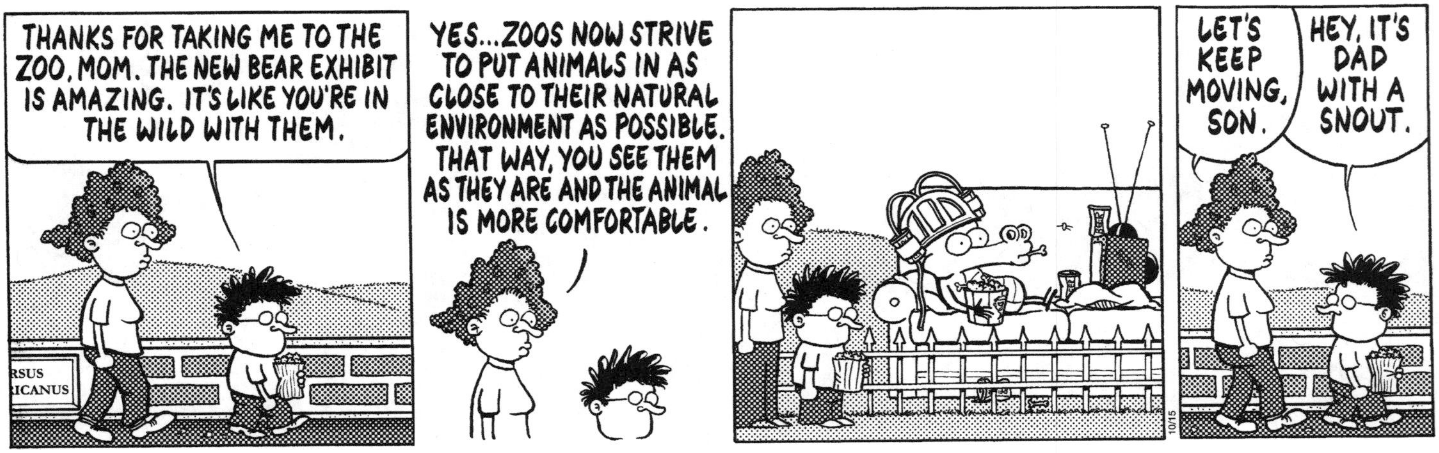
THANKS FOR TAKING ME TO THE ZOO, MOM. THE NEW BEAR EXHIBIT IS AMAZING. IT'S LIKE YOU'RE IN THE WILD WITH THEM.
RSUS
ICANUS
YES...ZOOS NOW STRIVE TO PUT ANIMALS IN AS CLOSE TO THEIR NATURAL ENVIRONMENT AS POSSIBLE. THAT WAY, YOU SEE THEM AS THEY ARE AND THE ANIMAL IS MORE COMFORTABLE.
10/15
LET'S KEEP MOVING, SON.
HEY, IT'S DAD WITH A SNOUT.

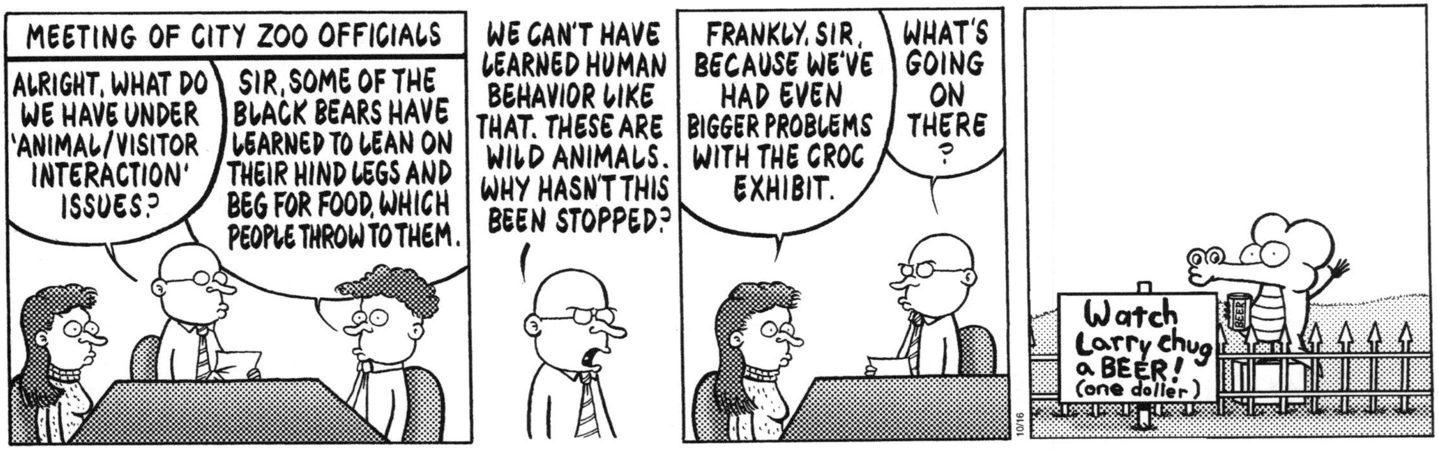
MEETING OF CITY ZOO OFFICIALS
ALRIGHT, WHAT DO WE HAVE UNDER 'ANIMAL/VISITOR INTERACTION' ISSUES?
SIR, SOME OF THE BLACK BEARS HAVE LEARNED TO LEAN ON THEIR HIND LEGS AND BEG FOR FOOD, WHICH PEOPLE THROW TO THEM.
WE CAN'T HAVE LEARNED HUMAN BEHAVIOR LIKE THAT. THESE ARE WILD ANIMALS. WHY HASN'T THIS BEEN STOPPED?
FRANKLY, SIR, BECAUSE WE'VE HAD EVEN BIGGER PROBLEMS WITH THE CROC EXHIBIT.
WHAT'S GOING ON THERE?
10/16
BEER
Watch Larry chug a BEER!
(one doller)

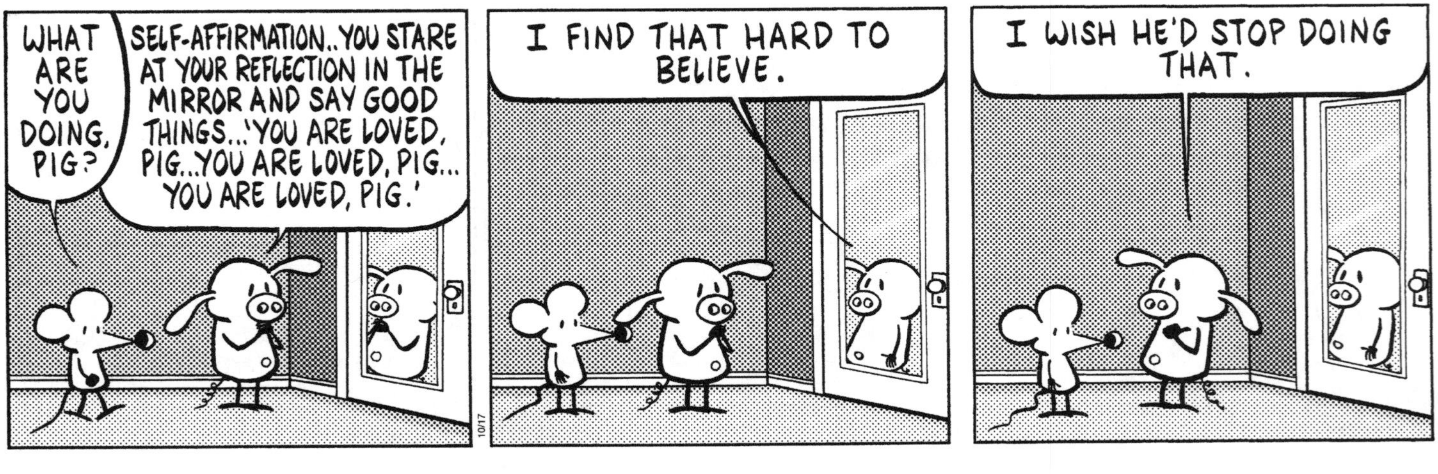
WHAT ARE YOU DOING, PIG?
SELF-AFFIRMATION..YOU STARE AT YOUR REFLECTION IN THE MIRROR AND SAY GOOD THINGS...'YOU ARE LOVED, PIG...YOU ARE LOVED, PIG... YOU ARE LOVED, PIG.'
10/17
I FIND THAT HARD TO BELIEVE.
I WISH HE'D STOP DOING THAT.

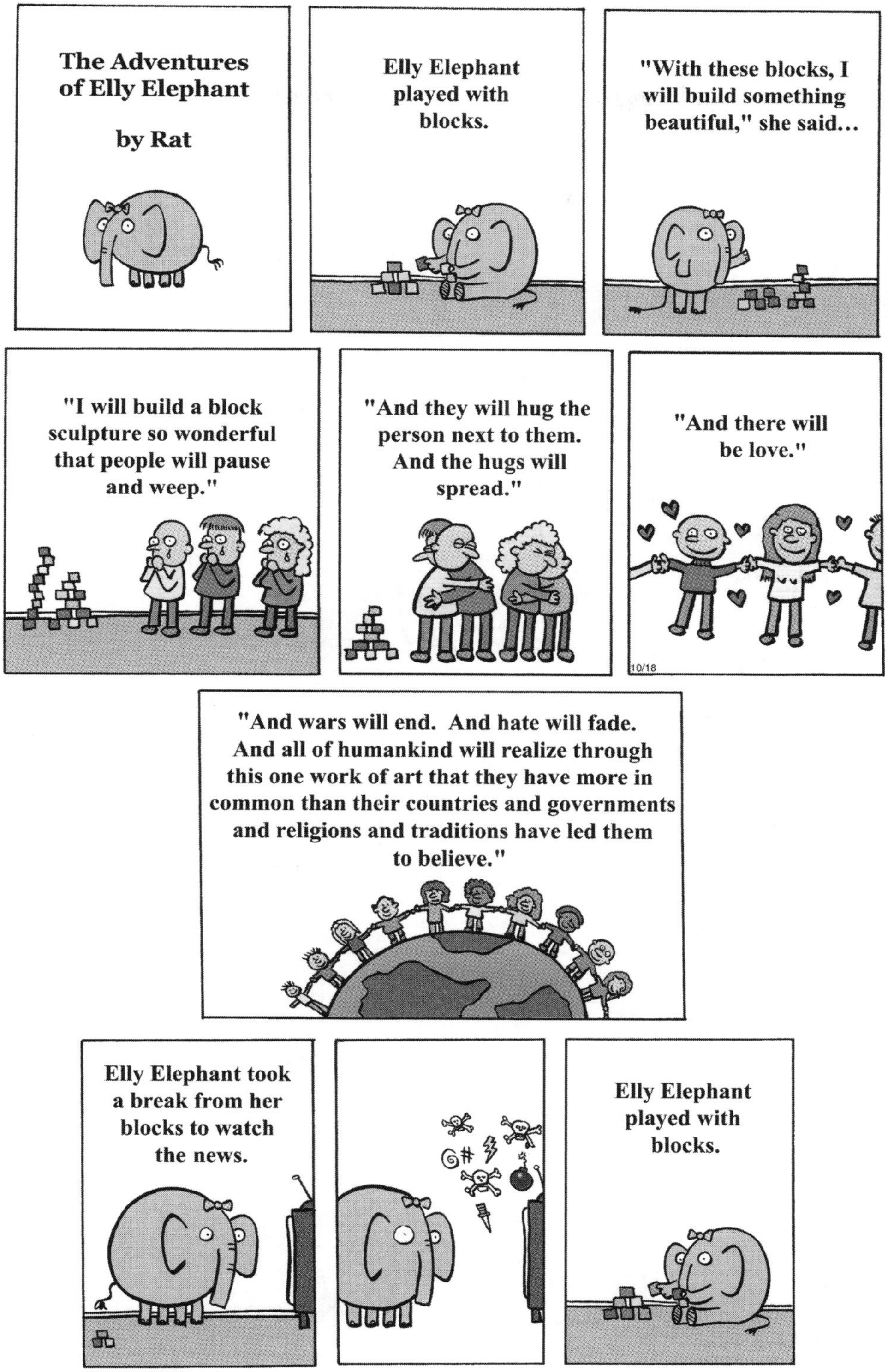
The Adventures of Elly Elephant
by Rat
Elly Elephant played with blocks.
"With these blocks, I will build something beautiful," she said...
"I will build a block sculpture so wonderful that people will pause and weep."
"And they will hug the person next to them. And the hugs will spread."
"And there will be love."
10/18
"And wars will end. And hate will fade. And all of humankind will realize through this one work of art that they have more in common than their countries and governments and religions and traditions have led them to believe."
Elly Elephant took a break from her blocks to watch the news.
Elly Elephant played with blocks.

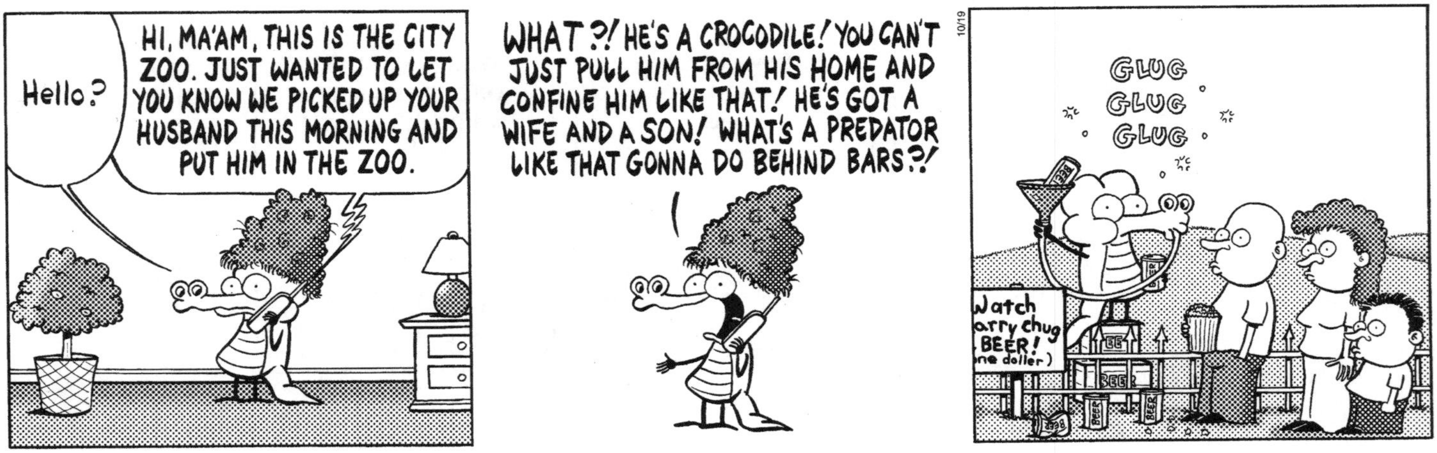
Hello?
HI, MA'AM, THIS IS THE CITY ZOO. JUST WANTED TO LET YOU KNOW WE PICKED UP YOUR HUSBAND THIS MORNING AND PUT HIM IN THE ZOO.
WHAT?! HE'S A CROCODILE! YOU CAN'T JUST PULL HIM FROM HIS HOME AND CONFINE HIM LIKE THAT! HE'S GOT A WIFE AND A SON! WHAT'S A PREDATOR LIKE THAT GONNA DO BEHIND BARS?!
10/19
GLUG
GLUG
GLUG
Watch
arry chug
BEER!
ne dollar)

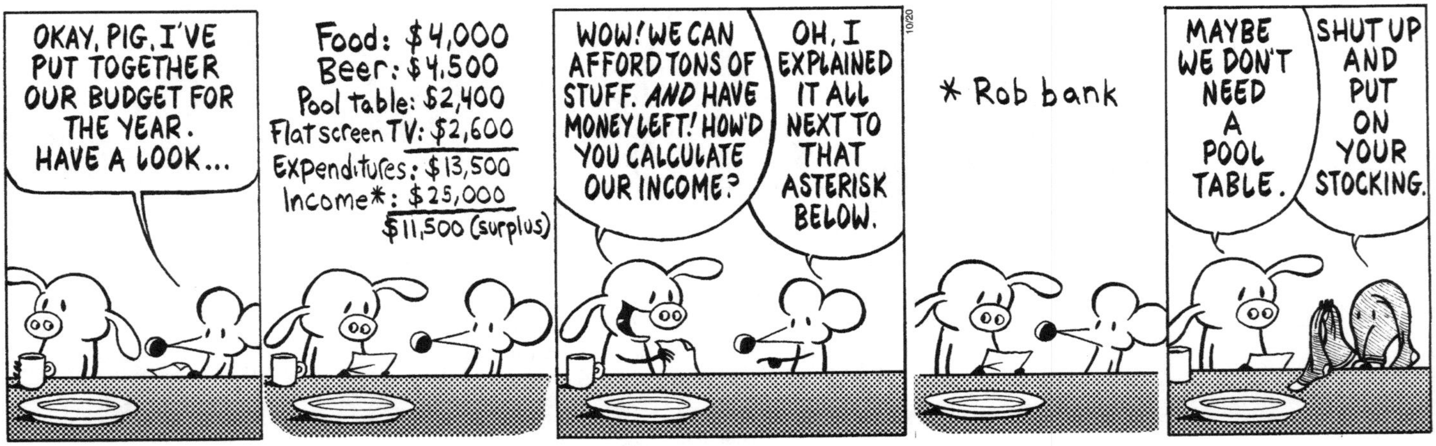
OKAY, PIG, I'VE PUT TOGETHER OUR BUDGET FOR THE YEAR. HAVE A LOOK...
Food: $4,000
Beer: $4,500
Pool table: $2,400
Flatscreen TV: $2,600
Expenditures: $13,500
Income*: $25,000
$11,500 (surplus)
WOW! WE CAN AFFORD TONS OF STUFF. AND HAVE MONEY LEFT! HOW'D YOU CALCULATE OUR INCOME?
OH, I EXPLAINED IT ALL NEXT TO THAT ASTERISK BELOW.
10/20
* Rob bank
MAYBE WE DON'T NEED A POOL TABLE.
SHUT UP AND PUT ON YOUR STOCKING.

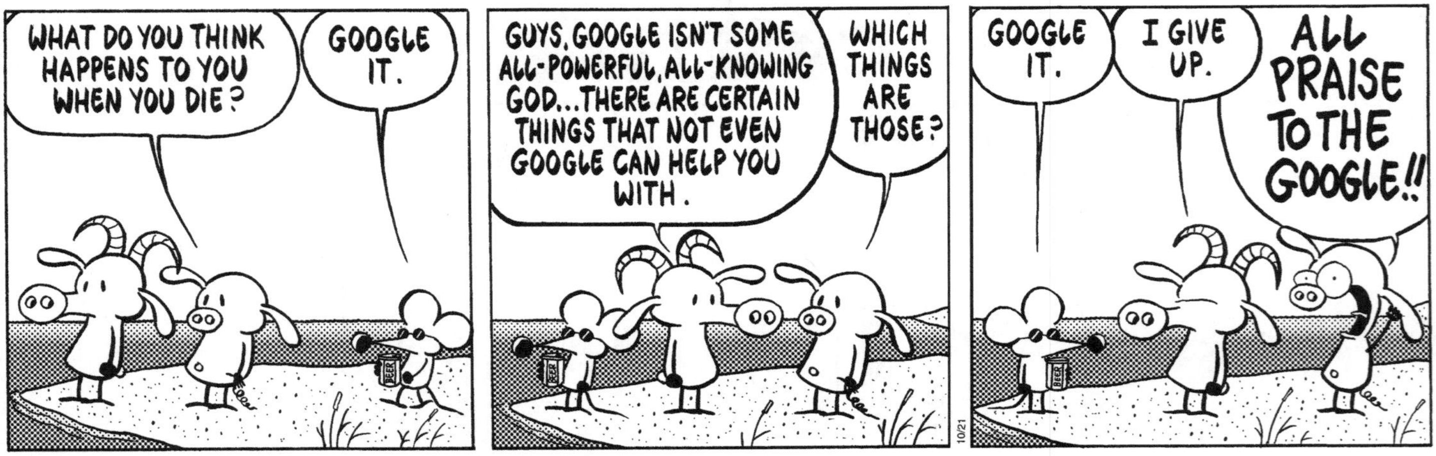
WHAT DO YOU THINK HAPPENS TO YOU WHEN YOU DIE?
GOOGLE IT.
GUYS, GOOGLE ISN'T SOME ALL-POWERFUL, ALL-KNOWING GOD...THERE ARE CERTAIN THINGS THAT NOT EVEN GOOGLE CAN HELP YOU WITH.
WHICH THINGS ARE THOSE?
10/21
GOOGLE IT.
I GIVE UP.
ALL PRAISE TO THE GOOGLE!!

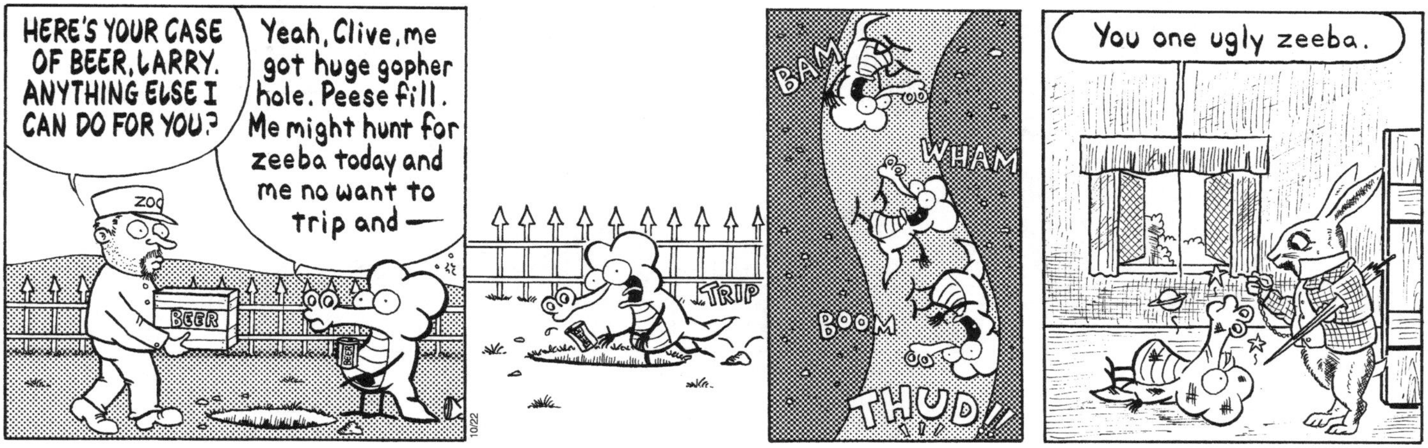
HERE'S YOUR CASE OF BEER, LARRY. ANYTHING ELSE I CAN DO FOR YOU?
Yeah, Clive, me got huge gopher hole. Peese fill. Me might hunt for zeeba today and me no want to trip and —
ZOO
BEER
TRIP
10/22
BAM
WHAM
BOOM
THUD!!
You one ugly zeeba.

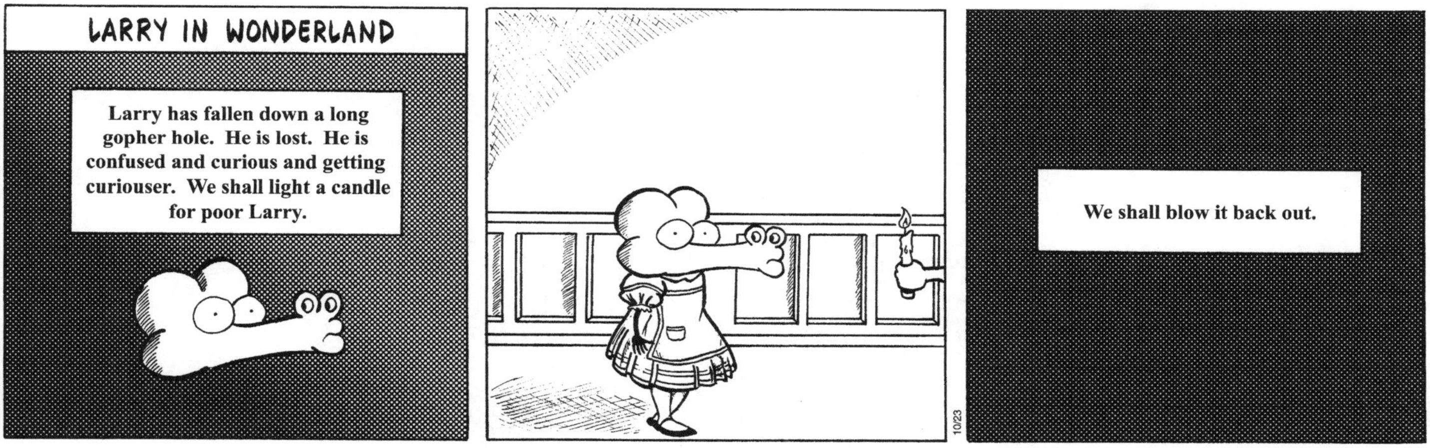
LARRY IN WONDERLAND
Larry has fallen down a long gopher hole. He is lost. He is confused and curious and getting curiouser. We shall light a candle for poor Larry.
10/23
We shall blow it back out.

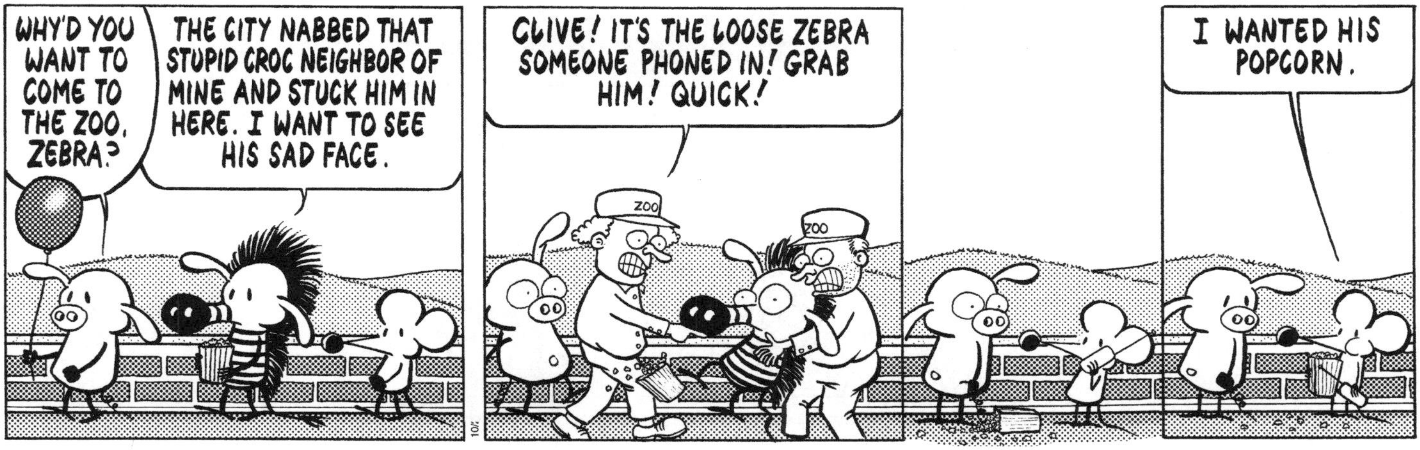
WHY'D YOU WANT TO COME TO THE ZOO, ZEBRA?
THE CITY NABBED THAT STUPID CROC NEIGHBOR OF MINE AND STUCK HIM IN HERE. I WANT TO SEE HIS SAD FACE.
CLIVE! IT'S THE LOOSE ZEBRA SOMEONE PHONED IN! GRAB HIM! QUICK!
ZOO
ZOO
I WANTED HIS POPCORN.

WHERE THE @☆#☆ ARE YOU GOING?
THERE'S A BULLFIGHT GOING ON DOWNTOWN.
A BULLFIGHT?! I'VE ALWAYS WANTED TO SEE A BULLFIGHT!

10/25

PUT 'EM UP, MIKE.
I'LL BREAK YOUR NOSE, CHIP.

I EXPECTED MORE.
YOUR MAMA IS SOOOOO FAT.
I KNOW YOU ARE, BUT WHAT AM I?

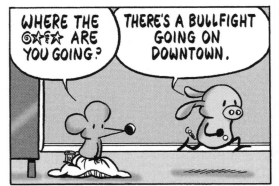

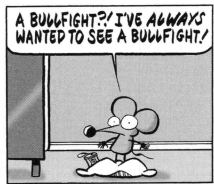

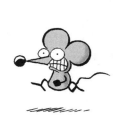

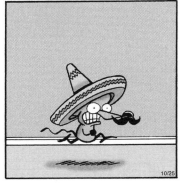

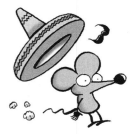

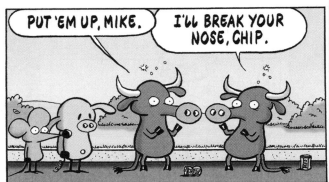

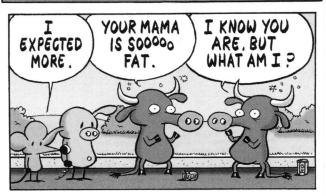

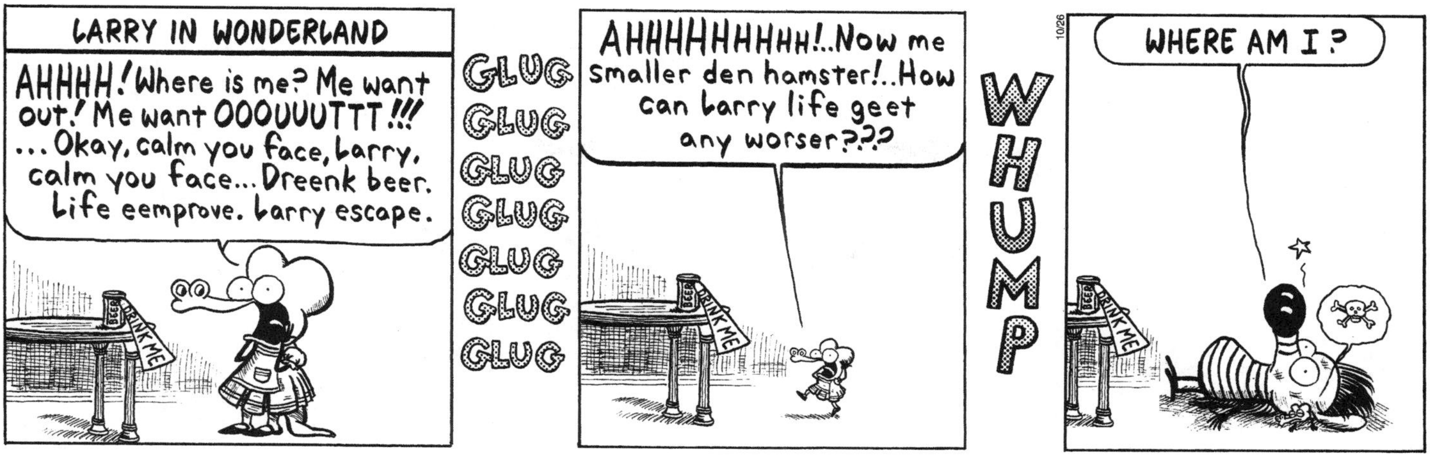
LARRY IN WONDERLAND
AHHHH! Where is me? Me want out! Me want OOOUUUTTT!!! ...Okay, calm you face, Larry, calm you face... Dreenk beer. Life eemprove. Larry escape.
BEER
DRINK ME
GLUG GLUG GLUG GLUG GLUG GLUG GLUG
AHHHHHHHHH!..Now me smaller den hamster!..How can Larry life geet any worser???
WHUMP
10/26
WHERE AM I?

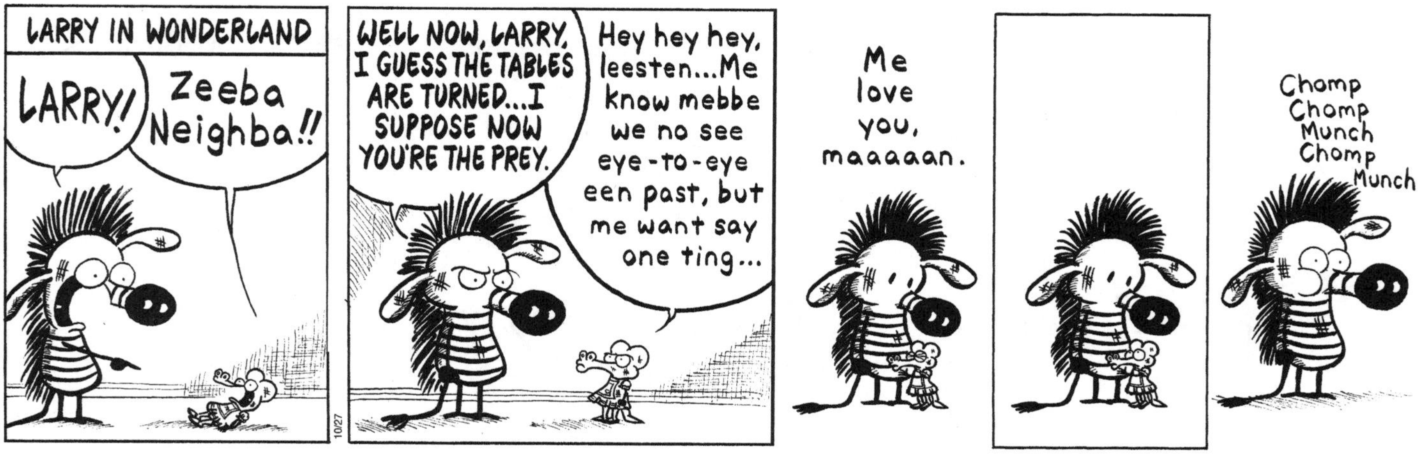
LARRY IN WONDERLAND
LARRY!
Zeeba Neighba!!
10/27
WELL NOW, LARRY, I GUESS THE TABLES ARE TURNED...I SUPPOSE NOW YOU'RE THE PREY.
Hey hey hey, leesten...Me know mebbe we no see eye-to-eye een past, but me want say one ting...
Me love you, maaaaan.
Chomp Chomp Munch Chomp Munch

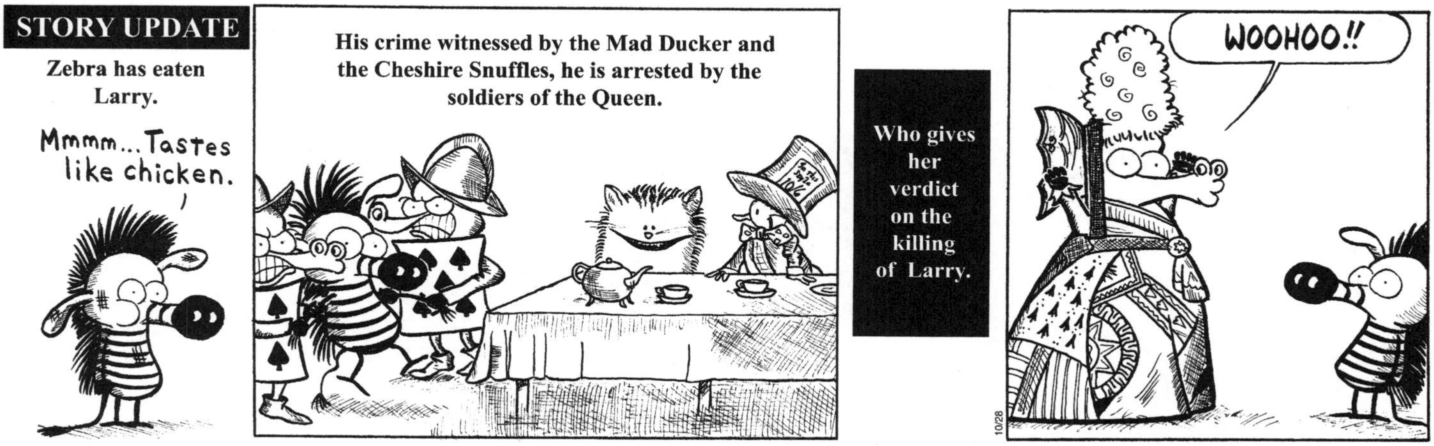
STORY UPDATE
Zebra has eaten Larry.
Mmmm...Tastes like chicken.
His crime witnessed by the Mad Ducker and the Cheshire Snuffles, he is arrested by the soldiers of the Queen.
Who gives her verdict on the killing of Larry.
10/28
WOOHOO!!

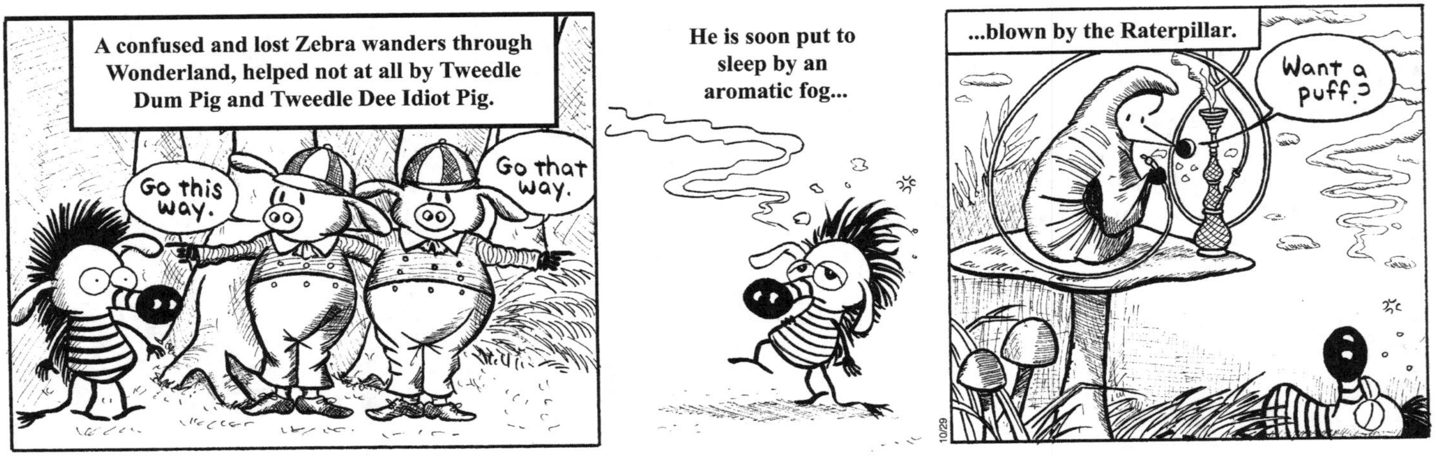
A confused and lost Zebra wanders through Wonderland, helped not at all by Tweedle Dum Pig and Tweedle Dee Idiot Pig.
Go this way.
Go that way.
He is soon put to sleep by an aromatic fog...
...blown by the Raterpillar.
Want a puff?
10/29

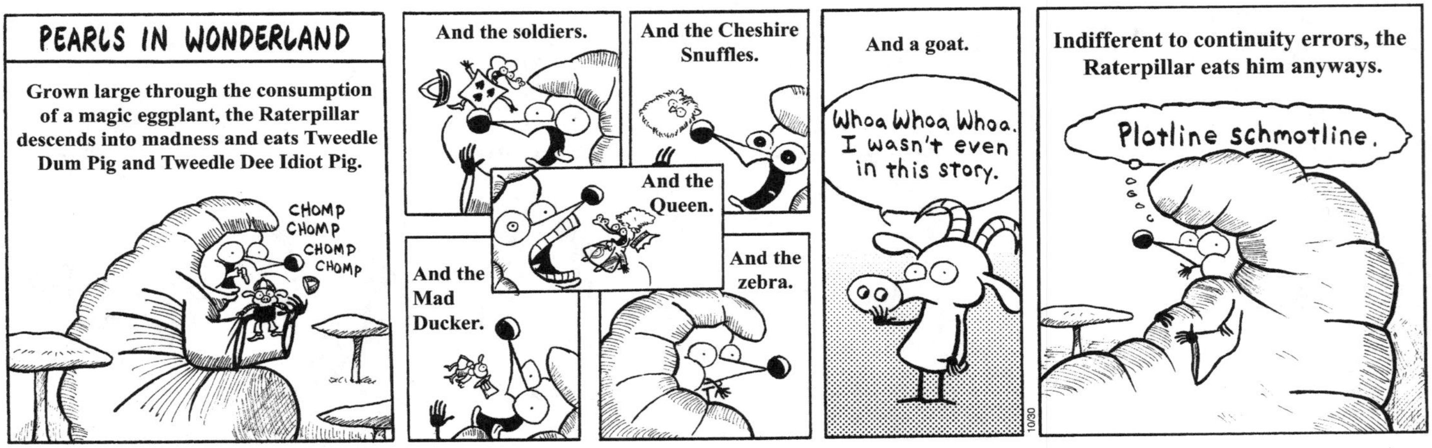
PEARLS IN WONDERLAND
Grown large through the consumption of a magic eggplant, the Raterpillar descends into madness and eats Tweedle Dum Pig and Tweedle Dee Idiot Pig.
CHOMP CHOMP CHOMP CHOMP
And the soldiers.
And the Cheshire Snuffles.
And the Queen.
And the Mad Ducker.
And the zebra.
And a goat.
Whoa Whoa Whoa. I wasn't even in this story.
10/30
Indifferent to continuity errors, the Raterpillar eats him anyways.
Plotline schmotline.

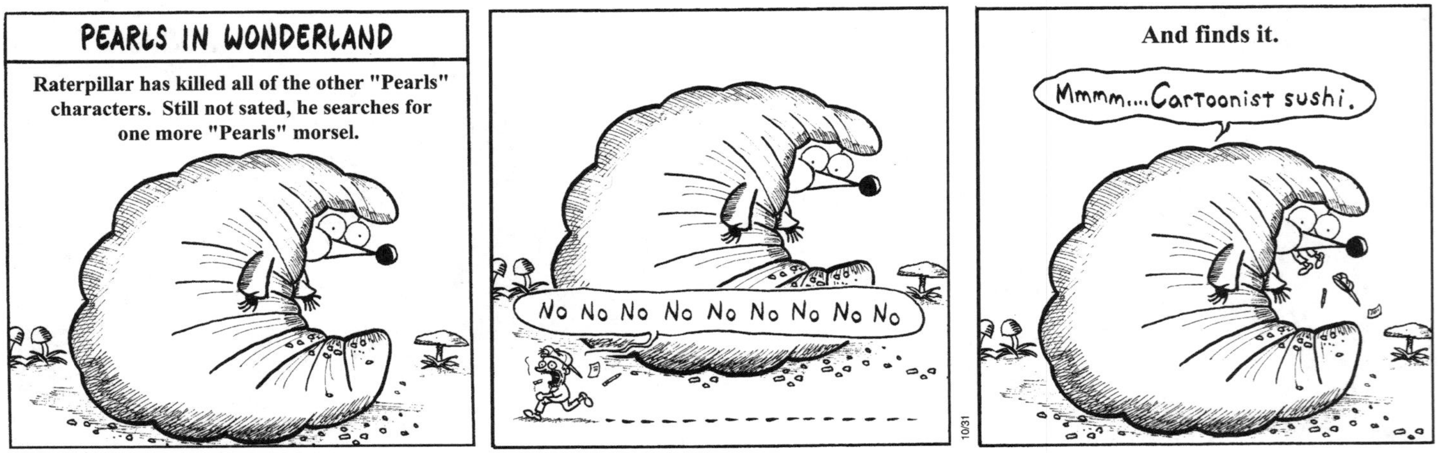
PEARLS IN WONDERLAND
Raterpillar has killed all of the other "Pearls" characters. Still not sated, he searches for one more "Pearls" morsel.
No No No No No No No No No
10/31
And finds it.
Mmmm....Cartoonist sushi.

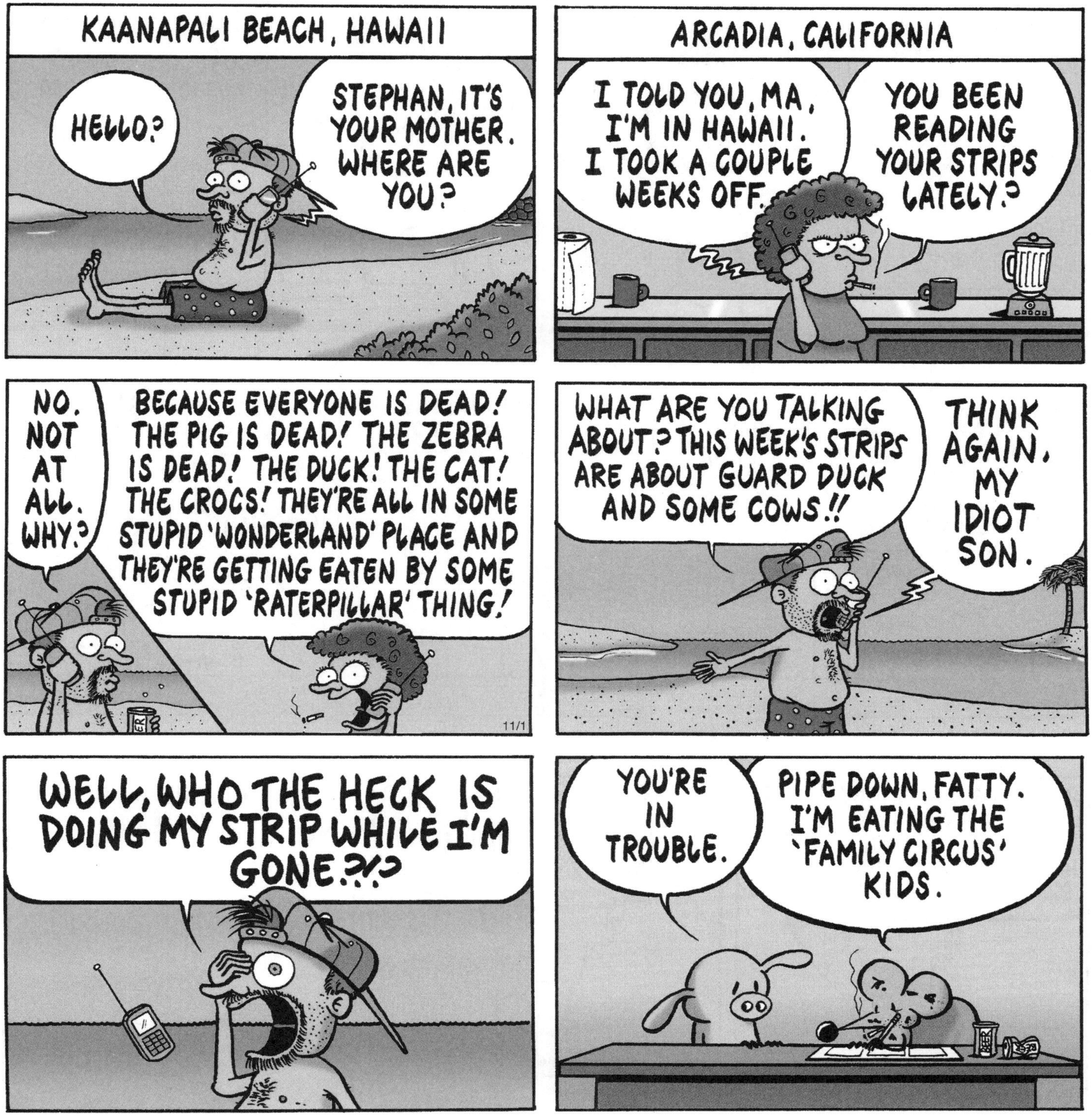
KAANAPALI BEACH, HAWAII
HELLO?
STEPHAN, IT'S YOUR MOTHER. WHERE ARE YOU?
ARCADIA, CALIFORNIA
I TOLD YOU, MA, I'M IN HAWAII. I TOOK A COUPLE WEEKS OFF.
YOU BEEN READING YOUR STRIPS LATELY?
NO. NOT AT ALL. WHY?
BECAUSE EVERYONE IS DEAD! THE PIG IS DEAD! THE ZEBRA IS DEAD! THE DUCK! THE CAT! THE CROCS! THEY'RE ALL IN SOME STUPID 'WONDERLAND' PLACE AND THEY'RE GETTING EATEN BY SOME STUPID 'RATERPILLAR' THING!
11/1
WHAT ARE YOU TALKING ABOUT? THIS WEEK'S STRIPS ARE ABOUT GUARD DUCK AND SOME COWS!!
THINK AGAIN, MY IDIOT SON.
WELL, WHO THE HECK IS DOING MY STRIP WHILE I'M GONE?!?
YOU'RE IN TROUBLE.
PIPE DOWN, FATTY. I'M EATING THE 'FAMILY CIRCUS' KIDS.

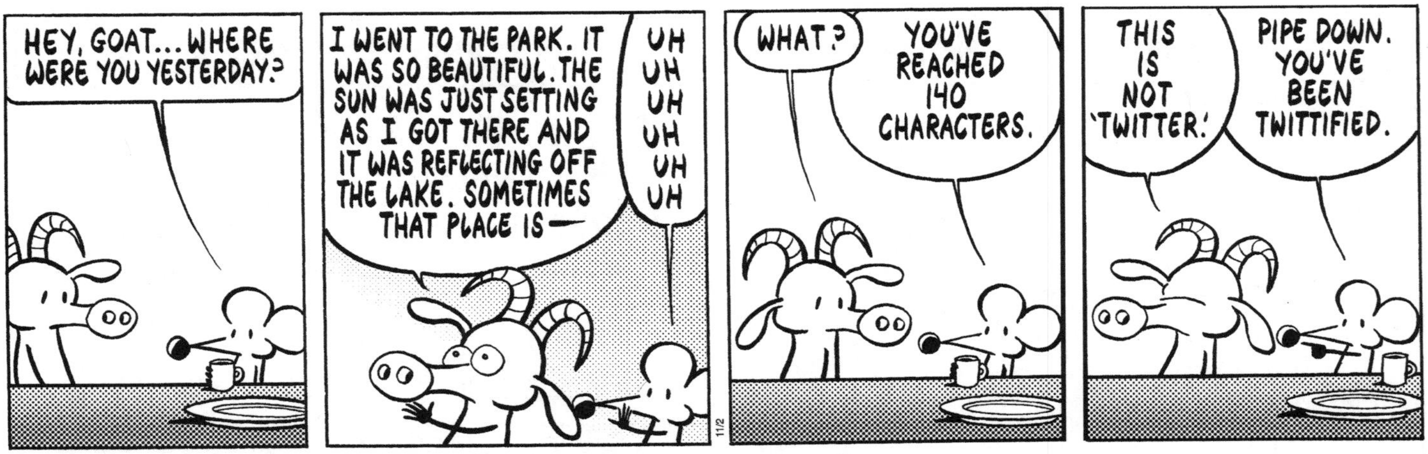
HEY, GOAT... WHERE WERE YOU YESTERDAY?
I WENT TO THE PARK. IT WAS SO BEAUTIFUL. THE SUN WAS JUST SETTING AS I GOT THERE AND IT WAS REFLECTING OFF THE LAKE. SOMETIMES THAT PLACE IS—
UH UH UH UH UH UH
11/2
WHAT?
YOU'VE REACHED 140 CHARACTERS.
THIS IS NOT 'TWITTER.'
PIPE DOWN. YOU'VE BEEN TWITTIFIED.

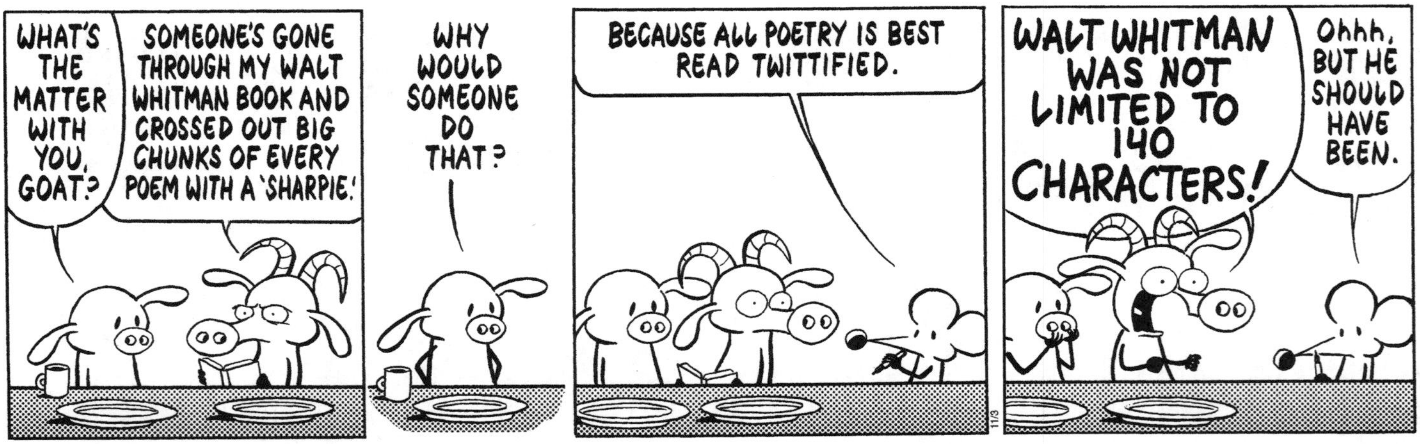
WHAT'S THE MATTER WITH YOU, GOAT?
SOMEONE'S GONE THROUGH MY WALT WHITMAN BOOK AND CROSSED OUT BIG CHUNKS OF EVERY POEM WITH A 'SHARPIE.'
WHY WOULD SOMEONE DO THAT?
BECAUSE ALL POETRY IS BEST READ TWITTIFIED.
11/3
WALT WHITMAN WAS NOT LIMITED TO 140 CHARACTERS!
Ohhh, BUT HE SHOULD HAVE BEEN.

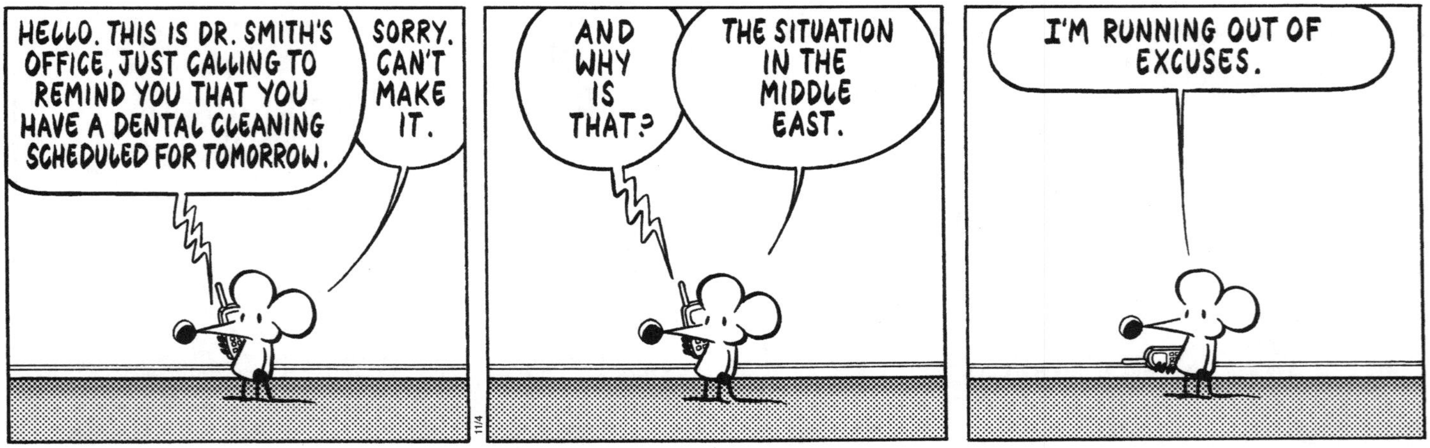
HELLO. THIS IS DR. SMITH'S OFFICE, JUST CALLING TO REMIND YOU THAT YOU HAVE A DENTAL CLEANING SCHEDULED FOR TOMORROW.
SORRY. CAN'T MAKE IT.
11/4
AND WHY IS THAT?
THE SITUATION IN THE MIDDLE EAST.
I'M RUNNING OUT OF EXCUSES.

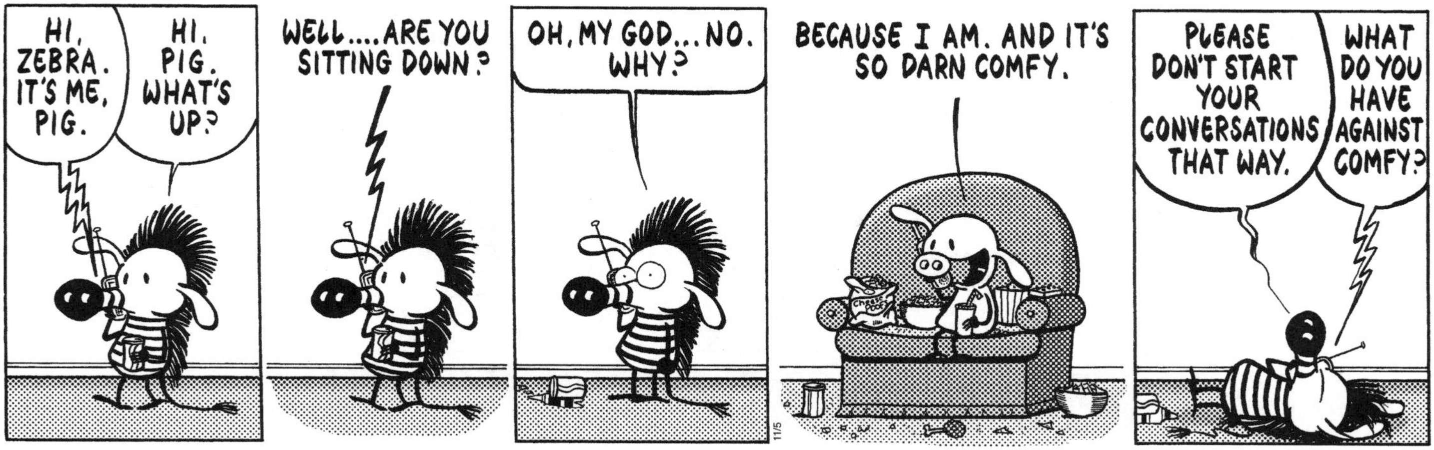
HI, ZEBRA. IT'S ME, PIG.
HI. PIG. WHAT'S UP?
WELL....ARE YOU SITTING DOWN?
OH, MY GOD...NO. WHY?
BECAUSE I AM. AND IT'S SO DARN COMFY.
PLEASE DON'T START YOUR CONVERSATIONS THAT WAY.
WHAT DO YOU HAVE AGAINST COMFY?

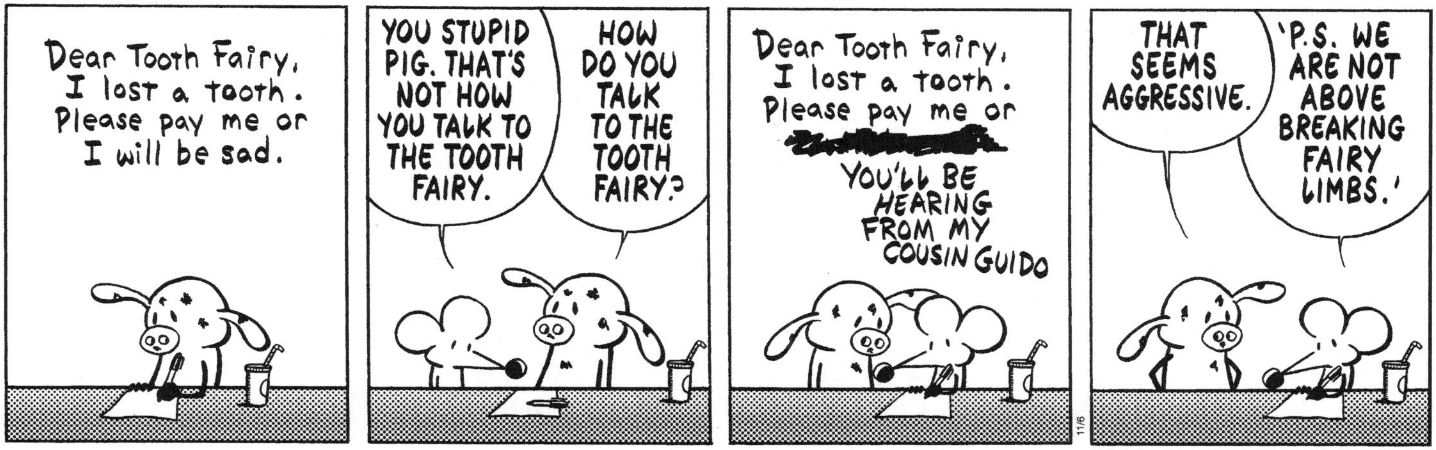
Dear Tooth Fairy, I lost a tooth. Please pay me or I will be sad.
YOU STUPID PIG. THAT'S NOT HOW YOU TALK TO THE TOOTH FAIRY.
HOW DO YOU TALK TO THE TOOTH FAIRY?
Dear Tooth Fairy, I lost a tooth. Please pay me or [redacted]
YOU'LL BE HEARING FROM MY COUSIN GUIDO
THAT SEEMS AGGRESSIVE.
'P.S. WE ARE NOT ABOVE BREAKING FAIRY LIMBS.'

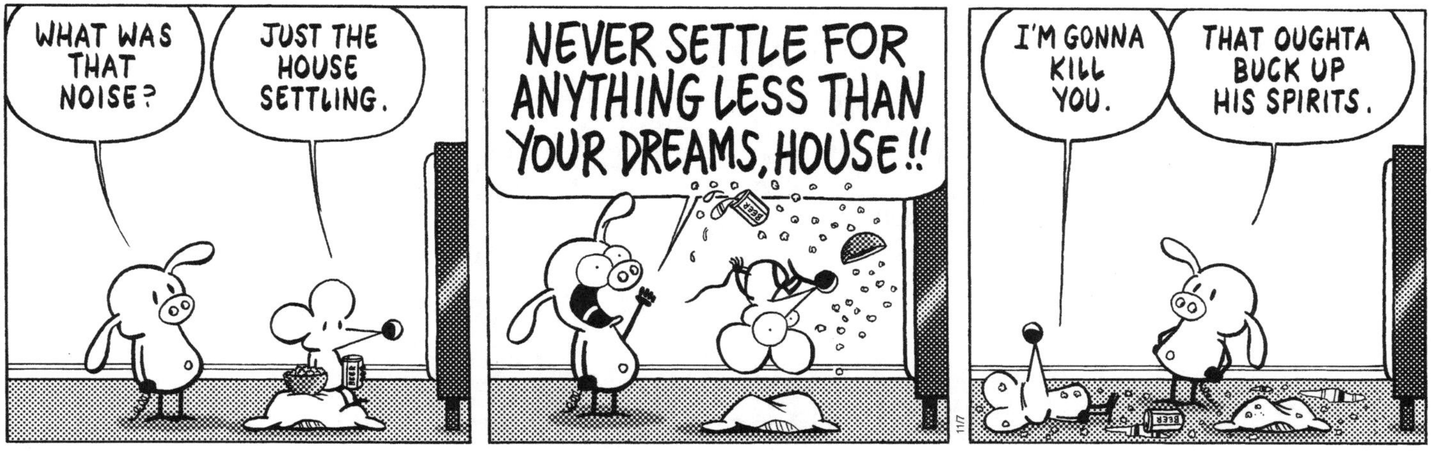
WHAT WAS THAT NOISE?
JUST THE HOUSE SETTLING.
NEVER SETTLE FOR ANYTHING LESS THAN YOUR DREAMS, HOUSE!!
I'M GONNA KILL YOU.
THAT OUGHTA BUCK UP HIS SPIRITS.

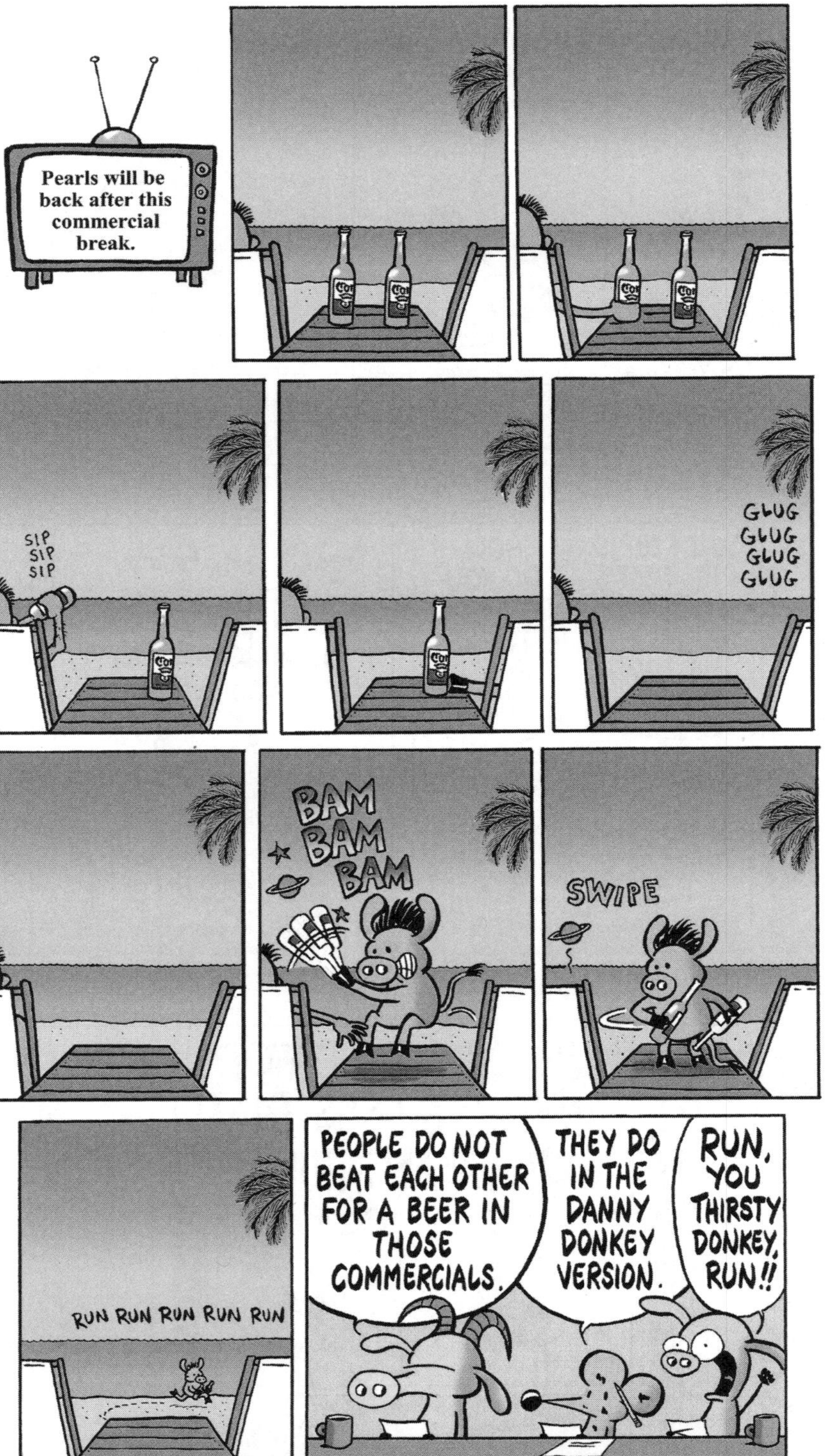
Pearls will be back after this commercial break.
SIP SIP SIP
GLUG GLUG GLUG GLUG
BAM BAM BAM
SWIPE
RUN RUN RUN RUN RUN
PEOPLE DO NOT BEAT EACH OTHER FOR A BEER IN THOSE COMMERCIALS.
THEY DO IN THE DANNY DONKEY VERSION.
RUN, YOU THIRSTY DONKEY, RUN!!

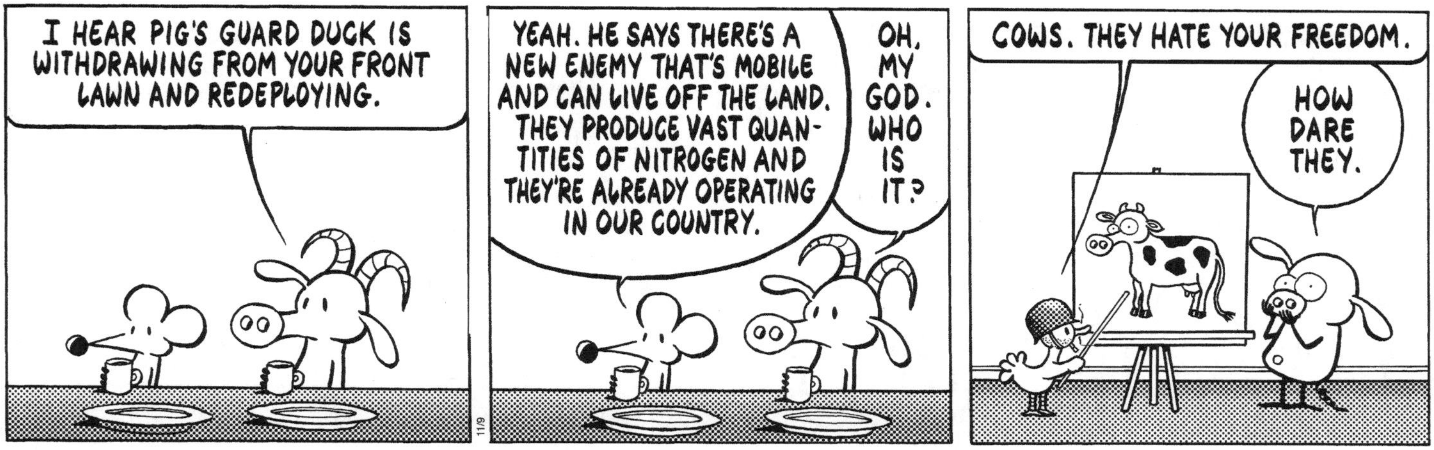
I HEAR PIG'S GUARD DUCK IS WITHDRAWING FROM YOUR FRONT LAWN AND REDEPLOYING.
11/9
YEAH. HE SAYS THERE'S A NEW ENEMY THAT'S MOBILE AND CAN LIVE OFF THE LAND. THEY PRODUCE VAST QUANTITIES OF NITROGEN AND THEY'RE ALREADY OPERATING IN OUR COUNTRY.
OH, MY GOD. WHO IS IT?
COWS. THEY HATE YOUR FREEDOM.
HOW DARE THEY.

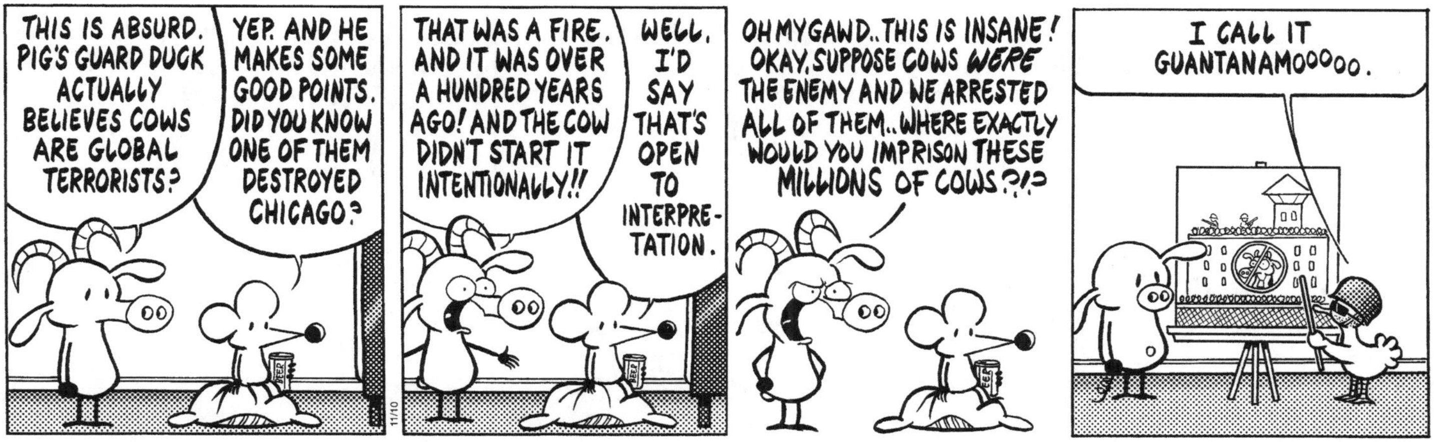
THIS IS ABSURD. PIG'S GUARD DUCK ACTUALLY BELIEVES COWS ARE GLOBAL TERRORISTS?
YEP. AND HE MAKES SOME GOOD POINTS. DID YOU KNOW ONE OF THEM DESTROYED CHICAGO?
BEER
11/10
THAT WAS A FIRE. AND IT WAS OVER A HUNDRED YEARS AGO! AND THE COW DIDN'T START IT INTENTIONALLY!!
WELL, I'D SAY THAT'S OPEN TO INTERPRETATION.
BEER
OHMYGAWD.. THIS IS INSANE! OKAY, SUPPOSE COWS *WERE* THE ENEMY AND WE ARRESTED ALL OF THEM.. WHERE EXACTLY WOULD YOU IMPRISON THESE MILLIONS OF COWS?!?
BEER
I CALL IT GUANTANAMOOOOO.

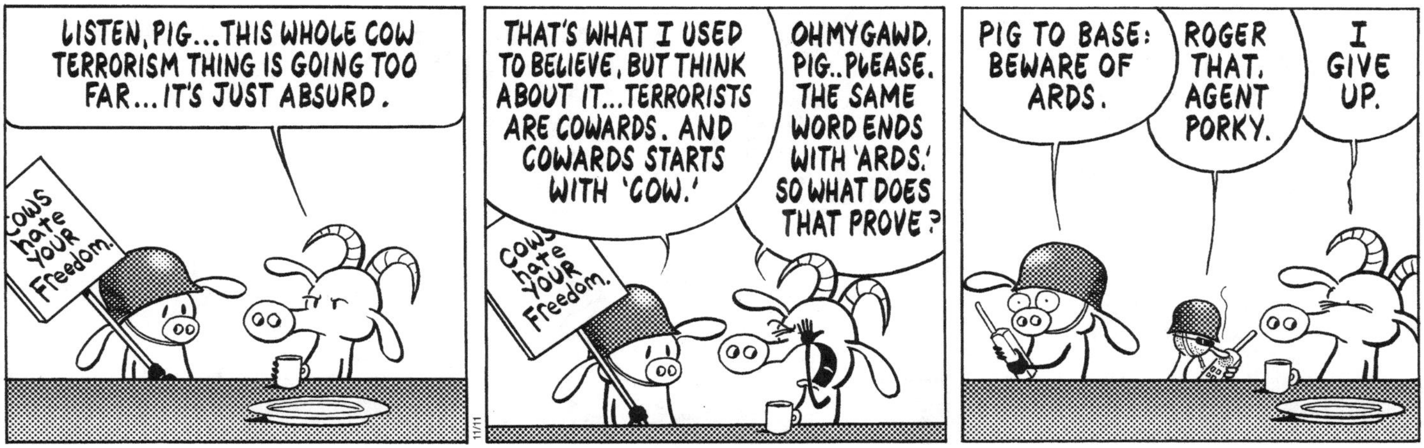
LISTEN, PIG... THIS WHOLE COW TERRORISM THING IS GOING TOO FAR... IT'S JUST ABSURD.
COWS hate YOUR Freedom.
11/11
THAT'S WHAT I USED TO BELIEVE, BUT THINK ABOUT IT... TERRORISTS ARE COWARDS. AND COWARDS STARTS WITH 'COW.'
OHMYGAWD. PIG.. PLEASE. THE SAME WORD ENDS WITH 'ARDS.' SO WHAT DOES THAT PROVE?
COWS hate YOUR Freedom.
PIG TO BASE: BEWARE OF ARDS.
ROGER THAT, AGENT PORKY.
I GIVE UP.

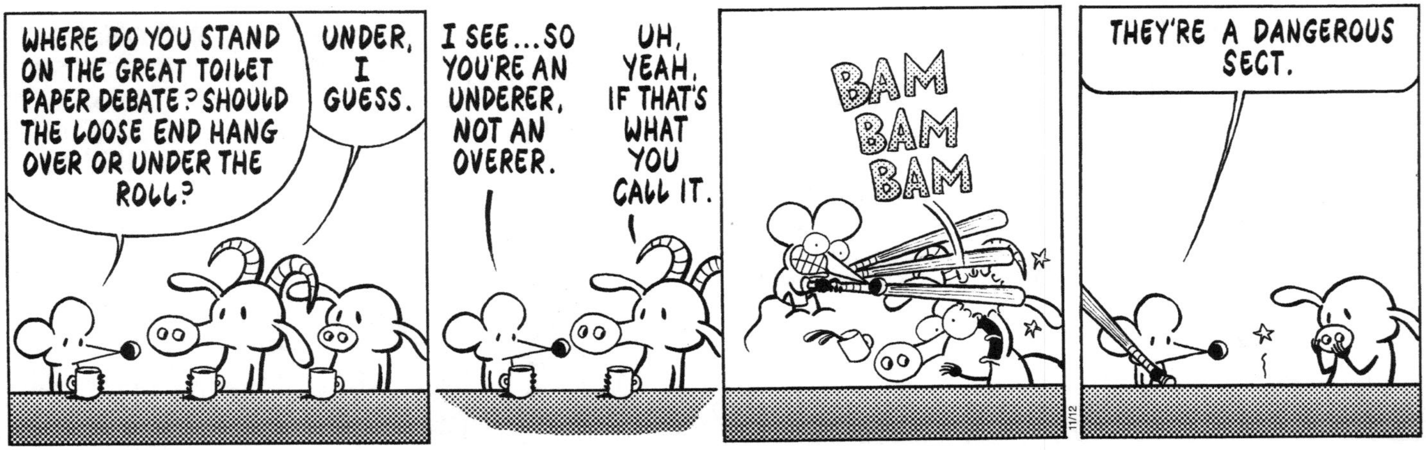
WHERE DO YOU STAND ON THE GREAT TOILET PAPER DEBATE? SHOULD THE LOOSE END HANG OVER OR UNDER THE ROLL?
UNDER, I GUESS.
I SEE...SO YOU'RE AN UNDERER, NOT AN OVERER.
UH, YEAH, IF THAT'S WHAT YOU CALL IT.
BAM
BAM
BAM
11/12
THEY'RE A DANGEROUS SECT.

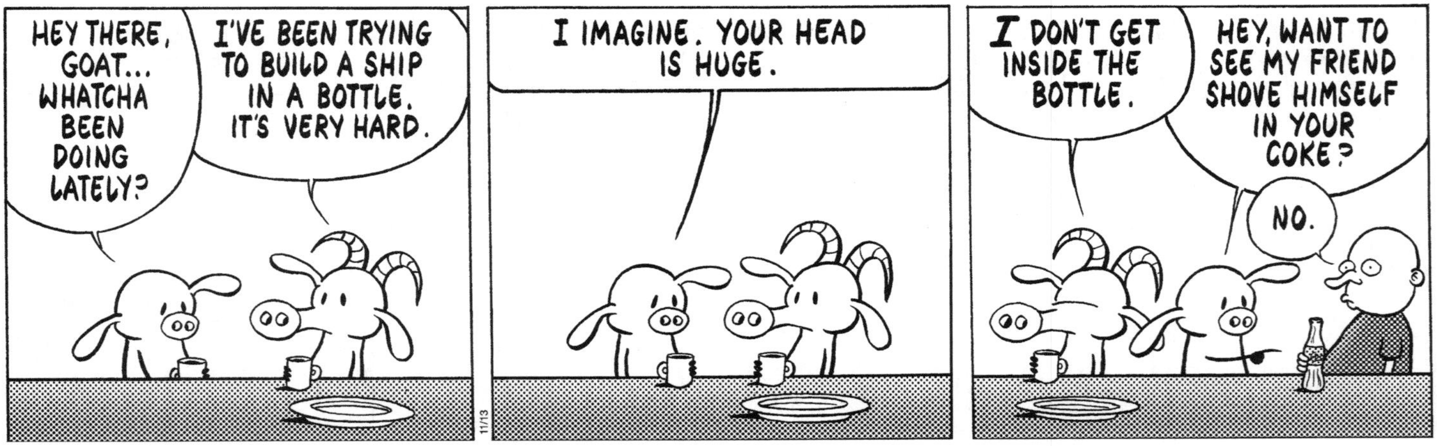
HEY THERE, GOAT... WHATCHA BEEN DOING LATELY?
I'VE BEEN TRYING TO BUILD A SHIP IN A BOTTLE. IT'S VERY HARD.
11/13
I IMAGINE. YOUR HEAD IS HUGE.
I DON'T GET INSIDE THE BOTTLE.
HEY, WANT TO SEE MY FRIEND SHOVE HIMSELF IN YOUR COKE?
NO.

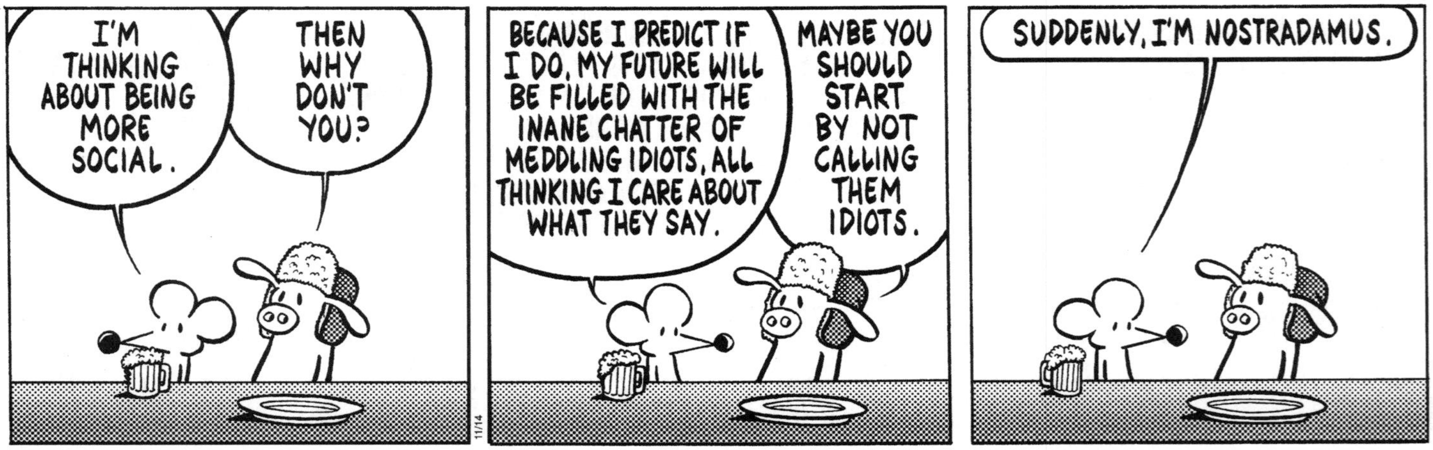
I'M THINKING ABOUT BEING MORE SOCIAL.
THEN WHY DON'T YOU?
11/14
BECAUSE I PREDICT IF I DO, MY FUTURE WILL BE FILLED WITH THE INANE CHATTER OF MEDDLING IDIOTS, ALL THINKING I CARE ABOUT WHAT THEY SAY.
MAYBE YOU SHOULD START BY NOT CALLING THEM IDIOTS.
SUDDENLY, I'M NOSTRADAMUS.

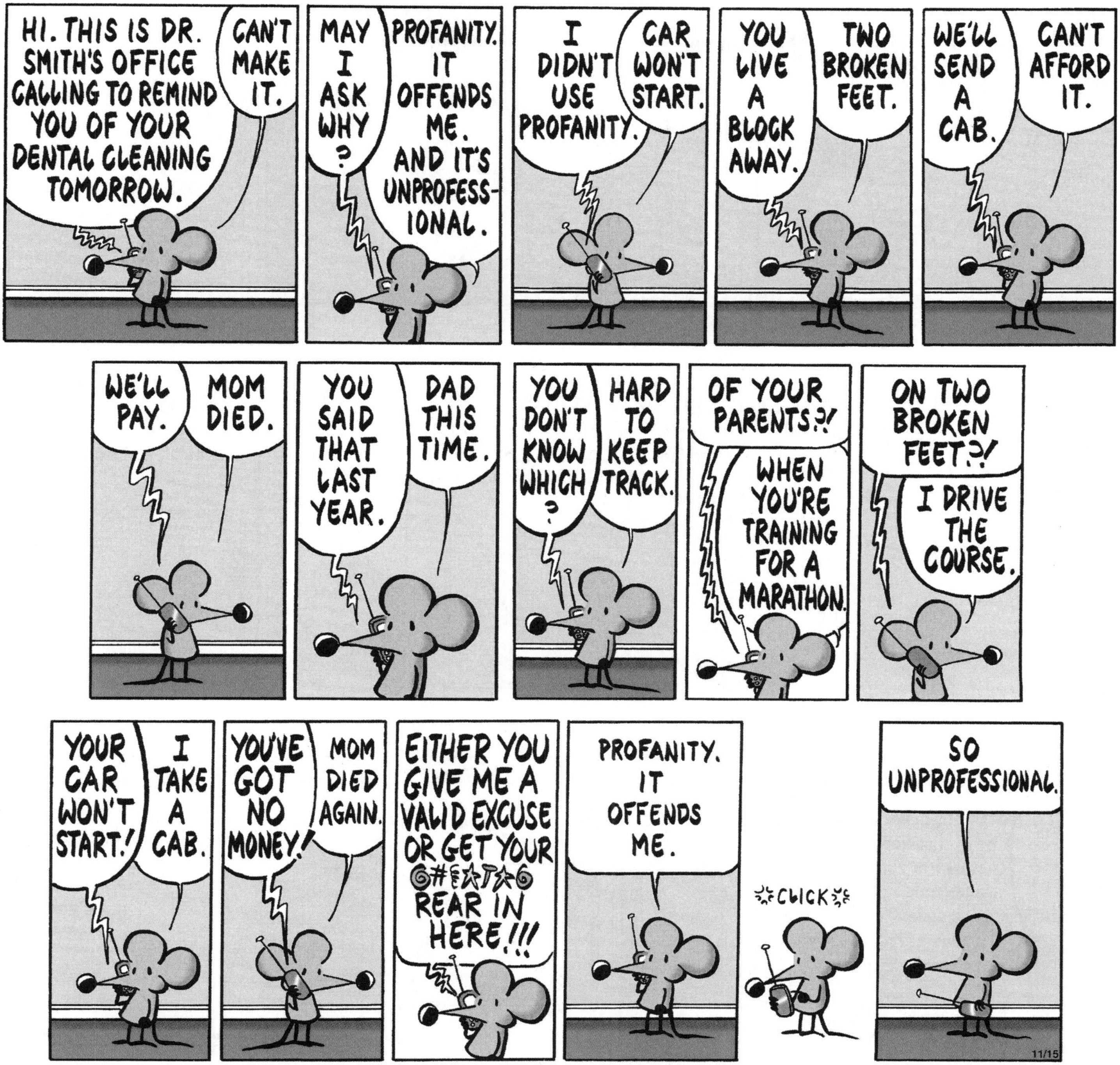
HI. THIS IS DR. SMITH'S OFFICE CALLING TO REMIND YOU OF YOUR DENTAL CLEANING TOMORROW.
CAN'T MAKE IT.
MAY I ASK WHY?
PROFANITY. IT OFFENDS ME. AND IT'S UNPROFESSIONAL.
I DIDN'T USE PROFANITY.
CAR WON'T START.
YOU LIVE A BLOCK AWAY.
TWO BROKEN FEET.
WE'LL SEND A CAB.
CAN'T AFFORD IT.
WE'LL PAY.
MOM DIED.
YOU SAID THAT LAST YEAR.
DAD THIS TIME.
YOU DON'T KNOW WHICH?
HARD TO KEEP TRACK.
OF YOUR PARENTS?!
WHEN YOU'RE TRAINING FOR A MARATHON.
ON TWO BROKEN FEET?!
I DRIVE THE COURSE.
YOUR CAR WON'T START!
I TAKE A CAB.
YOU'VE GOT NO MONEY!
MOM DIED AGAIN.
EITHER YOU GIVE ME A VALID EXCUSE OR GET YOUR
REAR IN HERE!!!
PROFANITY. IT OFFENDS ME.
CLICK
SO UNPROFESSIONAL.
11/15

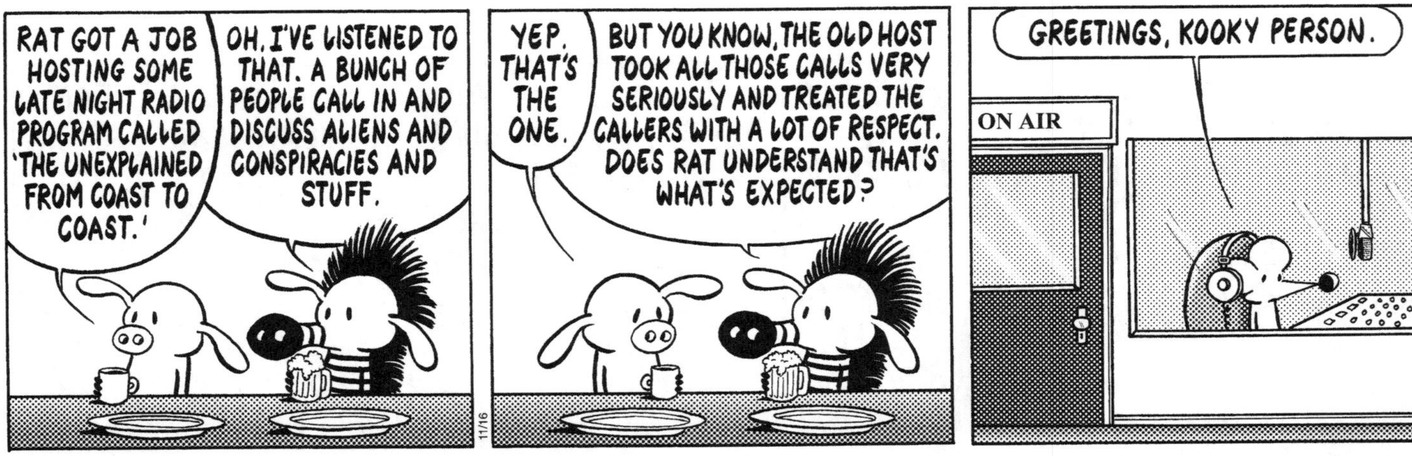
RAT GOT A JOB HOSTING SOME LATE NIGHT RADIO PROGRAM CALLED 'THE UNEXPLAINED FROM COAST TO COAST.'
OH, I'VE LISTENED TO THAT. A BUNCH OF PEOPLE CALL IN AND DISCUSS ALIENS AND CONSPIRACIES AND STUFF.
11/16
YEP. THAT'S THE ONE.
BUT YOU KNOW, THE OLD HOST TOOK ALL THOSE CALLS VERY SERIOUSLY AND TREATED THE CALLERS WITH A LOT OF RESPECT. DOES RAT UNDERSTAND THAT'S WHAT'S EXPECTED?
GREETINGS, KOOKY PERSON.
ON AIR

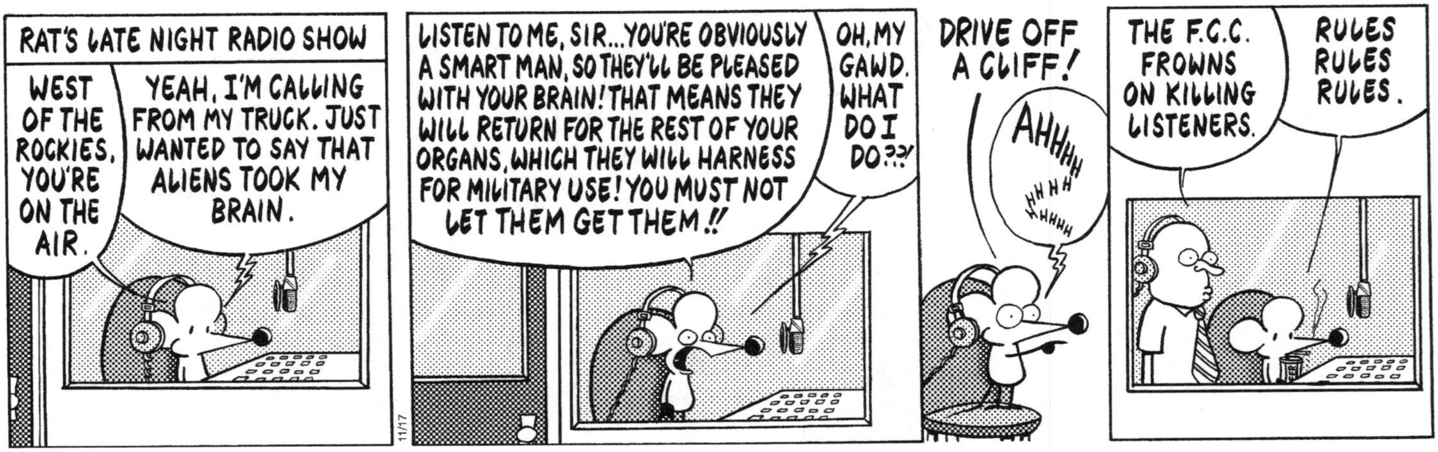
RAT'S LATE NIGHT RADIO SHOW
WEST OF THE ROCKIES, YOU'RE ON THE AIR.
YEAH, I'M CALLING FROM MY TRUCK. JUST WANTED TO SAY THAT ALIENS TOOK MY BRAIN.
11/17
LISTEN TO ME, SIR... YOU'RE OBVIOUSLY A SMART MAN, SO THEY'LL BE PLEASED WITH YOUR BRAIN! THAT MEANS THEY WILL RETURN FOR THE REST OF YOUR ORGANS, WHICH THEY WILL HARNESS FOR MILITARY USE! YOU MUST NOT LET THEM GET THEM!!
OH, MY GAWD. WHAT DO I DO?!?
DRIVE OFF A CLIFF!
AHHHHH HHHH HHHHH
THE F.C.C. FROWNS ON KILLING LISTENERS.
RULES RULES RULES.

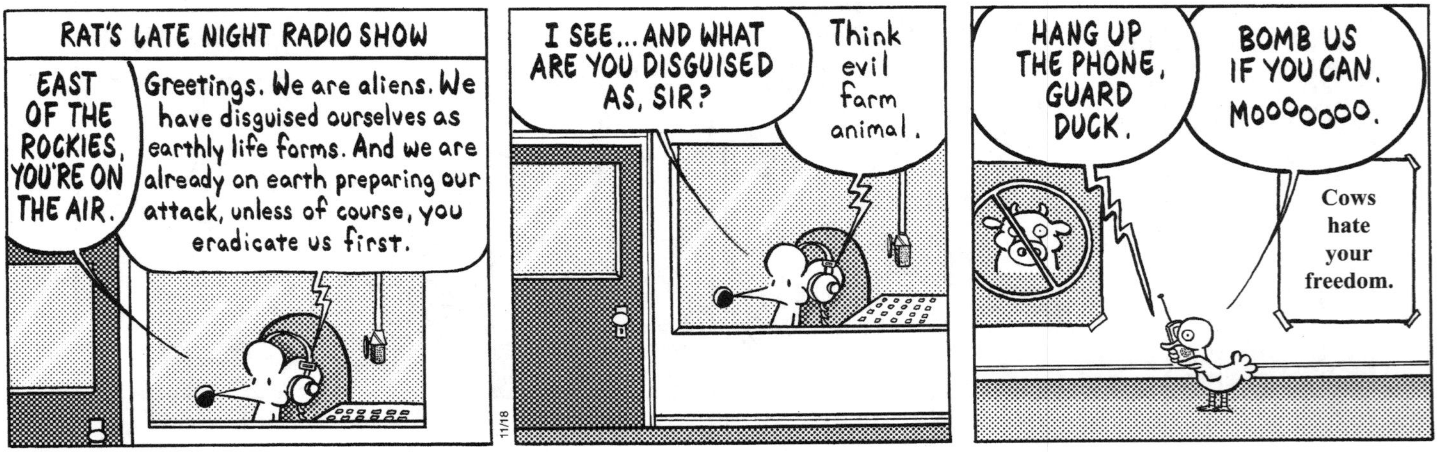
RAT'S LATE NIGHT RADIO SHOW
EAST OF THE ROCKIES, YOU'RE ON THE AIR.
Greetings. We are aliens. We have disguised ourselves as earthly life forms. And we are already on earth preparing our attack, unless of course, you eradicate us first.
11/18
I SEE... AND WHAT ARE YOU DISGUISED AS, SIR?
Think evil farm animal.
HANG UP THE PHONE, GUARD DUCK.
BOMB US IF YOU CAN. MOOOOOOO.
Cows hate your freedom.

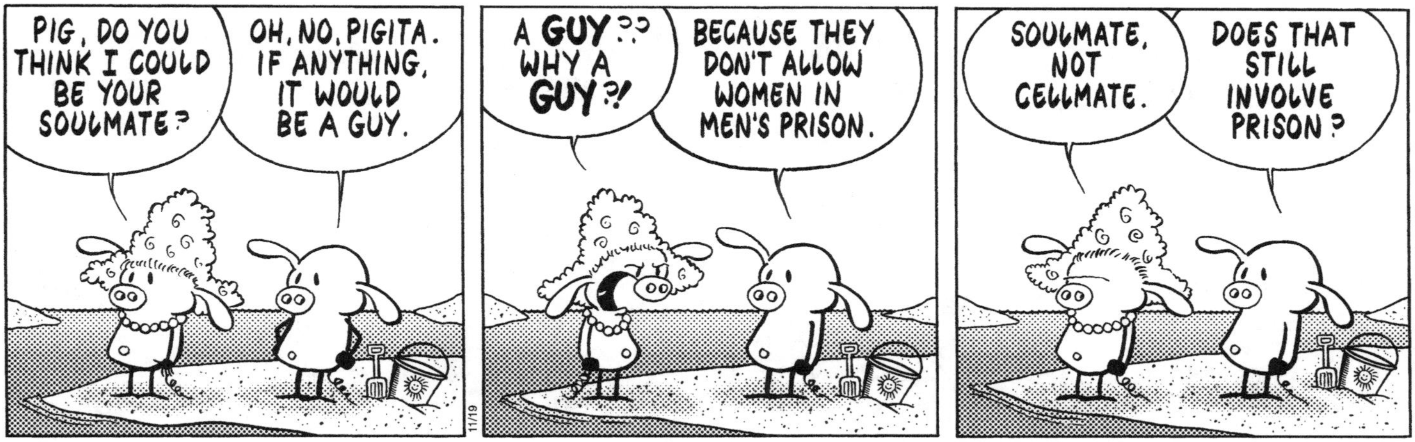
PIG, DO YOU THINK I COULD BE YOUR SOULMATE?
OH, NO, PIGITA. IF ANYTHING, IT WOULD BE A GUY.
11/19
A GUY?? WHY A GUY?!
BECAUSE THEY DON'T ALLOW WOMEN IN MEN'S PRISON.
SOULMATE, NOT CELLMATE.
DOES THAT STILL INVOLVE PRISON?

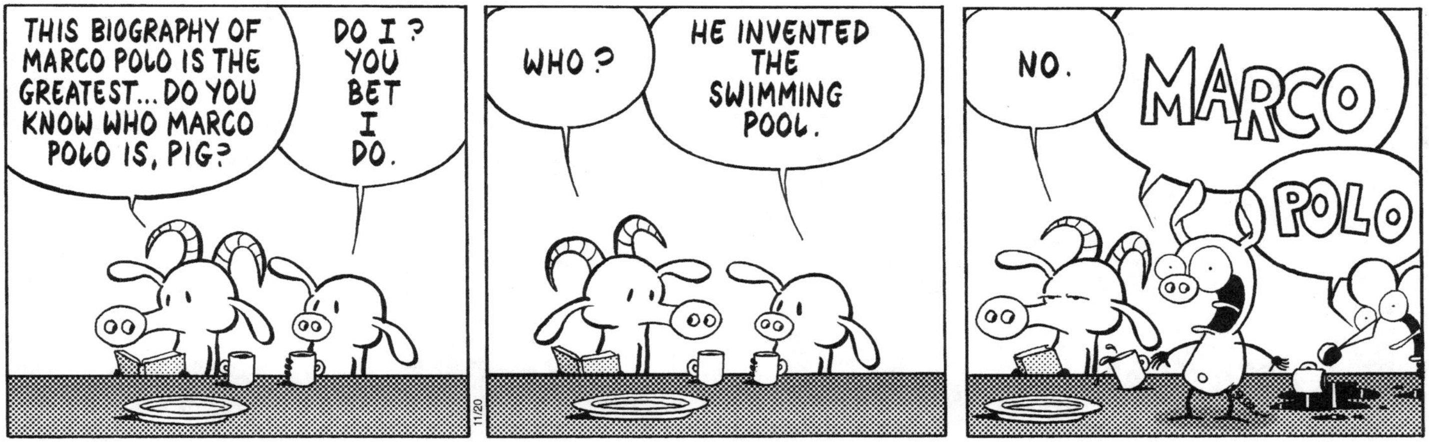
THIS BIOGRAPHY OF MARCO POLO IS THE GREATEST... DO YOU KNOW WHO MARCO POLO IS, PIG?
DO I? YOU BET I DO.
11/20
WHO?
HE INVENTED THE SWIMMING POOL.
NO.
MARCO
POLO

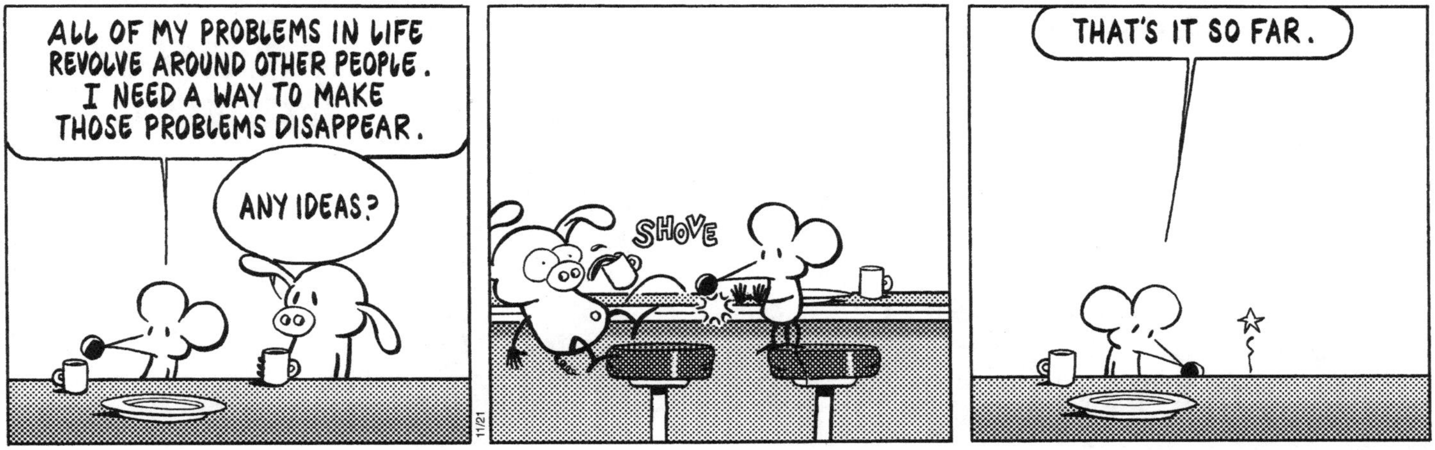
ALL OF MY PROBLEMS IN LIFE REVOLVE AROUND OTHER PEOPLE. I NEED A WAY TO MAKE THOSE PROBLEMS DISAPPEAR.
ANY IDEAS?
11/21
SHOVE
THAT'S IT SO FAR.

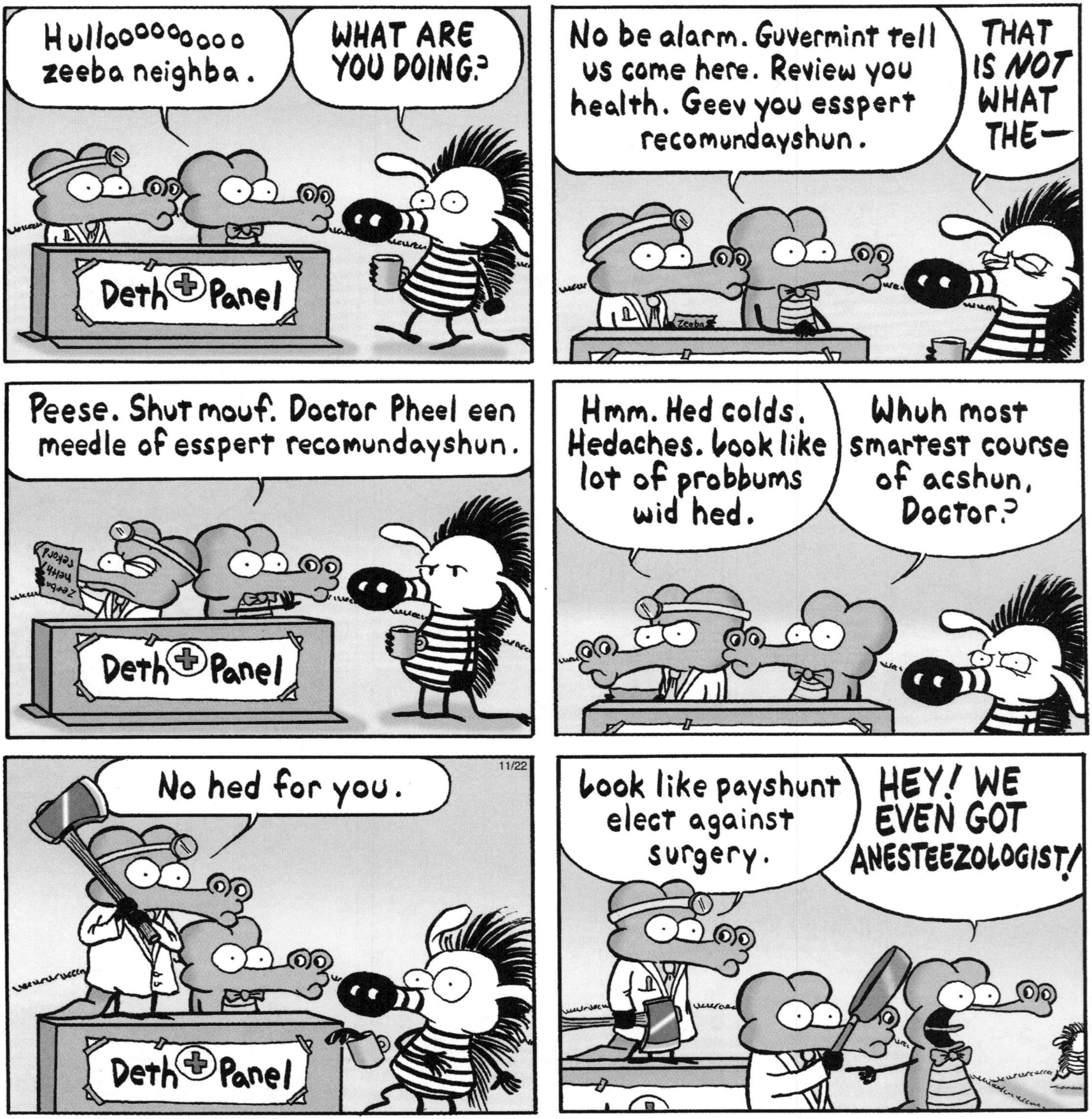
Hulloooooooo zeeba neighba.
WHAT ARE YOU DOING?
Deth Panel
No be alarm. Guvermint tell us come here. Review you health. Geev you essprt recomundayshun.
THAT IS NOT WHAT THE—
Zeeba
Peese. Shut mouf. Doctor Pheel een meedle of essprt recomundayshun.
Zeeba helth rekord
Deth Panel
Hmm. Hed colds. Hedaches. Look like lot of probbums wid hed.
Whuh most smartest course of acshun, Doctor?
No hed for you.
11/22
Deth Panel
Look like payshunt elect against surgery.
HEY! WE EVEN GOT ANESTEEZOLOGIST!

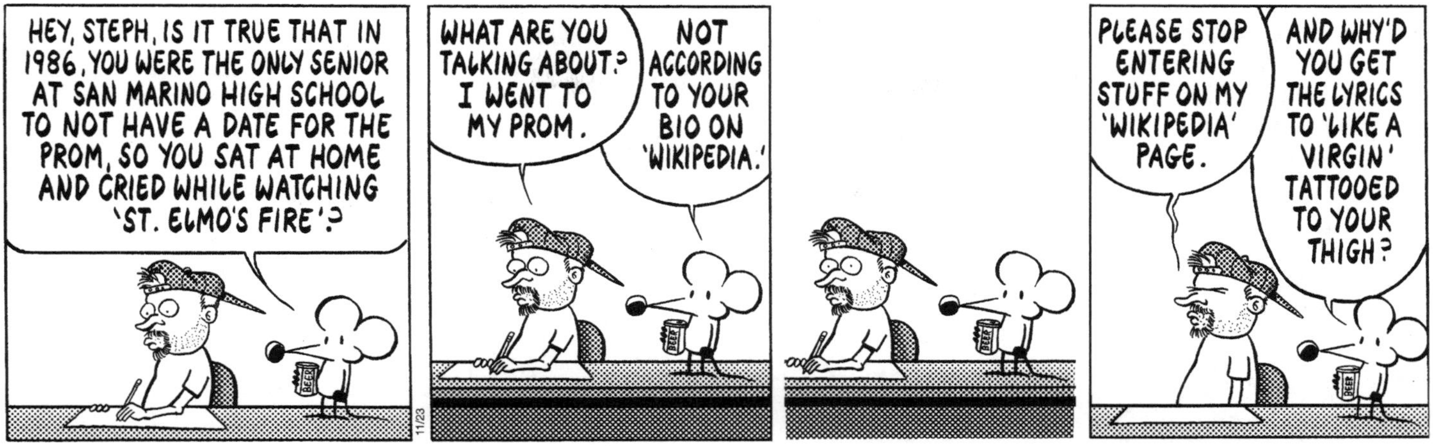
HEY, STEPH, IS IT TRUE THAT IN 1986, YOU WERE THE ONLY SENIOR AT SAN MARINO HIGH SCHOOL TO NOT HAVE A DATE FOR THE PROM, SO YOU SAT AT HOME AND CRIED WHILE WATCHING 'ST. ELMO'S FIRE'?
WHAT ARE YOU TALKING ABOUT? I WENT TO MY PROM.
NOT ACCORDING TO YOUR BIO ON 'WIKIPEDIA.'
PLEASE STOP ENTERING STUFF ON MY 'WIKIPEDIA' PAGE.
AND WHY'D YOU GET THE LYRICS TO 'LIKE A VIRGIN' TATTOOED TO YOUR THIGH?

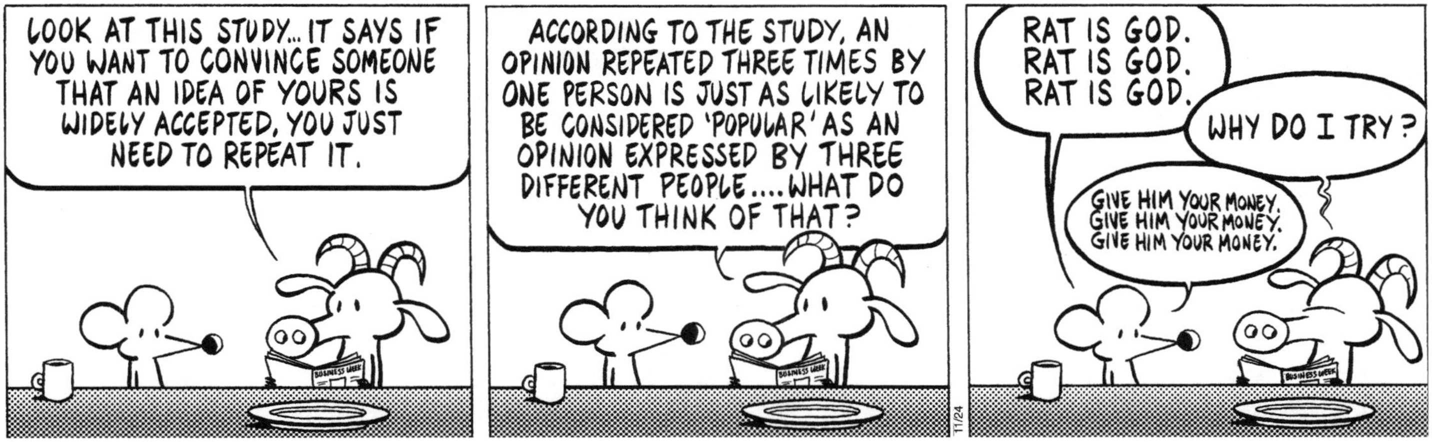
LOOK AT THIS STUDY... IT SAYS IF YOU WANT TO CONVINCE SOMEONE THAT AN IDEA OF YOURS IS WIDELY ACCEPTED, YOU JUST NEED TO REPEAT IT.
ACCORDING TO THE STUDY, AN OPINION REPEATED THREE TIMES BY ONE PERSON IS JUST AS LIKELY TO BE CONSIDERED 'POPULAR' AS AN OPINION EXPRESSED BY THREE DIFFERENT PEOPLE.... WHAT DO YOU THINK OF THAT?
RAT IS GOD. RAT IS GOD. RAT IS GOD.
GIVE HIM YOUR MONEY. GIVE HIM YOUR MONEY. GIVE HIM YOUR MONEY.
WHY DO I TRY?

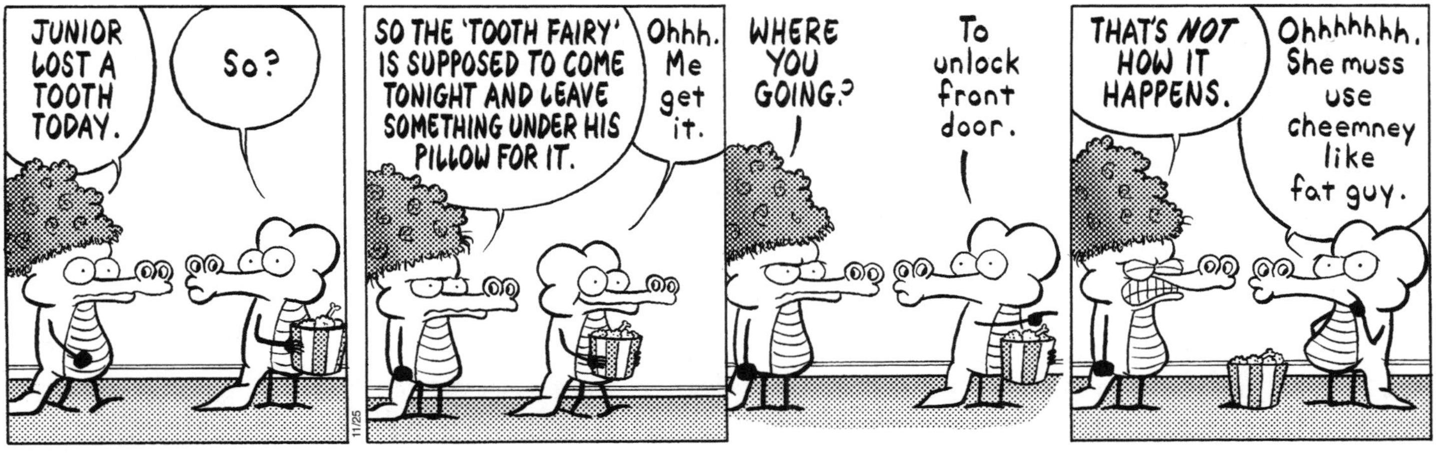
JUNIOR LOST A TOOTH TODAY.
So?
SO THE 'TOOTH FAIRY' IS SUPPOSED TO COME TONIGHT AND LEAVE SOMETHING UNDER HIS PILLOW FOR IT.
Ohhh. Me get it.
WHERE YOU GOING?
To unlock front door.
THAT'S NOT HOW IT HAPPENS.
Ohhhhhhh. She muss use cheemney like fat guy.

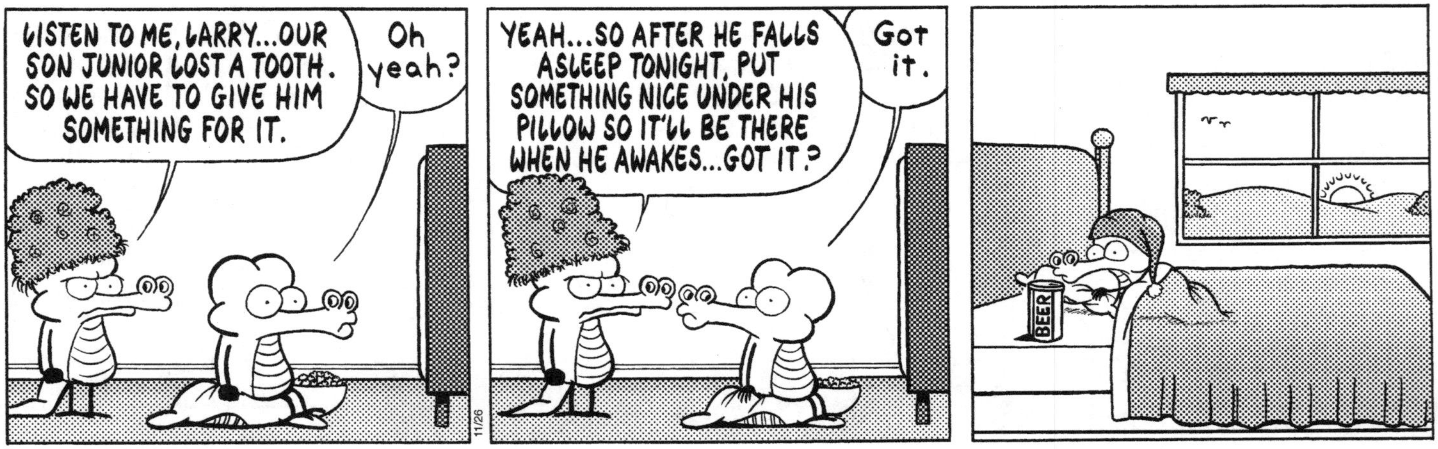
LISTEN TO ME, LARRY...OUR SON JUNIOR LOST A TOOTH. SO WE HAVE TO GIVE HIM SOMETHING FOR IT.
Oh yeah?
YEAH...SO AFTER HE FALLS ASLEEP TONIGHT, PUT SOMETHING NICE UNDER HIS PILLOW SO IT'LL BE THERE WHEN HE AWAKES...GOT IT?
Got it.
BEER
11/26

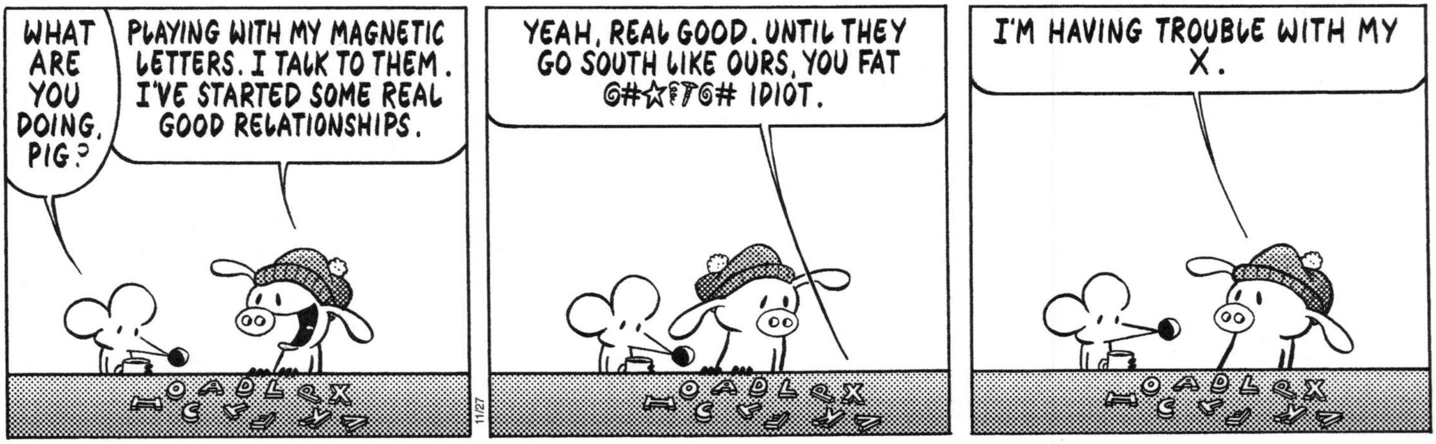
WHAT ARE YOU DOING, PIG?
PLAYING WITH MY MAGNETIC LETTERS. I TALK TO THEM. I'VE STARTED SOME REAL GOOD RELATIONSHIPS.
YEAH, REAL GOOD. UNTIL THEY GO SOUTH LIKE OURS, YOU FAT @#☆!?@# IDIOT.
I'M HAVING TROUBLE WITH MY X.
11/27

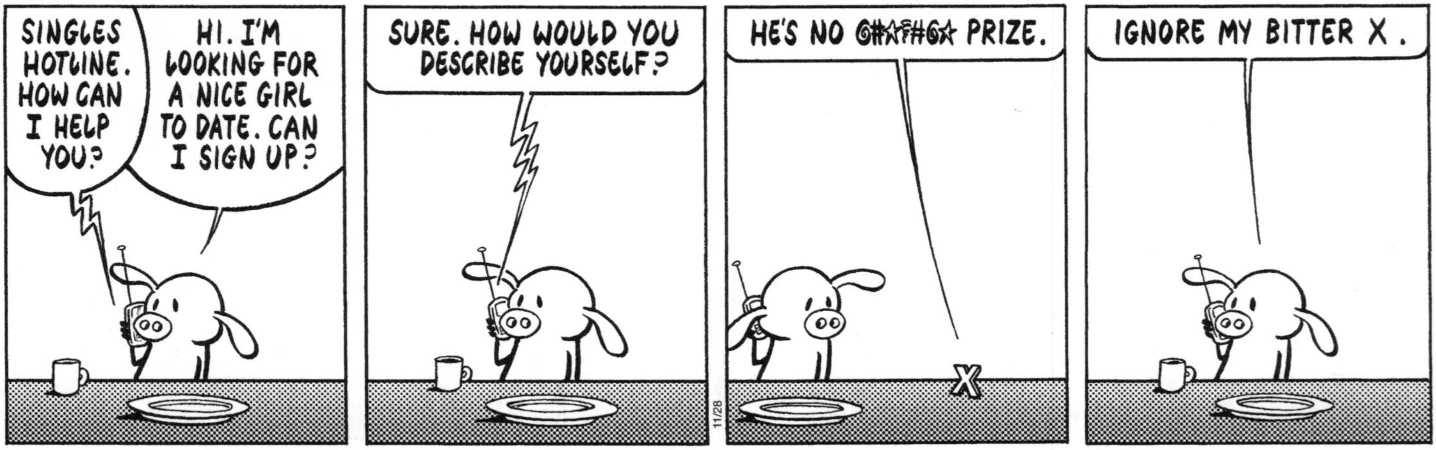
SINGLES HOTLINE. HOW CAN I HELP YOU?
HI. I'M LOOKING FOR A NICE GIRL TO DATE. CAN I SIGN UP?
SURE. HOW WOULD YOU DESCRIBE YOURSELF?
HE'S NO @#☆!@☆ PRIZE.
IGNORE MY BITTER X.
11/28

STORY UPDATE

Pig is playing with magnetic letters. He is having trouble with his 'X.'

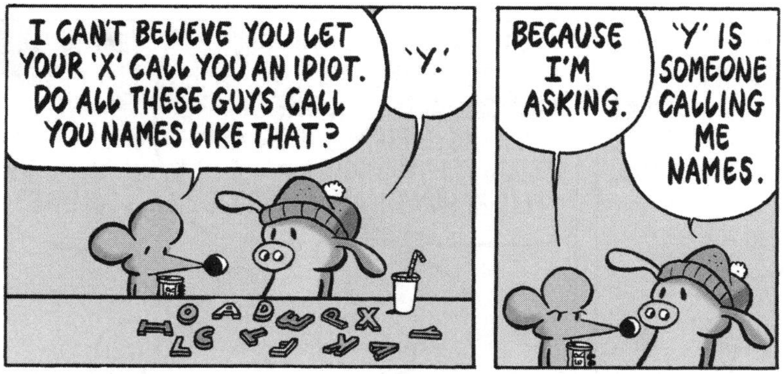
I CAN'T BELIEVE YOU LET YOUR 'X' CALL YOU AN IDIOT. DO ALL THESE GUYS CALL YOU NAMES LIKE THAT?
'Y.'
BECAUSE I'M ASKING.
'Y' IS SOMEONE CALLING ME NAMES.

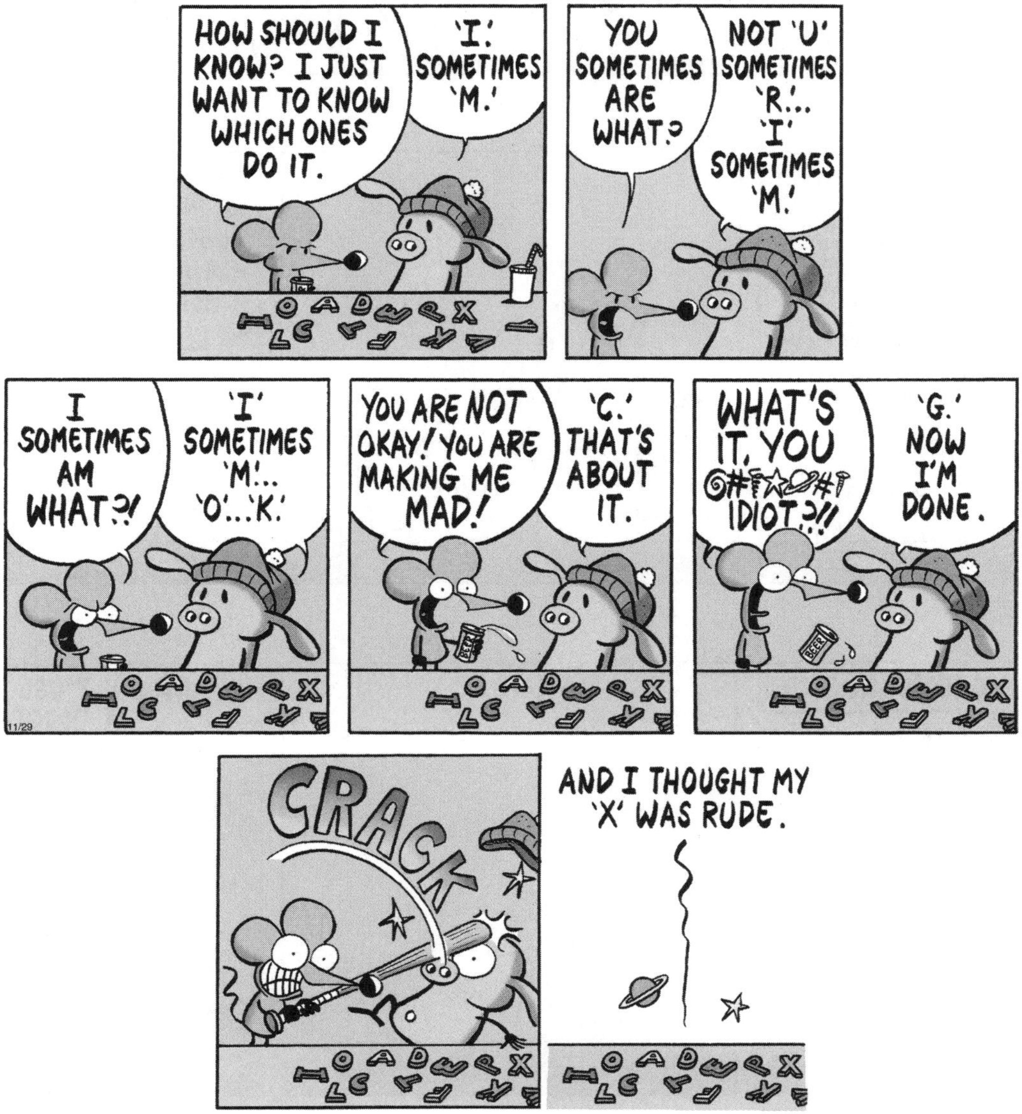
HOW SHOULD I KNOW? I JUST WANT TO KNOW WHICH ONES DO IT.
'I.' SOMETIMES 'M.'
YOU SOMETIMES ARE WHAT?
NOT 'U' SOMETIMES 'R.'... 'I' SOMETIMES 'M.'
I SOMETIMES AM WHAT?!
'I' SOMETIMES 'M.'... 'O.'...'K.'
YOU ARE NOT OKAY! YOU ARE MAKING ME MAD!
'C.' THAT'S ABOUT IT.
WHAT'S IT, YOU IDIOT?!!
'G.' NOW I'M DONE.
CRACK
AND I THOUGHT MY 'X' WAS RUDE.

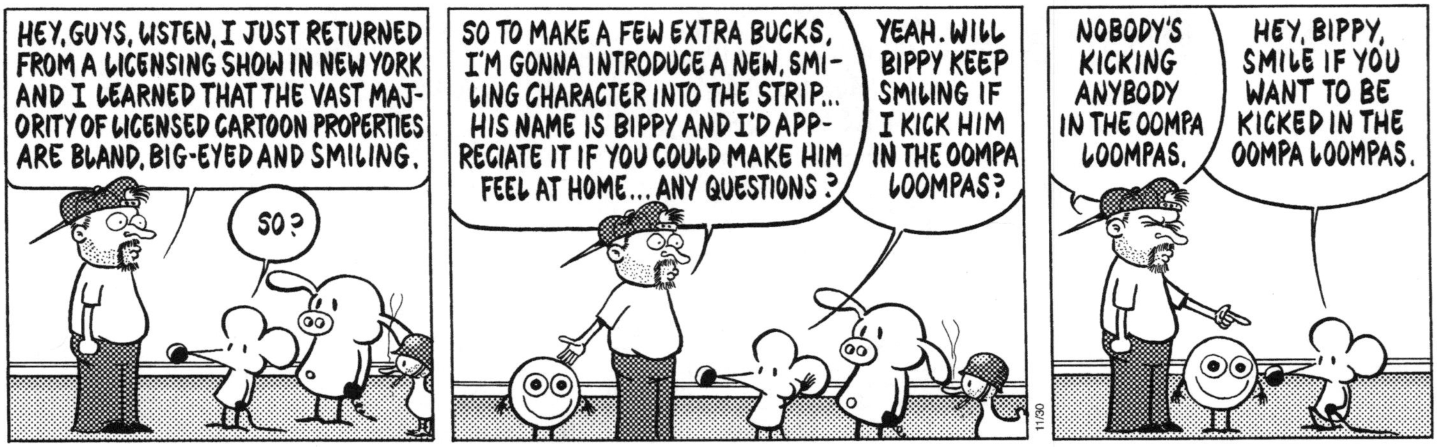
HEY, GUYS, LISTEN, I JUST RETURNED FROM A LICENSING SHOW IN NEW YORK AND I LEARNED THAT THE VAST MAJORITY OF LICENSED CARTOON PROPERTIES ARE BLAND, BIG-EYED AND SMILING.
SO?
SO TO MAKE A FEW EXTRA BUCKS, I'M GONNA INTRODUCE A NEW, SMILING CHARACTER INTO THE STRIP... HIS NAME IS BIPPY AND I'D APPRECIATE IT IF YOU COULD MAKE HIM FEEL AT HOME... ANY QUESTIONS?
YEAH. WILL BIPPY KEEP SMILING IF I KICK HIM IN THE OOMPA LOOMPAS?
11/30
NOBODY'S KICKING ANYBODY IN THE OOMPA LOOMPAS.
HEY, BIPPY, SMILE IF YOU WANT TO BE KICKED IN THE OOMPA LOOMPAS.

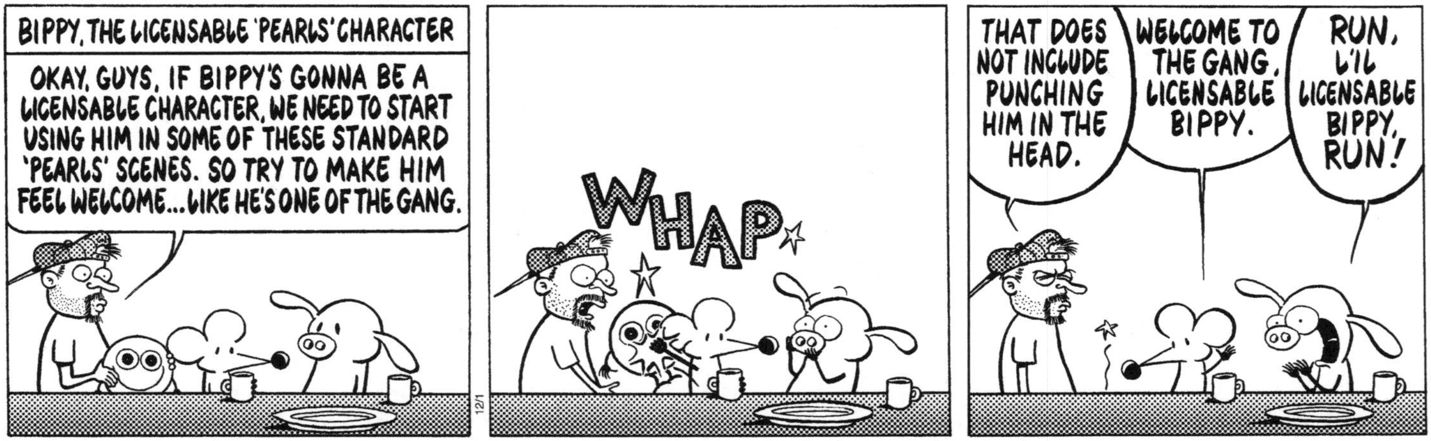
BIPPY, THE LICENSABLE 'PEARLS' CHARACTER
OKAY, GUYS, IF BIPPY'S GONNA BE A LICENSABLE CHARACTER, WE NEED TO START USING HIM IN SOME OF THESE STANDARD 'PEARLS' SCENES. SO TRY TO MAKE HIM FEEL WELCOME... LIKE HE'S ONE OF THE GANG.
12/1
WHAP
THAT DOES NOT INCLUDE PUNCHING HIM IN THE HEAD.
WELCOME TO THE GANG, LICENSABLE BIPPY.
RUN, L'IL LICENSABLE BIPPY, RUN!

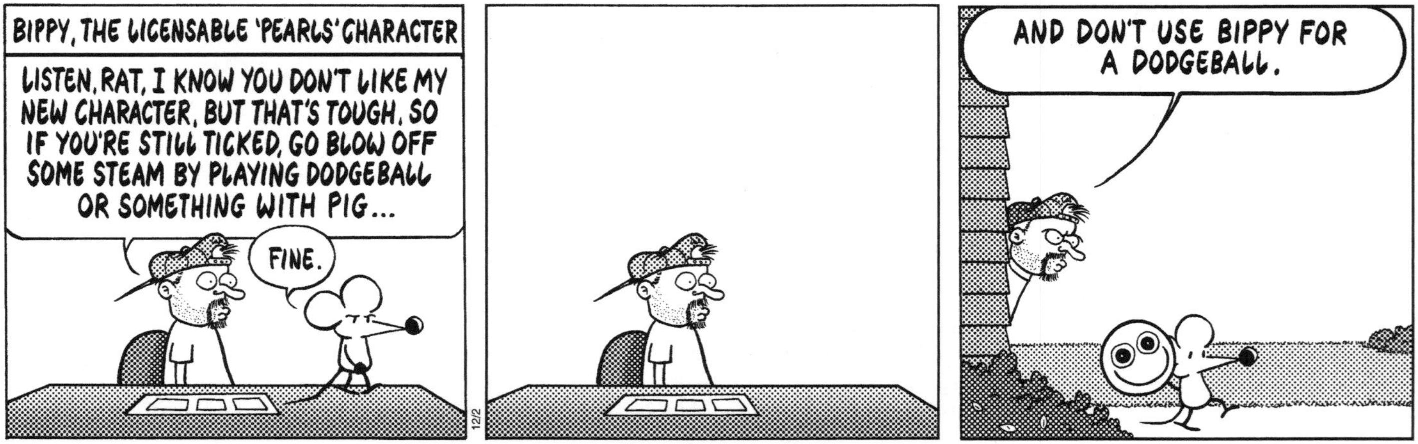
BIPPY, THE LICENSABLE 'PEARLS' CHARACTER
LISTEN, RAT, I KNOW YOU DON'T LIKE MY NEW CHARACTER, BUT THAT'S TOUGH, SO IF YOU'RE STILL TICKED, GO BLOW OFF SOME STEAM BY PLAYING DODGEBALL OR SOMETHING WITH PIG...
FINE.
12/2
AND DON'T USE BIPPY FOR A DODGEBALL.

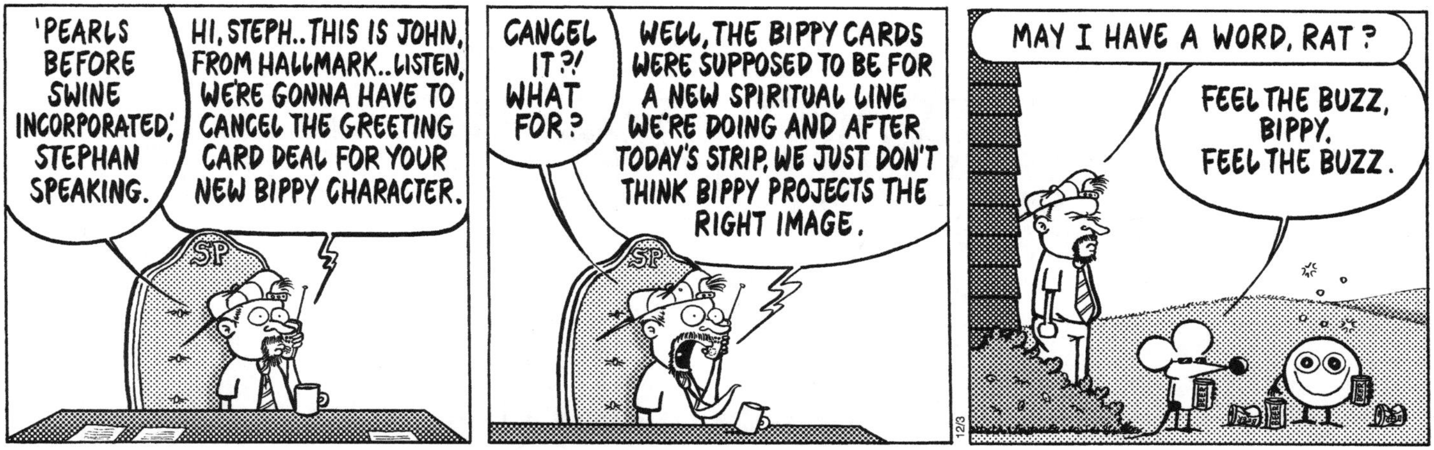
'PEARLS BEFORE SWINE INCORPORATED,' STEPHAN SPEAKING.
HI, STEPH.. THIS IS JOHN, FROM HALLMARK.. LISTEN, WE'RE GONNA HAVE TO CANCEL THE GREETING CARD DEAL FOR YOUR NEW BIPPY CHARACTER.
SP
CANCEL IT?! WHAT FOR?
WELL, THE BIPPY CARDS WERE SUPPOSED TO BE FOR A NEW SPIRITUAL LINE WE'RE DOING AND AFTER TODAY'S STRIP, WE JUST DON'T THINK BIPPY PROJECTS THE RIGHT IMAGE.
SP
12/3
MAY I HAVE A WORD, RAT?
FEEL THE BUZZ, BIPPY. FEEL THE BUZZ.

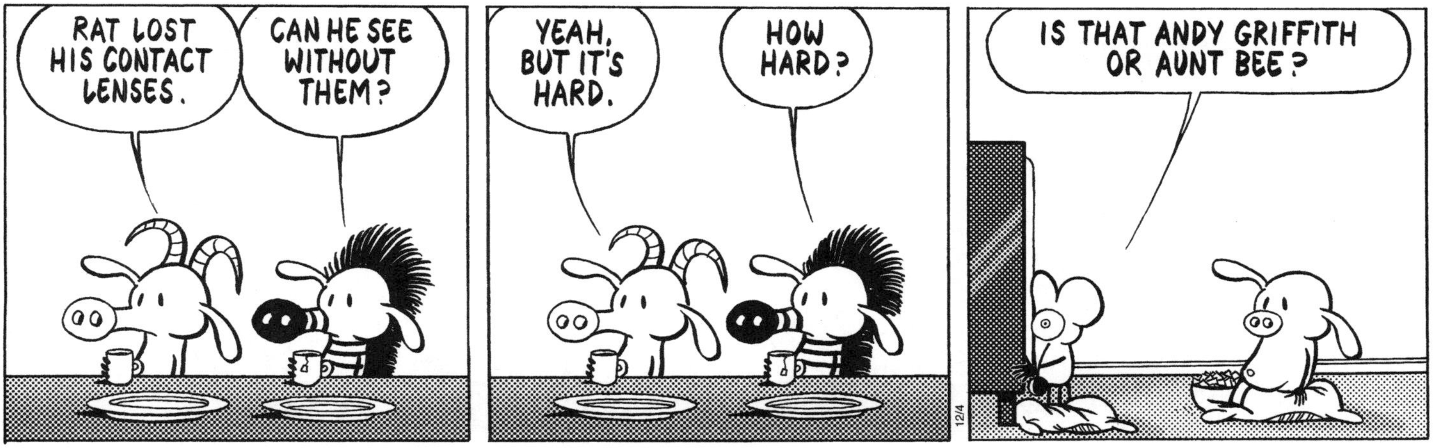
RAT LOST HIS CONTACT LENSES.
CAN HE SEE WITHOUT THEM?
YEAH, BUT IT'S HARD.
HOW HARD?
12/4
IS THAT ANDY GRIFFITH OR AUNT BEE?

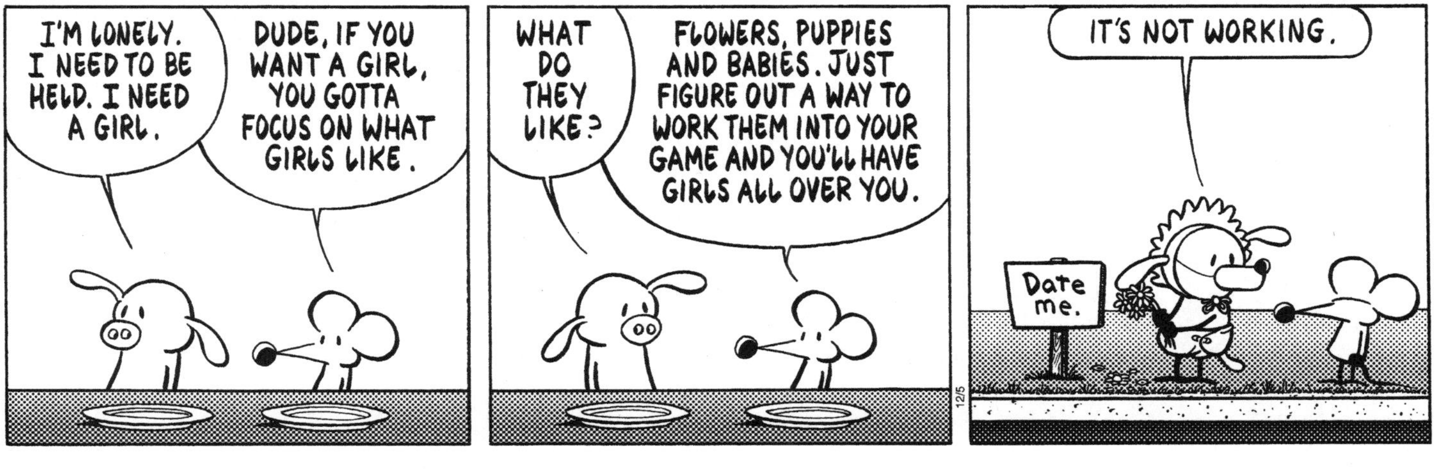
I'M LONELY. I NEED TO BE HELD. I NEED A GIRL.
DUDE, IF YOU WANT A GIRL, YOU GOTTA FOCUS ON WHAT GIRLS LIKE.
WHAT DO THEY LIKE?
FLOWERS, PUPPIES AND BABIES. JUST FIGURE OUT A WAY TO WORK THEM INTO YOUR GAME AND YOU'LL HAVE GIRLS ALL OVER YOU.
12/5
IT'S NOT WORKING.
Date me.

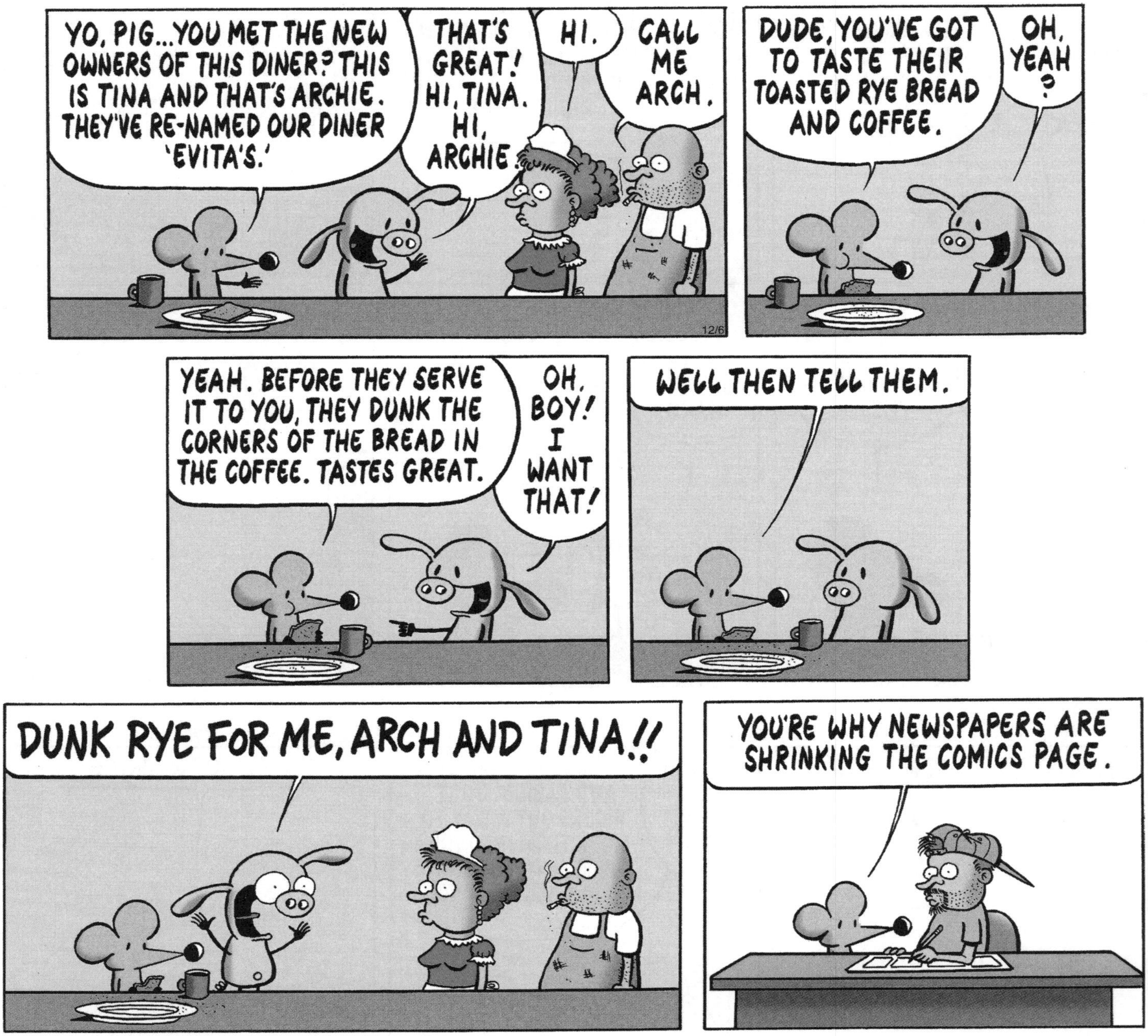
YO, PIG...YOU MET THE NEW OWNERS OF THIS DINER? THIS IS TINA AND THAT'S ARCHIE. THEY'VE RE-NAMED OUR DINER 'EVITA'S.'
THAT'S GREAT! HI, TINA. HI, ARCHIE.
HI.
CALL ME ARCH.
12/6
DUDE, YOU'VE GOT TO TASTE THEIR TOASTED RYE BREAD AND COFFEE.
OH, YEAH?
YEAH. BEFORE THEY SERVE IT TO YOU, THEY DUNK THE CORNERS OF THE BREAD IN THE COFFEE. TASTES GREAT.
OH, BOY! I WANT THAT!
WELL THEN TELL THEM.
DUNK RYE FOR ME, ARCH AND TINA!!
YOU'RE WHY NEWSPAPERS ARE SHRINKING THE COMICS PAGE.

Panel 1:

WHAT ARE YOU DOING, RAT?

WRITING A SCREENPLAY. I'VE ALREADY HIRED AN AGENT AND A MANAGER. WITH THEIR HELP, I WILL SELL IT FOR A MILLION BUCKS AND RETIRE ON THE COAST.

Panel 2:

YOU KNOW... THOSE GUYS TAKE TEN PERCENT OF WHATEVER YOU MAKE.

YEAH, WELL, IT'S WORTH IT. I RESEARCHED THESE GUYS ONLINE AND BELIEVE ME, IT SOUNDS LIKE THEY REALLY KNOW WHAT REPRESENTING TALENT IS ALL ABOUT.

Panel 3:

'STEP ONE: DO NOT RETURN PHONE CALLS.'

Panel 4:

ALRIGHT, MR. SNUFFLES, IF I'M GONNA BE A BIG-TIME HOLLYWOOD AGENT AND YOU'RE GONNA BE A MANAGER, WE FIRST HAVE TO FIGURE OUT THE DIFFERENCE.

Panel 5:

AHA...HERE IT IS...'WHILE BOTH TAKE TEN PERCENT, MANAGERS WILL SPEND THEIR FREE MOMENTS RIPPING ON THE INEPTITUDE OF AGENTS, WHILE AGENTS WILL CHOOSE INSTEAD TO RIP ON THE INEPTITUDE OF MANAGERS.'

Panel 6:

GOT IT, POOPYBRAIN?

Panel 7:

RAT MEETS HIS AGENT AND MANAGER

YOU TWO?! WHAT ARE YOU TWO DOING REPRESENTING YOURSELVES ONLINE AS HOLLYWOOD AGENTS?!?

Panel 8:

I MEAN, LOOK AT YOU! YOU'RE FRAUDS! YOU HAVE NO EXPERIENCE! YOU KNOW **NOTHING** ABOUT THE BUSINESS! AND YOU OBVIOUSLY KNOW NOTHING ABOUT REPRESENTATION! YOU'RE **FIRED!**

Panel 9:

TOLD YOU NOT TO PUT THE LITTER BOX IN THE RECEPTION AREA.

Panel 1:
I FIRED YOUR STUPID DUCK AND HIS MORON CAT FRIEND. THOSE FRAUDS TRIED TO POSE AS HOLLYWOOD AGENTS.

OH, I'M SURE THEY'LL BE OKAY. GUARD DUCK SAID HE JUST SIGNED ONE OF HIS ACTORS TO A FOUR-PICTURE DEAL FOR TWELVE MILLION DOLLARS.

Panel 2:
TWELVE MILLION DOLLARS?!! HOW IS THAT EVEN POSSIBLE?? WHAT CLIENT OF THEIRS MERITS THAT LEVEL OF CASH?!?

Panel 3:
A TOAST TO BIPPY.

HEAR HEAR!

Panel 4:
BEHOLD! I HAVE INVENTED A KITCHEN GADGET THAT SHALL MAKE ME RICH. IT IS CALLED THE 'SPOON PICKER UPPER.'

HOW'S IT WORK?

Panel 5:
WHEN YOU DON'T WANT TO WALK ALL THE WAY OVER TO THE SPOON DRAWER TO GET A SPOON, YOU CAN JUST REACH FOR ONE WITH THIS THING.

BUT THAT'S SILLY. IT'S JUST A COUPLE STEPS.

Panel 6:
POKE POKE JAB

Panel 7:
GOOD THING IT'S GOT OTHER USES.

Panel 8:
YOU EVER PARTICIPATED IN A PROTEST MOVEMENT, GOAT?

OH, YEAH. AGAINST WARS, WHALING, GLOBAL WARMING. A WHOLE BUNCH OF IMPORTANT CAUSES. WHY?

Panel 9:
BECAUSE RAT'S DOING IT.

WELL, GOOD FOR HIM. IT'S IMPORTANT TO STAND UP AND BE COUNTED IN THE GLOBAL COMMUNITY. WHAT'S THE CAUSE?

Panel 10:
PUT PANTS ON ZIGGY! +

FIGHT THE POWER!!

Check please.

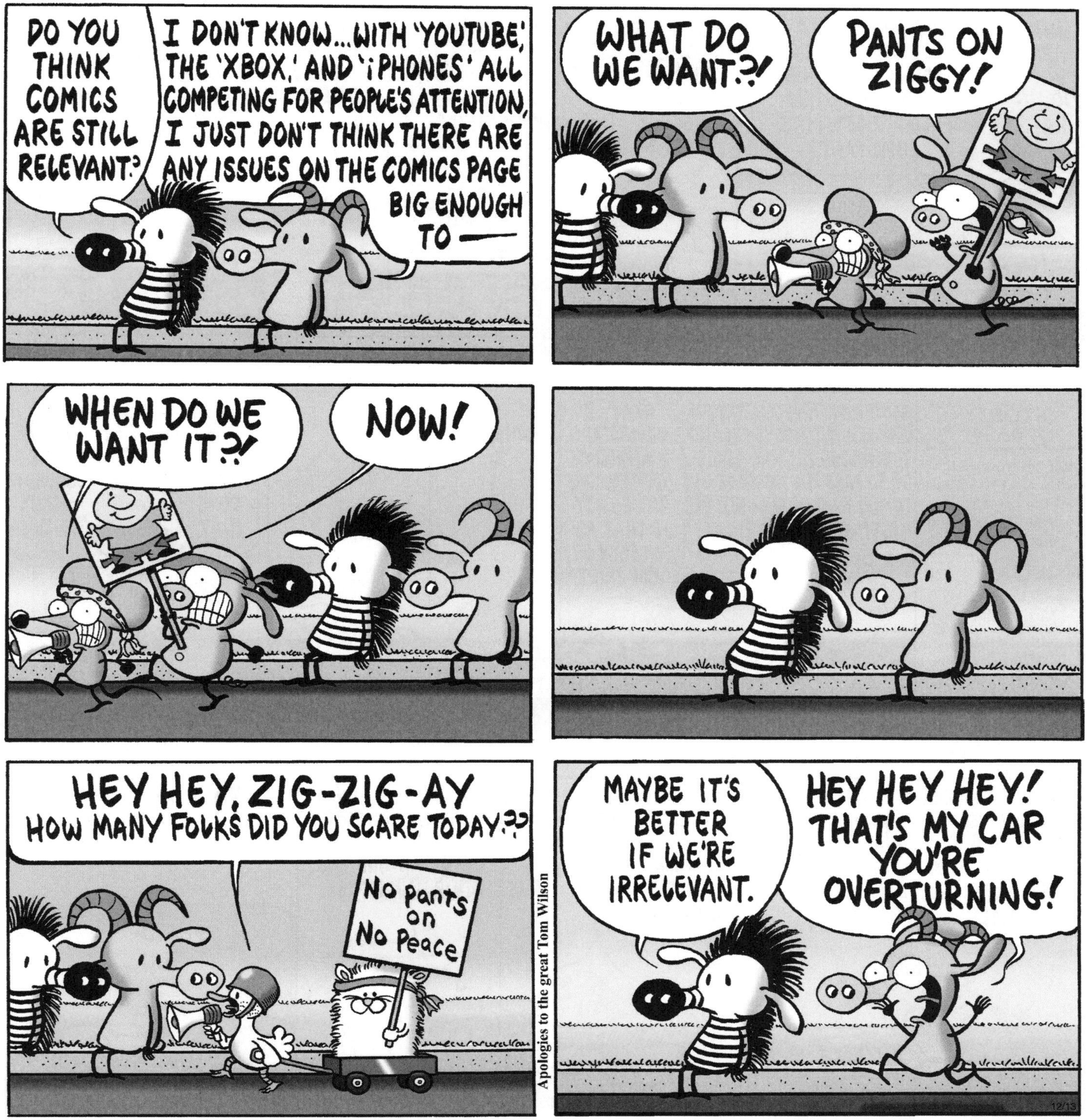
DO YOU THINK COMICS ARE STILL RELEVANT?
I DON'T KNOW... WITH 'YOUTUBE,' THE 'XBOX,' AND 'iPHONES' ALL COMPETING FOR PEOPLE'S ATTENTION, I JUST DON'T THINK THERE ARE ANY ISSUES ON THE COMICS PAGE BIG ENOUGH TO —
WHAT DO WE WANT?!
PANTS ON ZIGGY!
WHEN DO WE WANT IT?!
NOW!
HEY HEY, ZIG-ZIG-AY
HOW MANY FOLKS DID YOU SCARE TODAY??
No pants on No Peace
Apologies to the great Tom Wilson
MAYBE IT'S BETTER IF WE'RE IRRELEVANT.
HEY HEY HEY! THAT'S MY CAR YOU'RE OVERTURNING!
12/13

Panel 1: WHAT ARE YOU DOING, RAT? — WE'RE GOING ON A HUNGER STRIKE. WE'RE NOT GONNA EAT A THING UNTIL THE COMIC STRIP CHARACTER 'ZIGGY' PUTS ON SOME PANTS. THE ZIGGY FAST FOR PANTS

Panel 2: YOU'RE EATING A CHEESEBURGER. — YEAH, WELL I'M THE ORGANIZER. I HAVE TO KEEP A CLEAR HEAD. I'VE GOT OTHERS TO DO THE HUNGER STRIKE. THE ZIGG FAST FO PANT

Panel 3: SURE HOPE HE PUTS ON PANTS. — MAY I KILL HIM FOR THE FRIES, SIR? — PEOPLE, PEOPLE, REMAIN STRONG.

STORY UPDATE

Rat has traveled to the Kansas City offices of Universal Press Syndicate, the company that syndicates "Ziggy" to newspapers, to speak to Syndicate Vice President John Glynn about putting pants on Ziggy.

Panel 4: LISTEN, WE APPRECIATE YOUR CONCERN, BUT ZIGGY'S CREATOR TOM WILSON, JR., HAS ASKED US TO PASS THE MESSAGE ON TO YOU THAT HE WILL NOT BE PUTTING PANTS ON ZIGGY. — OKAY...I UNDERSTAND. I APPRECIATE YOUR TALKING TO US...HEY, IS THAT AN INK STAIN ON YOUR SHIRT?

Panel 5: WHERE?

Panel 6: WHAM WHAM WHAM

Panel 7: MAYBE WE SHOULDN'T HAVE DONE THAT. — HEY...WE'RE SENDING OUR OWN MESSAGE. — MAY I TAKE THE CHUBBY MAN'S ¡PHONE?

Panel 8: OUR LONG NATIONAL NIGHTMARE IS OVER. TOM WILSON, JR. HAS AGREED TO PUT PANTS ON ZIGGY IN TODAY'S 'ZIGGY' STRIP. — YOU'RE KIDDING. WHAT'D YOU HAVE TO BRIBE HIM WITH TO MAKE HIM DO THAT?

Panel 9: I GAVE HIM ONE OF OUR CHARACTERS. ALL HE ASKED FOR WAS SOMEONE SOFT AND CUDDLY AND CUTE THAT ZIGGY COULD SNUGGLE WITH. — OH, GREAT. SO WHAT YOU GAVE HIM SNUFFLES THE CAT?

Panel 10: NO NO NO...I DIDN'T GIVE HIM SNUFFLES. I MADE SURE IT WASN'T ANYONE THE STRIP WOULD MISS.

Panel 11: THIS MAKES ME FEEL UNCOMFORTABLE.

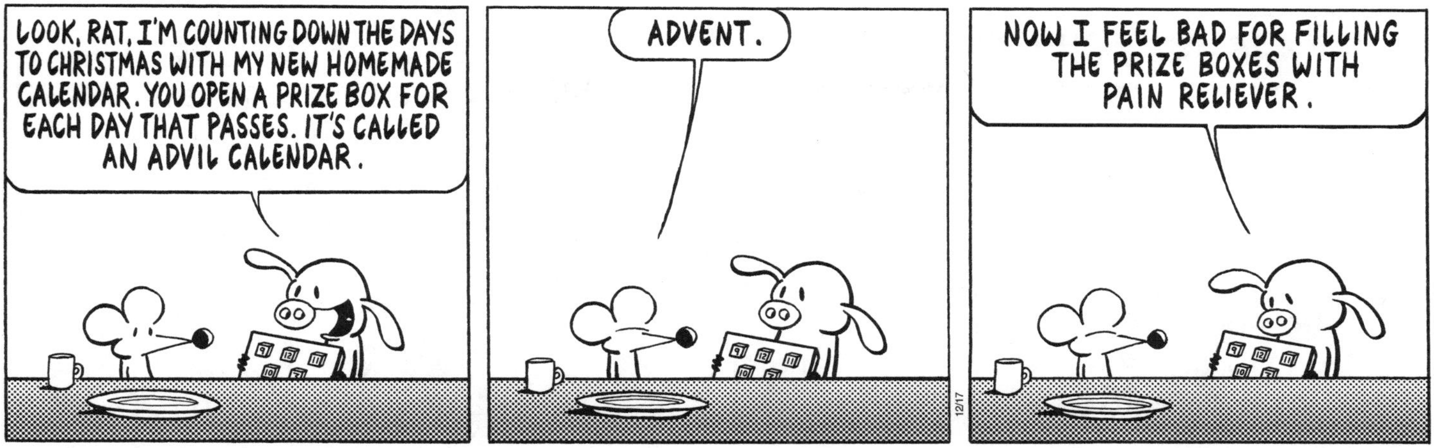
LOOK, RAT, I'M COUNTING DOWN THE DAYS TO CHRISTMAS WITH MY NEW HOMEMADE CALENDAR. YOU OPEN A PRIZE BOX FOR EACH DAY THAT PASSES. IT'S CALLED AN ADVIL CALENDAR.
ADVENT.
NOW I FEEL BAD FOR FILLING THE PRIZE BOXES WITH PAIN RELIEVER.
12/17

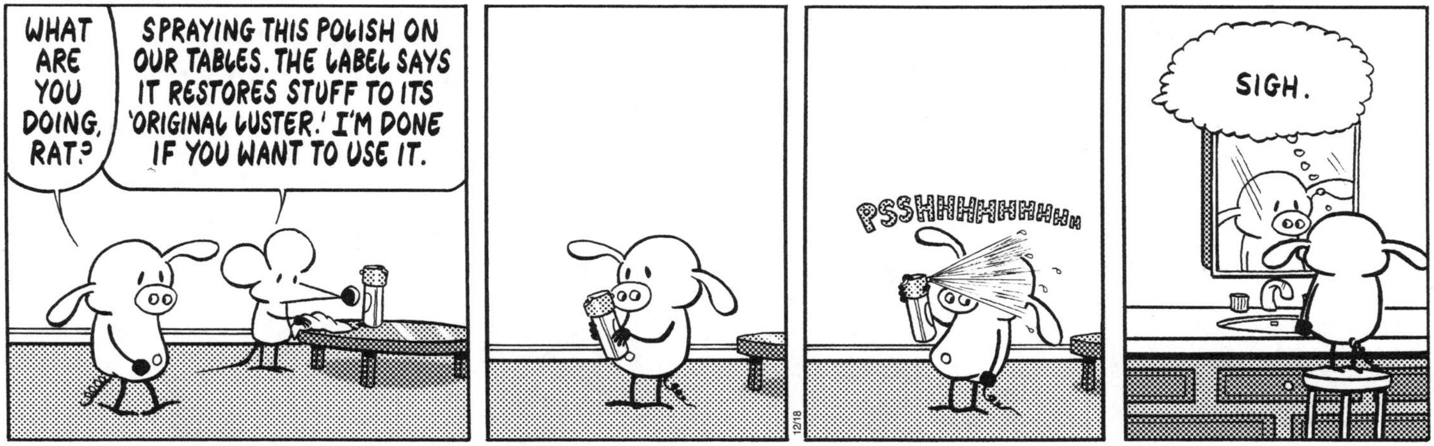
WHAT ARE YOU DOING, RAT?
SPRAYING THIS POLISH ON OUR TABLES. THE LABEL SAYS IT RESTORES STUFF TO ITS 'ORIGINAL LUSTER.' I'M DONE IF YOU WANT TO USE IT.
12/18
PSSHHHHHHHHHH
SIGH.

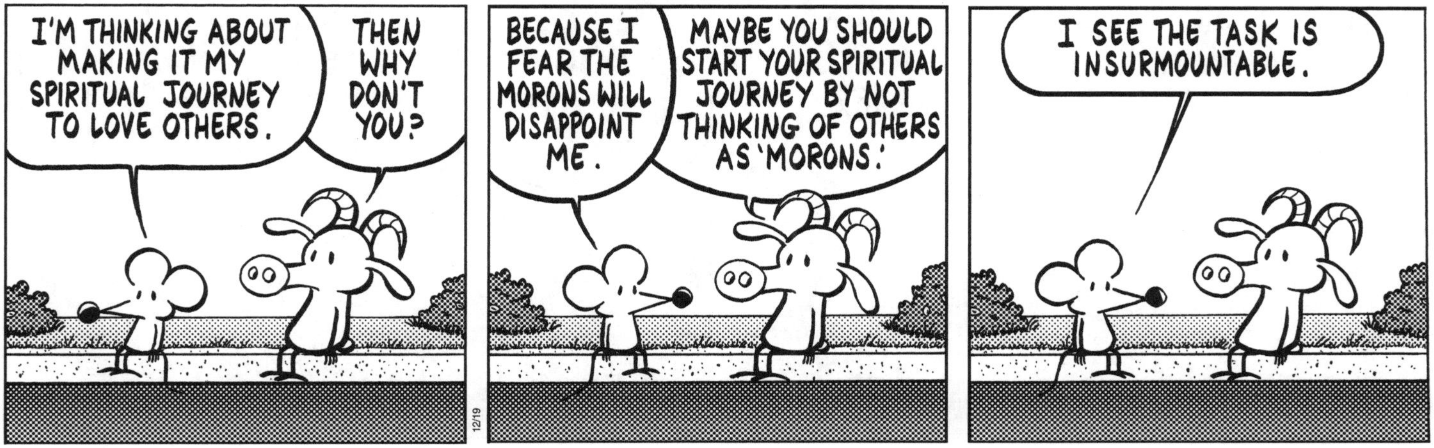
I'M THINKING ABOUT MAKING IT MY SPIRITUAL JOURNEY TO LOVE OTHERS.
THEN WHY DON'T YOU?
12/19
BECAUSE I FEAR THE MORONS WILL DISAPPOINT ME.
MAYBE YOU SHOULD START YOUR SPIRITUAL JOURNEY BY NOT THINKING OF OTHERS AS 'MORONS.'
I SEE THE TASK IS INSURMOUNTABLE.

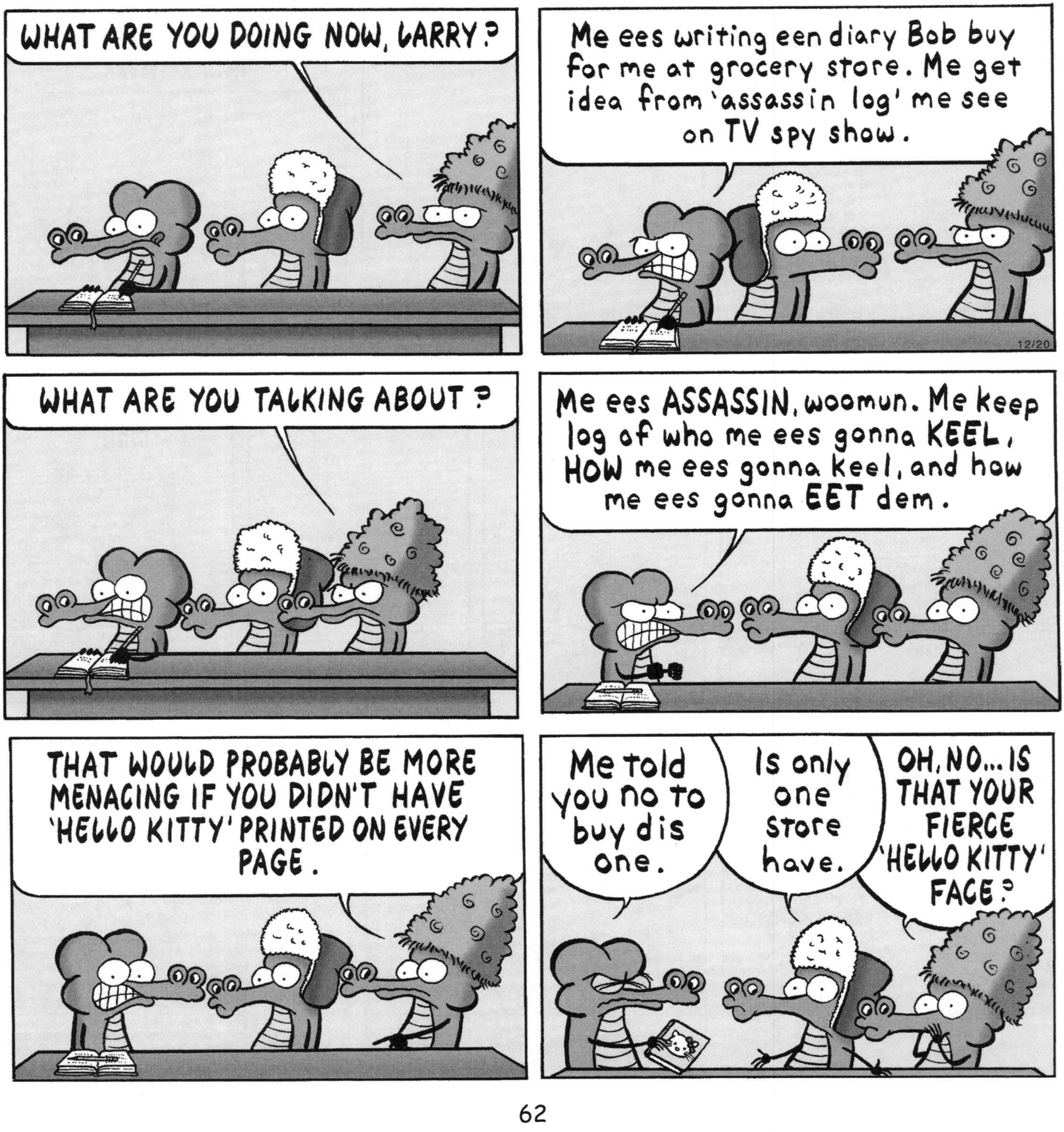
WHAT ARE YOU DOING NOW, LARRY?
Me ees writing een diary Bob buy for me at grocery store. Me get idea from 'assassin log' me see on TV spy show.
12/20
WHAT ARE YOU TALKING ABOUT?
Me ees ASSASSIN, woomun. Me keep log of who me ees gonna KEEL, HOW me ees gonna keel, and how me ees gonna EET dem.
THAT WOULD PROBABLY BE MORE MENACING IF YOU DIDN'T HAVE 'HELLO KITTY' PRINTED ON EVERY PAGE.
Me told you no to buy dis one.
Is only one store have.
OH, NO... IS THAT YOUR FIERCE 'HELLO KITTY' FACE?

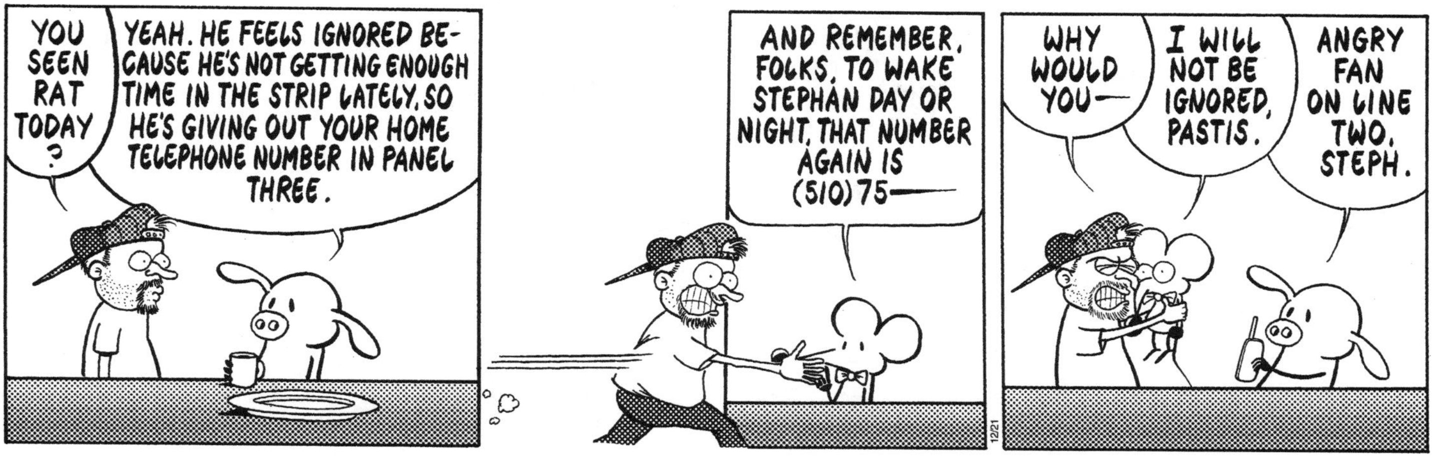
YOU SEEN RAT TODAY?
YEAH. HE FEELS IGNORED BECAUSE HE'S NOT GETTING ENOUGH TIME IN THE STRIP LATELY, SO HE'S GIVING OUT YOUR HOME TELEPHONE NUMBER IN PANEL THREE.
AND REMEMBER, FOLKS, TO WAKE STEPHAN DAY OR NIGHT, THAT NUMBER AGAIN IS (510) 75—
WHY WOULD YOU—
I WILL NOT BE IGNORED, PASTIS.
ANGRY FAN ON LINE TWO, STEPH.
12/21

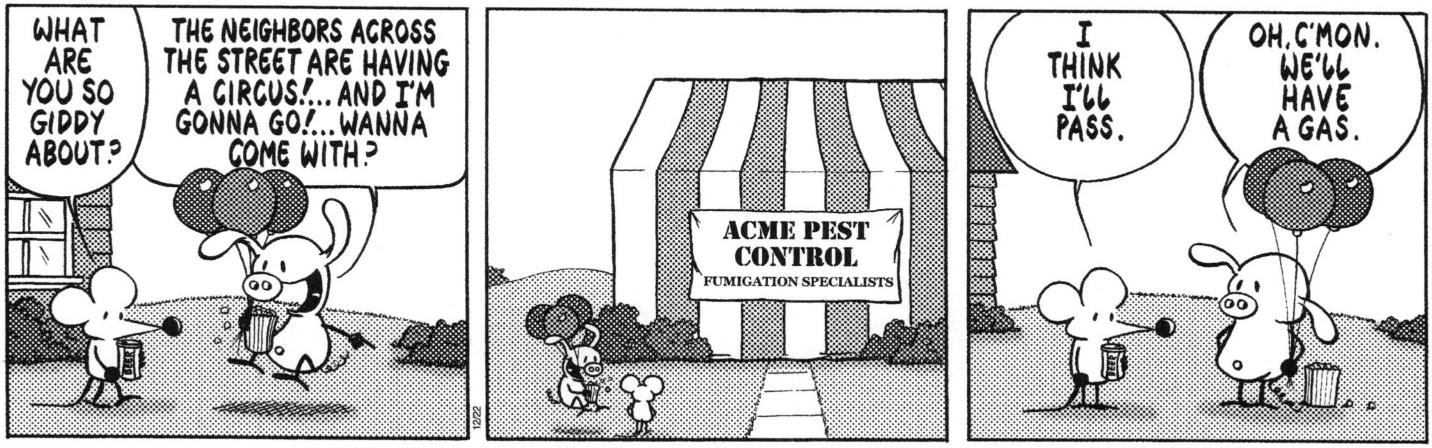
WHAT ARE YOU SO GIDDY ABOUT?
THE NEIGHBORS ACROSS THE STREET ARE HAVING A CIRCUS!... AND I'M GONNA GO!... WANNA COME WITH?
12/22
ACME PEST CONTROL
FUMIGATION SPECIALISTS
I THINK I'LL PASS.
OH, C'MON. WE'LL HAVE A GAS.

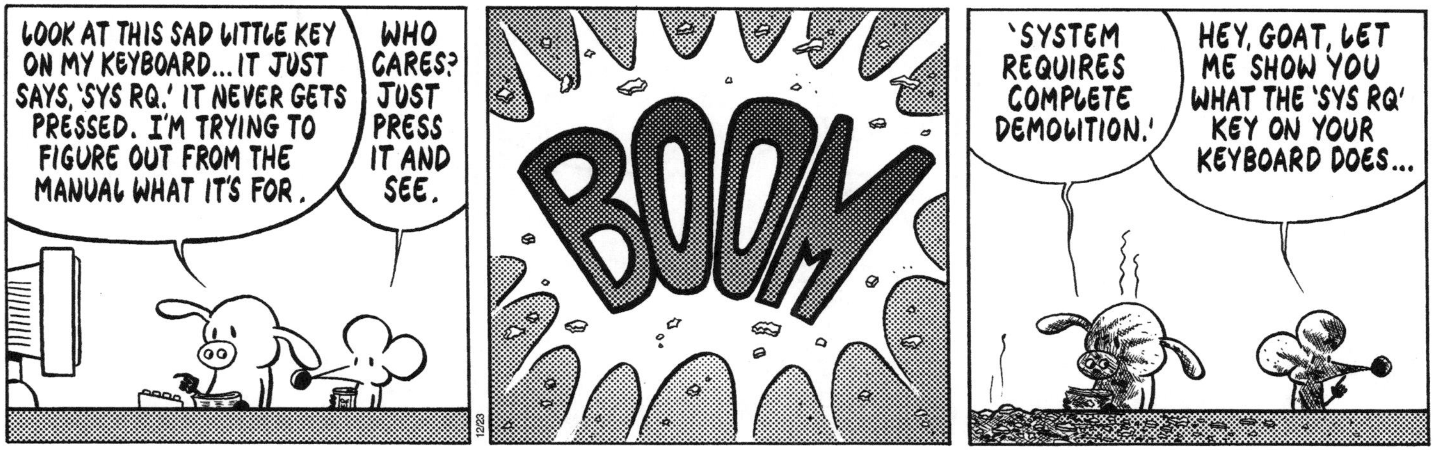
LOOK AT THIS SAD LITTLE KEY ON MY KEYBOARD... IT JUST SAYS, 'SYS RQ.' IT NEVER GETS PRESSED. I'M TRYING TO FIGURE OUT FROM THE MANUAL WHAT IT'S FOR.
WHO CARES? JUST PRESS IT AND SEE.
12/23
BOOM
'SYSTEM REQUIRES COMPLETE DEMOLITION.'
HEY, GOAT, LET ME SHOW YOU WHAT THE 'SYS RQ' KEY ON YOUR KEYBOARD DOES...

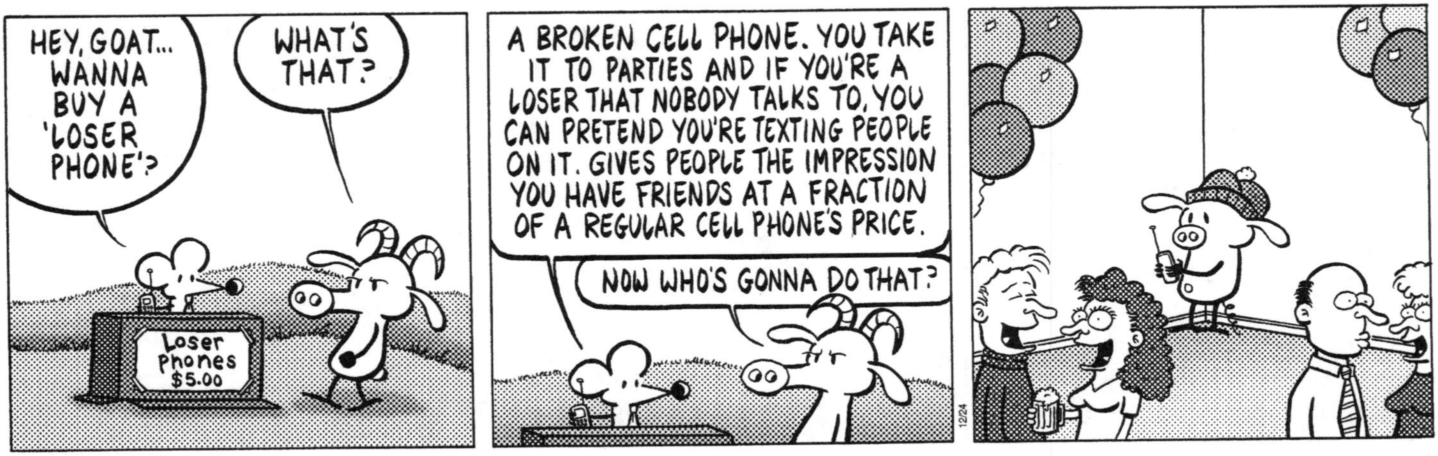
HEY, GOAT... WANNA BUY A 'LOSER PHONE'?
WHAT'S THAT?
Loser Phones $5.00
A BROKEN CELL PHONE. YOU TAKE IT TO PARTIES AND IF YOU'RE A LOSER THAT NOBODY TALKS TO, YOU CAN PRETEND YOU'RE TEXTING PEOPLE ON IT. GIVES PEOPLE THE IMPRESSION YOU HAVE FRIENDS AT A FRACTION OF A REGULAR CELL PHONE'S PRICE.
NOW WHO'S GONNA DO THAT?
12/24

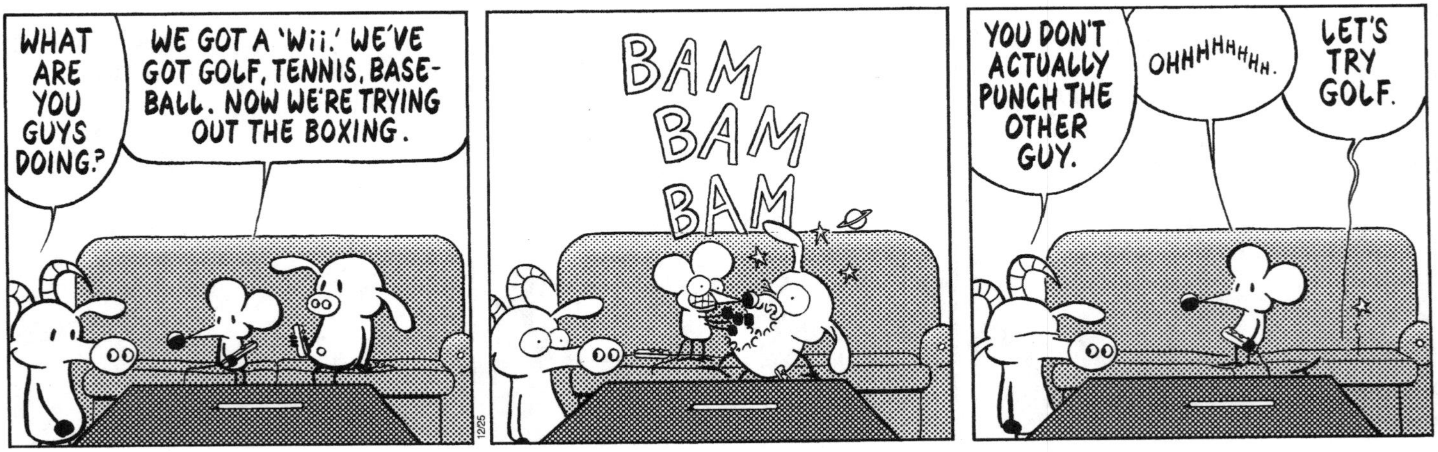
WHAT ARE YOU GUYS DOING?
WE GOT A 'Wii.' WE'VE GOT GOLF, TENNIS, BASEBALL. NOW WE'RE TRYING OUT THE BOXING.
12/25
BAM
BAM
BAM
YOU DON'T ACTUALLY PUNCH THE OTHER GUY.
OHHHHHHHH.
LET'S TRY GOLF.

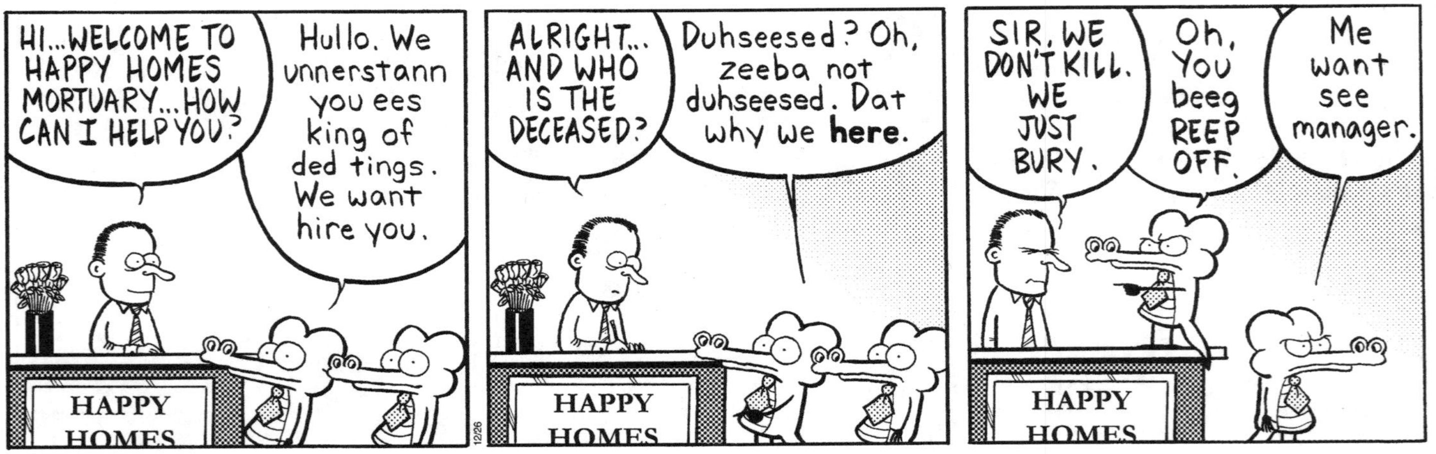
HI...WELCOME TO HAPPY HOMES MORTUARY...HOW CAN I HELP YOU?
Hullo. We unnerstann you ees king of ded tings. We want hire you.
HAPPY HOMES
12/26
ALRIGHT... AND WHO IS THE DECEASED?
Duhseesed? Oh, zeeba not duhseesed. Dat why we **here**.
HAPPY HOMES
SIR, WE DON'T KILL. WE JUST BURY.
Oh, You beeg REEP OFF.
Me want see manager.
HAPPY HOMES

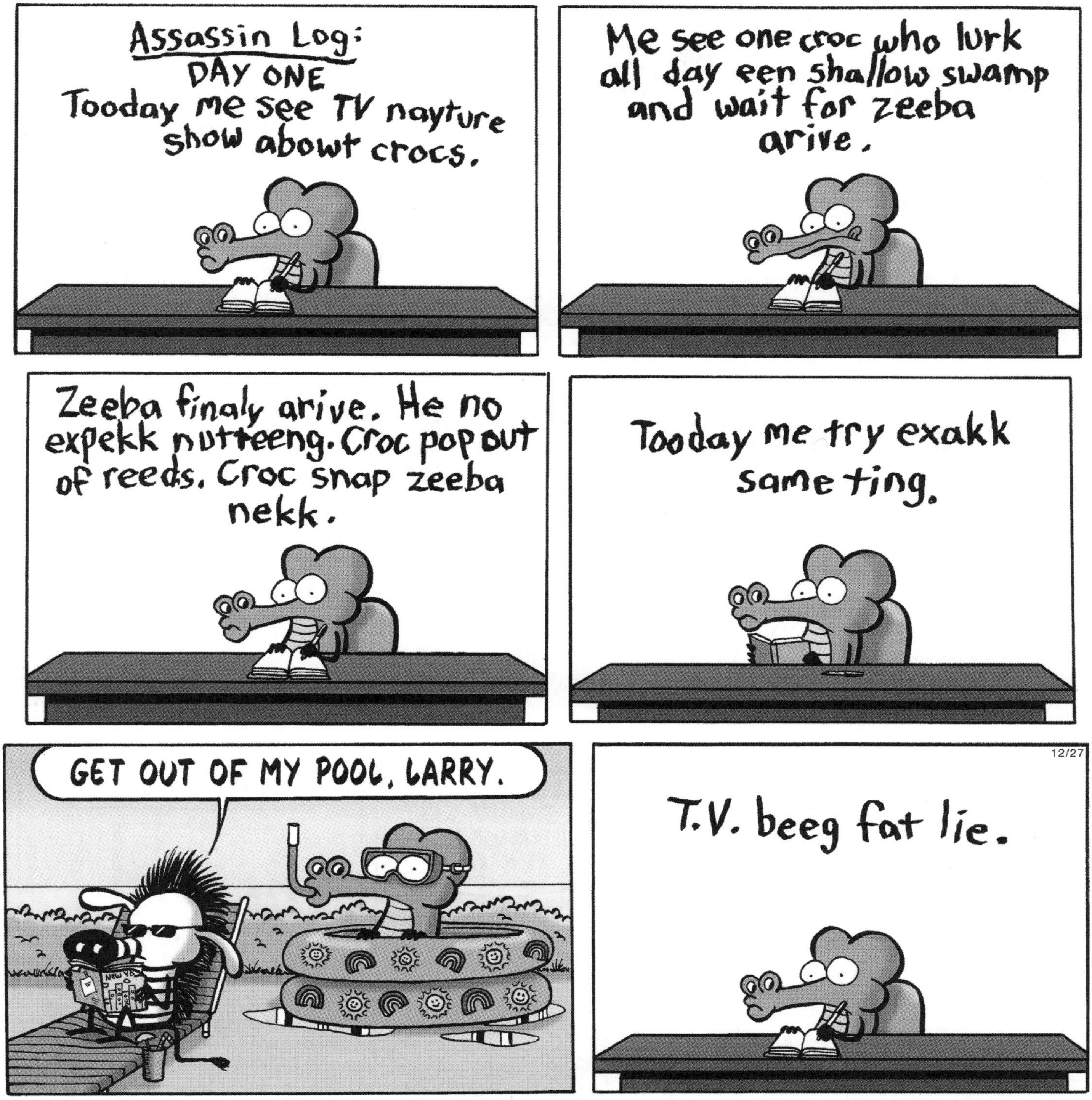
Assassin Log:
DAY ONE
Tooday me see TV nayture show abowt crocs.
Me see one croc who lurk all day een shallow swamp and wait for zeeba arive.
Zeeba finaly arive. He no expekk nutteeng. Croc pop out of reeds. Croc snap zeeba nekk.
Tooday me try exakk same ting.
GET OUT OF MY POOL, LARRY.
12/27
T.V. beeg fat lie.

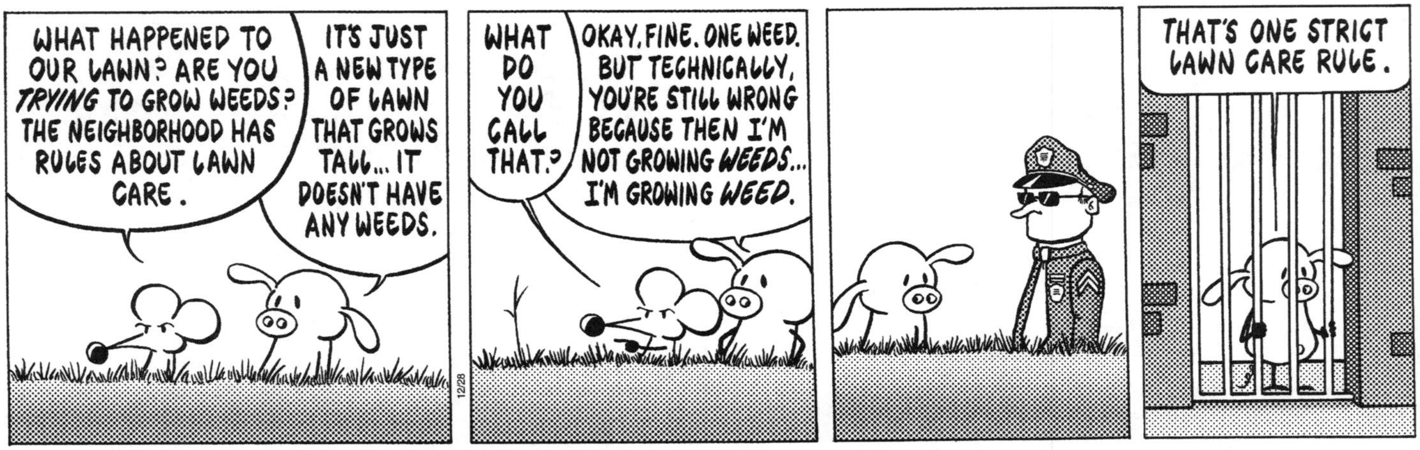
WHAT HAPPENED TO OUR LAWN? ARE YOU *TRYING* TO GROW WEEDS? THE NEIGHBORHOOD HAS RULES ABOUT LAWN CARE.
IT'S JUST A NEW TYPE OF LAWN THAT GROWS TALL... IT DOESN'T HAVE ANY WEEDS.
12/28
WHAT DO YOU CALL THAT?
OKAY, FINE. ONE WEED. BUT TECHNICALLY, YOU'RE STILL WRONG BECAUSE THEN I'M NOT GROWING *WEEDS*... I'M GROWING *WEED*.
THAT'S ONE STRICT LAWN CARE RULE.

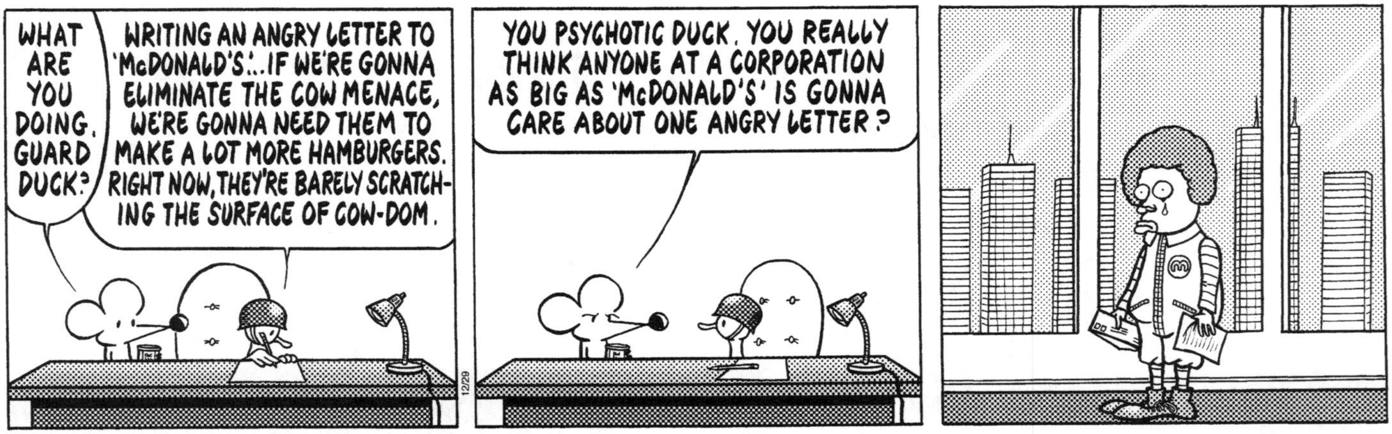
WHAT ARE YOU DOING, GUARD DUCK?
WRITING AN ANGRY LETTER TO 'McDONALD'S'... IF WE'RE GONNA ELIMINATE THE COW MENACE, WE'RE GONNA NEED THEM TO MAKE A LOT MORE HAMBURGERS. RIGHT NOW, THEY'RE BARELY SCRATCHING THE SURFACE OF COW-DOM.
12/29
YOU PSYCHOTIC DUCK. YOU REALLY THINK ANYONE AT A CORPORATION AS BIG AS 'McDONALD'S' IS GONNA CARE ABOUT ONE ANGRY LETTER?

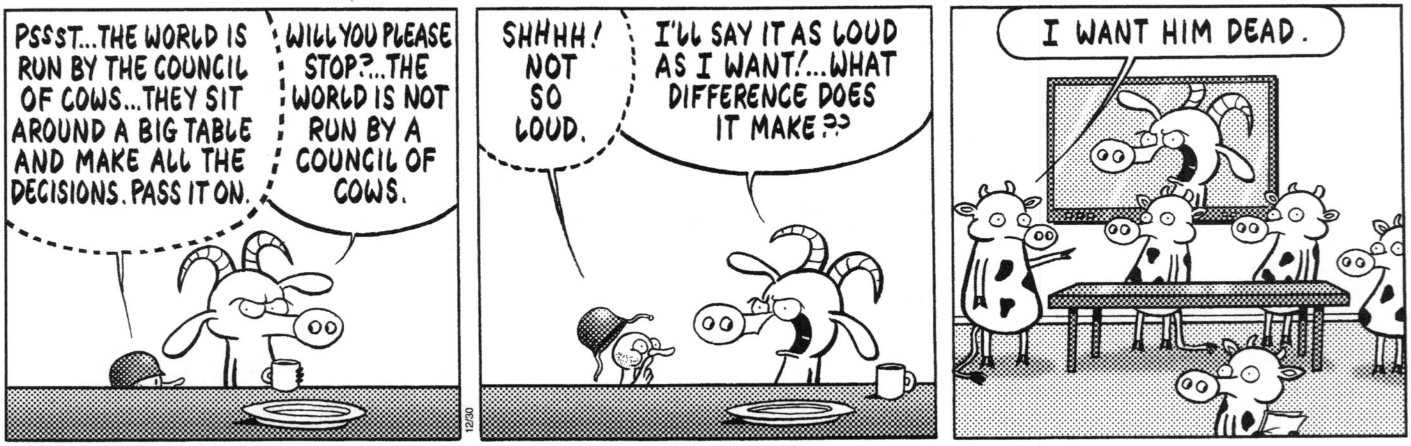
PSSST... THE WORLD IS RUN BY THE COUNCIL OF COWS... THEY SIT AROUND A BIG TABLE AND MAKE ALL THE DECISIONS. PASS IT ON.
WILL YOU PLEASE STOP?... THE WORLD IS NOT RUN BY A COUNCIL OF COWS.
12/30
SHHHH! NOT SO LOUD.
I'LL SAY IT AS LOUD AS I WANT!... WHAT DIFFERENCE DOES IT MAKE??
I WANT HIM DEAD.

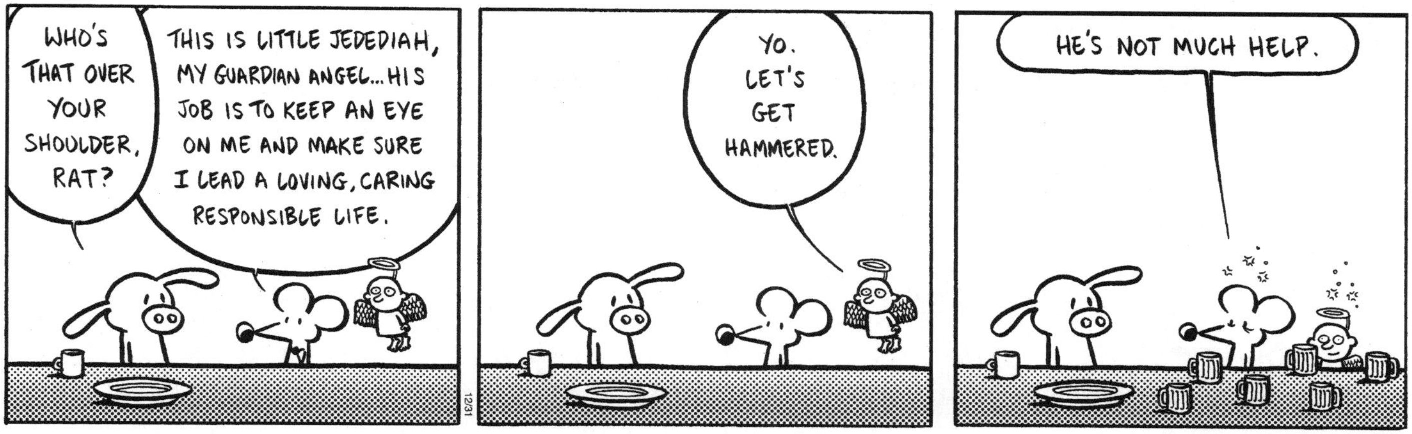
WHO'S THAT OVER YOUR SHOULDER, RAT?
THIS IS LITTLE JEDEDIAH, MY GUARDIAN ANGEL... HIS JOB IS TO KEEP AN EYE ON ME AND MAKE SURE I LEAD A LOVING, CARING RESPONSIBLE LIFE.
YO. LET'S GET HAMMERED.
HE'S NOT MUCH HELP.
12/31

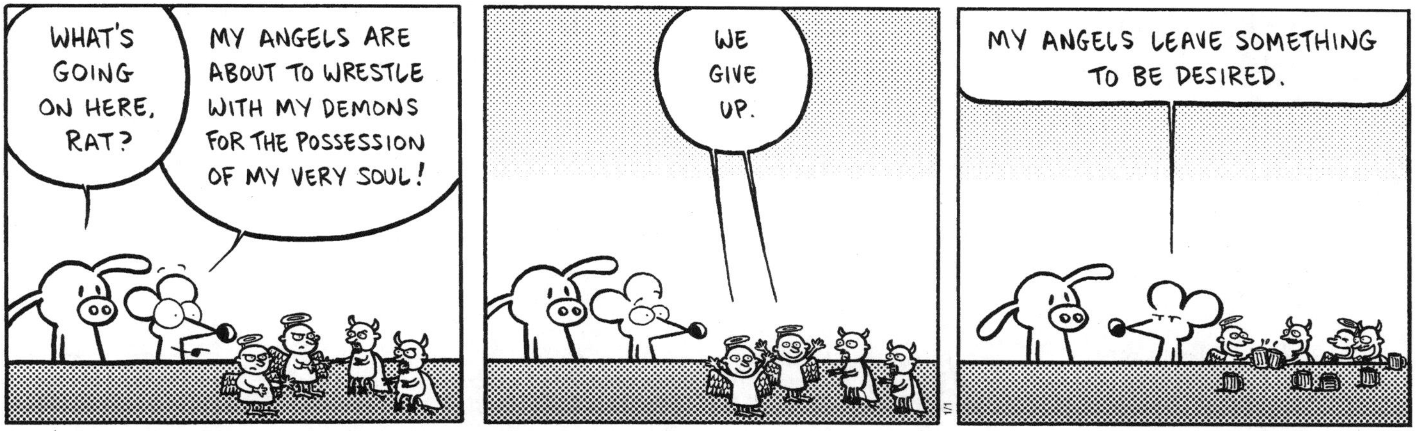
WHAT'S GOING ON HERE, RAT?
MY ANGELS ARE ABOUT TO WRESTLE WITH MY DEMONS FOR THE POSSESSION OF MY VERY SOUL!
WE GIVE UP.
MY ANGELS LEAVE SOMETHING TO BE DESIRED.
1/1

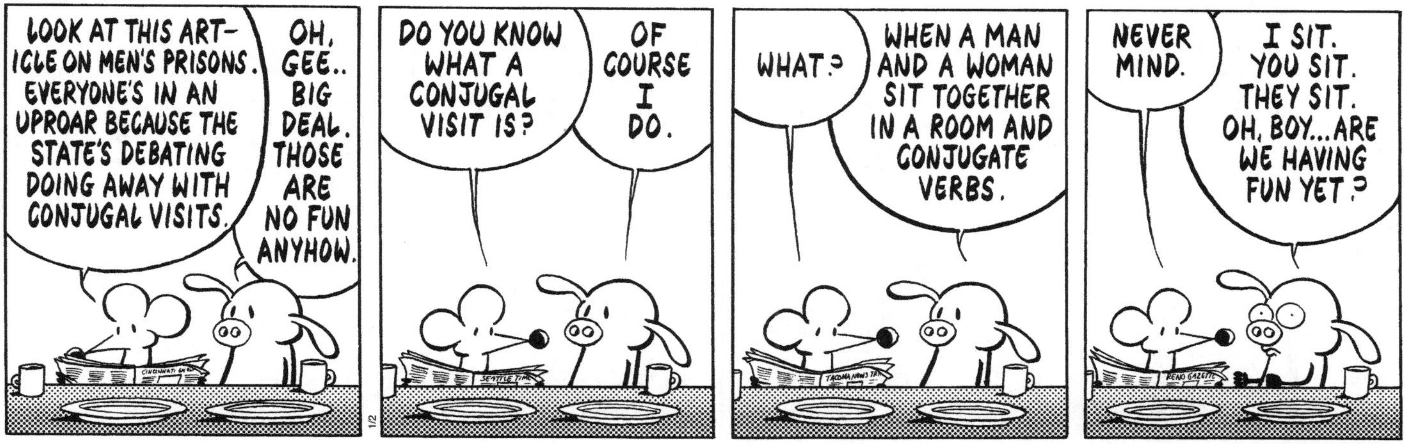
LOOK AT THIS ARTICLE ON MEN'S PRISONS. EVERYONE'S IN AN UPROAR BECAUSE THE STATE'S DEBATING DOING AWAY WITH CONJUGAL VISITS.
OH, GEE.. BIG DEAL. THOSE ARE NO FUN ANYHOW.
DO YOU KNOW WHAT A CONJUGAL VISIT IS?
OF COURSE I DO.
WHAT?
WHEN A MAN AND A WOMAN SIT TOGETHER IN A ROOM AND CONJUGATE VERBS.
NEVER MIND.
I SIT. YOU SIT. THEY SIT. OH, BOY... ARE WE HAVING FUN YET?
1/2

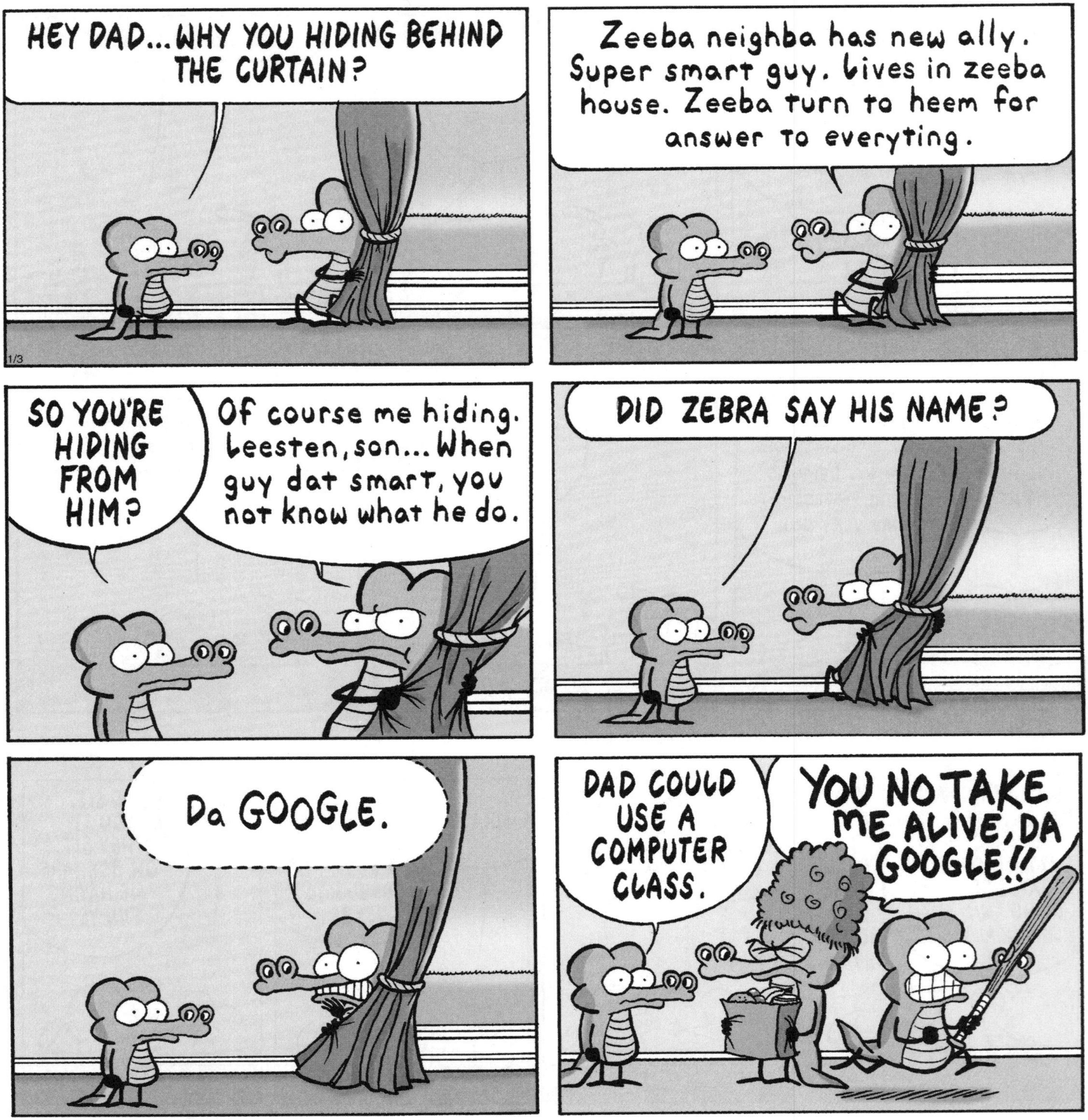
HEY DAD... WHY YOU HIDING BEHIND THE CURTAIN?
Zeeba neighba has new ally. Super smart guy. Lives in zeeba house. Zeeba turn to heem for answer to everyting.
SO YOU'RE HIDING FROM HIM?
Of course me hiding. Leesten, son... When guy dat smart, you not know what he do.
DID ZEBRA SAY HIS NAME?
Da GOOGLE.
DAD COULD USE A COMPUTER CLASS.
YOU NO TAKE ME ALIVE, DA GOOGLE!!

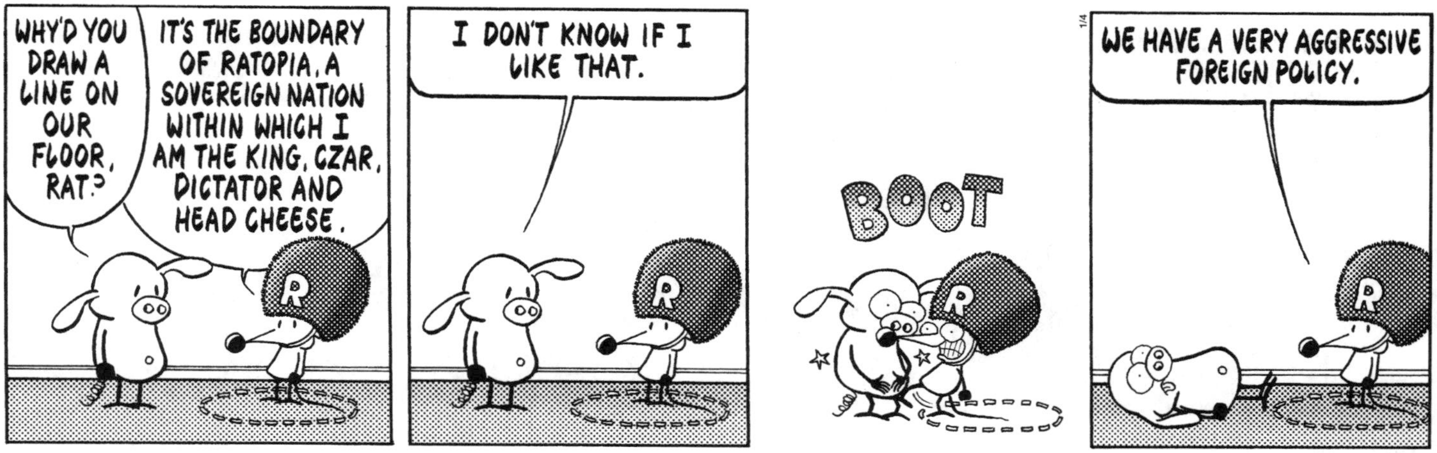
WHY'D YOU DRAW A LINE ON OUR FLOOR, RAT?
IT'S THE BOUNDARY OF RATOPIA, A SOVEREIGN NATION WITHIN WHICH I AM THE KING, CZAR, DICTATOR AND HEAD CHEESE.
I DON'T KNOW IF I LIKE THAT.
BOOT
WE HAVE A VERY AGGRESSIVE FOREIGN POLICY.

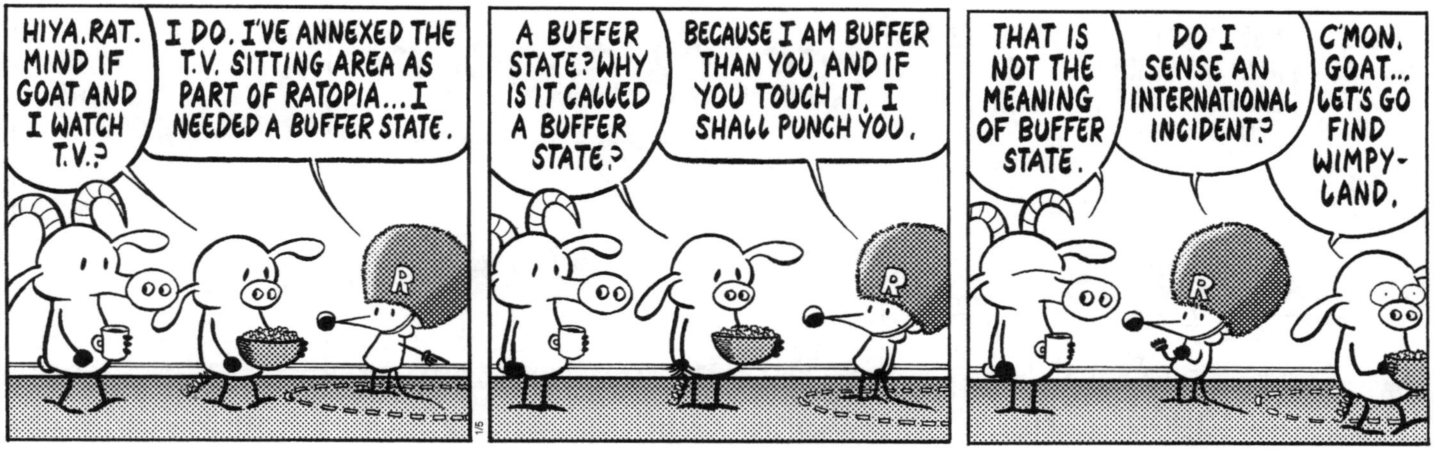
HIYA, RAT. MIND IF GOAT AND I WATCH T.V.?
I DO. I'VE ANNEXED THE T.V. SITTING AREA AS PART OF RATOPIA... I NEEDED A BUFFER STATE.
A BUFFER STATE? WHY IS IT CALLED A BUFFER STATE?
BECAUSE I AM BUFFER THAN YOU, AND IF YOU TOUCH IT, I SHALL PUNCH YOU.
THAT IS NOT THE MEANING OF BUFFER STATE.
DO I SENSE AN INTERNATIONAL INCIDENT?
C'MON, GOAT... LET'S GO FIND WIMPY-LAND.

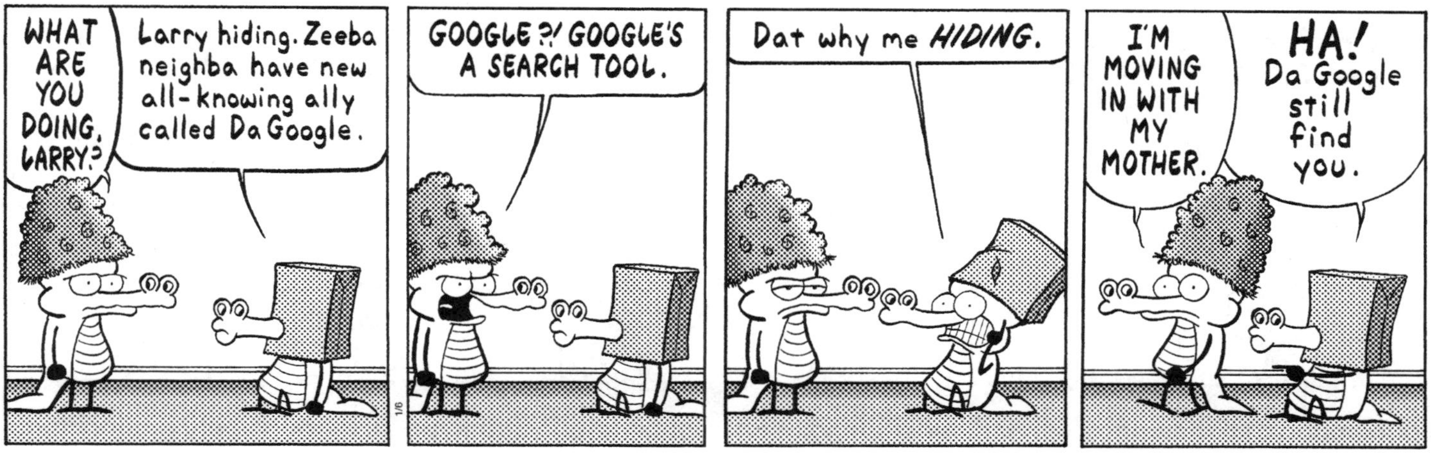
WHAT ARE YOU DOING, LARRY?
Larry hiding. Zeeba neighba have new all-knowing ally called Da Google.
GOOGLE?! GOOGLE'S A SEARCH TOOL.
Dat why me *HIDING*.
I'M MOVING IN WITH MY MOTHER.
HA! Da Google still find you.

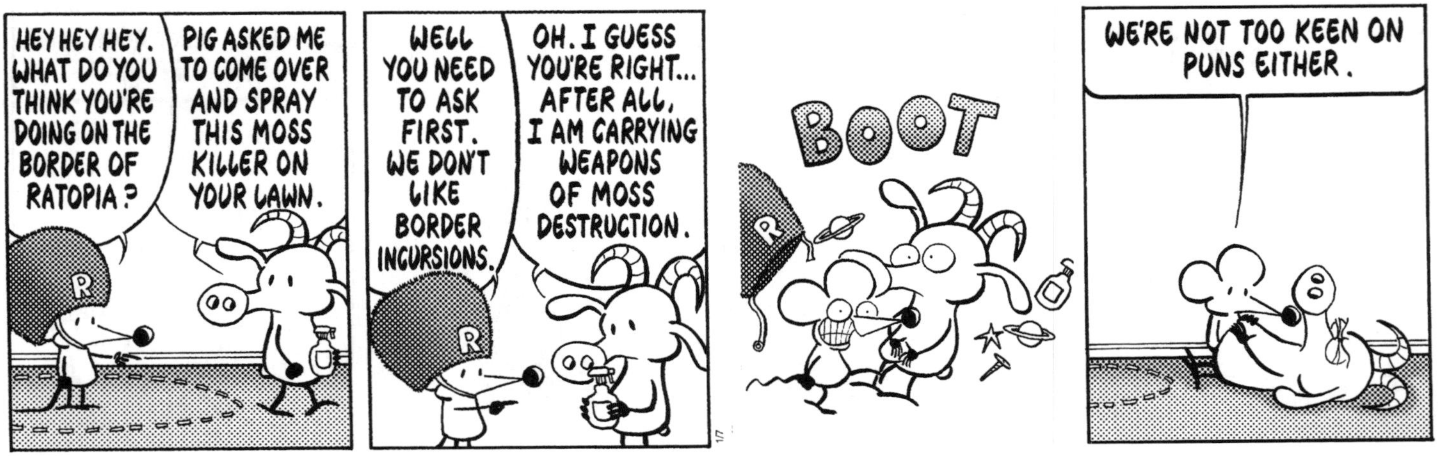
HEY HEY HEY. WHAT DO YOU THINK YOU'RE DOING ON THE BORDER OF RATOPIA?
PIG ASKED ME TO COME OVER AND SPRAY THIS MOSS KILLER ON YOUR LAWN.
WELL YOU NEED TO ASK FIRST. WE DON'T LIKE BORDER INCURSIONS.
OH. I GUESS YOU'RE RIGHT... AFTER ALL, I AM CARRYING WEAPONS OF MOSS DESTRUCTION.
1/7
BOOT
WE'RE NOT TOO KEEN ON PUNS EITHER.

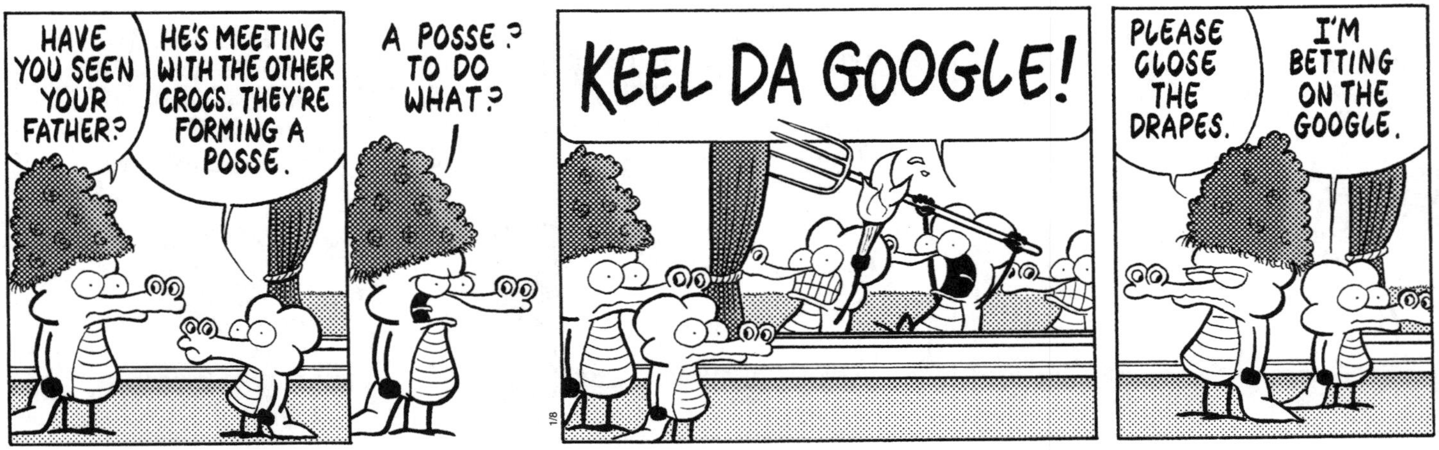
HAVE YOU SEEN YOUR FATHER?
HE'S MEETING WITH THE OTHER CROCS. THEY'RE FORMING A POSSE.
A POSSE? TO DO WHAT?
KEEL DA GOOGLE!
1/8
PLEASE CLOSE THE DRAPES.
I'M BETTING ON THE GOOGLE.

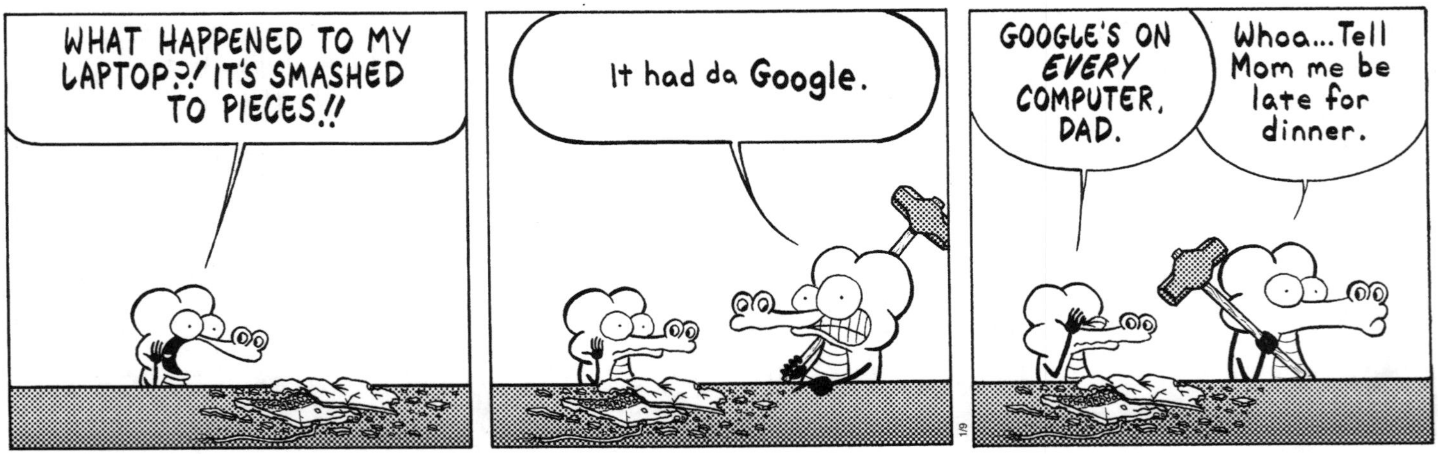
WHAT HAPPENED TO MY LAPTOP?! IT'S SMASHED TO PIECES!!
It had da Google.
1/9
GOOGLE'S ON EVERY COMPUTER, DAD.
Whoa...Tell Mom me be late for dinner.

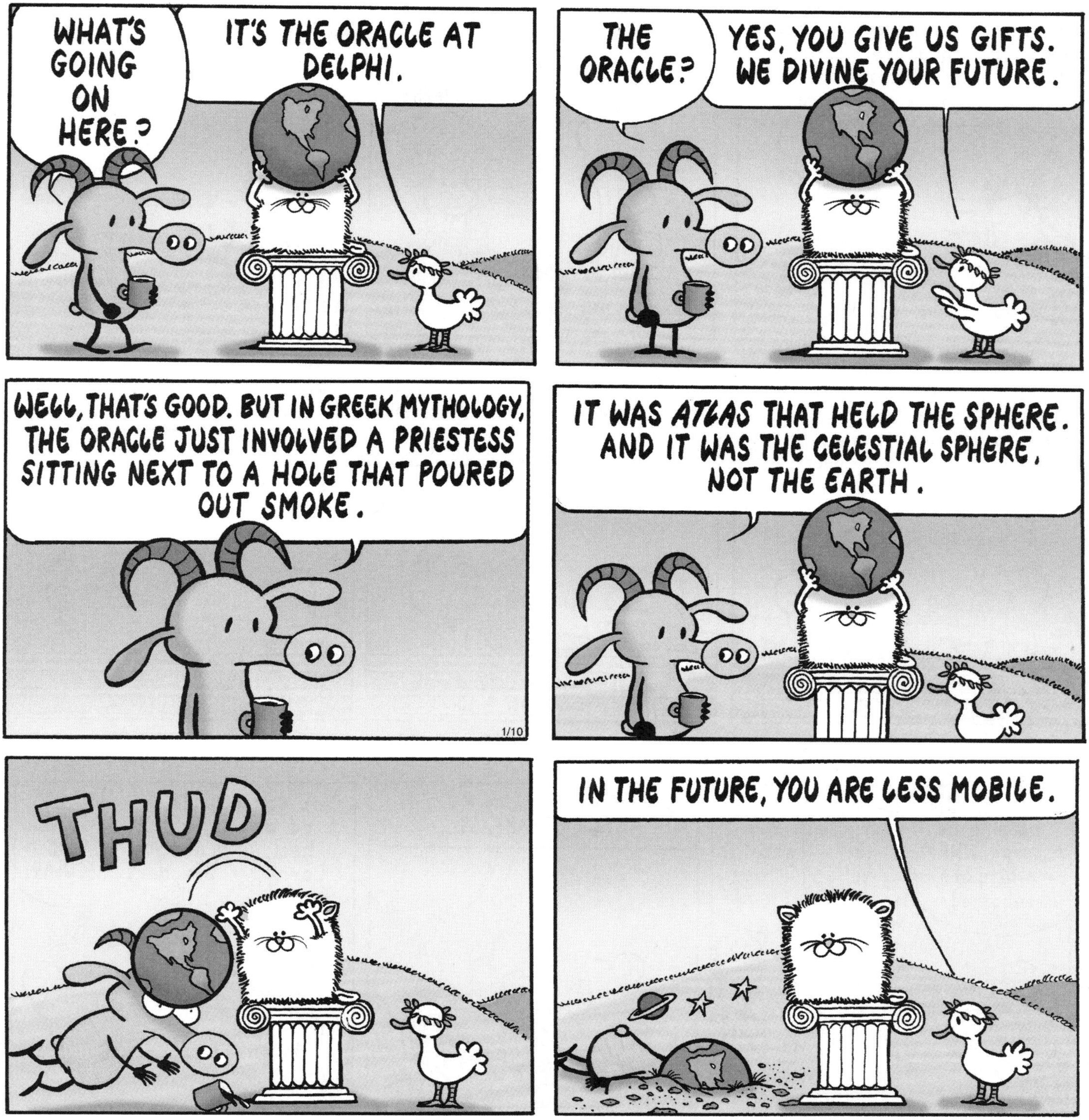
WHAT'S GOING ON HERE?
IT'S THE ORACLE AT DELPHI.
THE ORACLE?
YES, YOU GIVE US GIFTS. WE DIVINE YOUR FUTURE.
WELL, THAT'S GOOD. BUT IN GREEK MYTHOLOGY, THE ORACLE JUST INVOLVED A PRIESTESS SITTING NEXT TO A HOLE THAT POURED OUT SMOKE.
1/10
IT WAS *ATLAS* THAT HELD THE SPHERE. AND IT WAS THE CELESTIAL SPHERE, NOT THE EARTH.
THUD
IN THE FUTURE, YOU ARE LESS MOBILE.

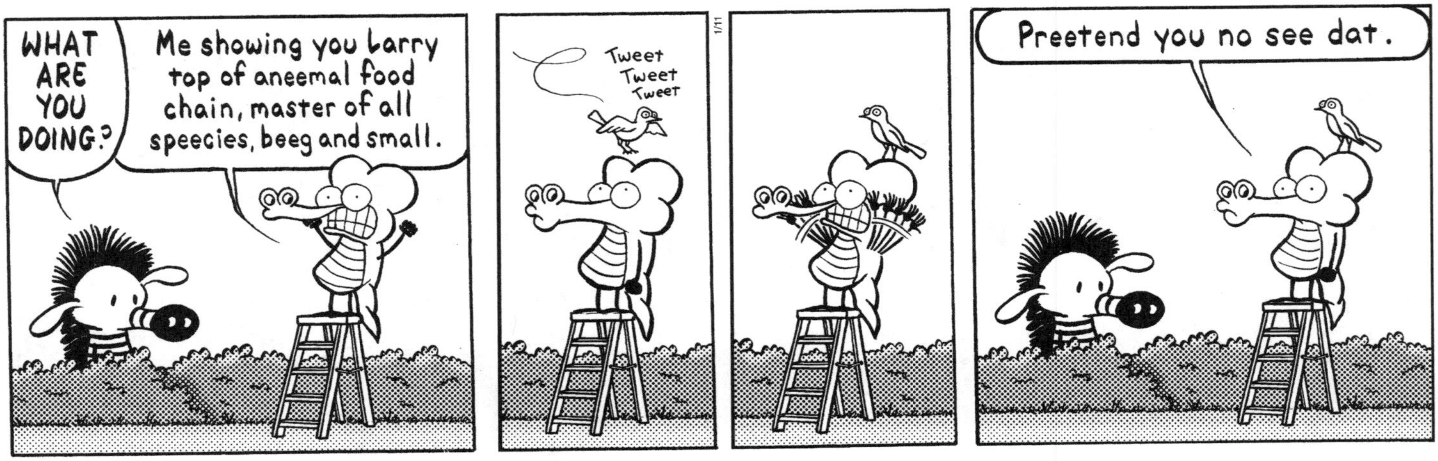
WHAT ARE YOU DOING?
Me showing you Larry top of aneemal food chain, master of all speecies, beeg and small.
Tweet Tweet Tweet
1/11
Preetend you no see dat.

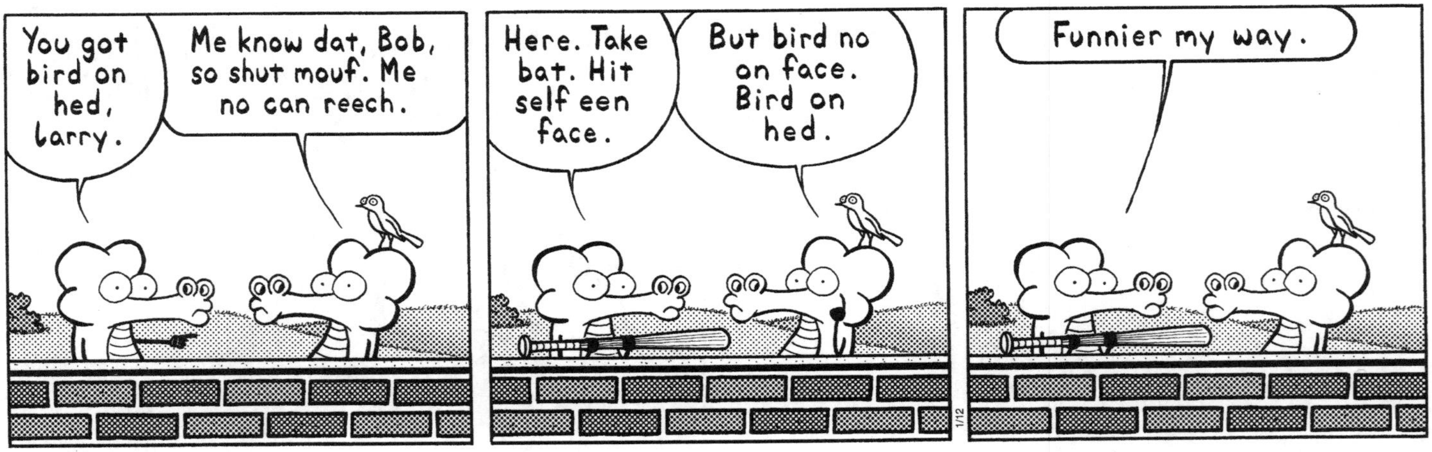
You got bird on hed, Larry.
Me know dat, Bob, so shut mouf. Me no can reech.
Here. Take bat. Hit self een face.
But bird no on face. Bird on hed.
1/12
Funnier my way.

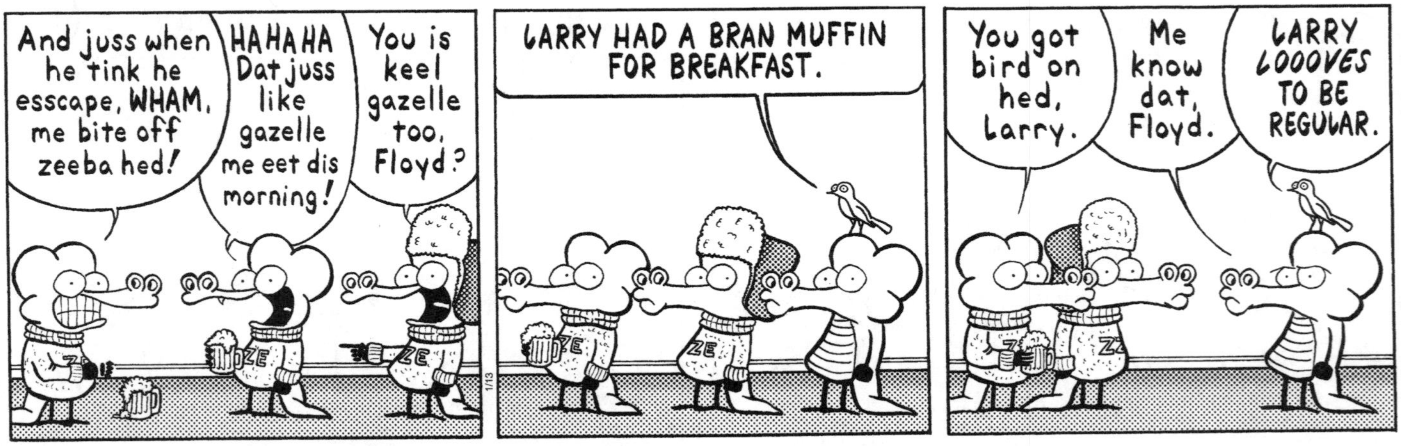
And juss when he tink he esscape, WHAM, me bite off zeeba hed!
HAHAHA Dat juss like gazelle me eet dis morning!
You is keel gazelle too, Floyd?
1/13
LARRY HAD A BRAN MUFFIN FOR BREAKFAST.
You got bird on hed, Larry.
Me know dat, Floyd.
LARRY LOOOVES TO BE REGULAR.

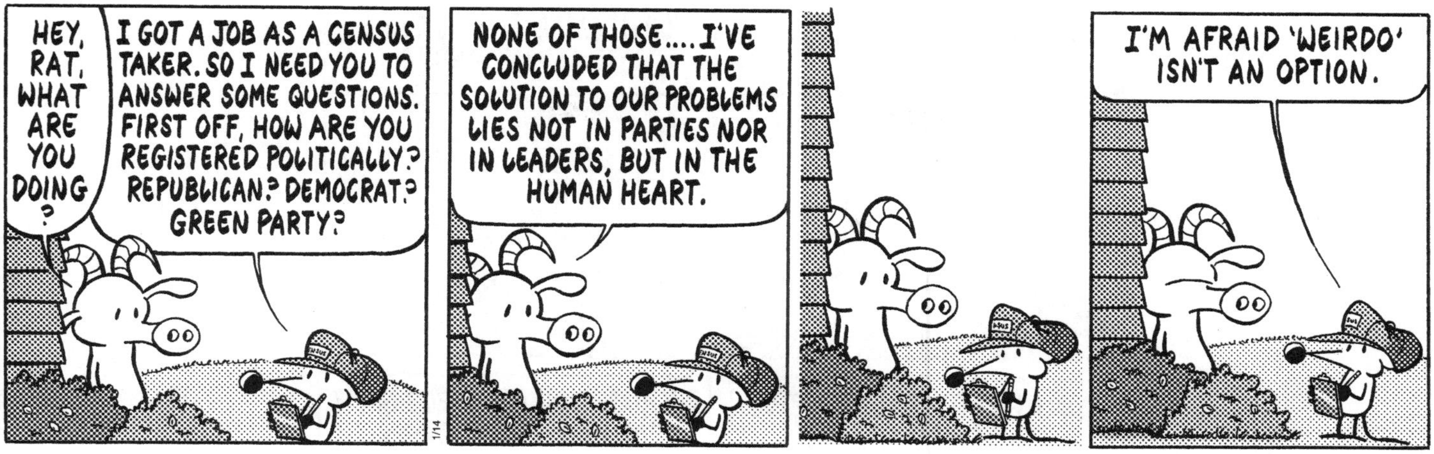
HEY, RAT, WHAT ARE YOU DOING?
I GOT A JOB AS A CENSUS TAKER. SO I NEED YOU TO ANSWER SOME QUESTIONS. FIRST OFF, HOW ARE YOU REGISTERED POLITICALLY? REPUBLICAN? DEMOCRAT? GREEN PARTY?
1/14
NONE OF THOSE.... I'VE CONCLUDED THAT THE SOLUTION TO OUR PROBLEMS LIES NOT IN PARTIES NOR IN LEADERS, BUT IN THE HUMAN HEART.
I'M AFRAID 'WEIRDO' ISN'T AN OPTION.

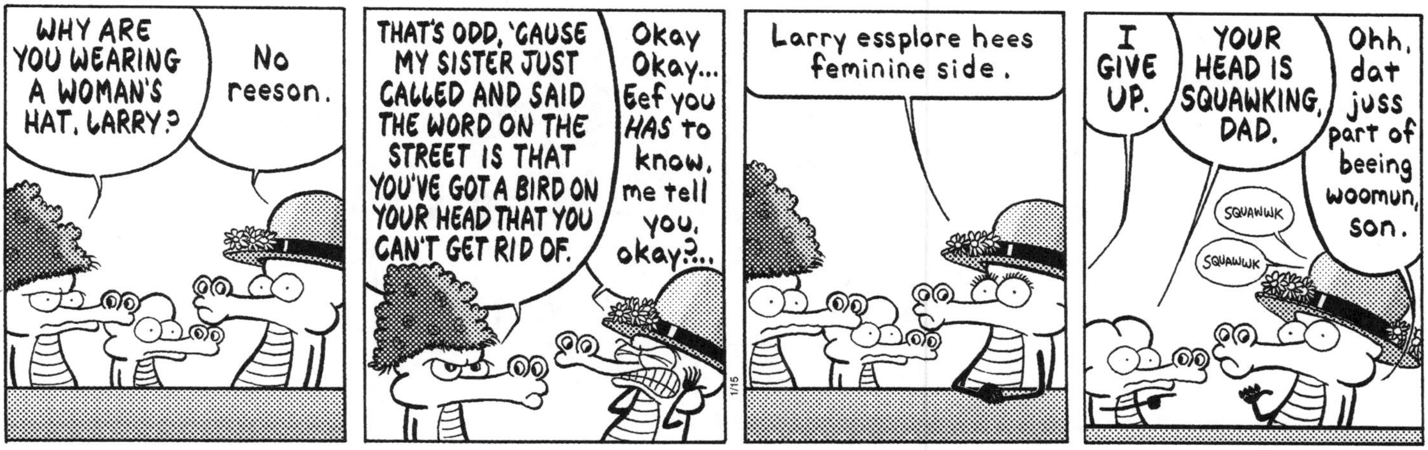
WHY ARE YOU WEARING A WOMAN'S HAT, LARRY?
No reeson.
THAT'S ODD, 'CAUSE MY SISTER JUST CALLED AND SAID THE WORD ON THE STREET IS THAT YOU'VE GOT A BIRD ON YOUR HEAD THAT YOU CAN'T GET RID OF.
Okay Okay... Eef you *HAS* to know, me tell you, okay?...
1/15
Larry esplore hees feminine side.
I GIVE UP.
YOUR HEAD IS SQUAWKING, DAD.
SQUAWWK
SQUAWWK
Ohh, dat juss part of beeing woomun, son.

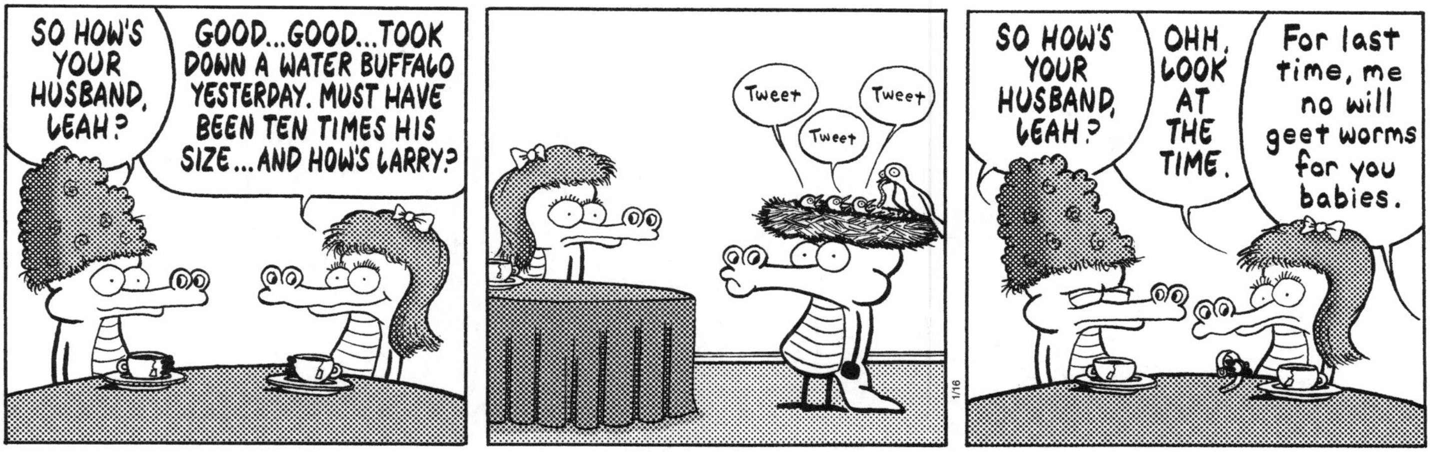
SO HOW'S YOUR HUSBAND, LEAH?
GOOD...GOOD...TOOK DOWN A WATER BUFFALO YESTERDAY. MUST HAVE BEEN TEN TIMES HIS SIZE... AND HOW'S LARRY?
Tweet
Tweet
Tweet
1/16
SO HOW'S YOUR HUSBAND, LEAH?
OHH, LOOK AT THE TIME.
For last time, me no will geet worms for you babies.

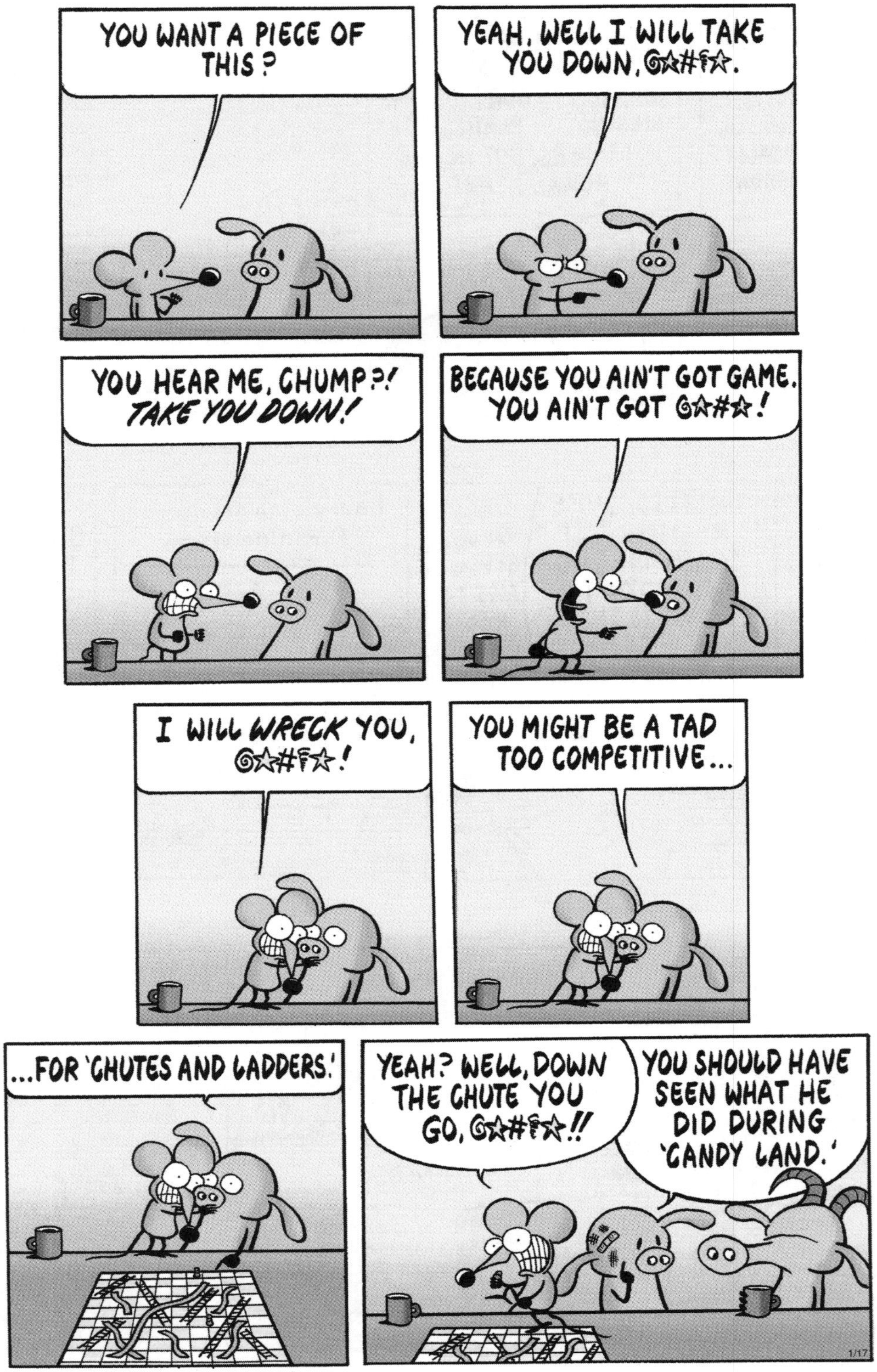
YOU WANT A PIECE OF THIS?
YEAH, WELL I WILL TAKE YOU DOWN, @☆#!☆.
YOU HEAR ME, CHUMP?! TAKE YOU DOWN!
BECAUSE YOU AIN'T GOT GAME. YOU AIN'T GOT @☆#☆!
I WILL WRECK YOU, @☆#!☆!
YOU MIGHT BE A TAD TOO COMPETITIVE...
...FOR 'CHUTES AND LADDERS.'
YEAH? WELL, DOWN THE CHUTE YOU GO, @☆#!☆!!
YOU SHOULD HAVE SEEN WHAT HE DID DURING 'CANDY LAND.'
1/17

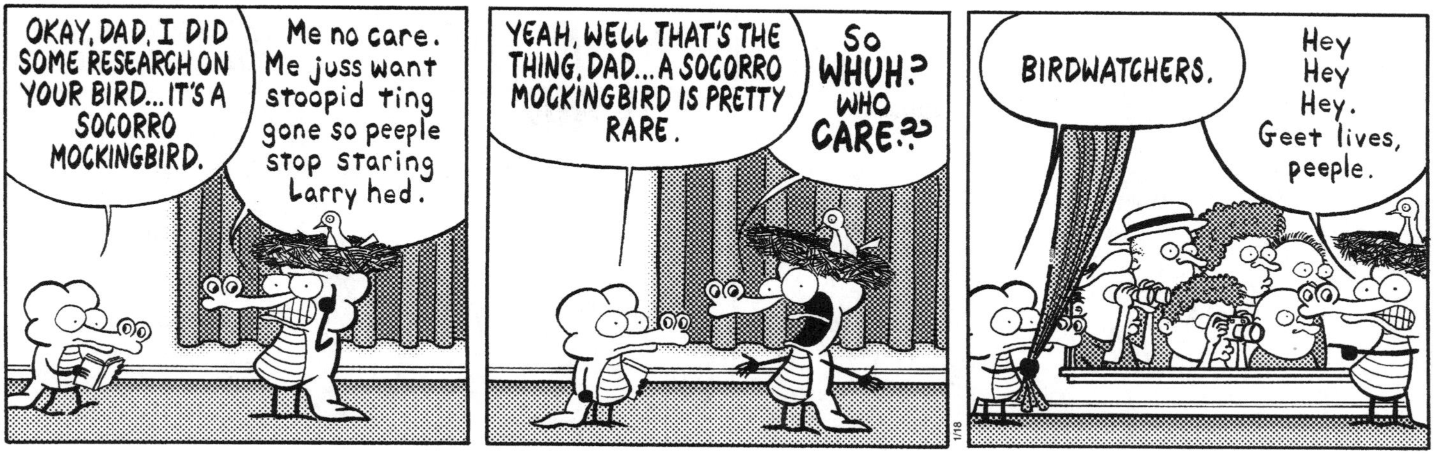

OKAY, DAD, I DID SOME RESEARCH ON YOUR BIRD... IT'S A SOCORRO MOCKINGBIRD.
Me no care. Me juss want stoopid ting gone so peeple stop staring Larry hed.
YEAH, WELL THAT'S THE THING, DAD... A SOCORRO MOCKINGBIRD IS PRETTY RARE.
So WHUH? WHO CARE?!
BIRDWATCHERS.
Hey Hey Hey. Geet lives, peeple.
1/18

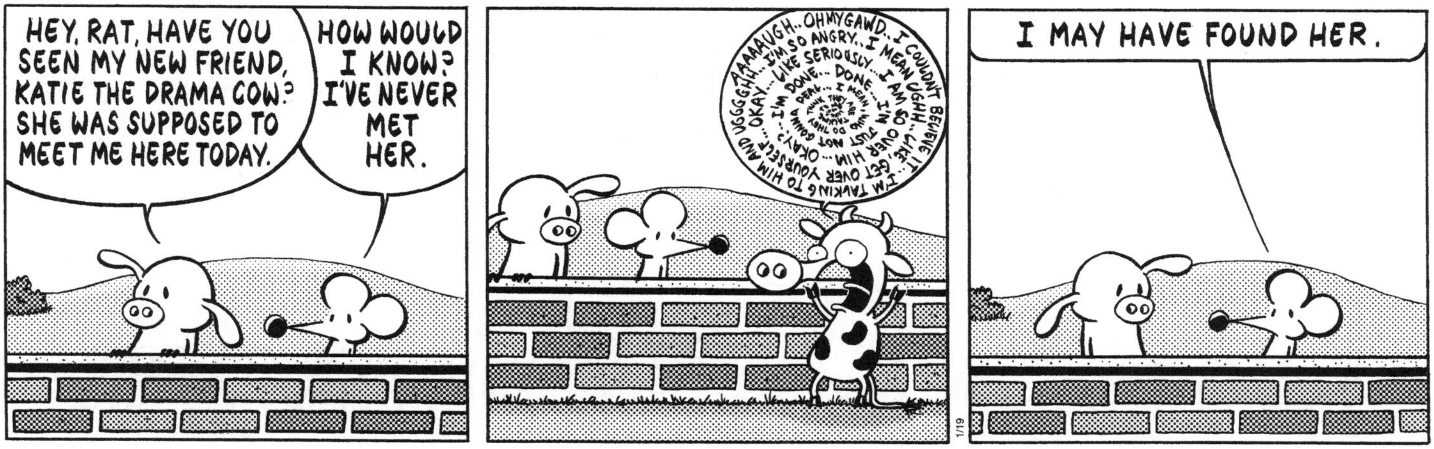

HEY, RAT, HAVE YOU SEEN MY NEW FRIEND, KATIE THE DRAMA COW? SHE WAS SUPPOSED TO MEET ME HERE TODAY.
HOW WOULD I KNOW? I'VE NEVER MET HER.
AAAAAUGH.. OHMYGAWD.. I COULDN'T BELIEVE IT.. I'M TALKING TO HIM AND UGGGGHH.. I'M SO ANGRY.. I MEAN UGHH.. LIKE, GET OVER YOURSELF... OKAY... LIKE SERIOUSLY... I AM SO OVER HIM... OKAY?... I'M DONE... DONE... I'M JUST NOT GONNA DEAL... I MEAN, WHO DO THEY THINK THEY ARE
I MAY HAVE FOUND HER.
1/19

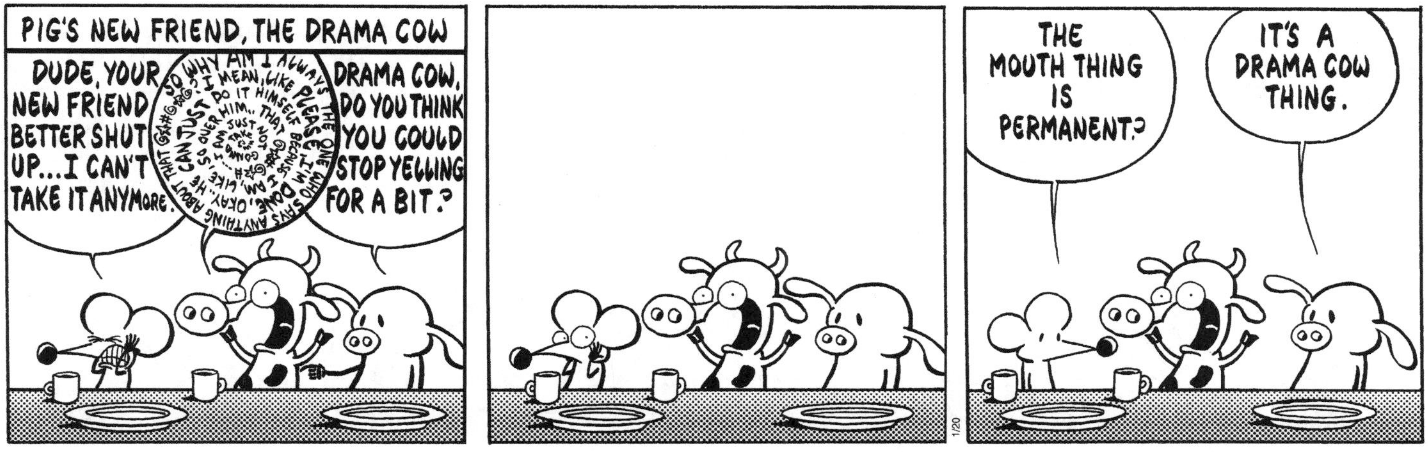

PIG'S NEW FRIEND, THE DRAMA COW
DUDE, YOUR NEW FRIEND BETTER SHUT UP... I CAN'T TAKE IT ANYMORE.
SO WHY AM I ALWAYS THE ONE WHO SAYS ANYTHING ABOUT THAT... I MEAN, LIKE PLEASE, I'M DONE, OKAY.. HE CAN JUST DO IT HIMSELF BECAUSE I AM, LIKE, SO OVER HIM.. THAT... I AM JUST NOT GONNA TAKE
DRAMA COW, DO YOU THINK YOU COULD STOP YELLING FOR A BIT?
THE MOUTH THING IS PERMANENT?
IT'S A DRAMA COW THING.
1/20

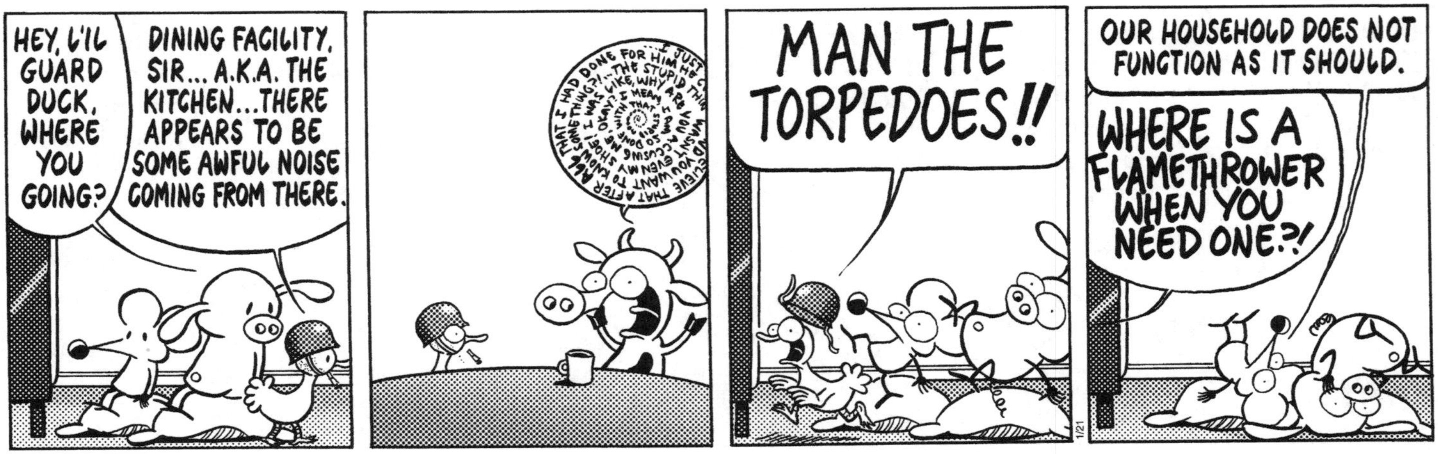
HEY, L'IL GUARD DUCK, WHERE YOU GOING?
DINING FACILITY, SIR... A.K.A. THE KITCHEN...THERE APPEARS TO BE SOME AWFUL NOISE COMING FROM THERE.
MAN THE TORPEDOES!!
OUR HOUSEHOLD DOES NOT FUNCTION AS IT SHOULD.
WHERE IS A FLAMETHROWER WHEN YOU NEED ONE?!
1/21

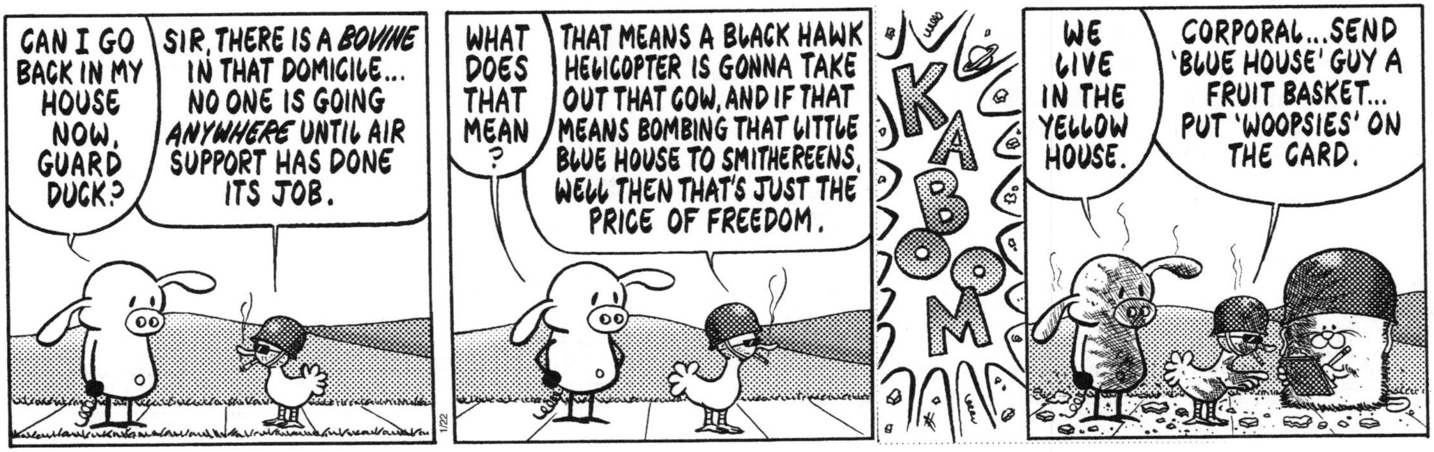
CAN I GO BACK IN MY HOUSE NOW, GUARD DUCK?
SIR, THERE IS A BOVINE IN THAT DOMICILE... NO ONE IS GOING ANYWHERE UNTIL AIR SUPPORT HAS DONE ITS JOB.
1/22
WHAT DOES THAT MEAN?
THAT MEANS A BLACK HAWK HELICOPTER IS GONNA TAKE OUT THAT COW, AND IF THAT MEANS BOMBING THAT LITTLE BLUE HOUSE TO SMITHEREENS, WELL THEN THAT'S JUST THE PRICE OF FREEDOM.
KABOOM
WE LIVE IN THE YELLOW HOUSE.
CORPORAL...SEND 'BLUE HOUSE' GUY A FRUIT BASKET... PUT 'WOOPSIES' ON THE CARD.

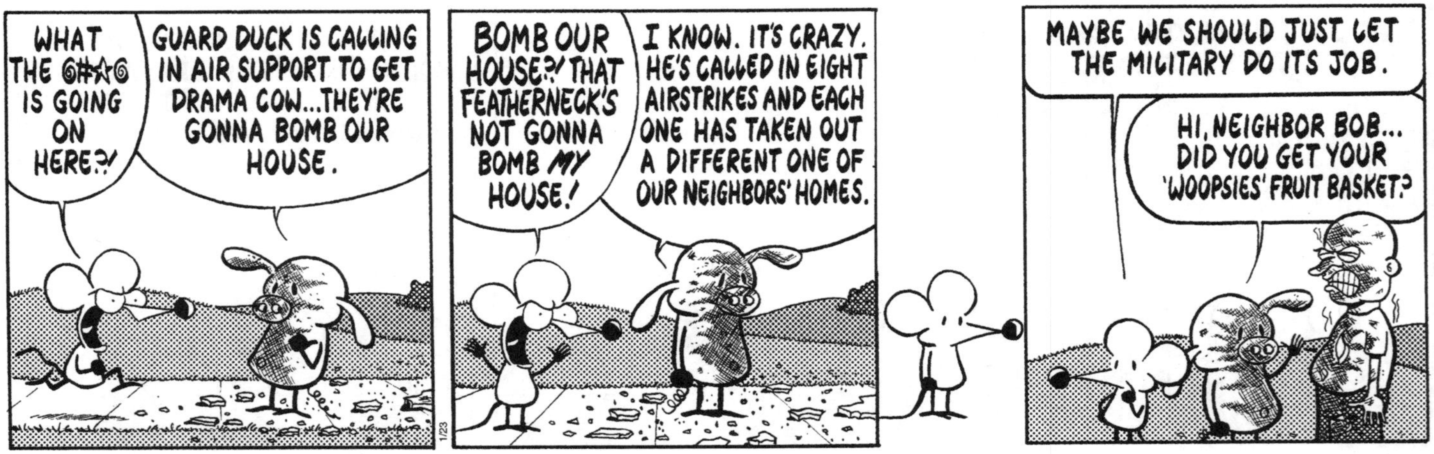
WHAT THE @#☆@ IS GOING ON HERE?!
GUARD DUCK IS CALLING IN AIR SUPPORT TO GET DRAMA COW...THEY'RE GONNA BOMB OUR HOUSE.
1/23
BOMB OUR HOUSE?! THAT FEATHERNECK'S NOT GONNA BOMB MY HOUSE!
I KNOW. IT'S CRAZY. HE'S CALLED IN EIGHT AIRSTRIKES AND EACH ONE HAS TAKEN OUT A DIFFERENT ONE OF OUR NEIGHBORS' HOMES.
MAYBE WE SHOULD JUST LET THE MILITARY DO ITS JOB.
HI, NEIGHBOR BOB... DID YOU GET YOUR 'WOOPSIES' FRUIT BASKET?

Danny Donkey hated people.
Stoopid People.
He hated their greed. He hated their pettiness. He hated their pigginess.
Bleah.
But most of all, he hated that there were 6,000,000,000 of them.
So Danny Donkey visited a spiritual guru.
"Climb a great mountain with a group of strangers," said the spiritual guru, "The shared challenge will bring you a new perspective."
So Danny Donkey climbed to the top of Mount Everest with a group of five strangers.
YAY
YAY
YAY
And pushed them off.
THIS IS 'DANNY DONKEY'S GUIDE TO SPIRITUAL FULFILLMENT'?
"'YAY,' SAID DANNY, 'ONLY 5,999,999,995 TO GO.'"
I AM SO FULFILLED I COULD CRY.

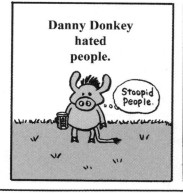

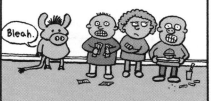

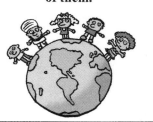

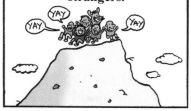

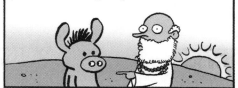

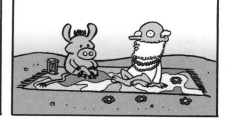

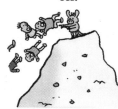

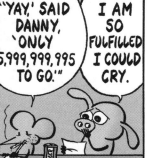

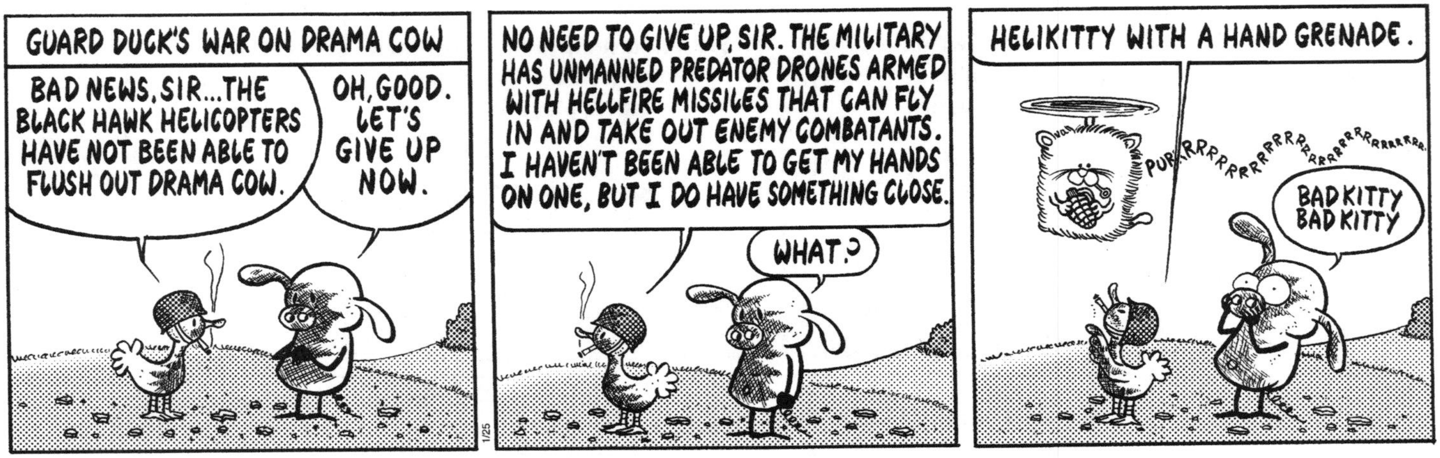
GUARD DUCK'S WAR ON DRAMA COW
BAD NEWS, SIR...THE BLACK HAWK HELICOPTERS HAVE NOT BEEN ABLE TO FLUSH OUT DRAMA COW.
OH, GOOD. LET'S GIVE UP NOW.
1/25
NO NEED TO GIVE UP, SIR. THE MILITARY HAS UNMANNED PREDATOR DRONES ARMED WITH HELLFIRE MISSILES THAT CAN FLY IN AND TAKE OUT ENEMY COMBATANTS. I HAVEN'T BEEN ABLE TO GET MY HANDS ON ONE, BUT I DO HAVE SOMETHING CLOSE.
WHAT?
HELIKITTY WITH A HAND GRENADE.
PURRRRRRRRRRRRRRRRRRRRRRRRRRR
BAD KITTY BAD KITTY

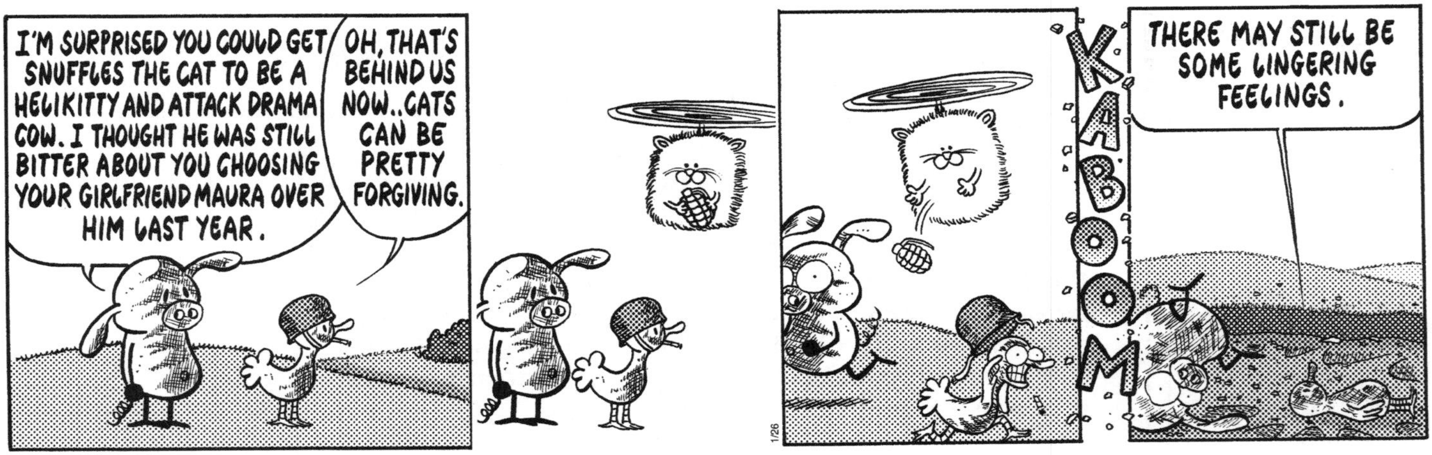
I'M SURPRISED YOU COULD GET SNUFFLES THE CAT TO BE A HELIKITTY AND ATTACK DRAMA COW. I THOUGHT HE WAS STILL BITTER ABOUT YOU CHOOSING YOUR GIRLFRIEND MAURA OVER HIM LAST YEAR.
OH, THAT'S BEHIND US NOW..CATS CAN BE PRETTY FORGIVING.
1/26
KABOOM
THERE MAY STILL BE SOME LINGERING FEELINGS.

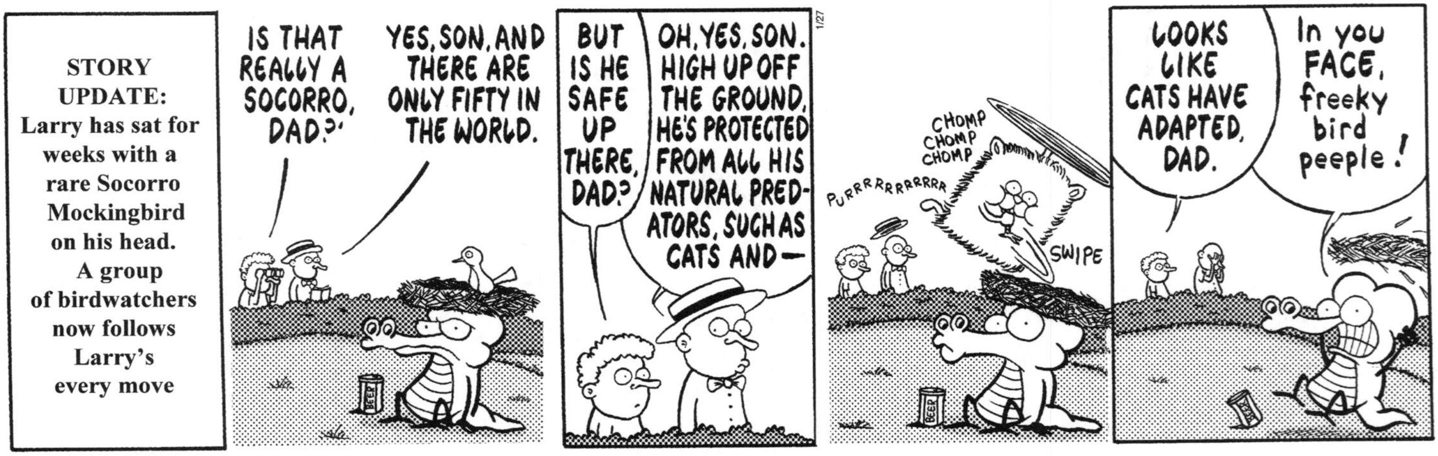
STORY UPDATE:
Larry has sat for weeks with a rare Socorro Mockingbird on his head. A group of birdwatchers now follows Larry's every move
IS THAT REALLY A SOCORRO, DAD?
YES, SON, AND THERE ARE ONLY FIFTY IN THE WORLD.
BEER
1/27
BUT IS HE SAFE UP THERE, DAD?
OH, YES, SON. HIGH UP OFF THE GROUND, HE'S PROTECTED FROM ALL HIS NATURAL PREDATORS, SUCH AS CATS AND—
CHOMP CHOMP CHOMP
PURRRRRRRRRRR
SWIPE
BEER
LOOKS LIKE CATS HAVE ADAPTED, DAD.
In you FACE, freeky bird peeple!

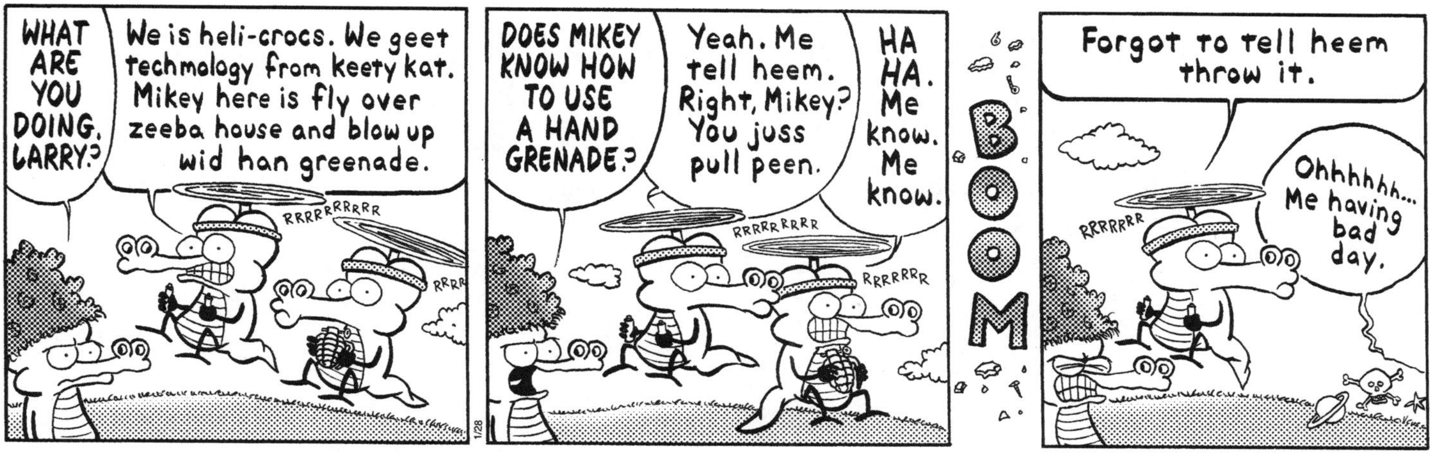
WHAT ARE YOU DOING, LARRY?
We is heli-crocs. We geet techmology from keety kat. Mikey here is fly over zeeba house and blow up wid han greenade.
RRRRRRRRRR
RRRR
DOES MIKEY KNOW HOW TO USE A HAND GRENADE?
Yeah. Me tell heem. Right, Mikey? You juss pull peen.
HA HA. Me know. Me know.
RRRRRRRRR
RRRRRRR
BOOM
Forgot to tell heem throw it.
RRRRRRR
Ohhhhhh... Me having bad day.
1/28

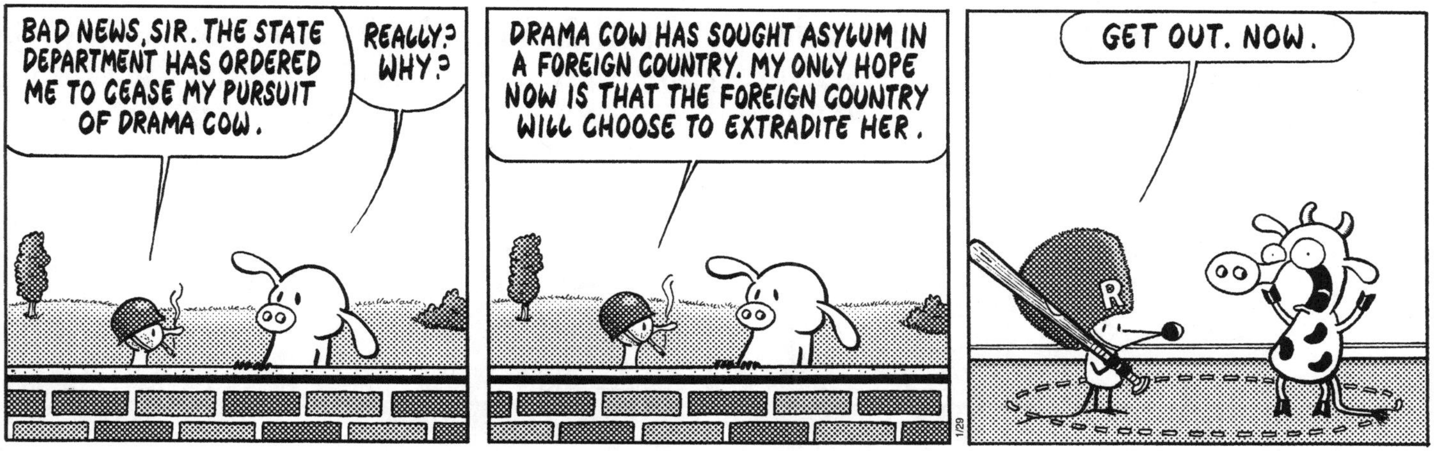
BAD NEWS, SIR. THE STATE DEPARTMENT HAS ORDERED ME TO CEASE MY PURSUIT OF DRAMA COW.
REALLY? WHY?
DRAMA COW HAS SOUGHT ASYLUM IN A FOREIGN COUNTRY. MY ONLY HOPE NOW IS THAT THE FOREIGN COUNTRY WILL CHOOSE TO EXTRADITE HER.
GET OUT. NOW.
1/29

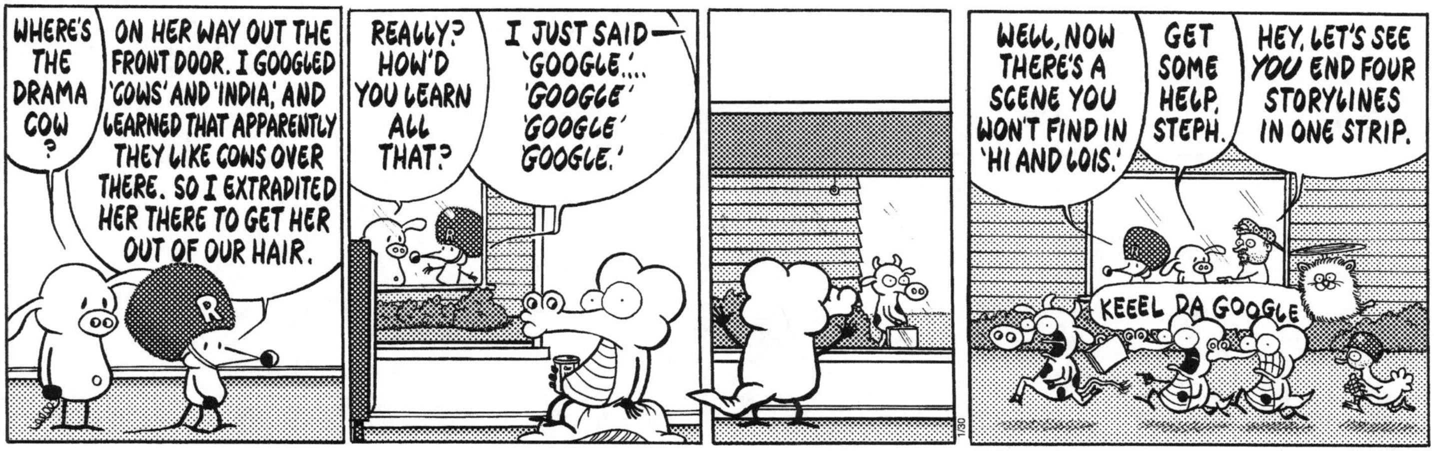
WHERE'S THE DRAMA COW?
ON HER WAY OUT THE FRONT DOOR. I GOOGLED 'COWS' AND 'INDIA,' AND LEARNED THAT APPARENTLY THEY LIKE COWS OVER THERE. SO I EXTRADITED HER THERE TO GET HER OUT OF OUR HAIR.
REALLY? HOW'D YOU LEARN ALL THAT?
I JUST SAID—'GOOGLE.'... 'GOOGLE' 'GOOGLE' 'GOOGLE.'
WELL, NOW THERE'S A SCENE YOU WON'T FIND IN 'HI AND LOIS.'
GET SOME HELP, STEPH.
HEY, LET'S SEE YOU END FOUR STORYLINES IN ONE STRIP.
KEEEL DA GOOGLE
1/30

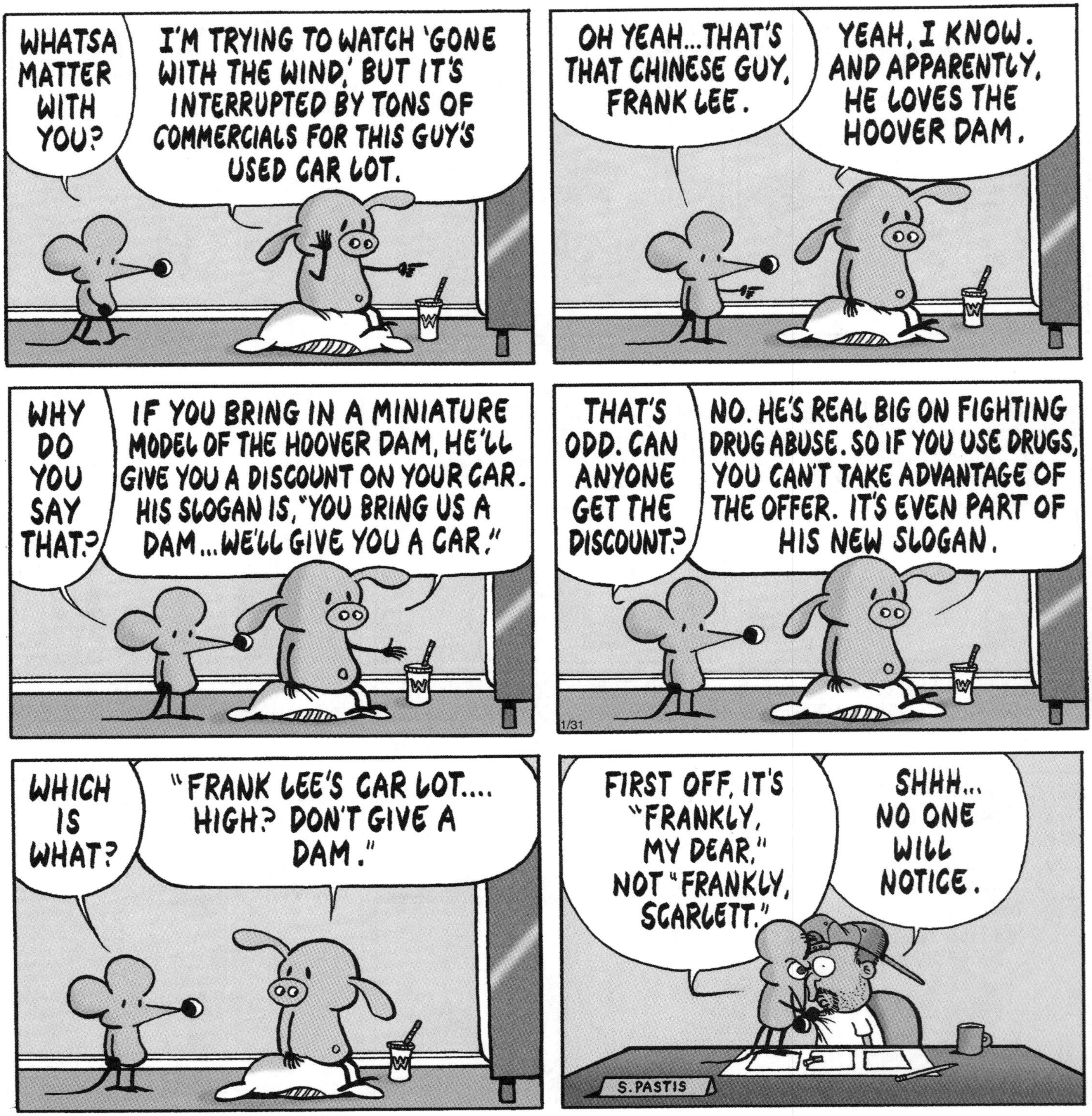
WHATSA MATTER WITH YOU?
I'M TRYING TO WATCH 'GONE WITH THE WIND,' BUT IT'S INTERRUPTED BY TONS OF COMMERCIALS FOR THIS GUY'S USED CAR LOT.
OH YEAH...THAT'S THAT CHINESE GUY, FRANK LEE.
YEAH, I KNOW. AND APPARENTLY, HE LOVES THE HOOVER DAM.
WHY DO YOU SAY THAT?
IF YOU BRING IN A MINIATURE MODEL OF THE HOOVER DAM, HE'LL GIVE YOU A DISCOUNT ON YOUR CAR. HIS SLOGAN IS, "YOU BRING US A DAM...WE'LL GIVE YOU A CAR."
THAT'S ODD. CAN ANYONE GET THE DISCOUNT?
NO. HE'S REAL BIG ON FIGHTING DRUG ABUSE. SO IF YOU USE DRUGS, YOU CAN'T TAKE ADVANTAGE OF THE OFFER. IT'S EVEN PART OF HIS NEW SLOGAN.
1/31
WHICH IS WHAT?
"FRANK LEE'S CAR LOT.... HIGH? DON'T GIVE A DAM."
FIRST OFF, IT'S "FRANKLY, MY DEAR," NOT "FRANKLY, SCARLETT."
SHHH... NO ONE WILL NOTICE.
S. PASTIS

Panel 1:

HOW COME YOU DON'T DRAW BICYCLES IN YOUR STRIP?

BECAUSE I CAN'T DRAW BICYCLES. AND YOU ALREADY KNOW THAT.

Panel 2:

Heeeeeeey... LOOK AT ME! I'M ON A BICYCLE!

WHAT THE ?? WHERE'D YOU GET THAT ?!

Panel 3:

I CUT IT OUT FROM A 'BABY BLUES' STRIP... NOW THAT RICK KIRKMAN GUY... HE CAN DRAW BIKES.

YOU CAN'T TAKE ART FROM OTHER COMIC STRIPS! WE'LL GET SUED!!

Panel 4:

YOU'LL GET SUED. I'M FICTIONAL.

RICK KIRKMAN ON LINE TWO....

AND HE'S GOT A POTTY MOUTH.

Panel 5:

THANKS FOR INVITING US OVER, TIMMY AND TAMMY SWAN. IT'S ALWAYS SO SPECIAL BEING WITH TWO BIRDS WHO HAVE BEEN TOGETHER FOR LIFE.

Panel 6:

WHAT'S SO SPECIAL ABOUT IT? I MEAN, TAMMY AND I LOVE EACH OTHER AND ALL, BUT ALL BIRDS MATE FOR LIFE.

NO, THEY DON'T. OTHER BIRDS HAVE NUMEROUS PARTNERS.

Panel 7:

DON'T WAIT UP.

Panel 8:

WHAT'S WRONG WITH YOU?

THE COMICS IN THIS PAPER HAVE BEEN SHRUNK TO THE POINT OF NEAR-ILLEGIBILITY. YOU CAN'T SEE ANY OF THE NUANCES OF THE ART.

Panel 9:

SO?

SO WHY SHOULD ANY OF THE BETTER CARTOONISTS BOTHER TO DRAW ELABORATE ART? NOW A GUY CAN GET AWAY WITH BEING A TOTALLY INCOMPETENT ARTIST.

Panel 10:

GOOD NEWS.

PASTIS

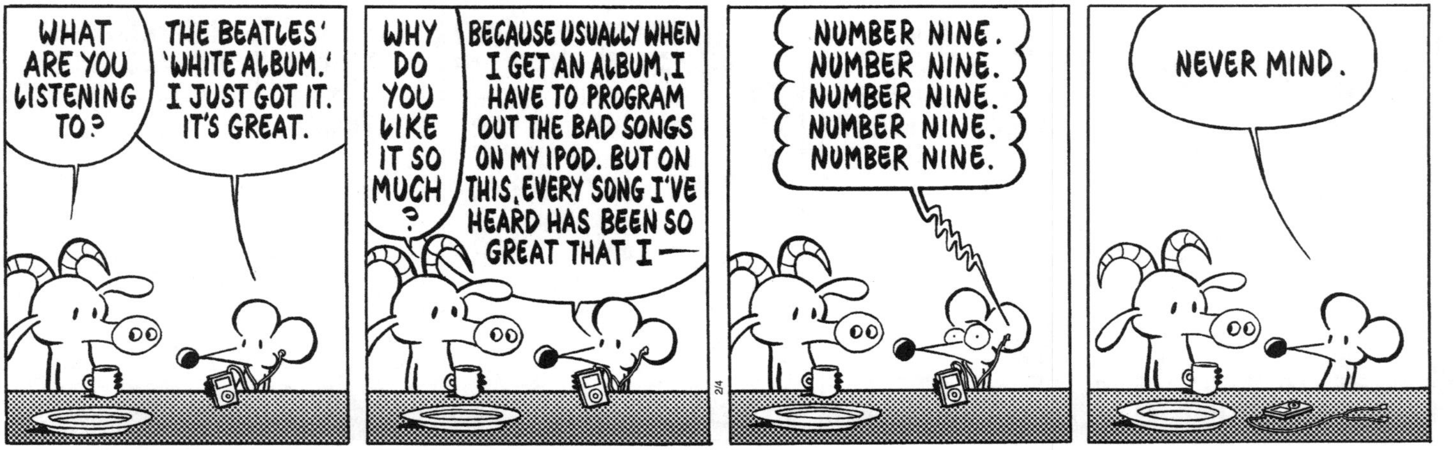
WHAT ARE YOU LISTENING TO?
THE BEATLES' 'WHITE ALBUM.' I JUST GOT IT. IT'S GREAT.
WHY DO YOU LIKE IT SO MUCH?
BECAUSE USUALLY WHEN I GET AN ALBUM, I HAVE TO PROGRAM OUT THE BAD SONGS ON MY IPOD. BUT ON THIS, EVERY SONG I'VE HEARD HAS BEEN SO GREAT THAT I—
2/4
NUMBER NINE. NUMBER NINE. NUMBER NINE. NUMBER NINE. NUMBER NINE.
NEVER MIND.

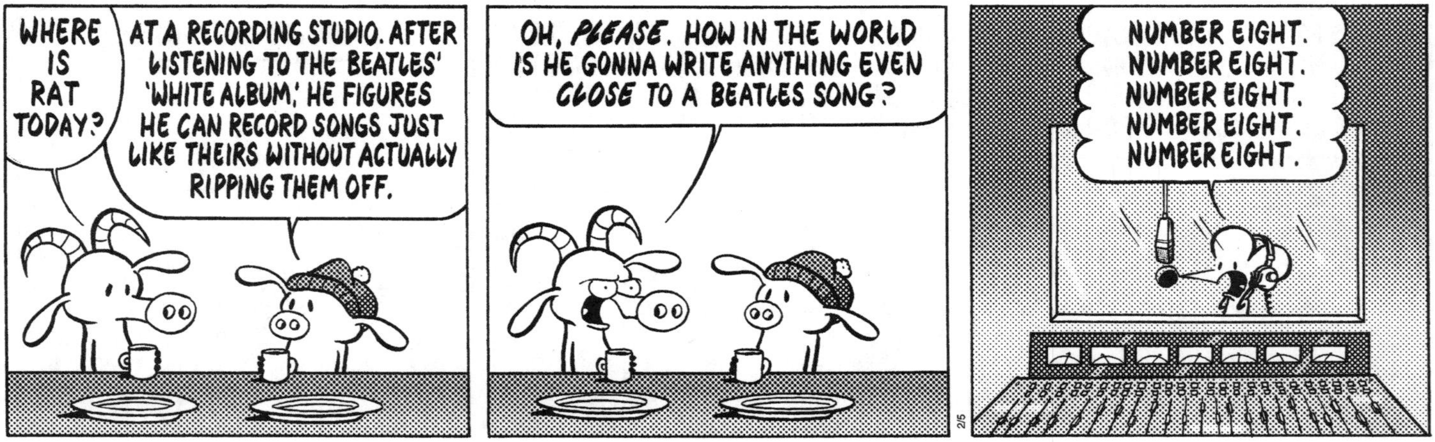
WHERE IS RAT TODAY?
AT A RECORDING STUDIO. AFTER LISTENING TO THE BEATLES' 'WHITE ALBUM,' HE FIGURES HE CAN RECORD SONGS JUST LIKE THEIRS WITHOUT ACTUALLY RIPPING THEM OFF.
OH, PLEASE. HOW IN THE WORLD IS HE GONNA WRITE ANYTHING EVEN CLOSE TO A BEATLES SONG?
2/5
NUMBER EIGHT. NUMBER EIGHT. NUMBER EIGHT. NUMBER EIGHT. NUMBER EIGHT.

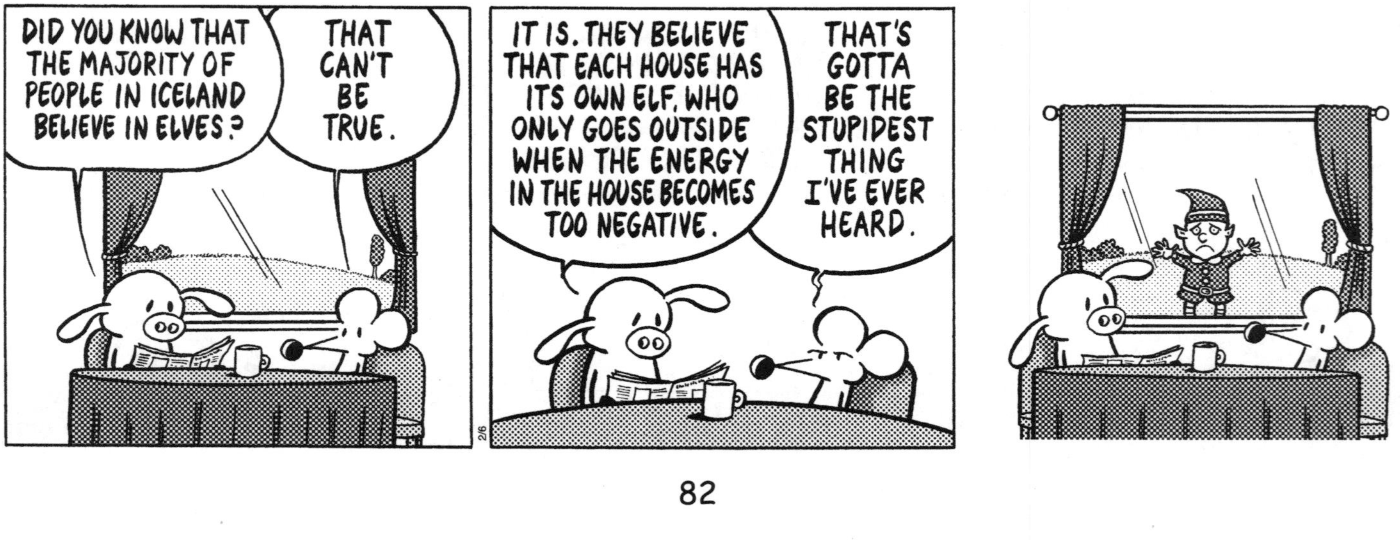
DID YOU KNOW THAT THE MAJORITY OF PEOPLE IN ICELAND BELIEVE IN ELVES?
THAT CAN'T BE TRUE.
2/6
IT IS. THEY BELIEVE THAT EACH HOUSE HAS ITS OWN ELF, WHO ONLY GOES OUTSIDE WHEN THE ENERGY IN THE HOUSE BECOMES TOO NEGATIVE.
THAT'S GOTTA BE THE STUPIDEST THING I'VE EVER HEARD.

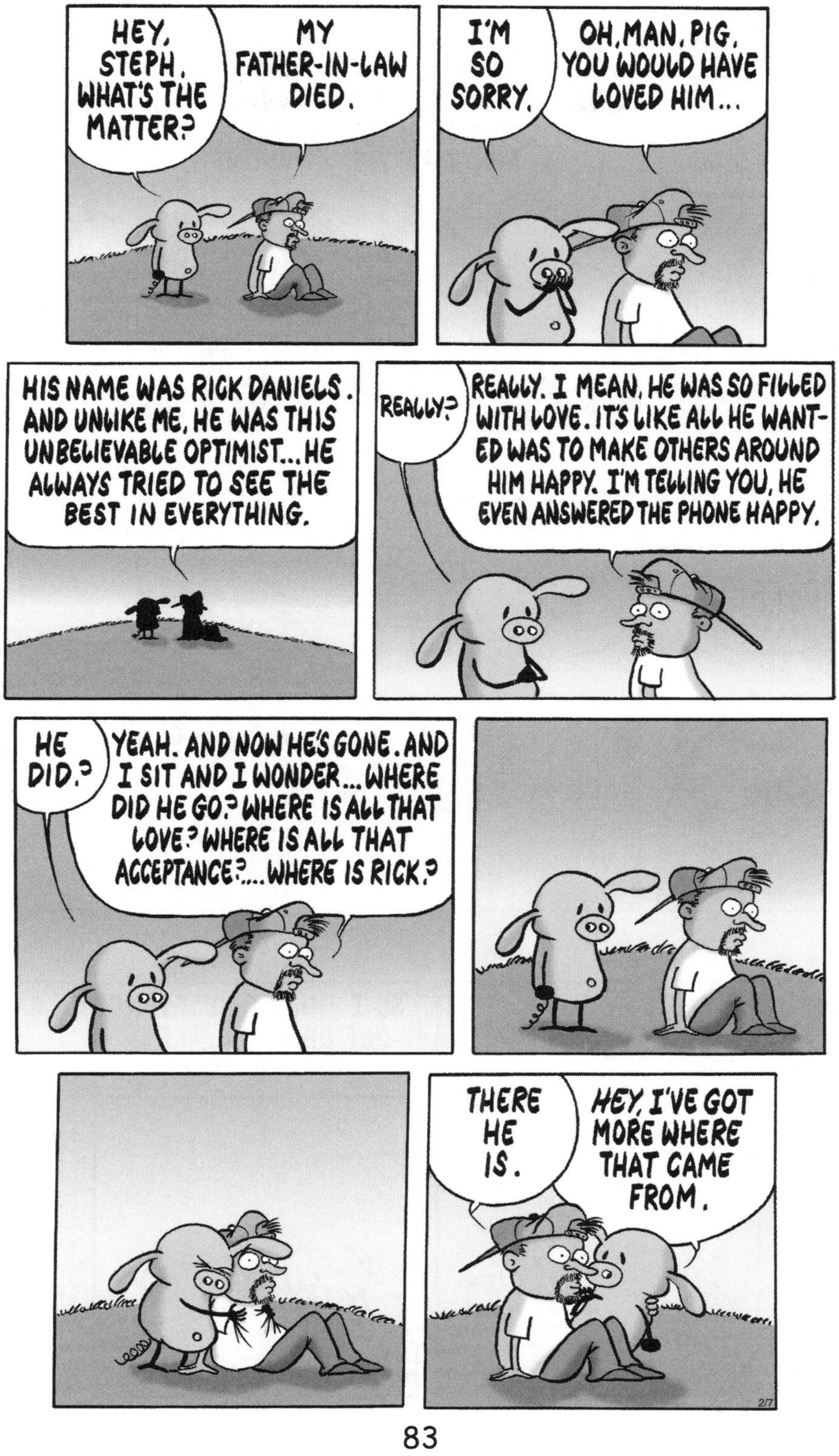
HEY, STEPH, WHAT'S THE MATTER?
MY FATHER-IN-LAW DIED.
I'M SO SORRY.
OH, MAN, PIG, YOU WOULD HAVE LOVED HIM...
HIS NAME WAS RICK DANIELS. AND UNLIKE ME, HE WAS THIS UNBELIEVABLE OPTIMIST... HE ALWAYS TRIED TO SEE THE BEST IN EVERYTHING.
REALLY?
REALLY. I MEAN, HE WAS SO FILLED WITH LOVE. IT'S LIKE ALL HE WANTED WAS TO MAKE OTHERS AROUND HIM HAPPY. I'M TELLING YOU, HE EVEN ANSWERED THE PHONE HAPPY.
HE DID?
YEAH. AND NOW HE'S GONE. AND I SIT AND I WONDER... WHERE DID HE GO? WHERE IS ALL THAT LOVE? WHERE IS ALL THAT ACCEPTANCE?... WHERE IS RICK?
THERE HE IS.
HEY, I'VE GOT MORE WHERE THAT CAME FROM.
2/7

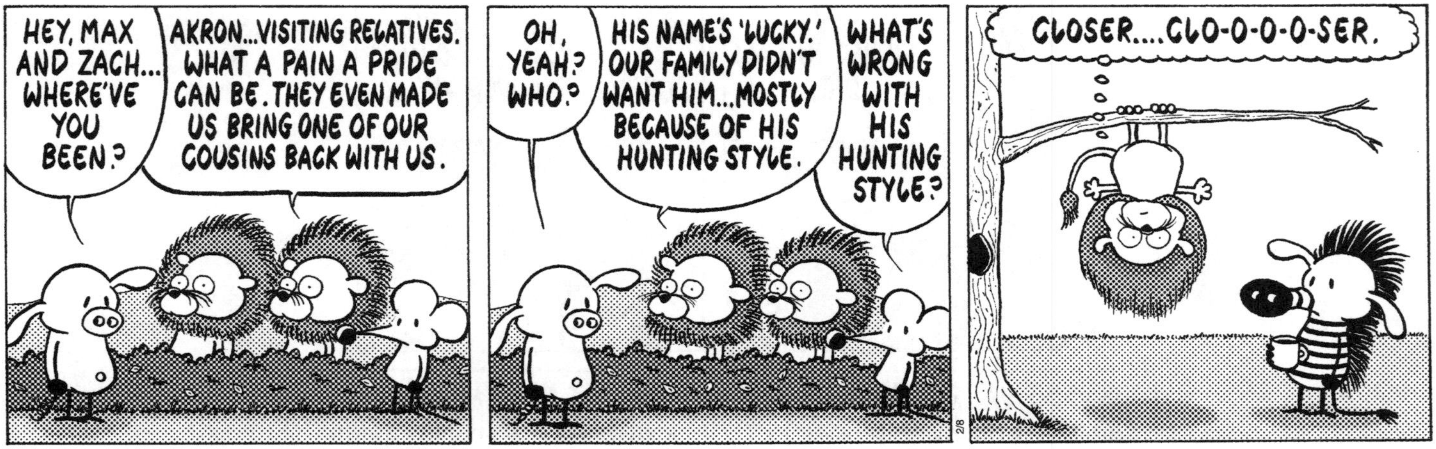
HEY, MAX AND ZACH... WHERE'VE YOU BEEN?
AKRON...VISITING RELATIVES. WHAT A PAIN A PRIDE CAN BE. THEY EVEN MADE US BRING ONE OF OUR COUSINS BACK WITH US.
OH, YEAH? WHO?
HIS NAME'S 'LUCKY.' OUR FAMILY DIDN'T WANT HIM...MOSTLY BECAUSE OF HIS HUNTING STYLE.
WHAT'S WRONG WITH HIS HUNTING STYLE?
2/8
CLOSER....CLO-O-O-O-SER.

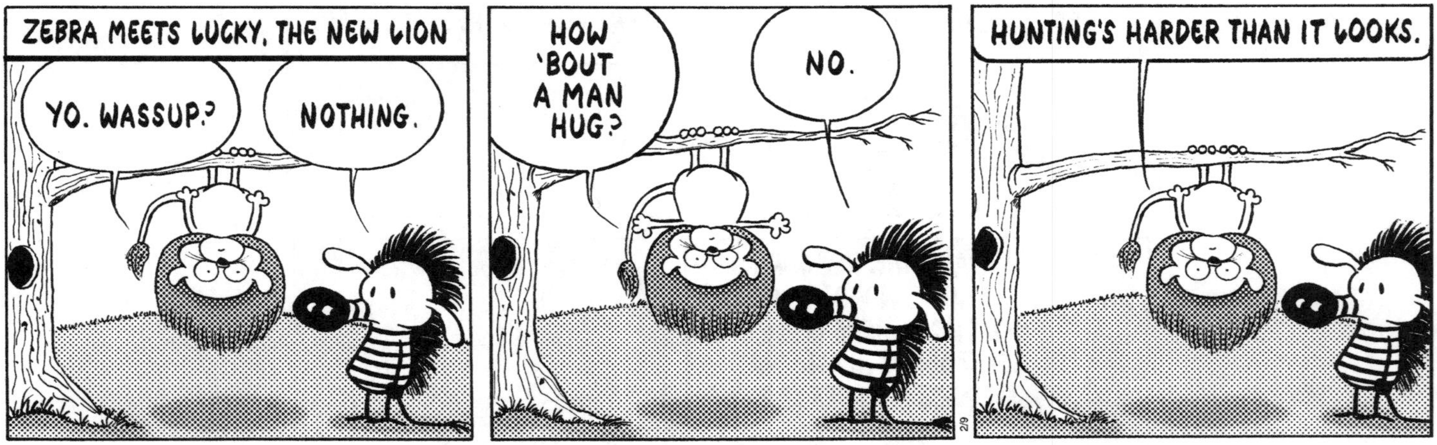
ZEBRA MEETS LUCKY, THE NEW LION
YO. WASSUP?
NOTHING.
HOW 'BOUT A MAN HUG?
NO.
2/9
HUNTING'S HARDER THAN IT LOOKS.

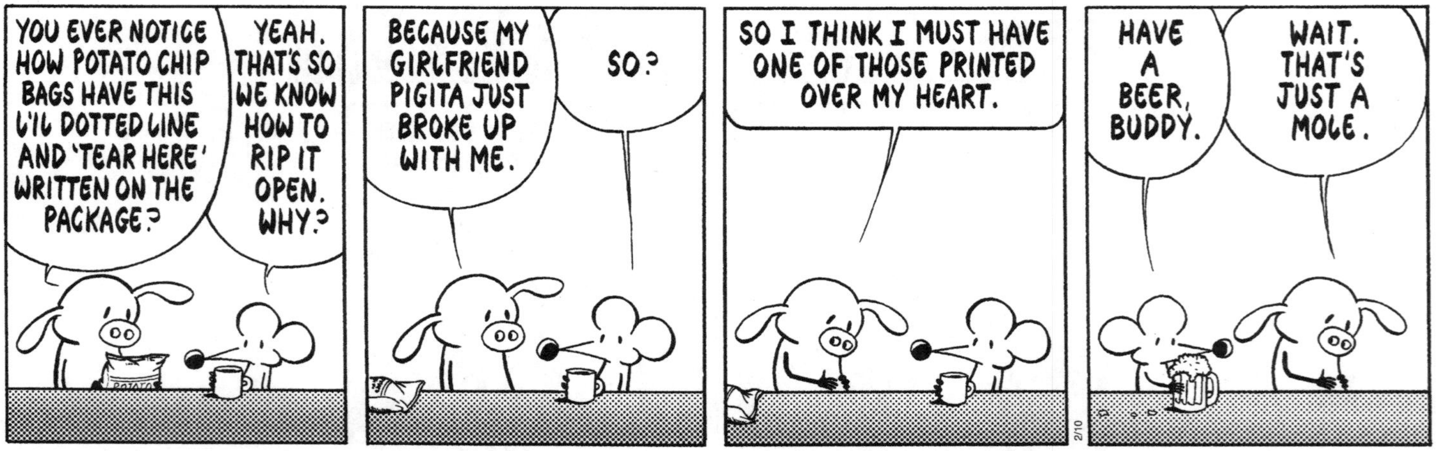
YOU EVER NOTICE HOW POTATO CHIP BAGS HAVE THIS L'IL DOTTED LINE AND 'TEAR HERE' WRITTEN ON THE PACKAGE?
YEAH. THAT'S SO WE KNOW HOW TO RIP IT OPEN. WHY?
BECAUSE MY GIRLFRIEND PIGITA JUST BROKE UP WITH ME.
SO?
SO I THINK I MUST HAVE ONE OF THOSE PRINTED OVER MY HEART.
2/10
HAVE A BEER, BUDDY.
WAIT. THAT'S JUST A MOLE.

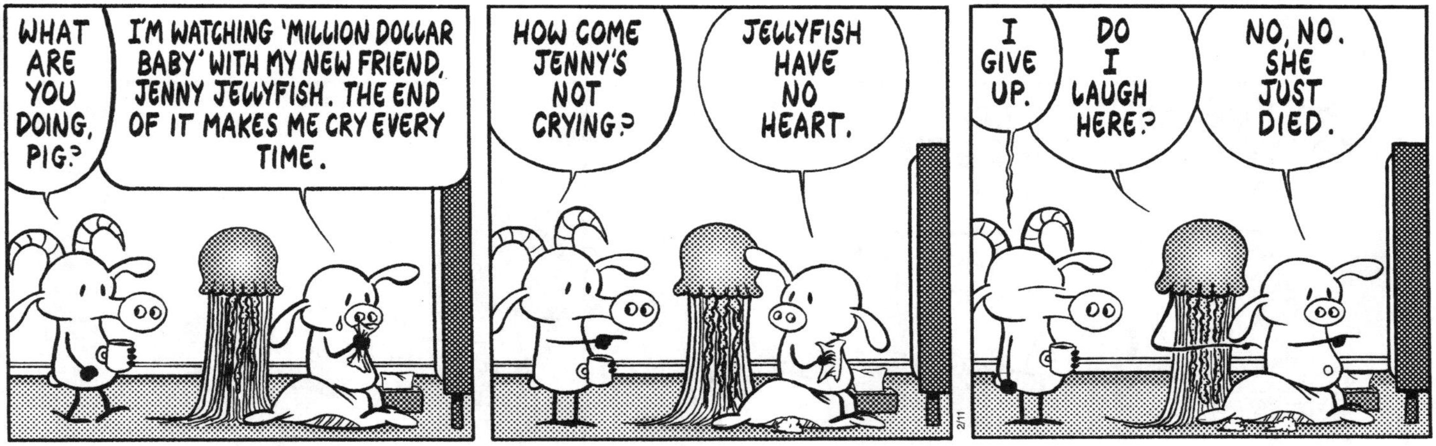
WHAT ARE YOU DOING, PIG?
I'M WATCHING 'MILLION DOLLAR BABY' WITH MY NEW FRIEND, JENNY JELLYFISH. THE END OF IT MAKES ME CRY EVERY TIME.
HOW COME JENNY'S NOT CRYING?
JELLYFISH HAVE NO HEART.
2/11
I GIVE UP.
DO I LAUGH HERE?
NO, NO. SHE JUST DIED.

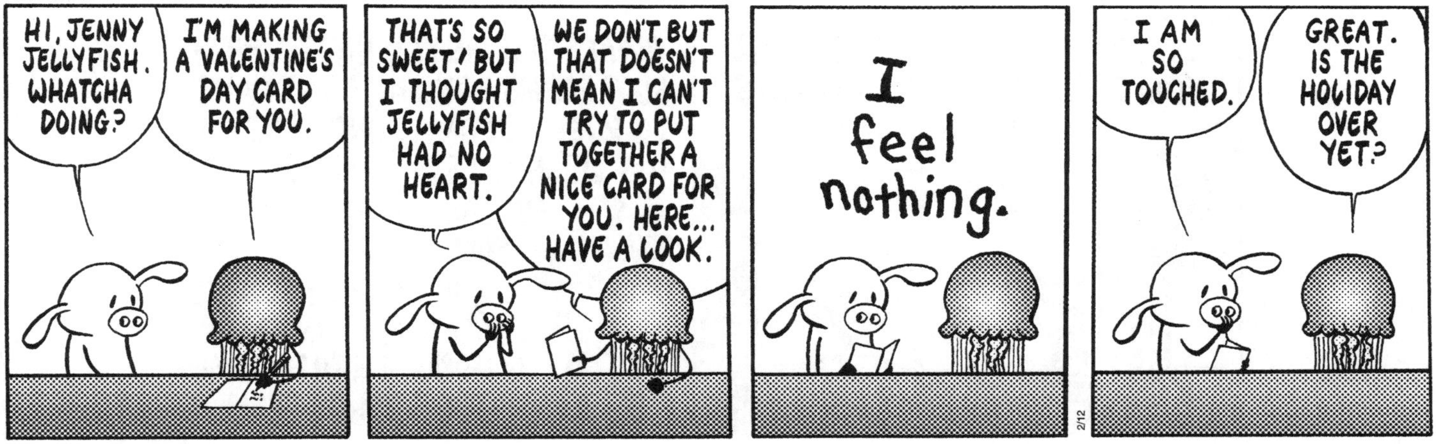
HI, JENNY JELLYFISH. WHATCHA DOING?
I'M MAKING A VALENTINE'S DAY CARD FOR YOU.
THAT'S SO SWEET! BUT I THOUGHT JELLYFISH HAD NO HEART.
WE DON'T, BUT THAT DOESN'T MEAN I CAN'T TRY TO PUT TOGETHER A NICE CARD FOR YOU. HERE... HAVE A LOOK.
I feel nothing.
2/12
I AM SO TOUCHED.
GREAT. IS THE HOLIDAY OVER YET?

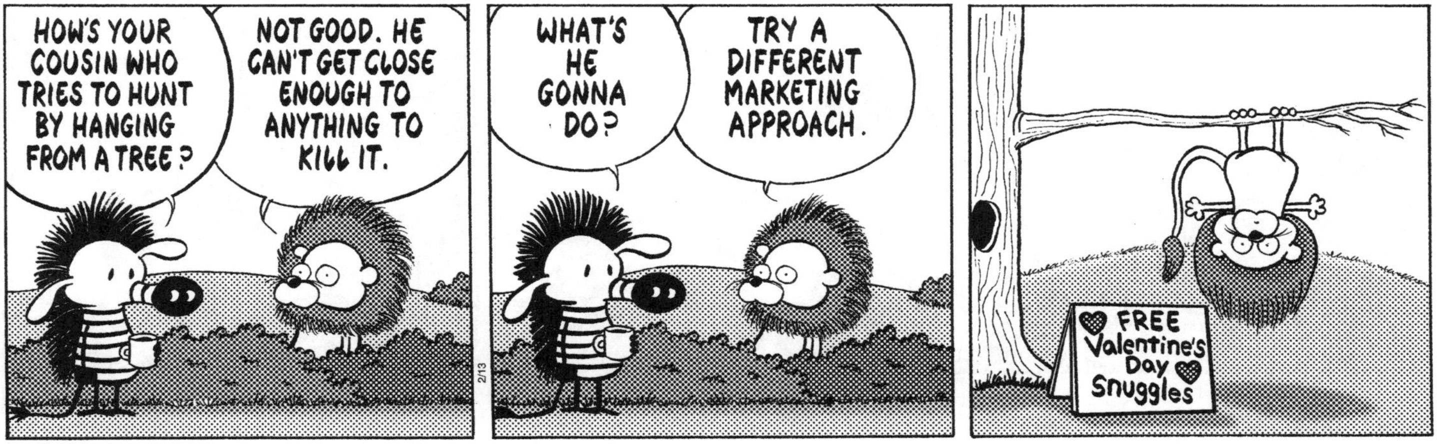
HOW'S YOUR COUSIN WHO TRIES TO HUNT BY HANGING FROM A TREE?
NOT GOOD. HE CAN'T GET CLOSE ENOUGH TO ANYTHING TO KILL IT.
2/13
WHAT'S HE GONNA DO?
TRY A DIFFERENT MARKETING APPROACH.
FREE Valentine's Day Snuggles

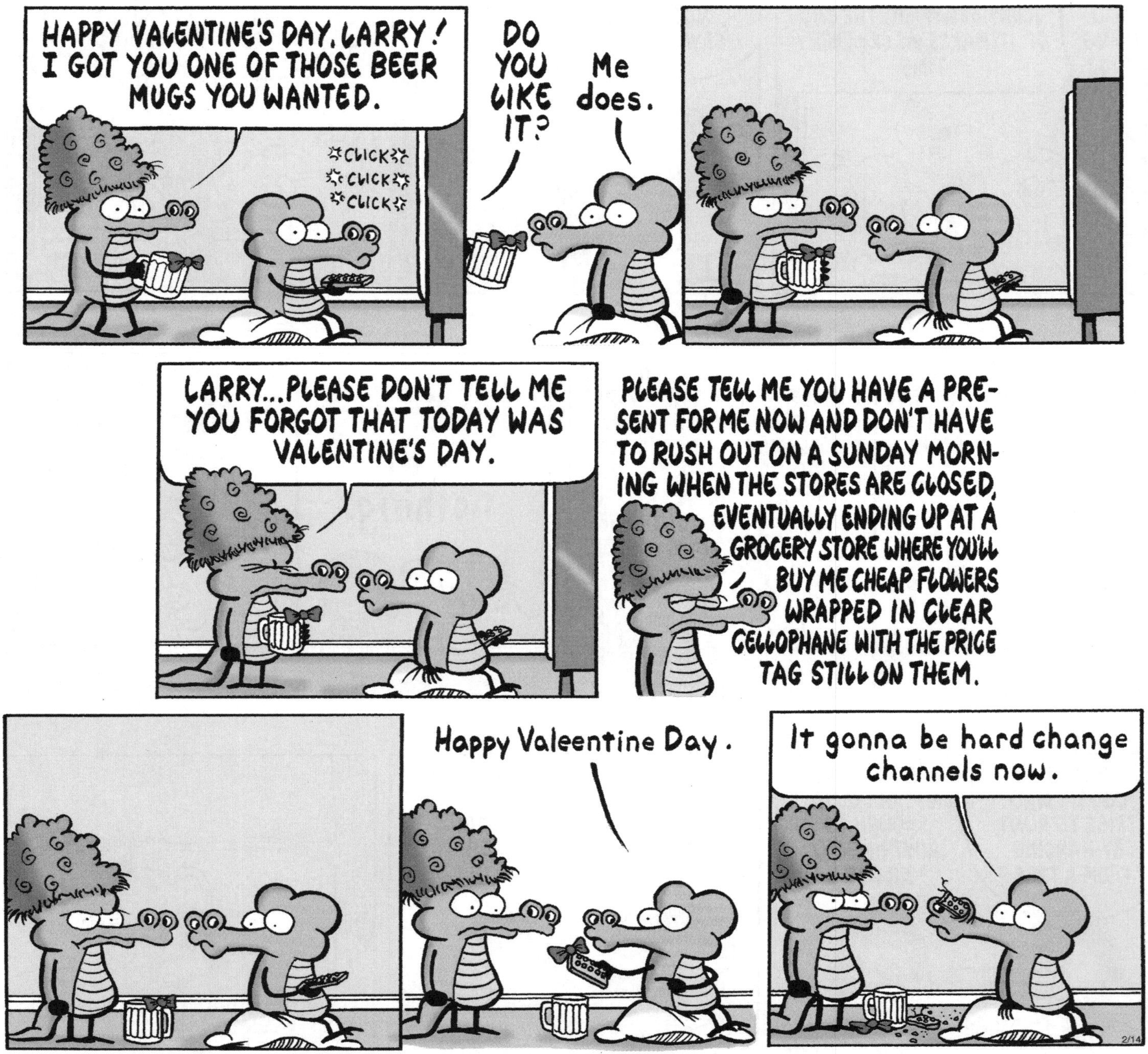
HAPPY VALENTINE'S DAY, LARRY! I GOT YOU ONE OF THOSE BEER MUGS YOU WANTED.
CLICK
CLICK
CLICK
DO YOU LIKE IT?
Me does.
LARRY...PLEASE DON'T TELL ME YOU FORGOT THAT TODAY WAS VALENTINE'S DAY.
PLEASE TELL ME YOU HAVE A PRESENT FOR ME NOW AND DON'T HAVE TO RUSH OUT ON A SUNDAY MORNING WHEN THE STORES ARE CLOSED, EVENTUALLY ENDING UP AT A GROCERY STORE WHERE YOU'LL BUY ME CHEAP FLOWERS WRAPPED IN CLEAR CELLOPHANE WITH THE PRICE TAG STILL ON THEM.
Happy Valeentine Day.
It gonna be hard change channels now.
2/14

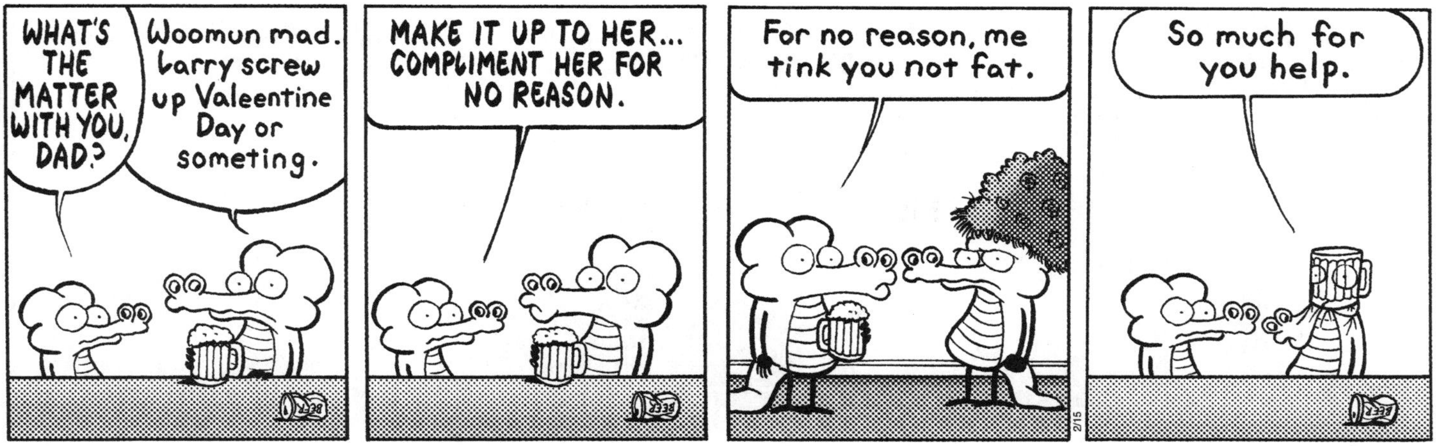
WHAT'S THE MATTER WITH YOU, DAD?
Woomun mad. Larry screw up Valeentine Day or someting.
MAKE IT UP TO HER... COMPLIMENT HER FOR NO REASON.
For no reason, me tink you not fat.
So much for you help.

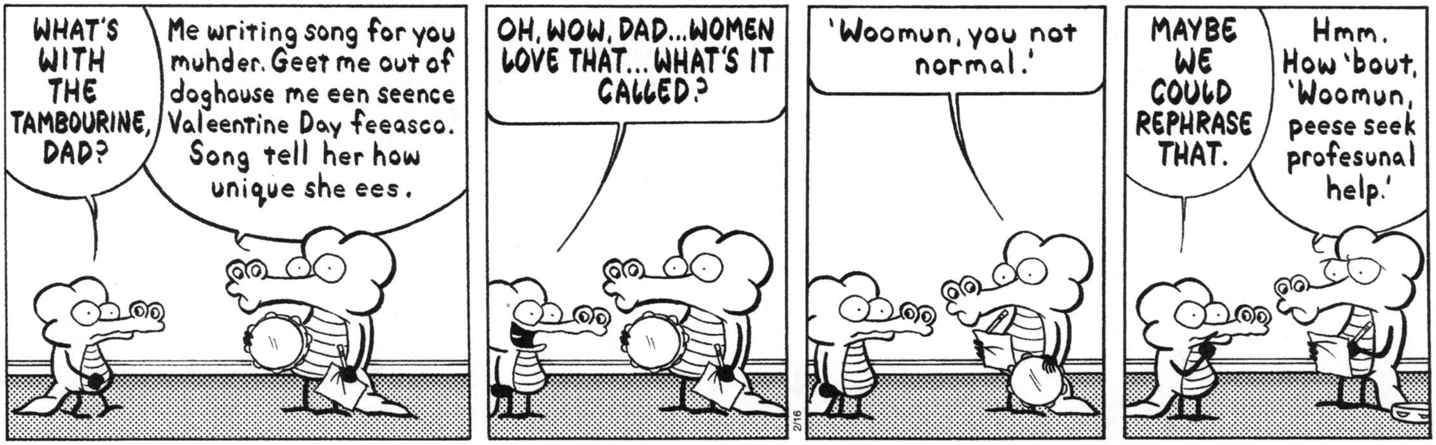
WHAT'S WITH THE TAMBOURINE, DAD?
Me writing song for you muhder. Geet me out of doghouse me een seence Valeentine Day feeasco. Song tell her how unique she ees.
OH, WOW, DAD... WOMEN LOVE THAT... WHAT'S IT CALLED?
'Woomun, you not normal.'
MAYBE WE COULD REPHRASE THAT.
Hmm. How 'bout, 'Woomun, peese seek profesunal help.'

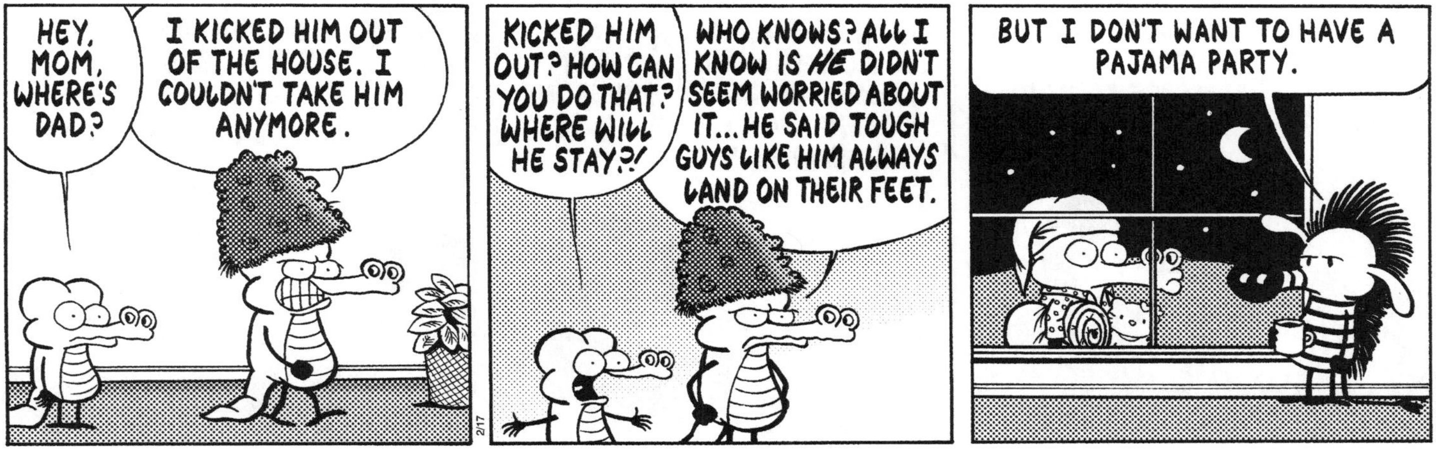
HEY, MOM, WHERE'S DAD?
I KICKED HIM OUT OF THE HOUSE. I COULDN'T TAKE HIM ANYMORE.
KICKED HIM OUT? HOW CAN YOU DO THAT? WHERE WILL HE STAY?!
WHO KNOWS? ALL I KNOW IS HE DIDN'T SEEM WORRIED ABOUT IT... HE SAID TOUGH GUYS LIKE HIM ALWAYS LAND ON THEIR FEET.
BUT I DON'T WANT TO HAVE A PAJAMA PARTY.

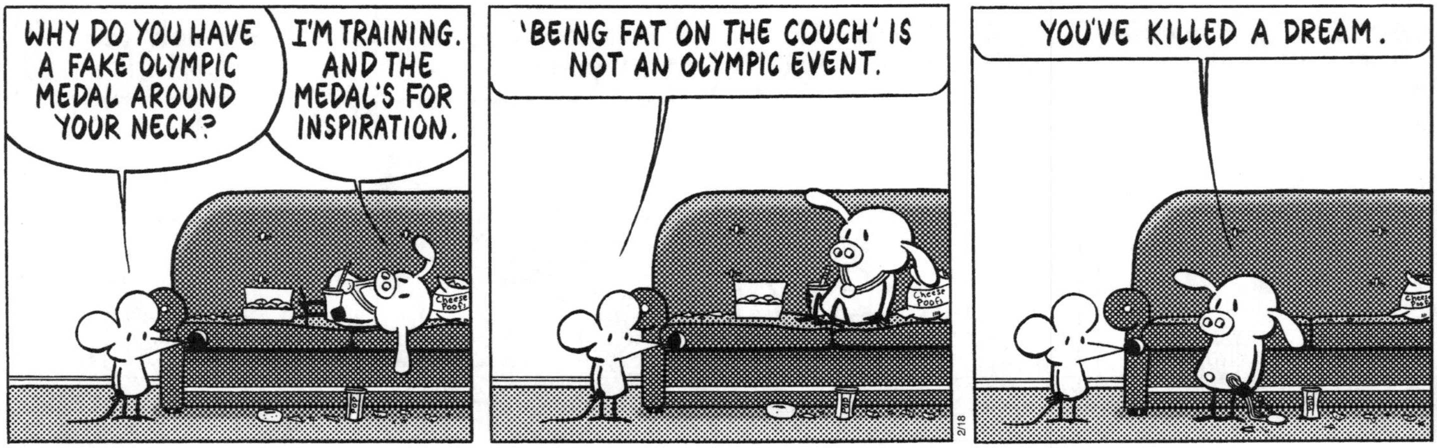
WHY DO YOU HAVE A FAKE OLYMPIC MEDAL AROUND YOUR NECK?
I'M TRAINING. AND THE MEDAL'S FOR INSPIRATION.
'BEING FAT ON THE COUCH' IS NOT AN OLYMPIC EVENT.
YOU'VE KILLED A DREAM.
Cheese Poofs
2/18

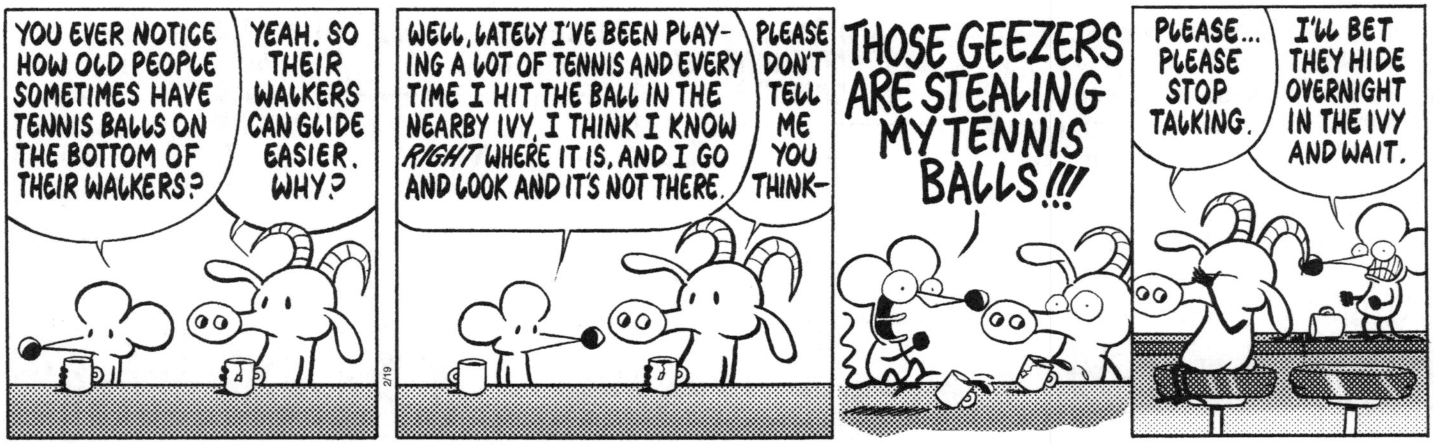
YOU EVER NOTICE HOW OLD PEOPLE SOMETIMES HAVE TENNIS BALLS ON THE BOTTOM OF THEIR WALKERS?
YEAH. SO THEIR WALKERS CAN GLIDE EASIER. WHY?
2/19
WELL, LATELY I'VE BEEN PLAYING A LOT OF TENNIS AND EVERY TIME I HIT THE BALL IN THE NEARBY IVY, I THINK I KNOW *RIGHT* WHERE IT IS, AND I GO AND LOOK AND IT'S NOT THERE.
PLEASE DON'T TELL ME YOU THINK-
THOSE GEEZERS ARE STEALING MY TENNIS BALLS!!!
PLEASE... PLEASE STOP TALKING.
I'LL BET THEY HIDE OVERNIGHT IN THE IVY AND WAIT.

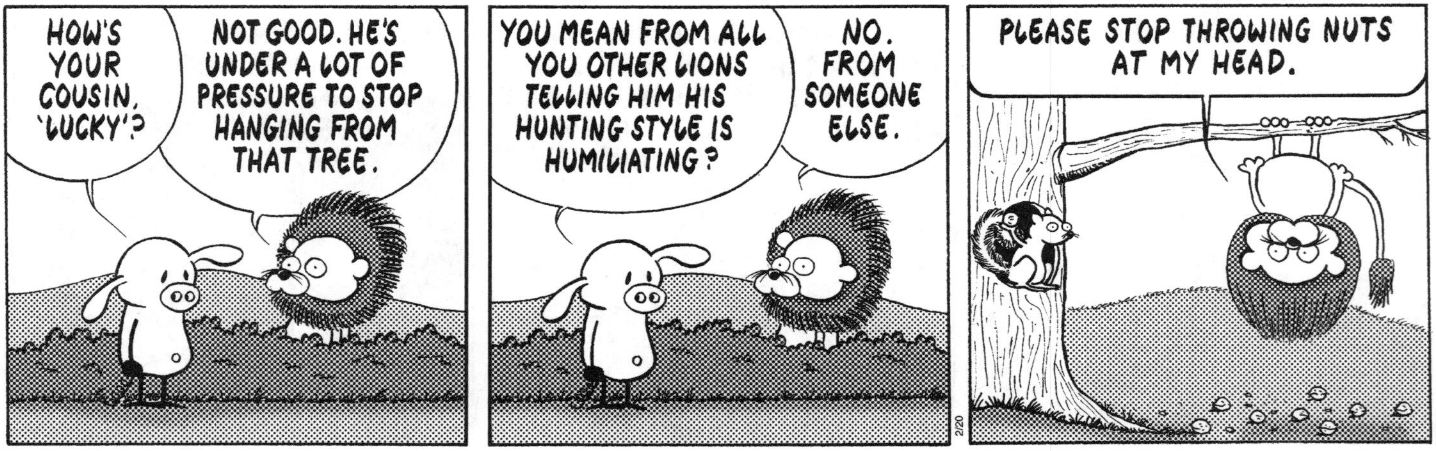
HOW'S YOUR COUSIN, 'LUCKY'?
NOT GOOD. HE'S UNDER A LOT OF PRESSURE TO STOP HANGING FROM THAT TREE.
YOU MEAN FROM ALL YOU OTHER LIONS TELLING HIM HIS HUNTING STYLE IS HUMILIATING?
NO. FROM SOMEONE ELSE.
2/20
PLEASE STOP THROWING NUTS AT MY HEAD.

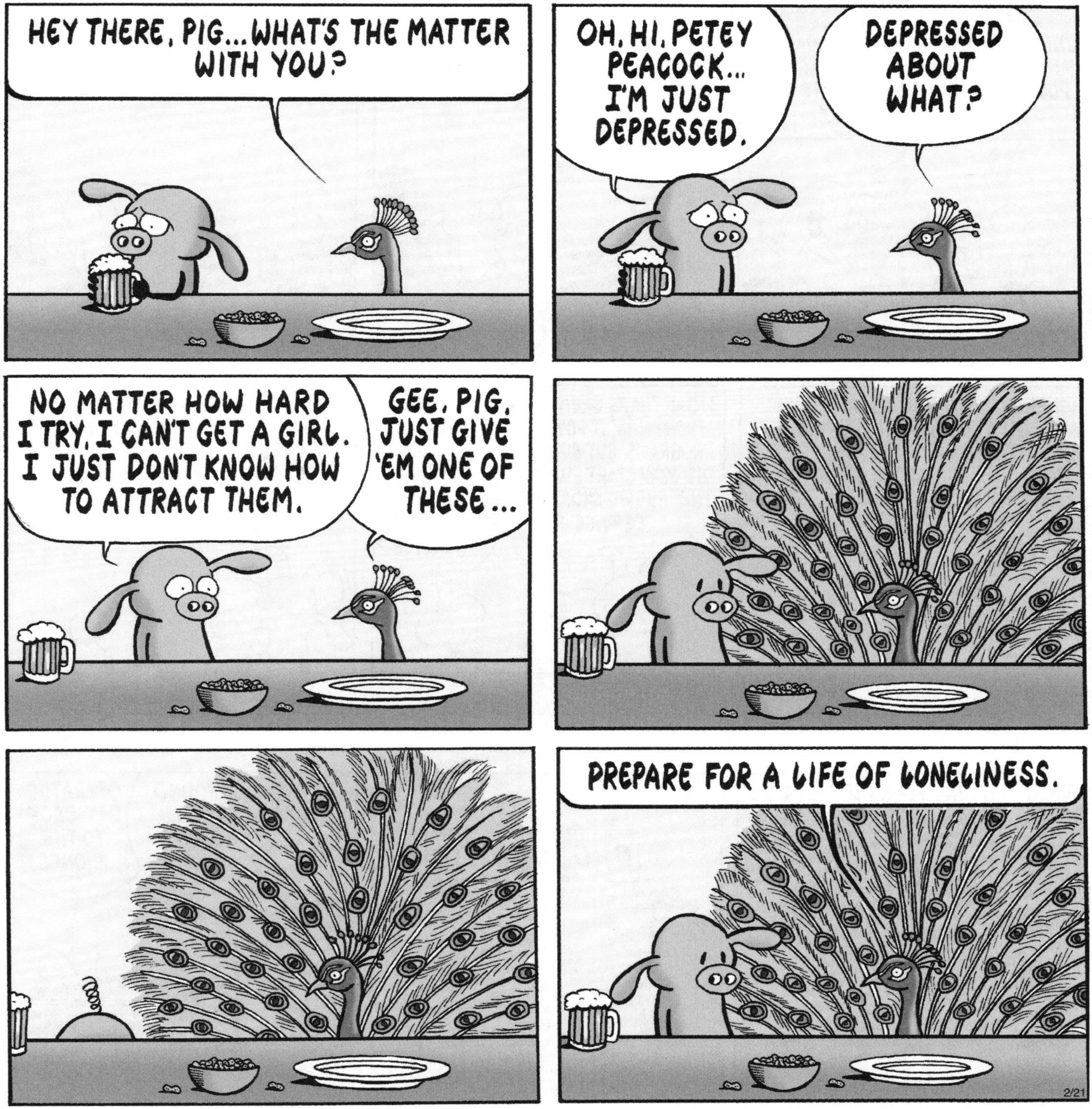
HEY THERE, PIG...WHAT'S THE MATTER WITH YOU?
OH, HI, PETEY PEACOCK... I'M JUST DEPRESSED.
DEPRESSED ABOUT WHAT?
NO MATTER HOW HARD I TRY, I CAN'T GET A GIRL. I JUST DON'T KNOW HOW TO ATTRACT THEM.
GEE, PIG, JUST GIVE 'EM ONE OF THESE...
PREPARE FOR A LIFE OF LONELINESS.
2/21

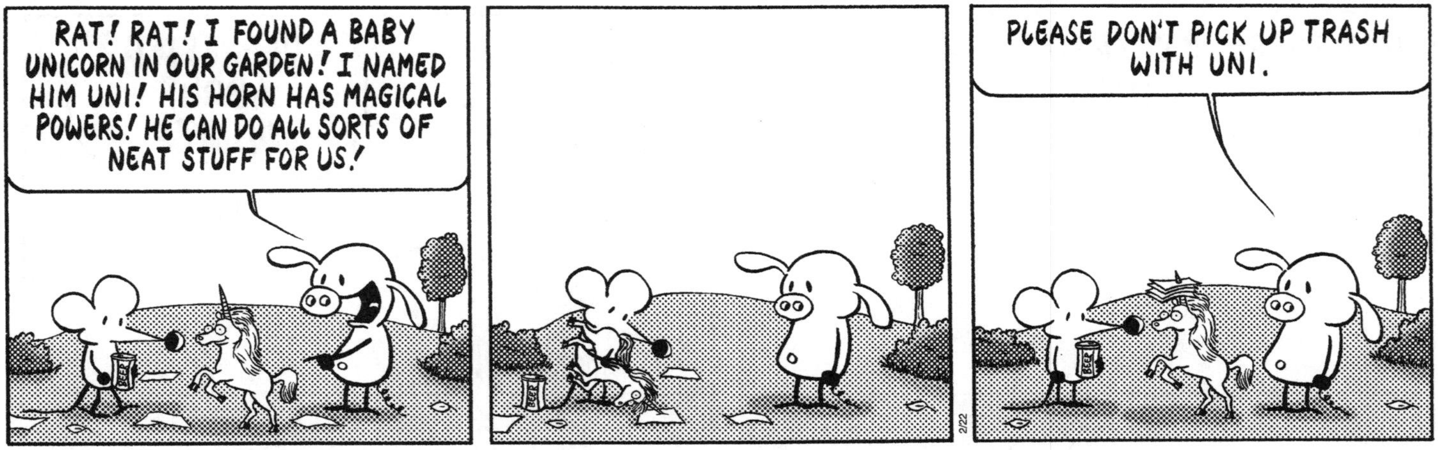
RAT! RAT! I FOUND A BABY UNICORN IN OUR GARDEN! I NAMED HIM UNI! HIS HORN HAS MAGICAL POWERS! HE CAN DO ALL SORTS OF NEAT STUFF FOR US!
BEER
BEER
PLEASE DON'T PICK UP TRASH WITH UNI.
BEER
2/22

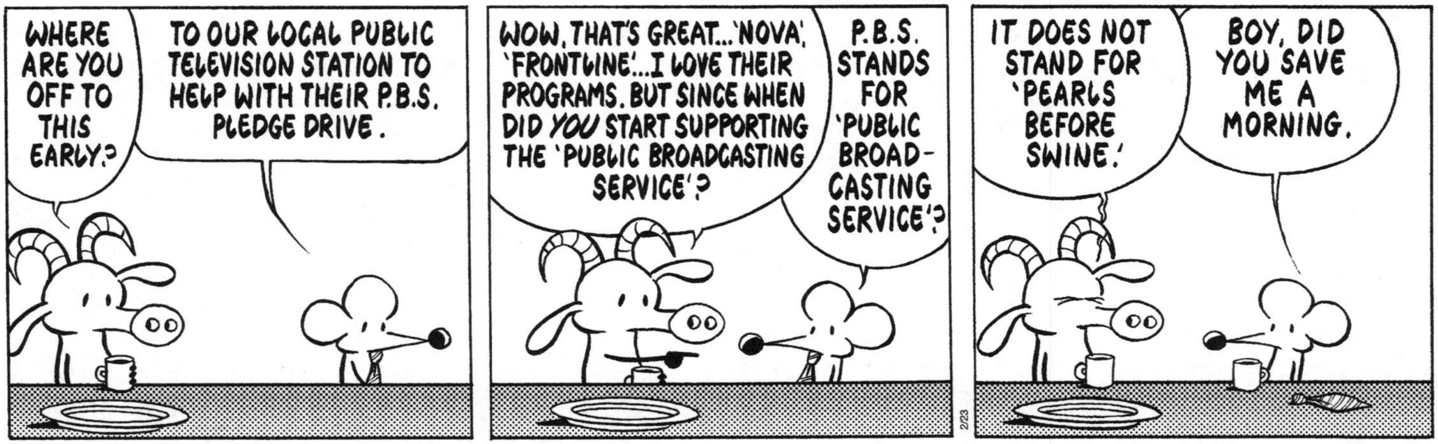
WHERE ARE YOU OFF TO THIS EARLY?
TO OUR LOCAL PUBLIC TELEVISION STATION TO HELP WITH THEIR P.B.S. PLEDGE DRIVE.
WOW, THAT'S GREAT...'NOVA', 'FRONTLINE'...I LOVE THEIR PROGRAMS. BUT SINCE WHEN DID *YOU* START SUPPORTING THE 'PUBLIC BROADCASTING SERVICE'?
P.B.S. STANDS FOR 'PUBLIC BROAD-CASTING SERVICE'?
IT DOES NOT STAND FOR 'PEARLS BEFORE SWINE.'
BOY, DID YOU SAVE ME A MORNING.
2/23

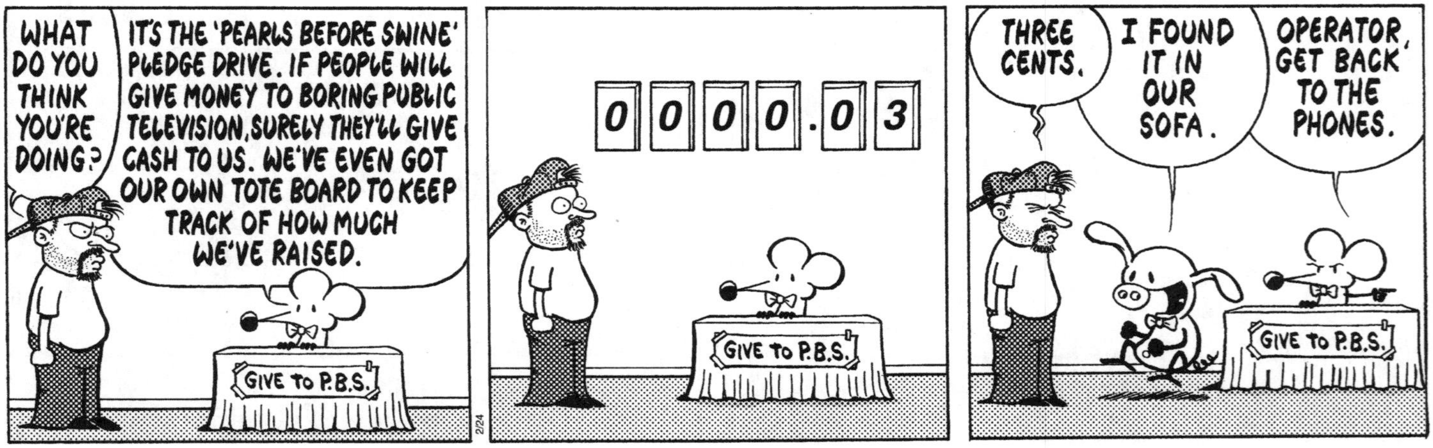
WHAT DO YOU THINK YOU'RE DOING?
IT'S THE 'PEARLS BEFORE SWINE' PLEDGE DRIVE. IF PEOPLE WILL GIVE MONEY TO BORING PUBLIC TELEVISION, SURELY THEY'LL GIVE CASH TO US. WE'VE EVEN GOT OUR OWN TOTE BOARD TO KEEP TRACK OF HOW MUCH WE'VE RAISED.
GIVE TO P.B.S.
2/24
0000.03
GIVE TO P.B.S.
THREE CENTS.
I FOUND IT IN OUR SOFA.
OPERATOR, GET BACK TO THE PHONES.
GIVE TO P.B.S.

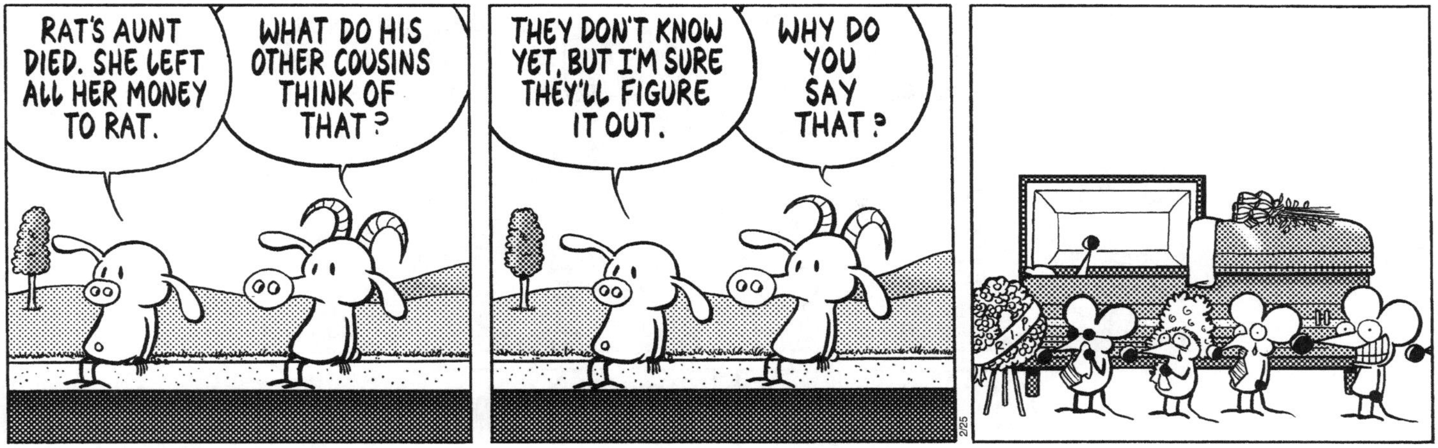
RAT'S AUNT DIED. SHE LEFT ALL HER MONEY TO RAT.
WHAT DO HIS OTHER COUSINS THINK OF THAT?
THEY DON'T KNOW YET, BUT I'M SURE THEY'LL FIGURE IT OUT.
WHY DO YOU SAY THAT?
2/25

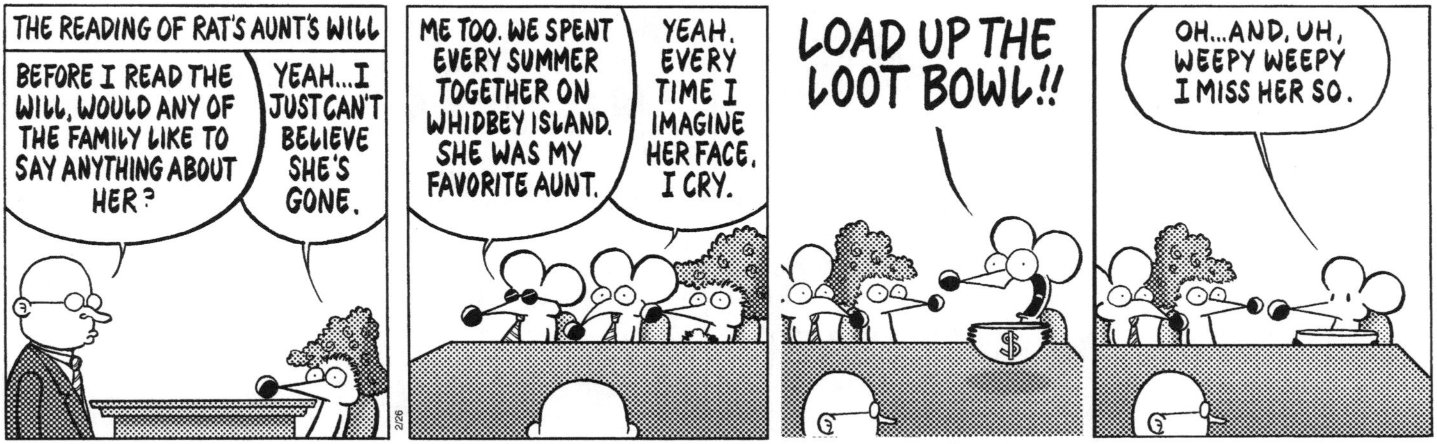
THE READING OF RAT'S AUNT'S WILL
BEFORE I READ THE WILL, WOULD ANY OF THE FAMILY LIKE TO SAY ANYTHING ABOUT HER?
YEAH...I JUST CAN'T BELIEVE SHE'S GONE.
2/26
ME TOO. WE SPENT EVERY SUMMER TOGETHER ON WHIDBEY ISLAND. SHE WAS MY FAVORITE AUNT.
YEAH. EVERY TIME I IMAGINE HER FACE, I CRY.
LOAD UP THE LOOT BOWL!!
$
OH...AND, UH, WEEPY WEEPY I MISS HER SO.

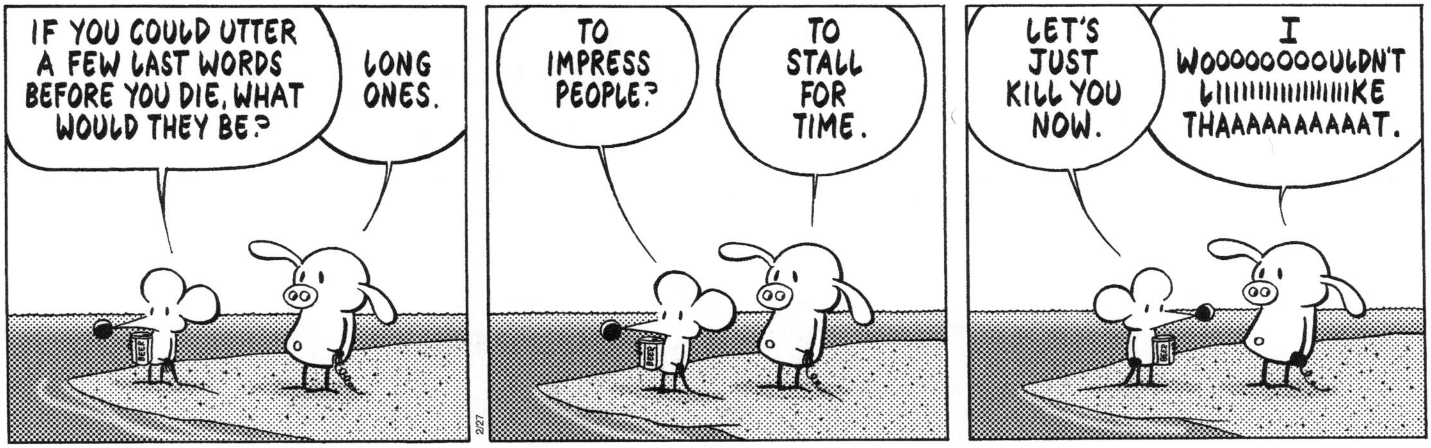
IF YOU COULD UTTER A FEW LAST WORDS BEFORE YOU DIE, WHAT WOULD THEY BE?
LONG ONES.
2/27
TO IMPRESS PEOPLE?
TO STALL FOR TIME.
LET'S JUST KILL YOU NOW.
I WOOOOOOOOULDN'T LIIIIIIIIIIIIIIKE THAAAAAAAAAAT.

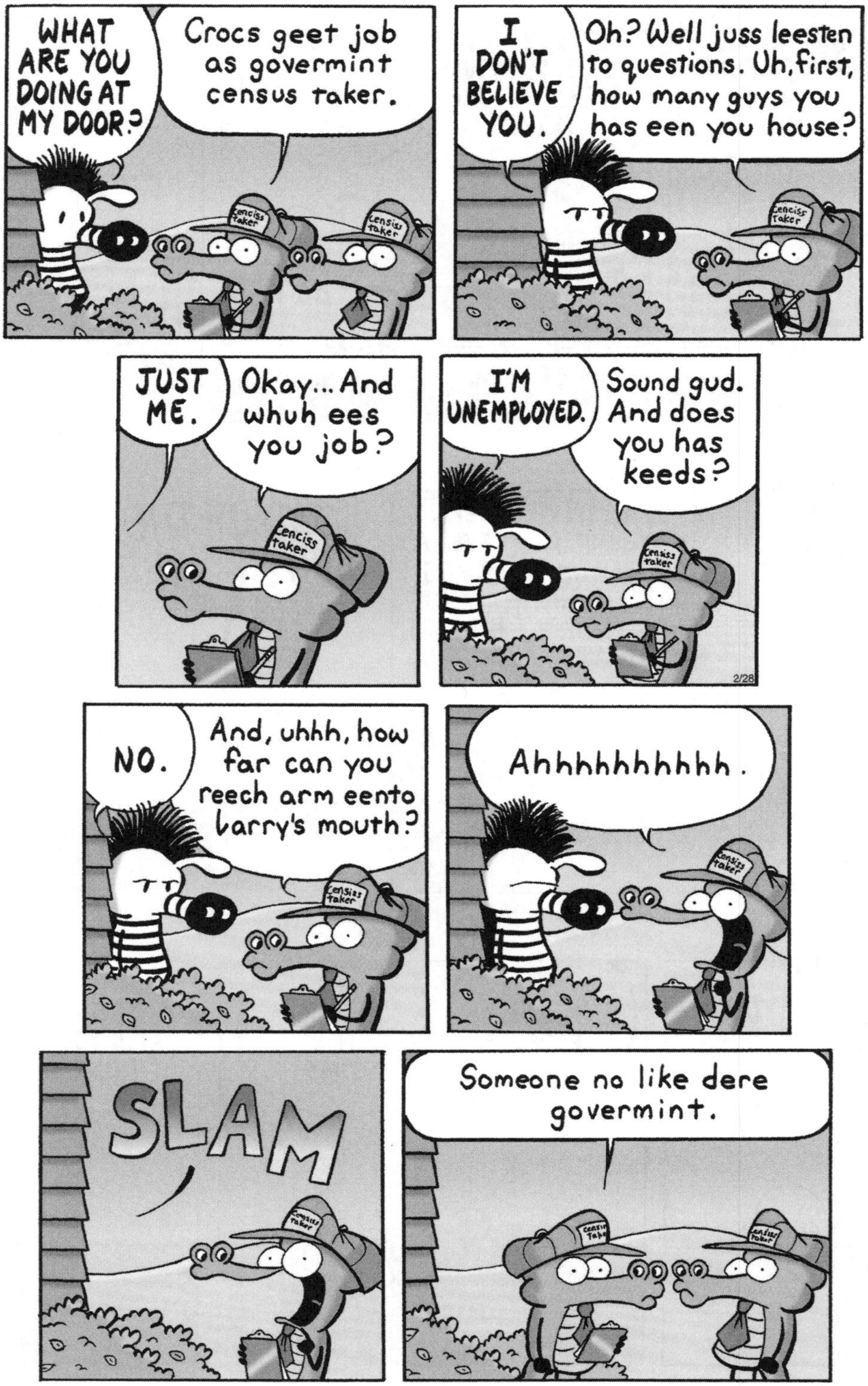
WHAT ARE YOU DOING AT MY DOOR?
Crocs geet job as govermint census taker.
Cenciss taker
Censiss taker
I DON'T BELIEVE YOU.
Oh? Well juss leesten to questions. Uh, first, how many guys you has een you house?
JUST ME.
Okay... And whuh ees you job?
I'M UNEMPLOYED.
Sound gud. And does you has keeds?
2/28
NO.
And, uhhh, how far can you reech arm eento larry's mouth?
Ahhhhhhhhhh.
SLAM
Someone no like dere govermint.

Panel 1:
HEY, PIG, WHERE WERE YOU?

INTERVIEWING FOR THE 'FRIENDLY GREETER' JOB AT WALMOTOPIA. YOU KNOW, THE GUY WHO SMILES AND SAYS HI TO PEOPLE WHEN THEY WALK IN THE STORE?

Panel 2:
OH, PIG, YOU'D BE PERFECT! WHO IN THE WORLD COULD CLAIM TO BE BETTER SUITED FOR THAT THAN YOU?

Panel 3:
I ADORE HUMANITY.

WALM

Panel 4:
DID GOAT TELL YOU I INTERVIEWED FOR THE 'FRIENDLY GREETER' JOB AT WALMOTOPIA?

THAT'S GREAT. YOU THINK YOU'LL GET IT?

Panel 5:
I DUNNO. THEY ASKED WHAT MY BIGGEST REGRET WAS IN TERMS OF HOW I RELATE TO PEOPLE AND I TOLD THEM THAT SOMETIMES OTHER PEOPLE MAKE ME MAD.

Panel 6:
WHAT'S WRONG WITH THAT? IT'S HONEST. WHAT DO YOU THINK OTHER CANDIDATES SAID THEY REGRETTED?

Panel 7:
THAT MY SHORT ARMS DO NOT ALLOW ME TO HOLD ALL HUMANITY IN ONE BIG EMBRACE.

Panel 8:
HELLO?

PIG, IT'S ME, RAT. LISTEN, I JUST WANT TO SAY I'LL BE HOME LATE. I GOT THE 'FRIENDLY GREETER' JOB AT WALMOTOPIA.

Panel 9:
YOU? WHY'D YOU GET THE JOB?

BECAUSE I'M GOOD WITH PEOPLE. AND I KNOW HOW TO TREAT THEM. AND HOW TO WELCOME THEM.

Panel 10:
PARDON ME, BUT I'M LOOKING FOR—

YO. BIG BONES. CAN YOU SEE I'M ON THE PHONE?

Panel 11:
MAYBE I SHOULD LET YOU GO BACK TO YOUR FRIENDLY GREETER JOB.

HANG ON, PIG...I'M SHOVING A FAT GUY OUT THE DOOR.

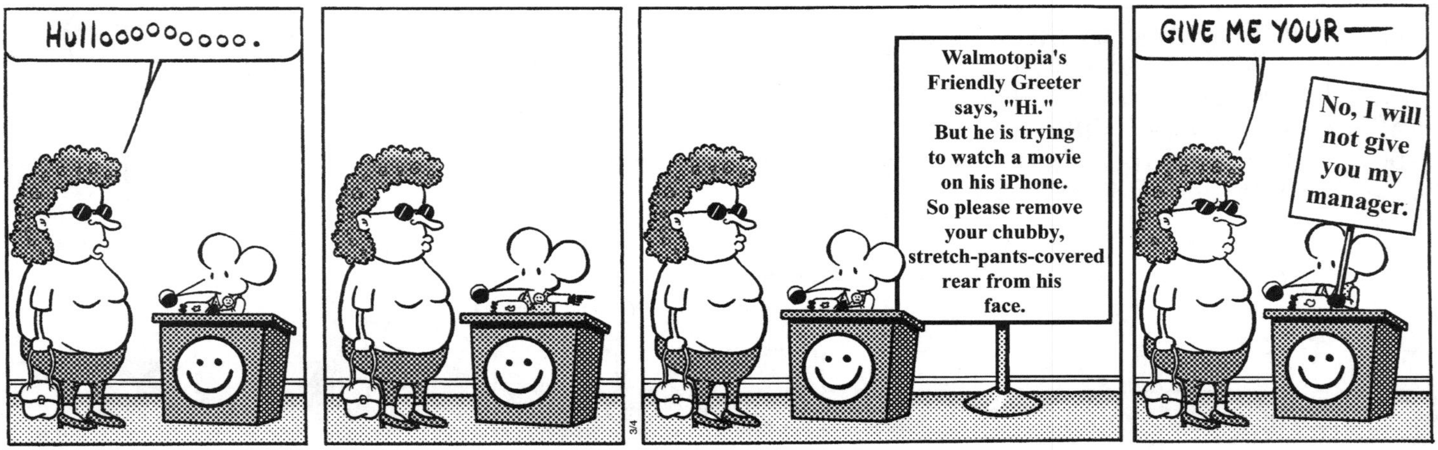
Hulloooooooooo.
Walmotopia's Friendly Greeter says, "Hi." But he is trying to watch a movie on his iPhone. So please remove your chubby, stretch-pants-covered rear from his face.
GIVE ME YOUR—
No, I will not give you my manager.

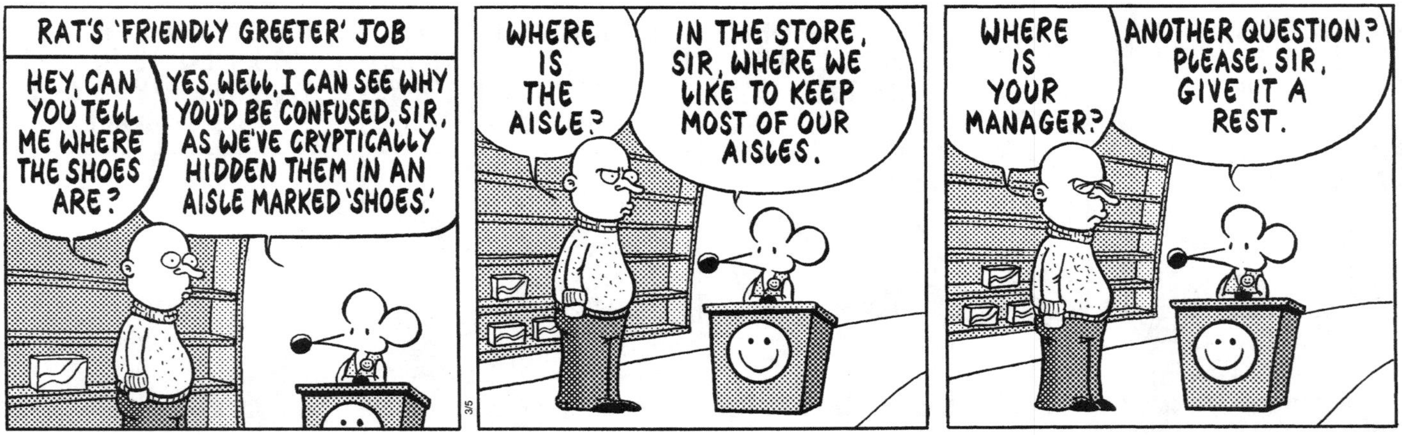
RAT'S 'FRIENDLY GREETER' JOB
HEY, CAN YOU TELL ME WHERE THE SHOES ARE?
YES, WELL, I CAN SEE WHY YOU'D BE CONFUSED, SIR, AS WE'VE CRYPTICALLY HIDDEN THEM IN AN AISLE MARKED 'SHOES.'
WHERE IS THE AISLE?
IN THE STORE, SIR, WHERE WE LIKE TO KEEP MOST OF OUR AISLES.
WHERE IS YOUR MANAGER?
ANOTHER QUESTION? PLEASE, SIR, GIVE IT A REST.

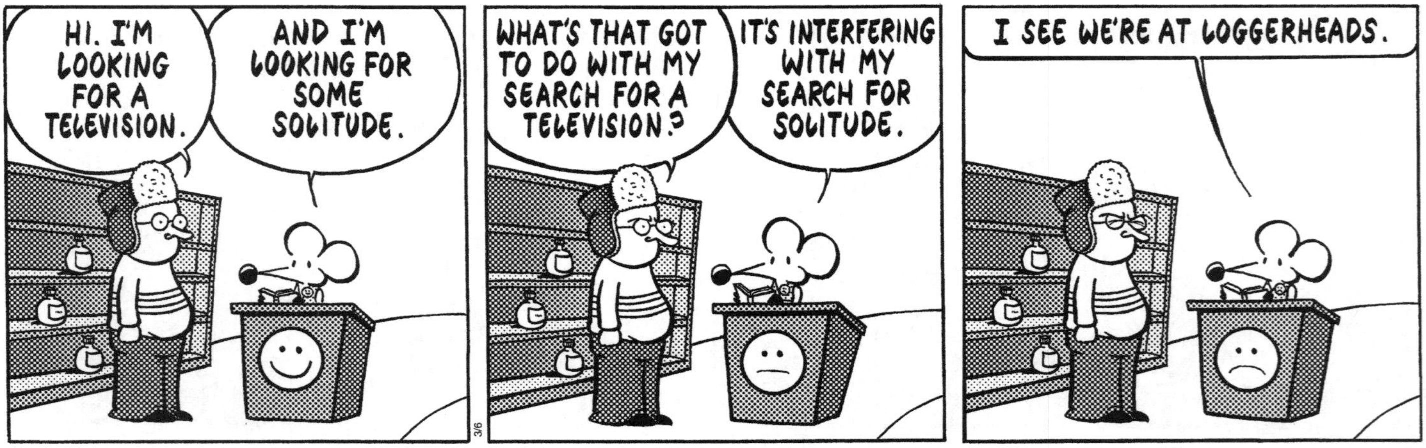
HI. I'M LOOKING FOR A TELEVISION.
AND I'M LOOKING FOR SOME SOLITUDE.
WHAT'S THAT GOT TO DO WITH MY SEARCH FOR A TELEVISION?
IT'S INTERFERING WITH MY SEARCH FOR SOLITUDE.
I SEE WE'RE AT LOGGERHEADS.

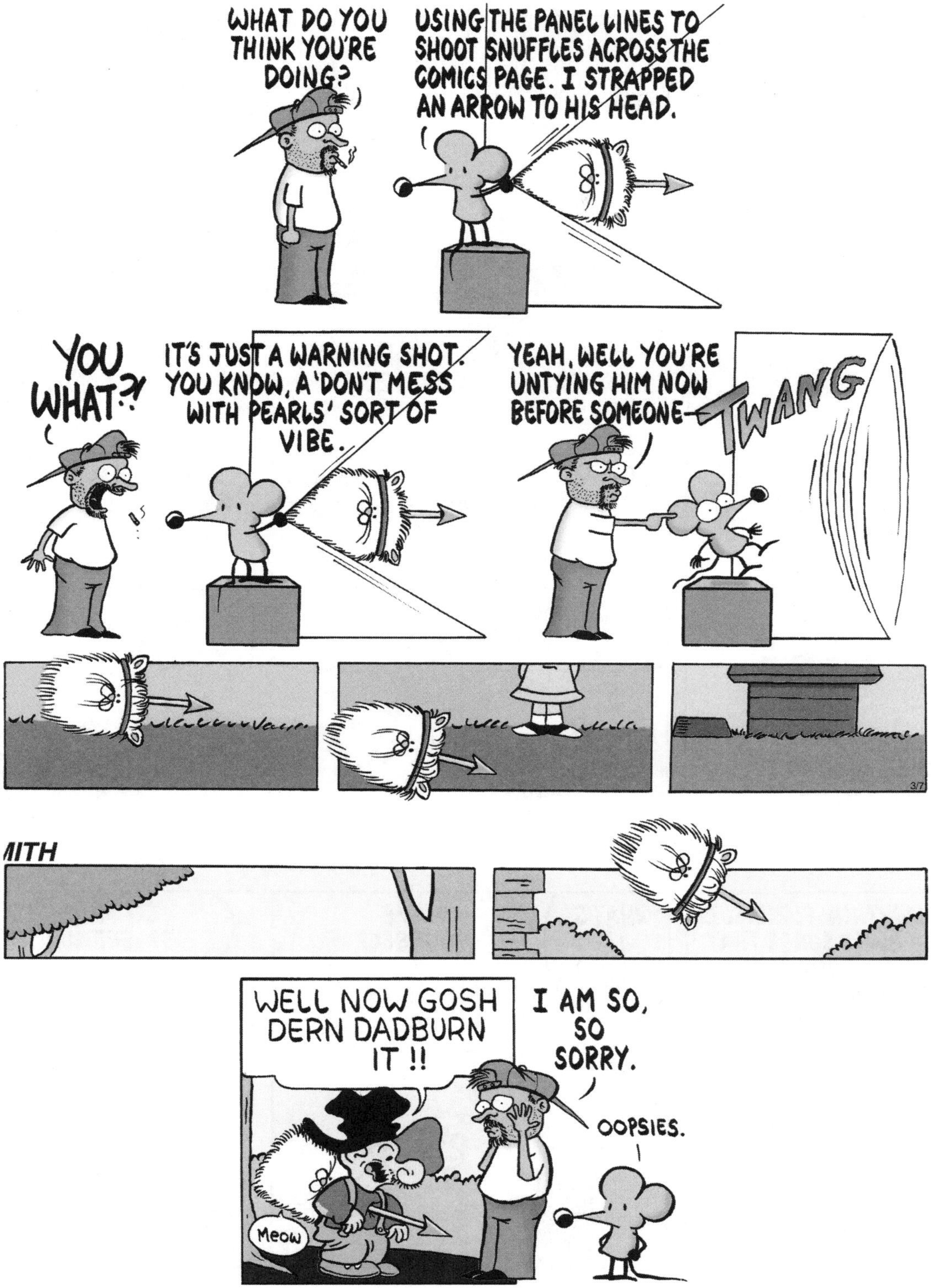
WHAT DO YOU THINK YOU'RE DOING?
USING THE PANEL LINES TO SHOOT SNUFFLES ACROSS THE COMICS PAGE. I STRAPPED AN ARROW TO HIS HEAD.
YOU WHAT?!
IT'S JUST A WARNING SHOT. YOU KNOW, A 'DON'T MESS WITH PEARLS' SORT OF VIBE.
YEAH, WELL YOU'RE UNTYING HIM NOW BEFORE SOMEONE—
TWANG
3/7
WELL NOW GOSH DERN DADBURN IT !!
Meow
I AM SO, SO SORRY.
OOPSIES.

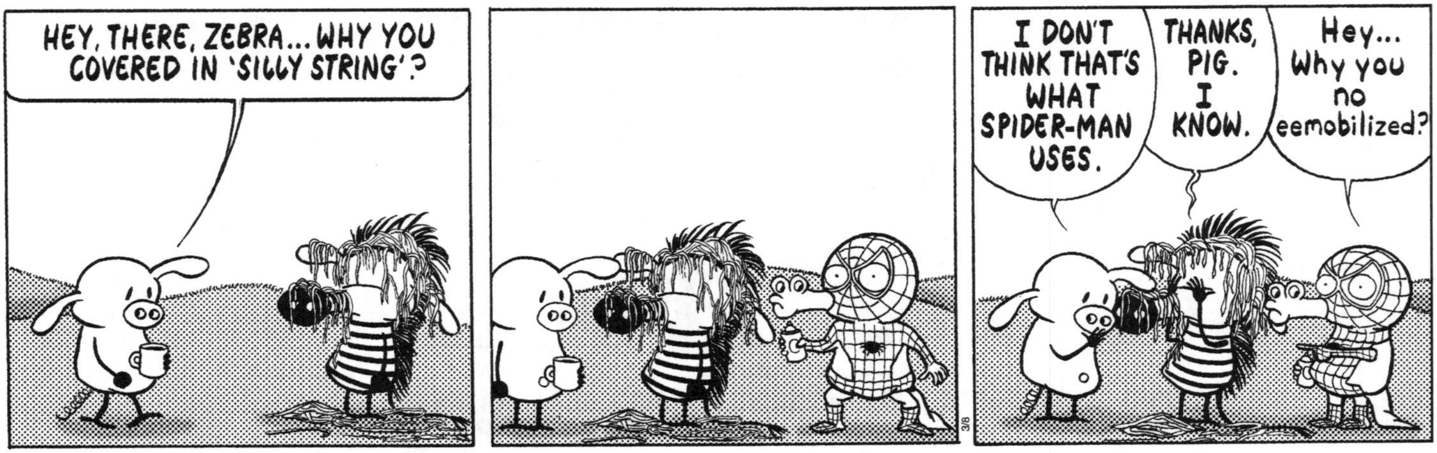
HEY, THERE, ZEBRA... WHY YOU COVERED IN 'SILLY STRING'?
I DON'T THINK THAT'S WHAT SPIDER-MAN USES.
THANKS, PIG. I KNOW.
Hey... Why you no eemobilized?
3/8

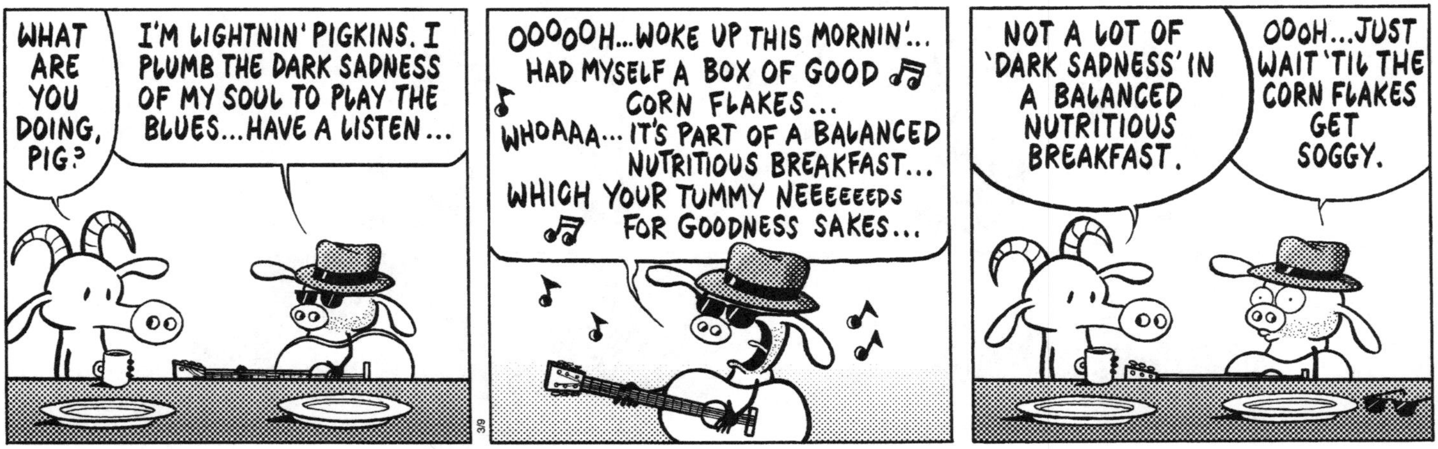
WHAT ARE YOU DOING, PIG?
I'M LIGHTNIN' PIGKINS. I PLUMB THE DARK SADNESS OF MY SOUL TO PLAY THE BLUES...HAVE A LISTEN...
3/9
OOOOOH...WOKE UP THIS MORNIN'... HAD MYSELF A BOX OF GOOD CORN FLAKES... WHOAAA... IT'S PART OF A BALANCED NUTRITIOUS BREAKFAST... WHICH YOUR TUMMY NEEEEEEDS FOR GOODNESS SAKES...
NOT A LOT OF 'DARK SADNESS' IN A BALANCED NUTRITIOUS BREAKFAST.
OOOH...JUST WAIT 'TIL THE CORN FLAKES GET SOGGY.

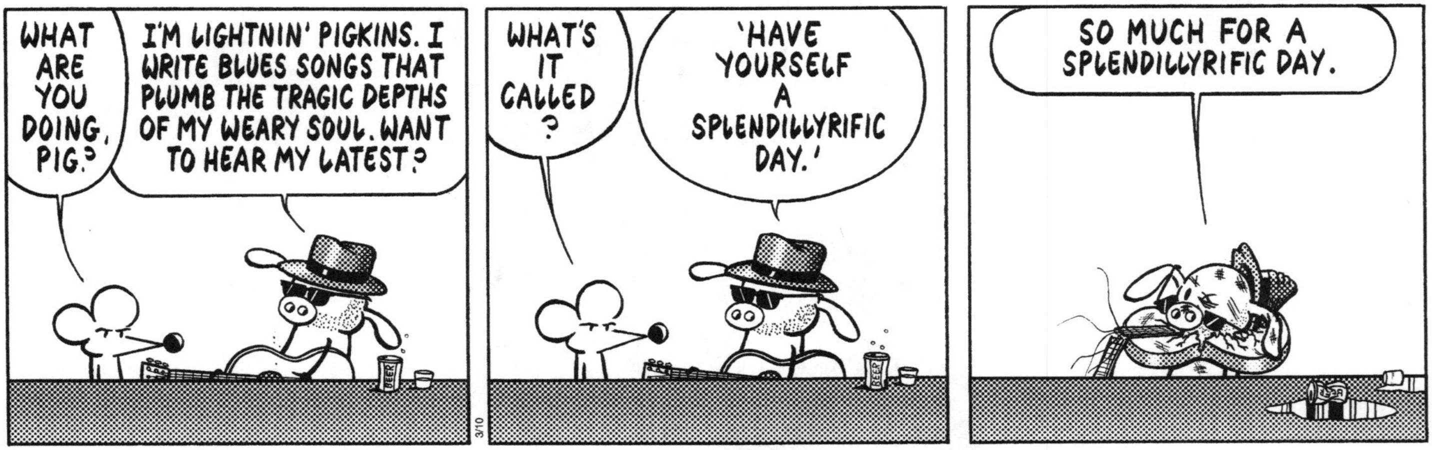
WHAT ARE YOU DOING, PIG?
I'M LIGHTNIN' PIGKINS. I WRITE BLUES SONGS THAT PLUMB THE TRAGIC DEPTHS OF MY WEARY SOUL. WANT TO HEAR MY LATEST?
3/10
WHAT'S IT CALLED?
'HAVE YOURSELF A SPLENDILLYRIFIC DAY.'
SO MUCH FOR A SPLENDILLYRIFIC DAY.

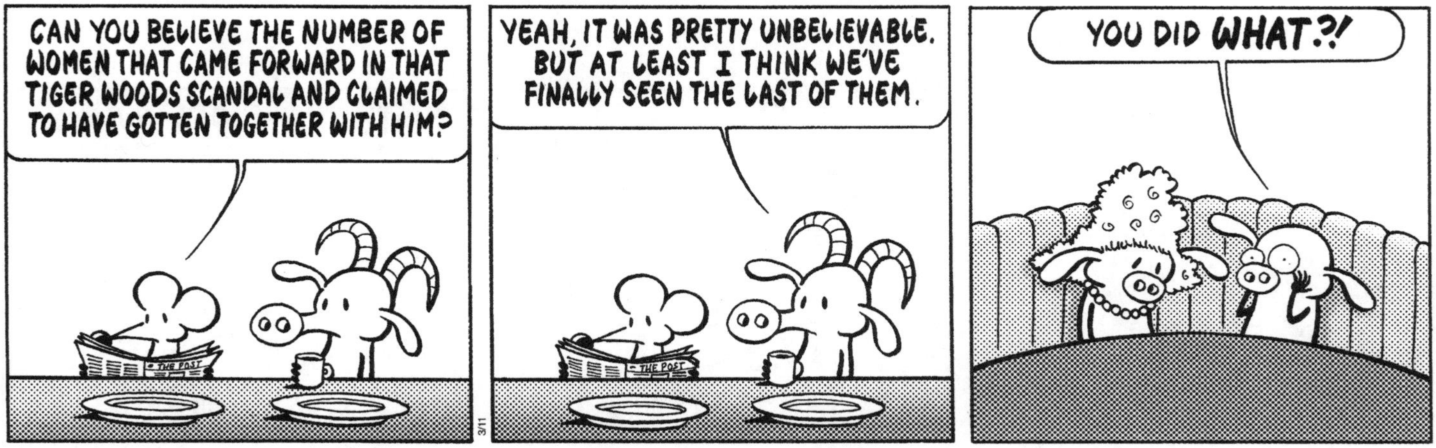
CAN YOU BELIEVE THE NUMBER OF WOMEN THAT CAME FORWARD IN THAT TIGER WOODS SCANDAL AND CLAIMED TO HAVE GOTTEN TOGETHER WITH HIM?
THE POST
YEAH, IT WAS PRETTY UNBELIEVABLE. BUT AT LEAST I THINK WE'VE FINALLY SEEN THE LAST OF THEM.
THE POST
YOU DID WHAT?!
3/11

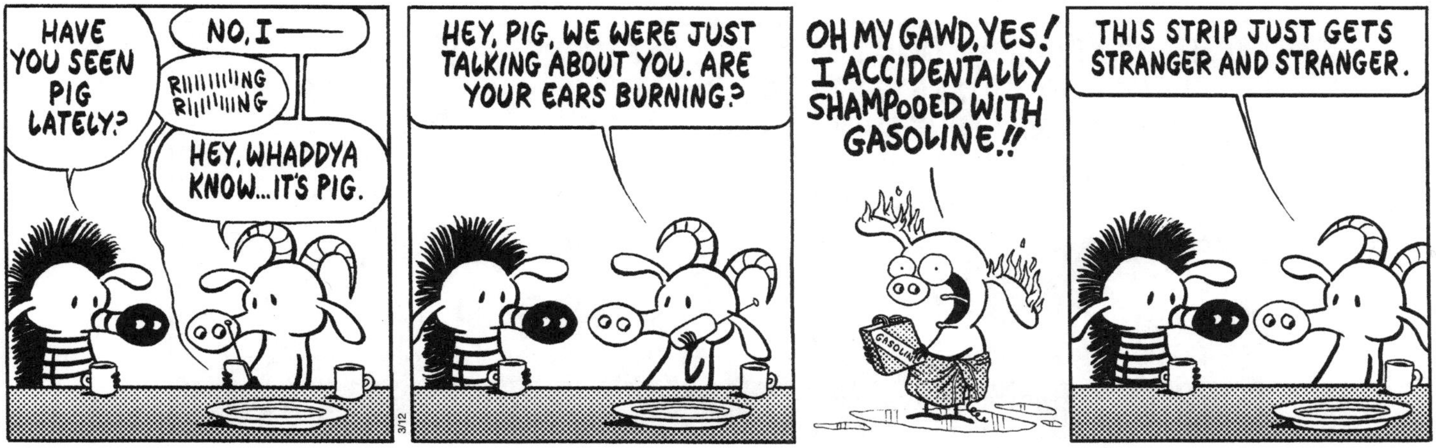
HAVE YOU SEEN PIG LATELY?
NO, I——
HEY, WHADDYA KNOW...IT'S PIG.
HEY, PIG, WE WERE JUST TALKING ABOUT YOU. ARE YOUR EARS BURNING?
OH MY GAWD, YES! I ACCIDENTALLY SHAMPOOED WITH GASOLINE!!
GASOLINE
THIS STRIP JUST GETS STRANGER AND STRANGER.
3/12

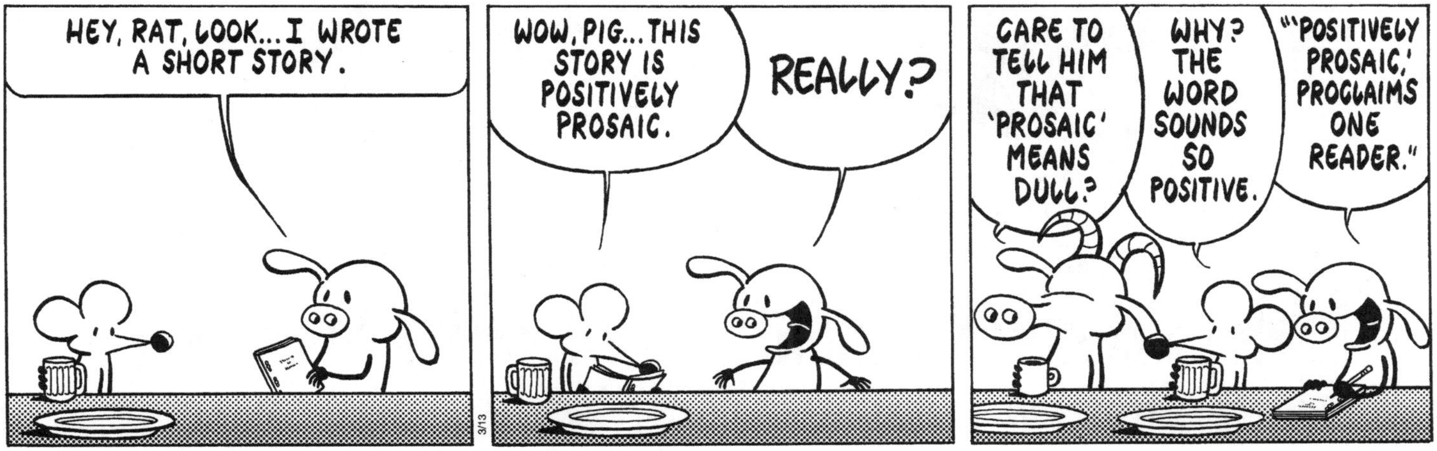
HEY, RAT, LOOK...I WROTE A SHORT STORY.
WOW, PIG...THIS STORY IS POSITIVELY PROSAIC.
REALLY?
CARE TO TELL HIM THAT 'PROSAIC' MEANS DULL?
WHY? THE WORD SOUNDS SO POSITIVE.
"'POSITIVELY PROSAIC,' PROCLAIMS ONE READER."
3/13

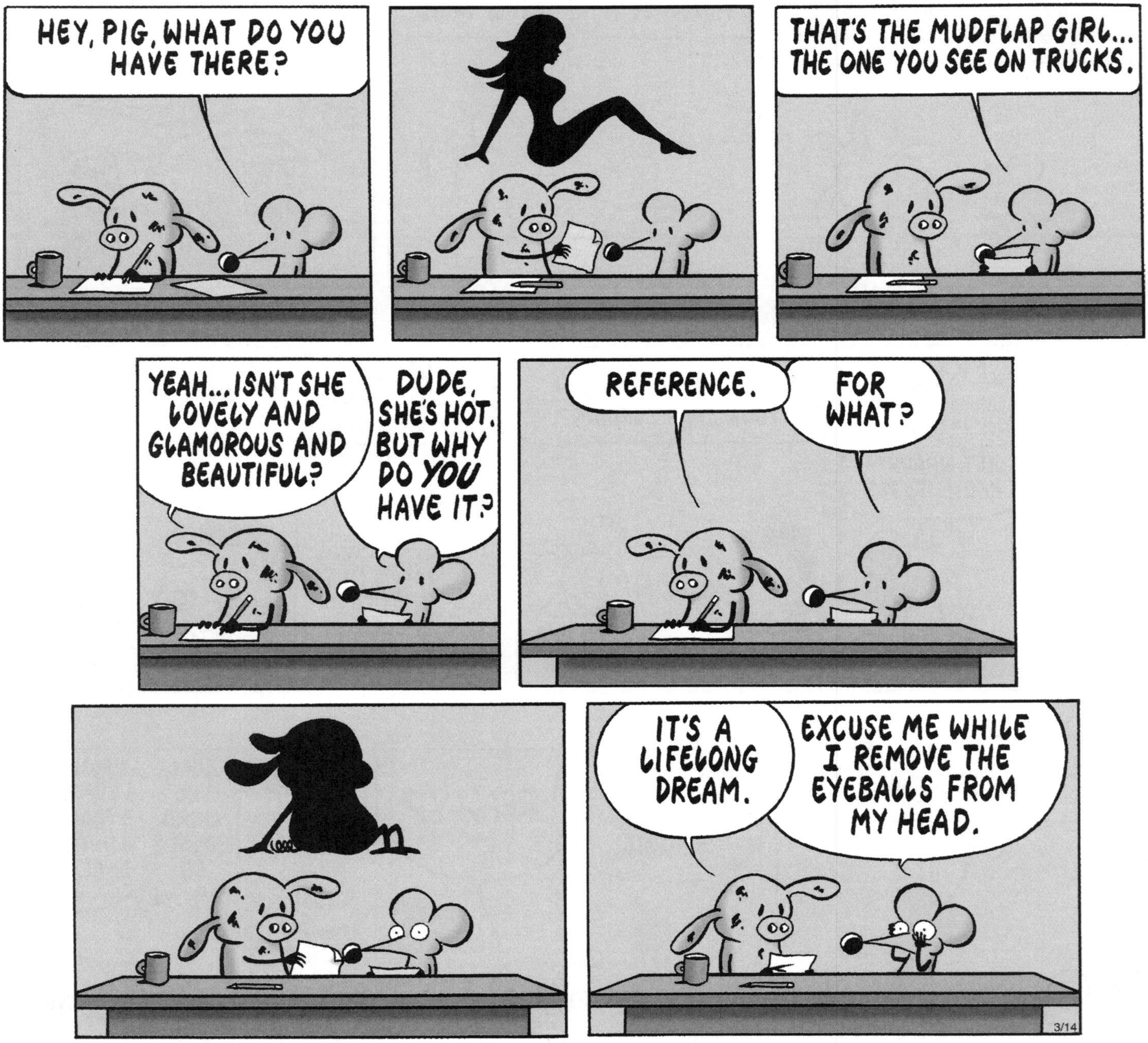
HEY, PIG, WHAT DO YOU HAVE THERE?
THAT'S THE MUDFLAP GIRL... THE ONE YOU SEE ON TRUCKS.
YEAH... ISN'T SHE LOVELY AND GLAMOROUS AND BEAUTIFUL?
DUDE, SHE'S HOT. BUT WHY DO *YOU* HAVE IT?
REFERENCE.
FOR WHAT?
IT'S A LIFELONG DREAM.
EXCUSE ME WHILE I REMOVE THE EYEBALLS FROM MY HEAD.
3/14

Strip 1:

 HEY, WHAT'S THAT THING IN THE CORNER OF THE PANEL?

IT'S OUR LOGO. SO PEOPLE KNOW WHAT COMIC STRIP THEY'RE READING. I GOT THE IDEA FROM CABLE T.V.

 BUT I HATE THOSE LITTLE THINGS. THEY ALWAYS CATCH MY EYE WHEN I'M TRYING TO WATCH A SHOW.

RELAX. IT WON'T HURT A THING.

 THUD

 PROVIDED WE ALL WEAR CUPS.

OHHHHHHHHHH MY OOMPA LOOMPAS.

Strip 2:

 WHAT DO YOU GOT THERE, RAT?

IT'S MY 'I'M HAVING AN OH-SO-HAPPY DAY' DIARY. I USE IT TO KEEP TRACK OF ALL THE DAYS IN MY LIFE THAT I WAS HAPPY.

 OH, YEAH? CAN I SEE IT?

SURE.

March 1, 2010	NOPE
March 2, 2010	NOPE
March 3, 2010	NOPE
March 4, 2010	NOPE
March 5, 2010	NOPE
March 6, 2010	NOPE
March 7, 2010	NOPE
March 8, 2010	NOPE
March 9, 2010	NOPE
March 10, 2010	NOPE

 I'M THINKING OF RE-NAMING IT.

Strip 3:

 HI, NEIGHBOR BOB. ARE YOU ENJOYING MY GARAGE SALE?

YEAH, PIG. BUT I HAVE TO SAY, I'M FEELING A LOT OF PRESSURE TO BUY.

 OH, GOSH, NEIGHBOR BOB, I'M NOT TRYING TO PRESSURE YOU.

IT'S NOT YOU, PIG. IT'S YOUR SALES STAFF.

 BUY SOMETHING.

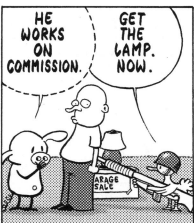 HE WORKS ON COMMISSION.

GET THE LAMP. NOW.

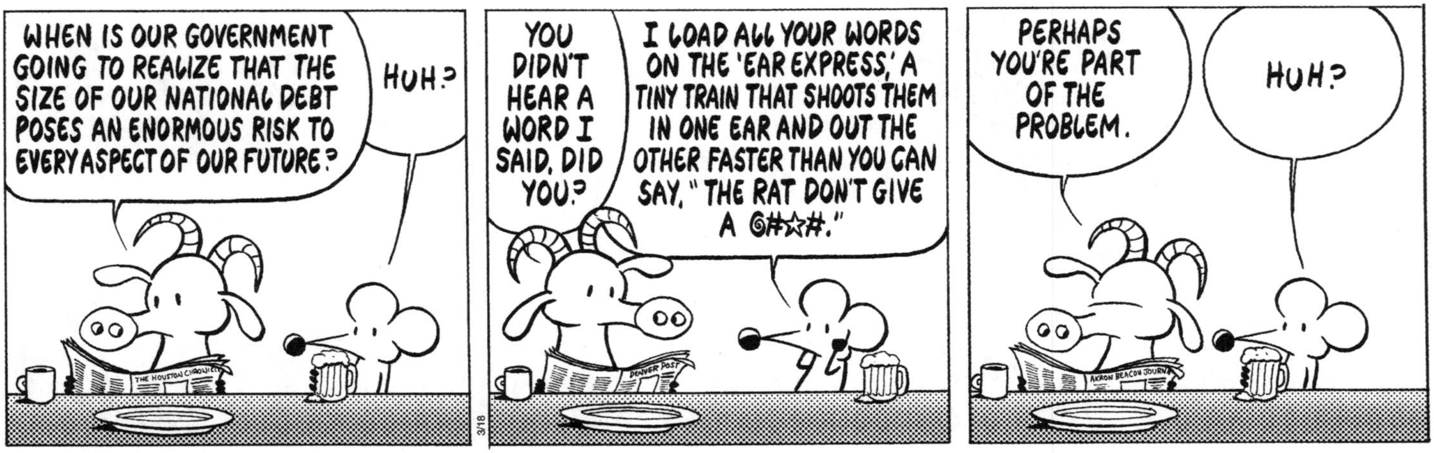
WHEN IS OUR GOVERNMENT GOING TO REALIZE THAT THE SIZE OF OUR NATIONAL DEBT POSES AN ENORMOUS RISK TO EVERY ASPECT OF OUR FUTURE?
HUH?
YOU DIDN'T HEAR A WORD I SAID, DID YOU?
I LOAD ALL YOUR WORDS ON THE 'EAR EXPRESS,' A TINY TRAIN THAT SHOOTS THEM IN ONE EAR AND OUT THE OTHER FASTER THAN YOU CAN SAY, "THE RAT DON'T GIVE A @#☆#."
PERHAPS YOU'RE PART OF THE PROBLEM.
HUH?
3/18

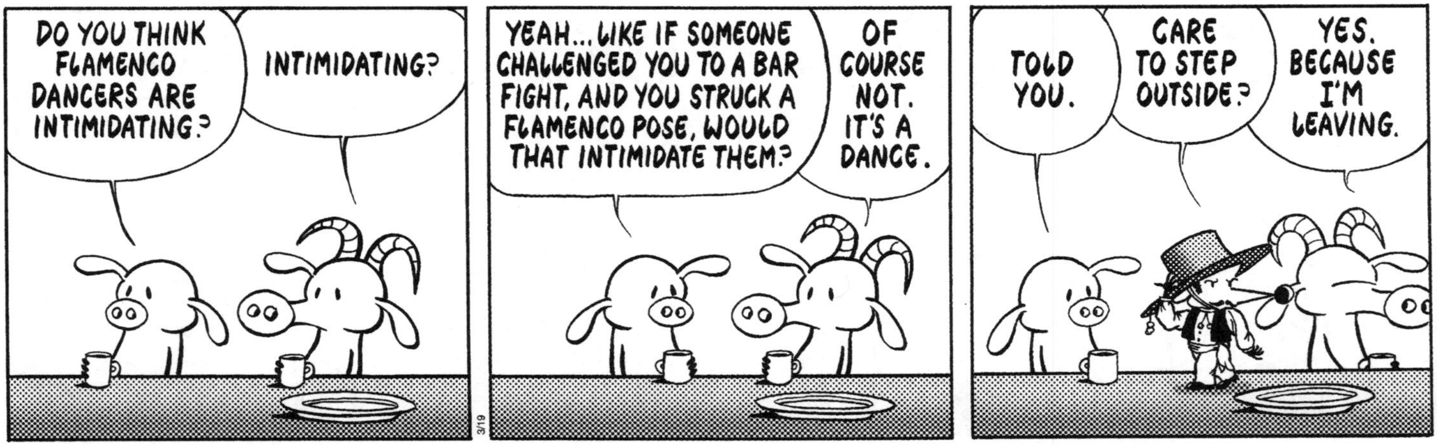
DO YOU THINK FLAMENCO DANCERS ARE INTIMIDATING?
INTIMIDATING?
YEAH... LIKE IF SOMEONE CHALLENGED YOU TO A BAR FIGHT, AND YOU STRUCK A FLAMENCO POSE, WOULD THAT INTIMIDATE THEM?
OF COURSE NOT. IT'S A DANCE.
TOLD YOU.
CARE TO STEP OUTSIDE?
YES. BECAUSE I'M LEAVING.
3/19

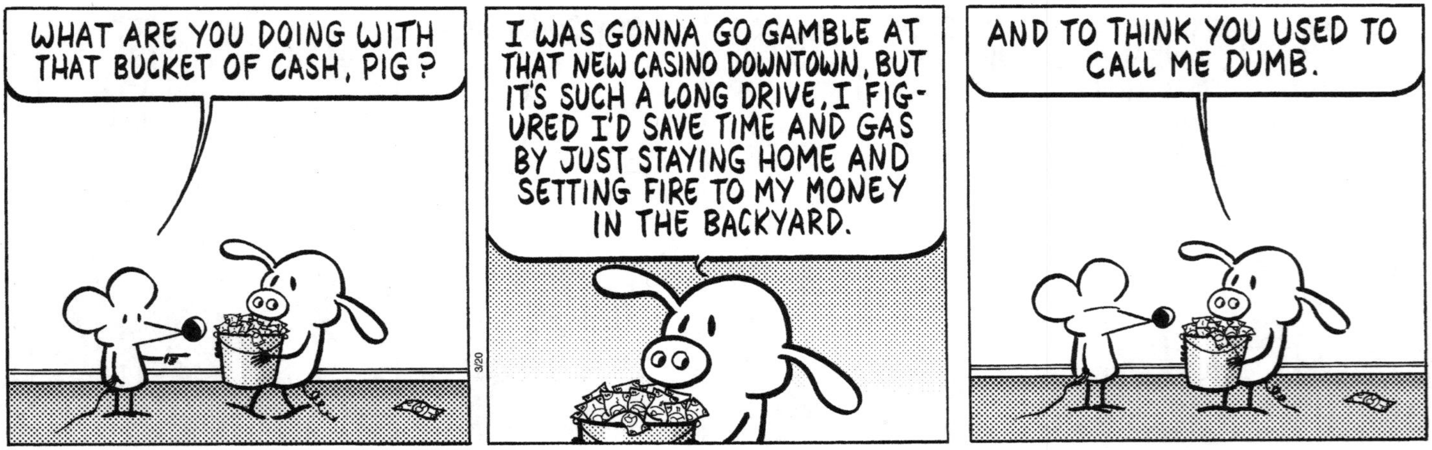
WHAT ARE YOU DOING WITH THAT BUCKET OF CASH, PIG?
I WAS GONNA GO GAMBLE AT THAT NEW CASINO DOWNTOWN, BUT IT'S SUCH A LONG DRIVE, I FIGURED I'D SAVE TIME AND GAS BY JUST STAYING HOME AND SETTING FIRE TO MY MONEY IN THE BACKYARD.
AND TO THINK YOU USED TO CALL ME DUMB.
3/20

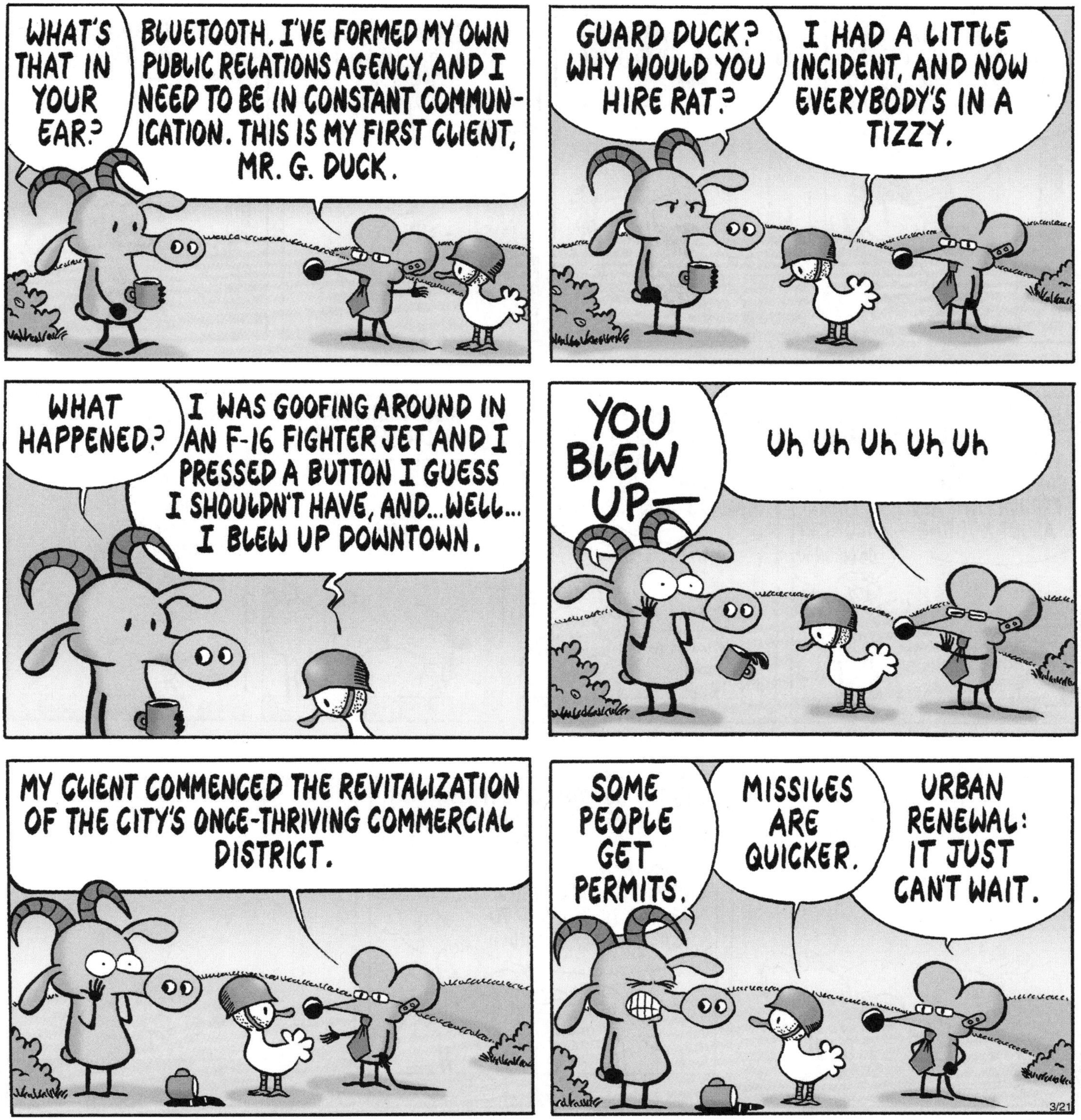
WHAT'S THAT IN YOUR EAR?
BLUETOOTH. I'VE FORMED MY OWN PUBLIC RELATIONS AGENCY, AND I NEED TO BE IN CONSTANT COMMUNICATION. THIS IS MY FIRST CLIENT, MR. G. DUCK.
GUARD DUCK? WHY WOULD YOU HIRE RAT?
I HAD A LITTLE INCIDENT, AND NOW EVERYBODY'S IN A TIZZY.
WHAT HAPPENED?
I WAS GOOFING AROUND IN AN F-16 FIGHTER JET AND I PRESSED A BUTTON I GUESS I SHOULDN'T HAVE, AND...WELL... I BLEW UP DOWNTOWN.
YOU BLEW UP—
Uh Uh Uh Uh Uh
MY CLIENT COMMENCED THE REVITALIZATION OF THE CITY'S ONCE-THRIVING COMMERCIAL DISTRICT.
SOME PEOPLE GET PERMITS.
MISSILES ARE QUICKER.
URBAN RENEWAL: IT JUST CAN'T WAIT.
3/21

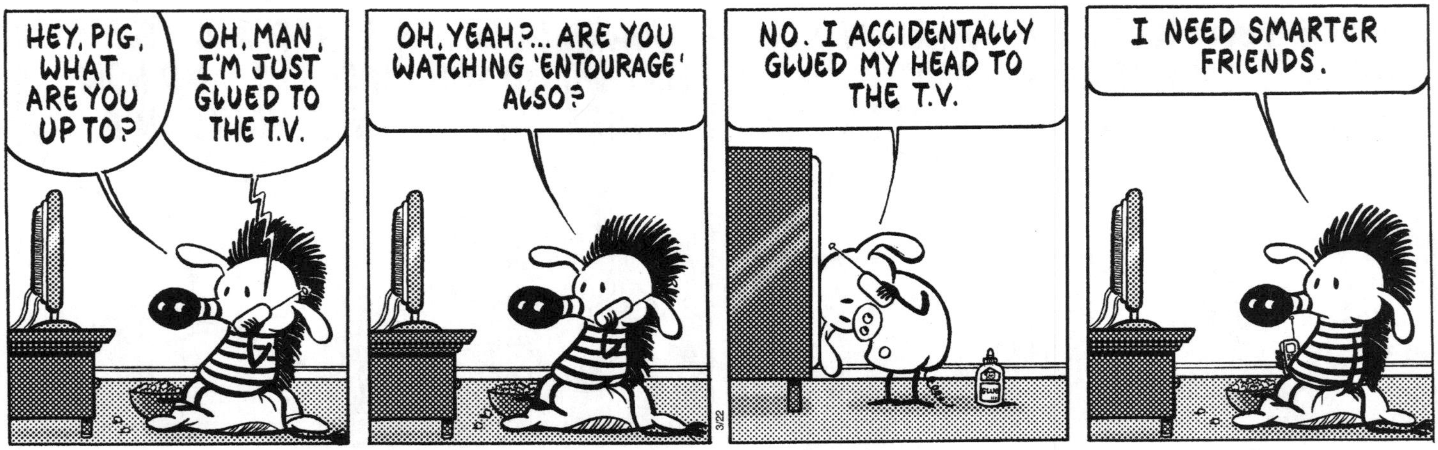
HEY, PIG, WHAT ARE YOU UP TO?
OH, MAN, I'M JUST GLUED TO THE T.V.
OH, YEAH?... ARE YOU WATCHING 'ENTOURAGE' ALSO?
NO. I ACCIDENTALLY GLUED MY HEAD TO THE T.V.
I NEED SMARTER FRIENDS.
3/22

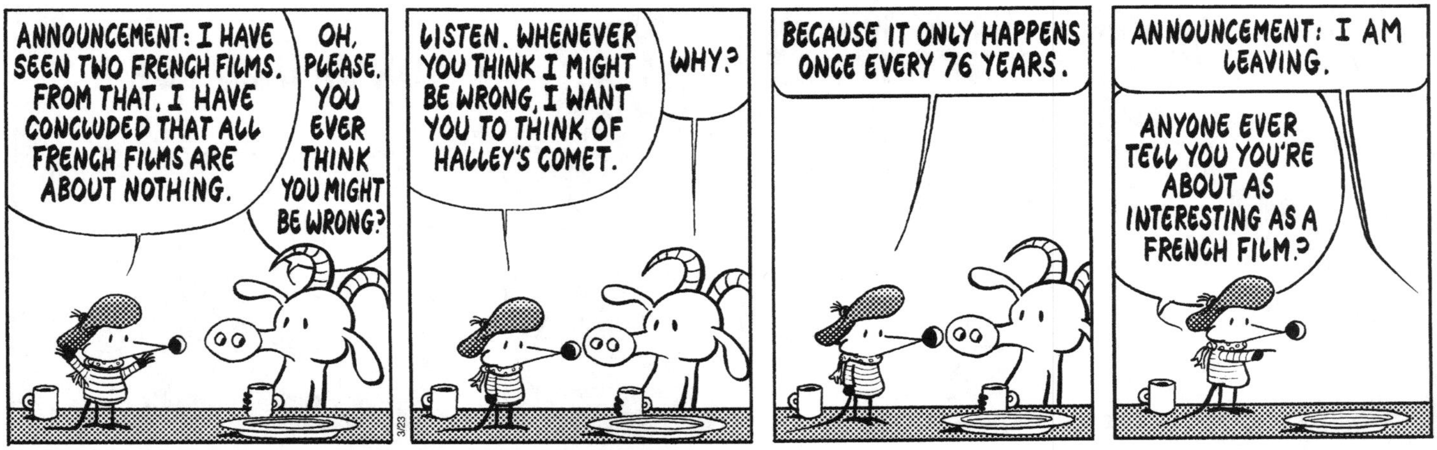
ANNOUNCEMENT: I HAVE SEEN TWO FRENCH FILMS. FROM THAT, I HAVE CONCLUDED THAT ALL FRENCH FILMS ARE ABOUT NOTHING.
OH, PLEASE. YOU EVER THINK YOU MIGHT BE WRONG?
LISTEN. WHENEVER YOU THINK I MIGHT BE WRONG, I WANT YOU TO THINK OF HALLEY'S COMET.
WHY?
BECAUSE IT ONLY HAPPENS ONCE EVERY 76 YEARS.
ANNOUNCEMENT: I AM LEAVING.
ANYONE EVER TELL YOU YOU'RE ABOUT AS INTERESTING AS A FRENCH FILM?
3/23

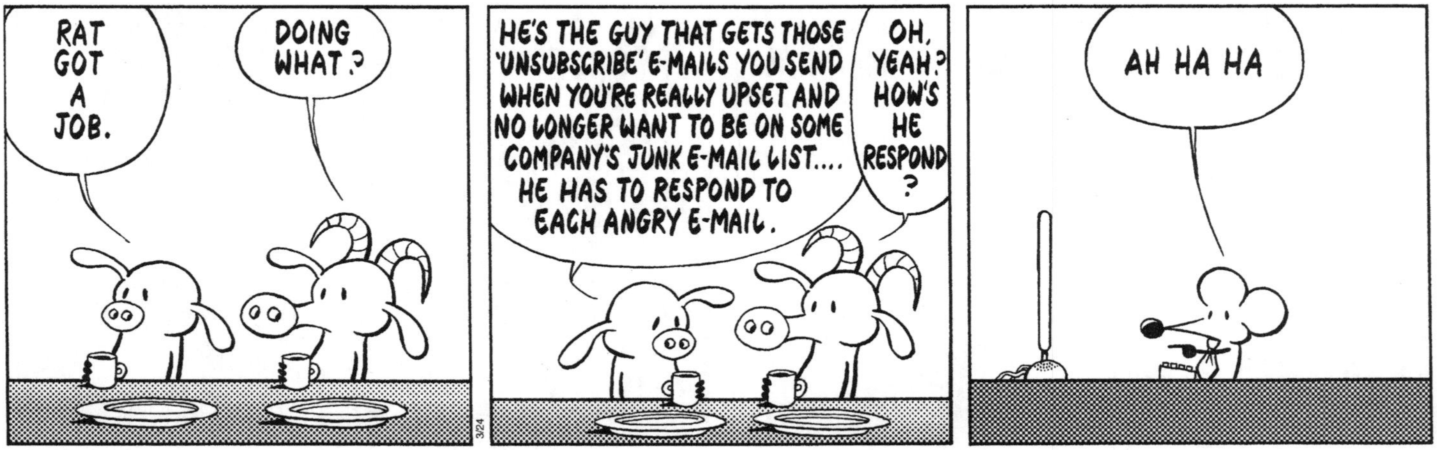
RAT GOT A JOB.
DOING WHAT?
HE'S THE GUY THAT GETS THOSE 'UNSUBSCRIBE' E-MAILS YOU SEND WHEN YOU'RE REALLY UPSET AND NO LONGER WANT TO BE ON SOME COMPANY'S JUNK E-MAIL LIST.... HE HAS TO RESPOND TO EACH ANGRY E-MAIL.
OH, YEAH? HOW'S HE RESPOND?
AH HA HA
3/24

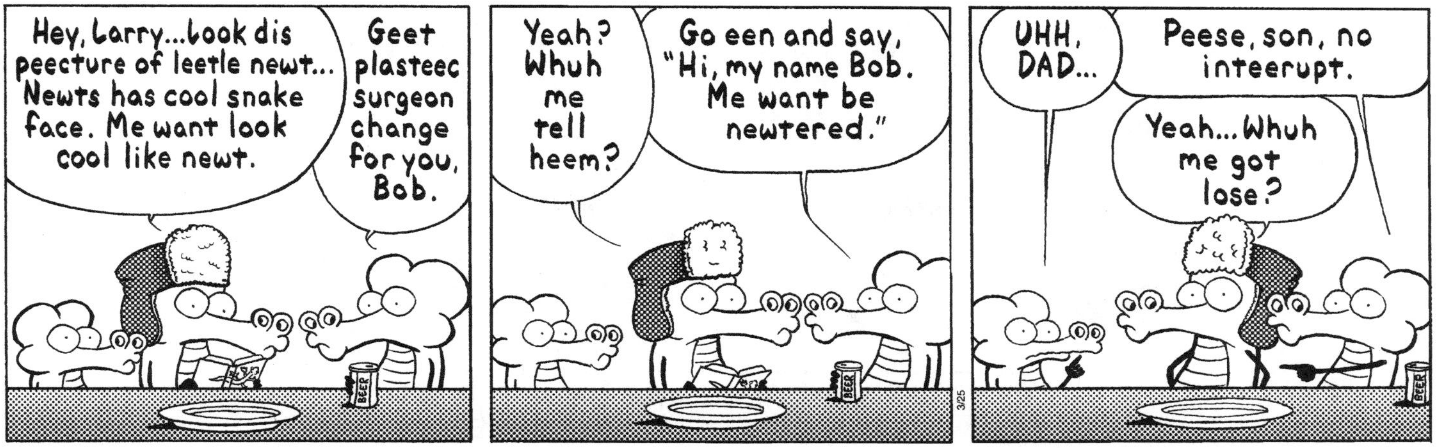
Hey, Larry...Look dis peecture of leetle newt... Newts has cool snake face. Me want look cool like newt.
Geet plasteec surgeon change for you, Bob.
BEER
Yeah? Whuh me tell heem?
Go een and say, "Hi, my name Bob. Me want be newtered."
BEER
3/25
UHH, DAD...
Peese, son, no inteerupt.
Yeah... Whuh me got lose?
BEER

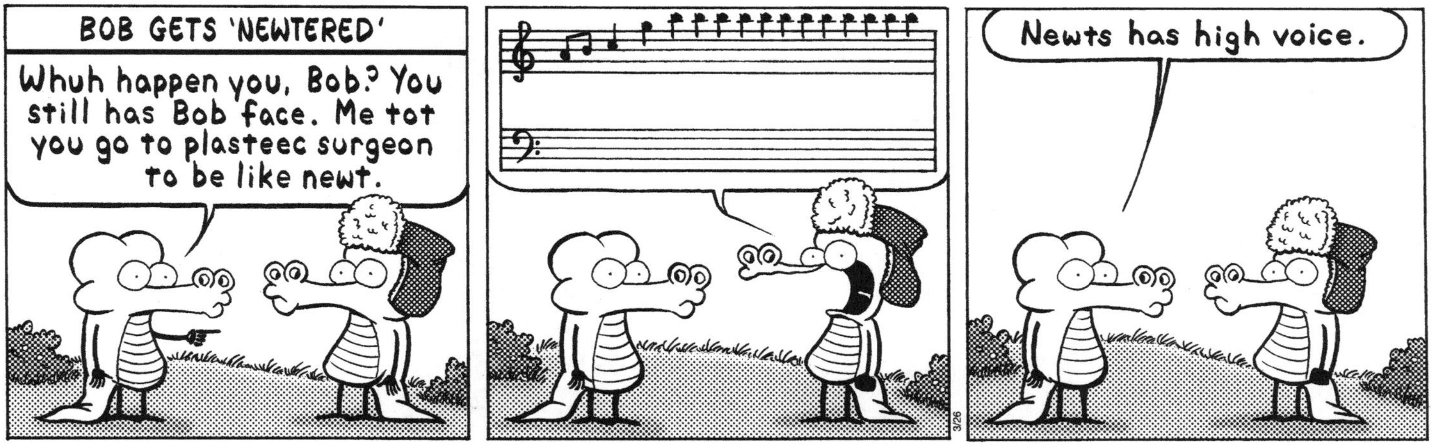
BOB GETS 'NEWTERED'
Whuh happen you, Bob? You still has Bob face. Me tot you go to plasteec surgeon to be like newt.
3/26
Newts has high voice.

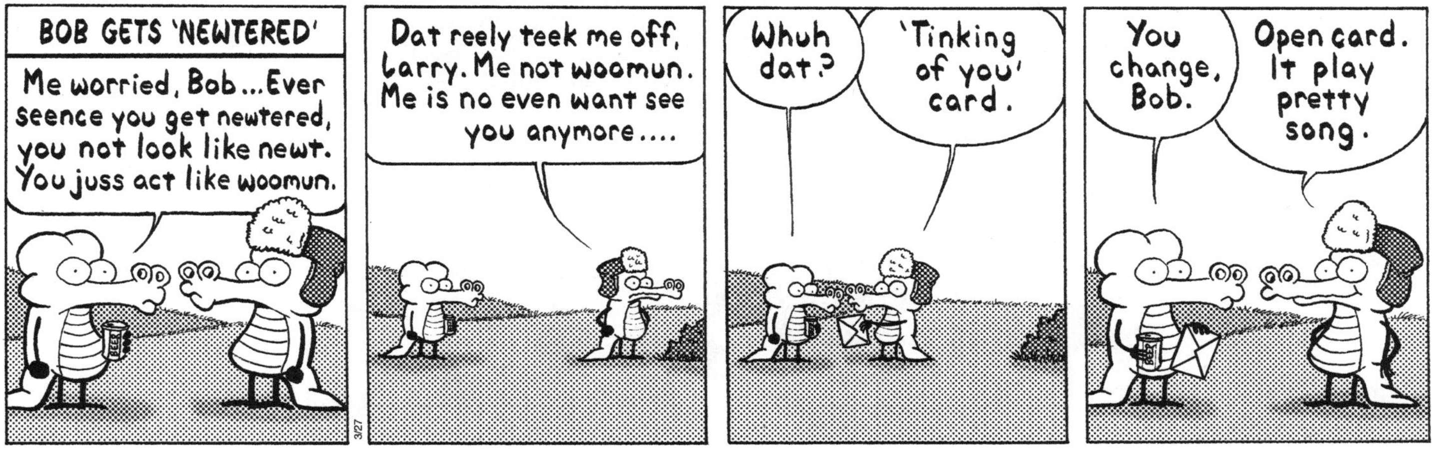
BOB GETS 'NEWTERED'
Me worried, Bob...Ever seence you get newtered, you not look like newt. You juss act like woomun.
BEER
3/27
Dat reely teek me off, Larry. Me not woomun. Me is no even want see you anymore....
Whuh dat?
'Tinking of you' card.
You change, Bob.
Open card. It play pretty song.
BEER

I, RAT EMERITUS, HAVE WRITTEN OUT THE MATHEMATICS OF DOING GOOD FOR YOUR FELLOW MAN.

WHAT ARE YOU TALKING ABOUT?

I'LL SHOW YOU...SEE, I START WITH THE SIMPLE PRINCIPLE THAT GIVING TO OTHERS PRODUCES GOOD.

Giving to others = GOOD

BUT THEN I HAVE TO ACCOUNT FOR THE SLOTH COROLLARY.

Giving to others → Makes them lazy

AND THE HAPPINESS PRINCIPLE.

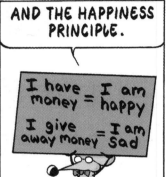

I have money = I am happy

I give away money = I am sad

AND THE FUTILITY ALGORITHM.

WORLD'S problems = Large

MY contribution = Drop in Bucket

THEN I ADD IT ALL UP, CARRY THE 3, DIVIDE BY 2, AND ARRIVE AT MY GRAND THEOREM OF HOW ONE SHOULD CONDUCT ONESELF.

WHICH IS WHAT?

Do nothing.

NOTHING. HOW OBVIOUS.

WELL...NOT *REALLY* NOTHING. YOU CAN SIT AROUND AND DRINK BEER.

3/28

104

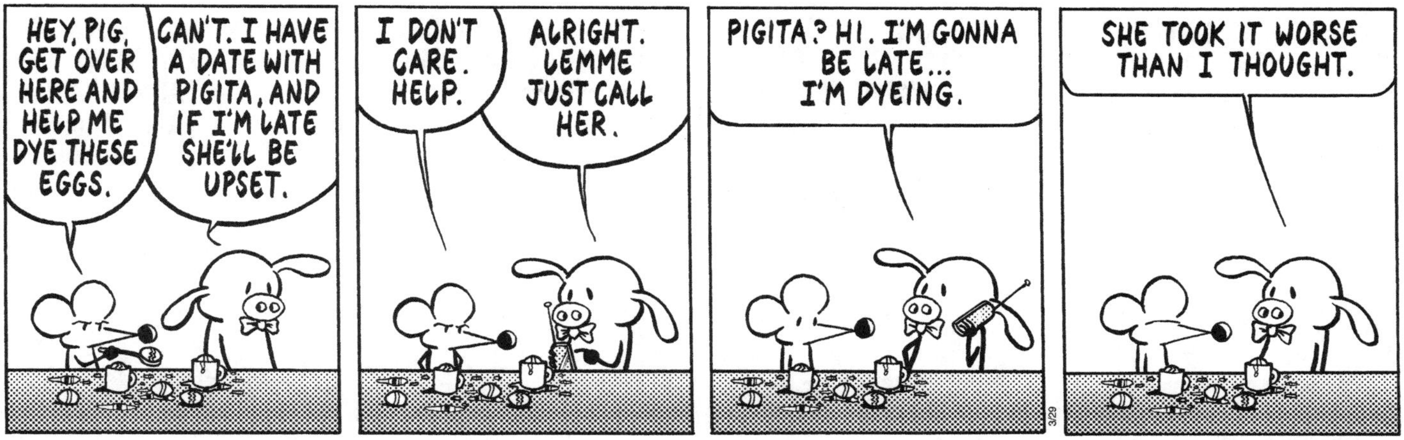
HEY, PIG, GET OVER HERE AND HELP ME DYE THESE EGGS.
CAN'T. I HAVE A DATE WITH PIGITA, AND IF I'M LATE SHE'LL BE UPSET.
I DON'T CARE. HELP.
ALRIGHT. LEMME JUST CALL HER.
PIGITA? HI. I'M GONNA BE LATE... I'M DYEING.
SHE TOOK IT WORSE THAN I THOUGHT.
3/29

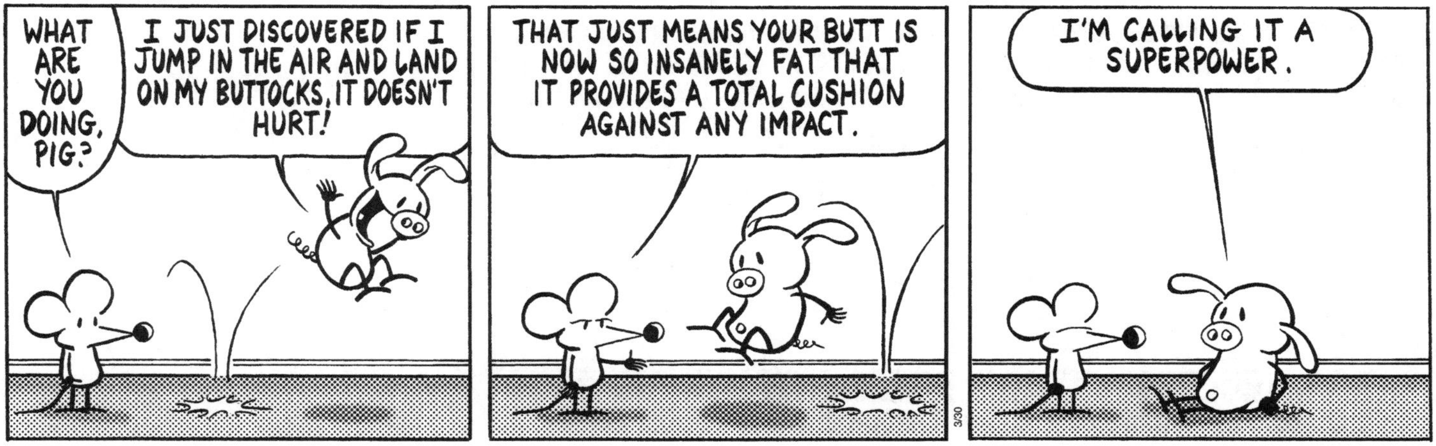
WHAT ARE YOU DOING, PIG?
I JUST DISCOVERED IF I JUMP IN THE AIR AND LAND ON MY BUTTOCKS, IT DOESN'T HURT!
THAT JUST MEANS YOUR BUTT IS NOW SO INSANELY FAT THAT IT PROVIDES A TOTAL CUSHION AGAINST ANY IMPACT.
I'M CALLING IT A SUPERPOWER.
3/30

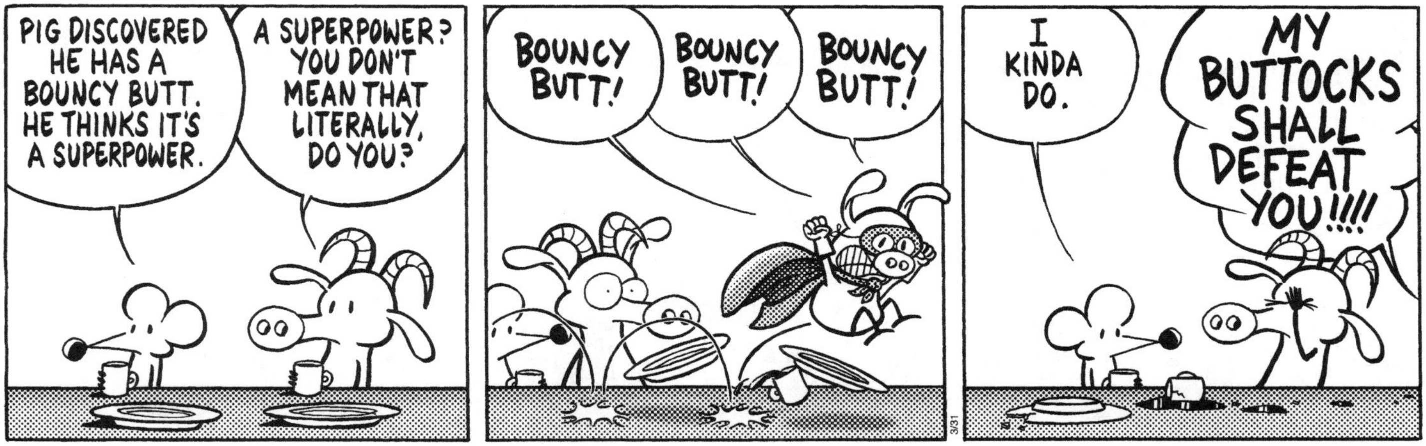
PIG DISCOVERED HE HAS A BOUNCY BUTT. HE THINKS IT'S A SUPERPOWER.
A SUPERPOWER? YOU DON'T MEAN THAT LITERALLY, DO YOU?
BOUNCY BUTT!
BOUNCY BUTT!
BOUNCY BUTT!
I KINDA DO.
MY BUTTOCKS SHALL DEFEAT YOU!!!!
3/31

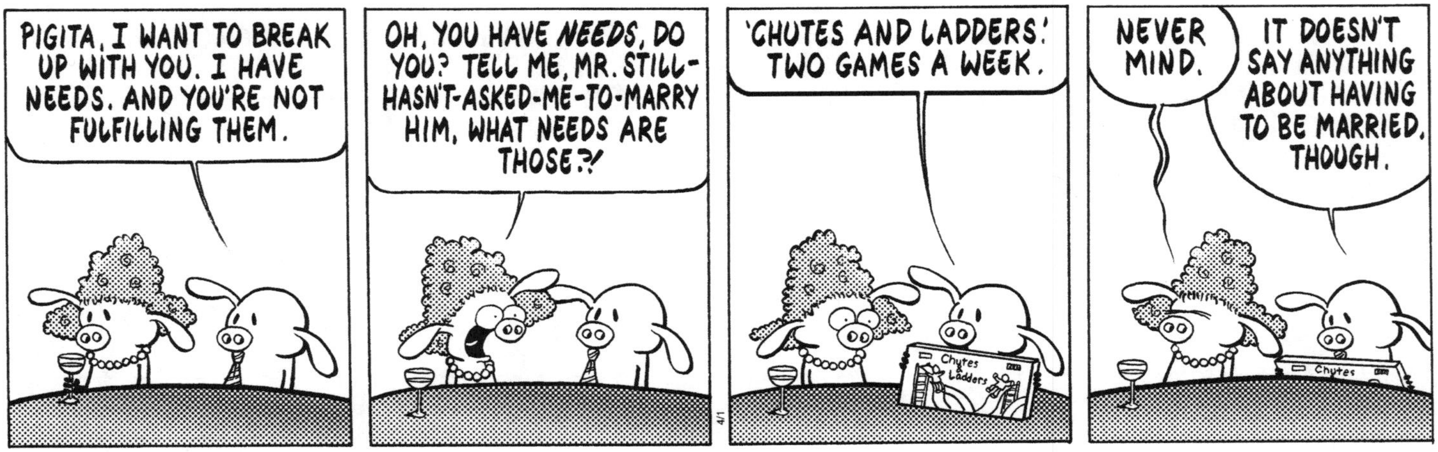
PIGITA, I WANT TO BREAK UP WITH YOU. I HAVE NEEDS. AND YOU'RE NOT FULFILLING THEM.
OH, YOU HAVE *NEEDS*, DO YOU? TELL ME, MR. STILL-HASN'T-ASKED-ME-TO-MARRY HIM, WHAT NEEDS ARE THOSE?!
'CHUTES AND LADDERS.' TWO GAMES A WEEK.
Chutes & Ladders
NEVER MIND.
IT DOESN'T SAY ANYTHING ABOUT HAVING TO BE MARRIED, THOUGH.
4/1

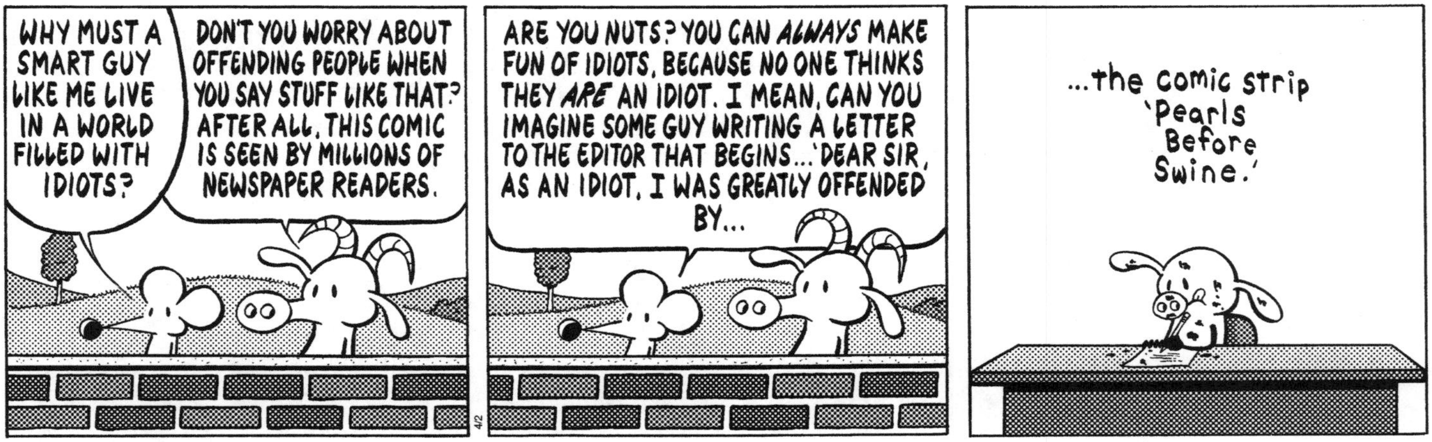
WHY MUST A SMART GUY LIKE ME LIVE IN A WORLD FILLED WITH IDIOTS?
DON'T YOU WORRY ABOUT OFFENDING PEOPLE WHEN YOU SAY STUFF LIKE THAT? AFTER ALL, THIS COMIC IS SEEN BY MILLIONS OF NEWSPAPER READERS.
ARE YOU NUTS? YOU CAN *ALWAYS* MAKE FUN OF IDIOTS, BECAUSE NO ONE THINKS THEY *ARE* AN IDIOT. I MEAN, CAN YOU IMAGINE SOME GUY WRITING A LETTER TO THE EDITOR THAT BEGINS...'DEAR SIR, AS AN IDIOT, I WAS GREATLY OFFENDED BY...
...the comic strip 'Pearls Before Swine.'
4/2

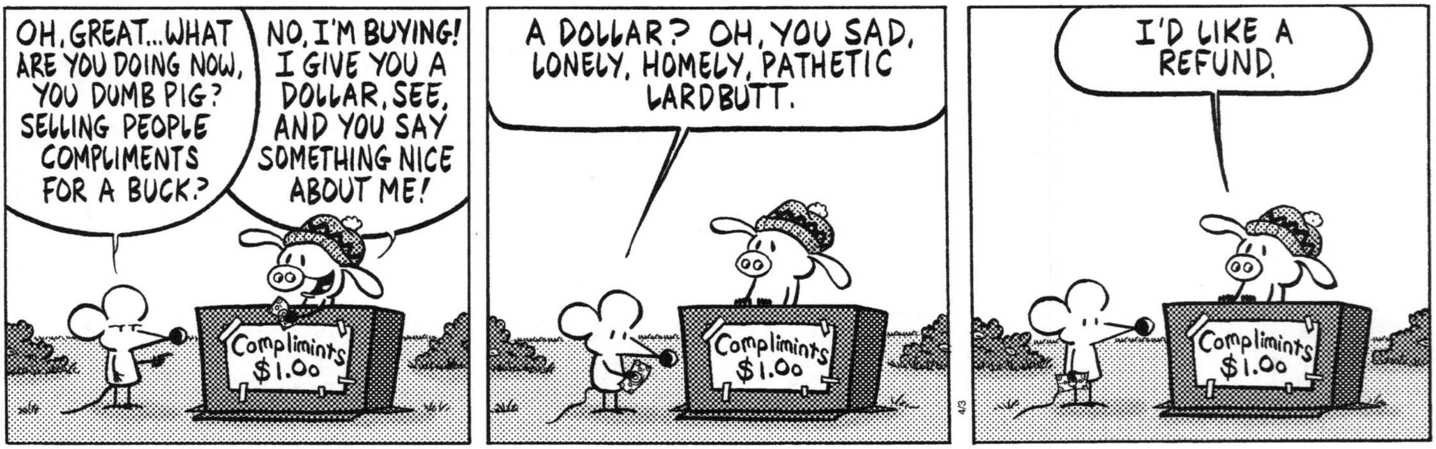
OH, GREAT...WHAT ARE YOU DOING NOW, YOU DUMB PIG? SELLING PEOPLE COMPLIMENTS FOR A BUCK?
NO, I'M BUYING! I GIVE YOU A DOLLAR, SEE, AND YOU SAY SOMETHING NICE ABOUT ME!
Complimints $1.00
A DOLLAR? OH, YOU SAD, LONELY, HOMELY, PATHETIC LARDBUTT.
I'D LIKE A REFUND.
4/3

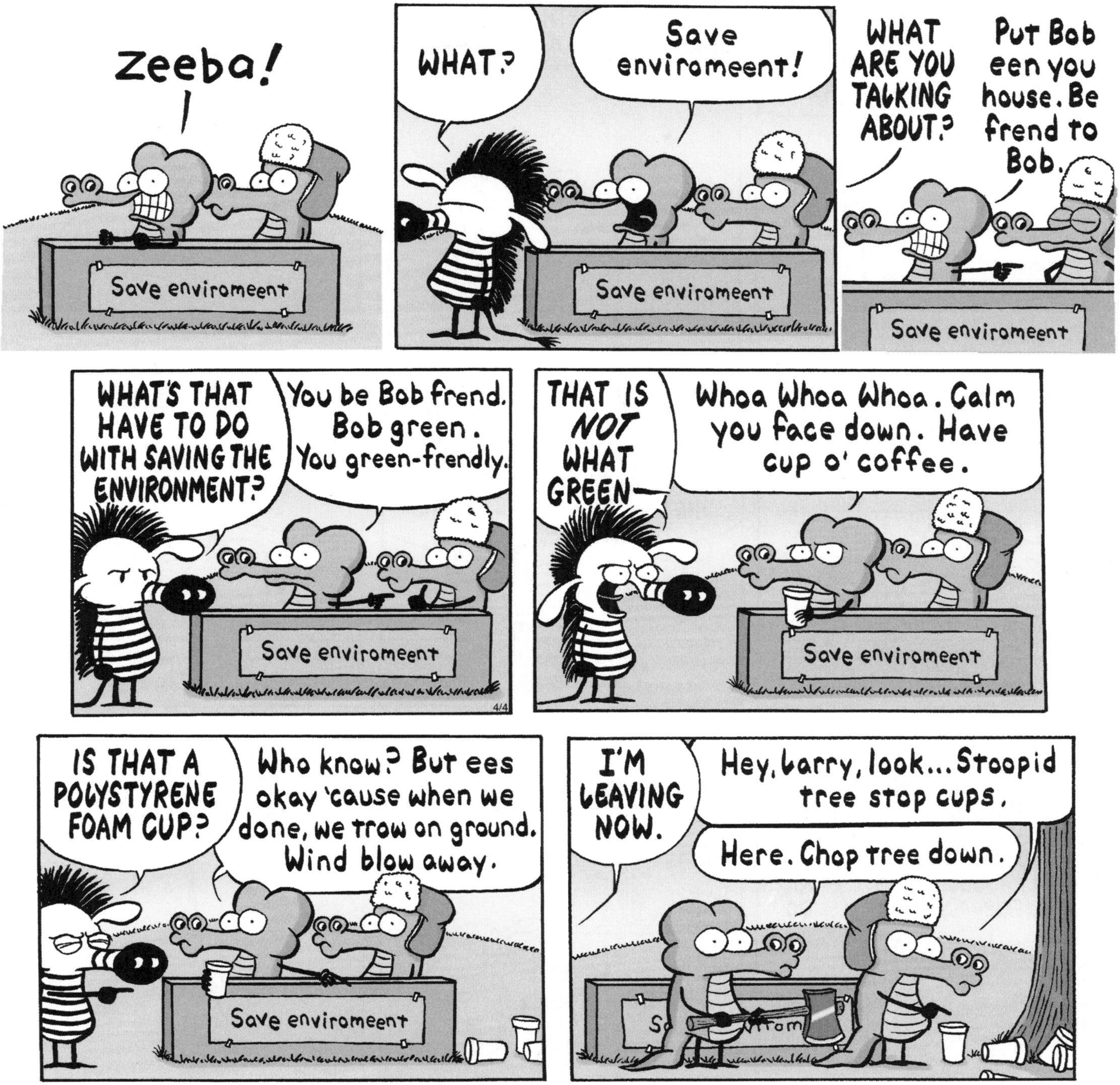
Zeeba!
Save enviromeent
WHAT?
Save enviromeent!
Save enviromeent
WHAT ARE YOU TALKING ABOUT?
Put Bob een you house. Be frend to Bob.
Save enviromeent
WHAT'S THAT HAVE TO DO WITH SAVING THE ENVIRONMENT?
You be Bob frend. Bob green. You green-frendly.
Save enviromeent
4/4
THAT IS NOT WHAT GREEN—
Whoa Whoa Whoa. Calm you face down. Have cup o' coffee.
Save enviromeent
IS THAT A POLYSTYRENE FOAM CUP?
Who know? But ees okay 'cause when we done, we trow on ground. Wind blow away.
Save enviromeent
I'M LEAVING NOW.
Hey, Larry, look... Stoopid tree stop cups.
Here. Chop tree down.

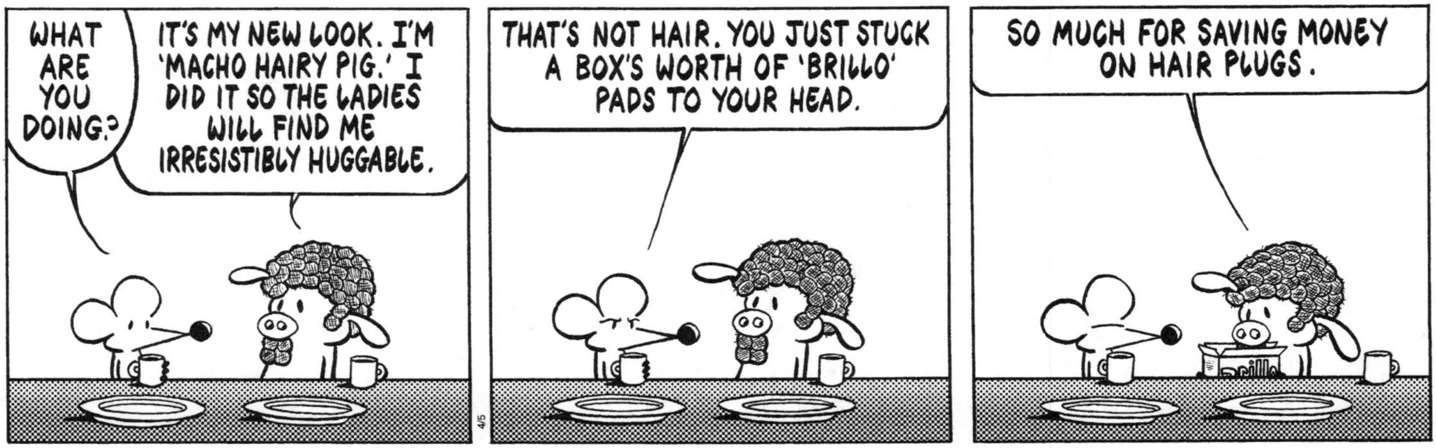
WHAT ARE YOU DOING?
IT'S MY NEW LOOK. I'M 'MACHO HAIRY PIG.' I DID IT SO THE LADIES WILL FIND ME IRRESISTIBLY HUGGABLE.
THAT'S NOT HAIR. YOU JUST STUCK A BOX'S WORTH OF 'BRILLO' PADS TO YOUR HEAD.
SO MUCH FOR SAVING MONEY ON HAIR PLUGS.

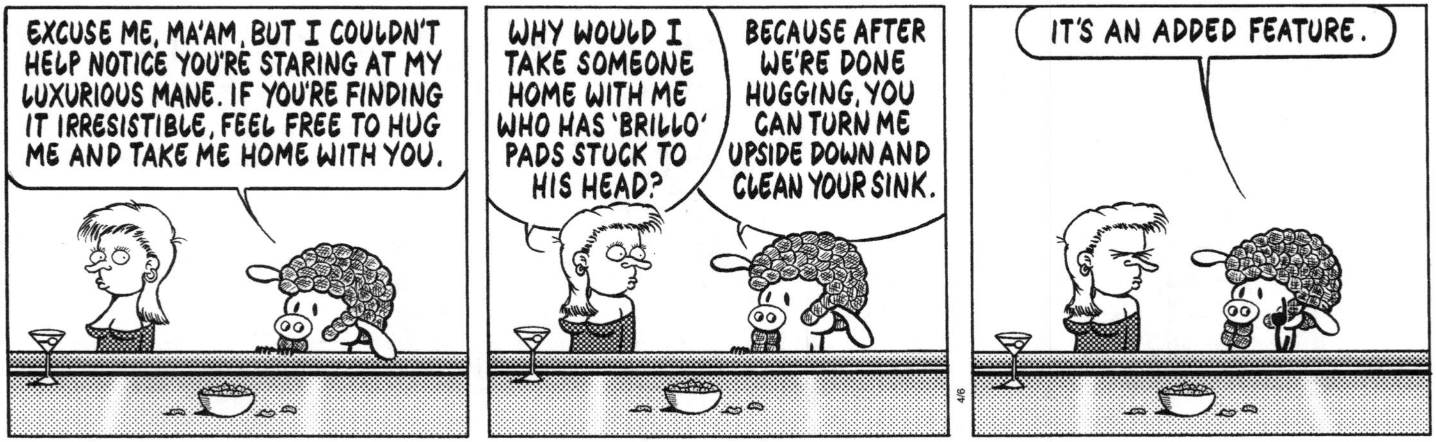
EXCUSE ME, MA'AM, BUT I COULDN'T HELP NOTICE YOU'RE STARING AT MY LUXURIOUS MANE. IF YOU'RE FINDING IT IRRESISTIBLE, FEEL FREE TO HUG ME AND TAKE ME HOME WITH YOU.
WHY WOULD I TAKE SOMEONE HOME WITH ME WHO HAS 'BRILLO' PADS STUCK TO HIS HEAD?
BECAUSE AFTER WE'RE DONE HUGGING, YOU CAN TURN ME UPSIDE DOWN AND CLEAN YOUR SINK.
IT'S AN ADDED FEATURE.

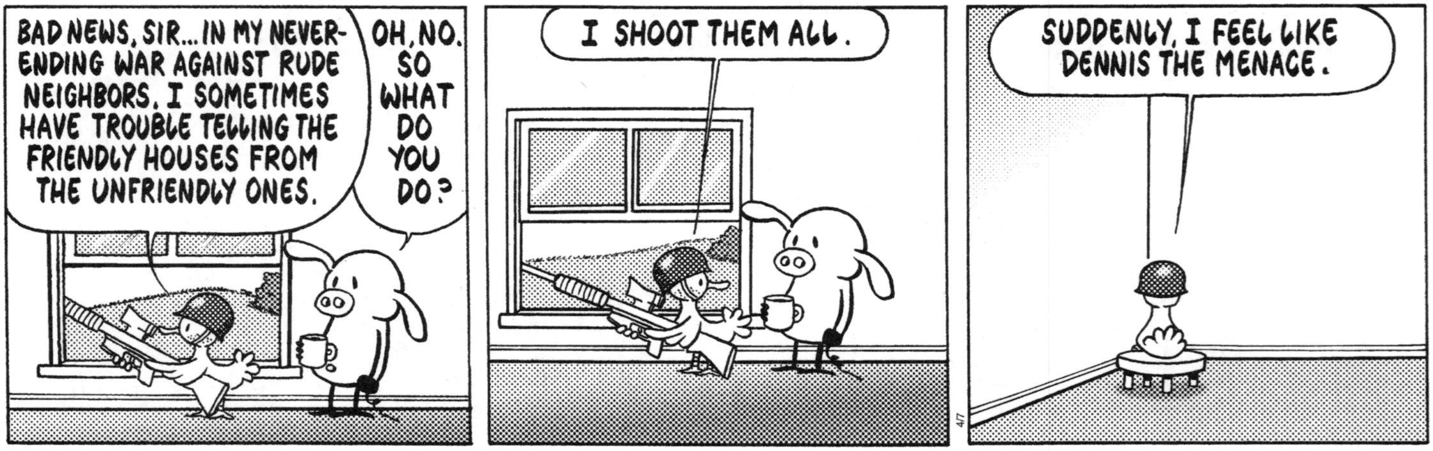
BAD NEWS, SIR... IN MY NEVER-ENDING WAR AGAINST RUDE NEIGHBORS, I SOMETIMES HAVE TROUBLE TELLING THE FRIENDLY HOUSES FROM THE UNFRIENDLY ONES.
OH, NO. SO WHAT DO YOU DO?
I SHOOT THEM ALL.
SUDDENLY, I FEEL LIKE DENNIS THE MENACE.

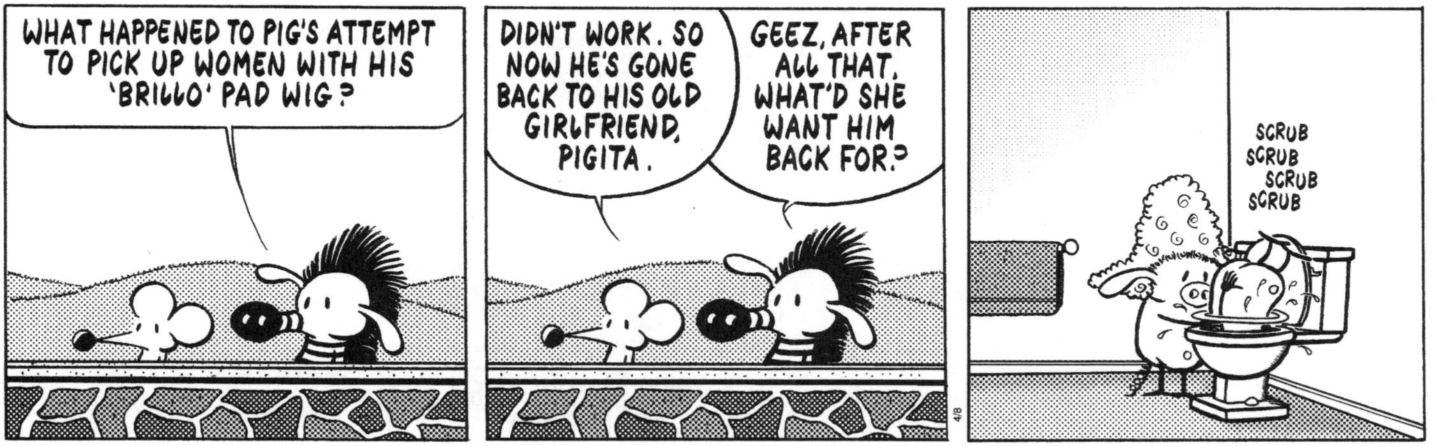
WHAT HAPPENED TO PIG'S ATTEMPT TO PICK UP WOMEN WITH HIS 'BRILLO' PAD WIG?
DIDN'T WORK. SO NOW HE'S GONE BACK TO HIS OLD GIRLFRIEND, PIGITA.
GEEZ, AFTER ALL THAT, WHAT'D SHE WANT HIM BACK FOR?
4/8
SCRUB
SCRUB
SCRUB
SCRUB

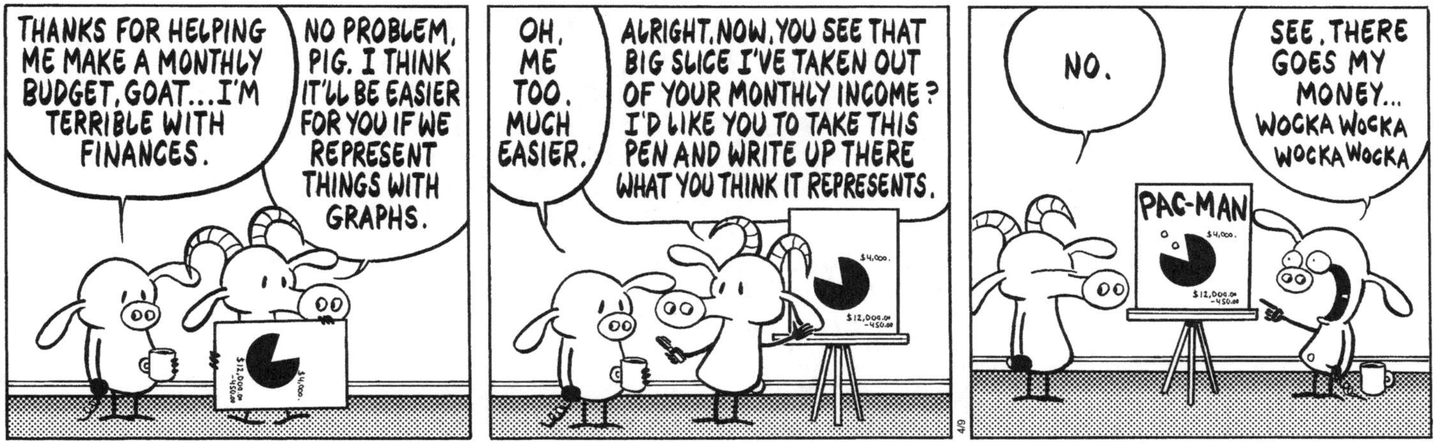
THANKS FOR HELPING ME MAKE A MONTHLY BUDGET, GOAT... I'M TERRIBLE WITH FINANCES.
NO PROBLEM, PIG. I THINK IT'LL BE EASIER FOR YOU IF WE REPRESENT THINGS WITH GRAPHS.
$12,000.00 -450.00
$4,000.
OH, ME TOO. MUCH EASIER.
ALRIGHT, NOW, YOU SEE THAT BIG SLICE I'VE TAKEN OUT OF YOUR MONTHLY INCOME? I'D LIKE YOU TO TAKE THIS PEN AND WRITE UP THERE WHAT YOU THINK IT REPRESENTS.
4/9
NO.
SEE, THERE GOES MY MONEY... WOCKA WOCKA WOCKA WOCKA
PAC-MAN

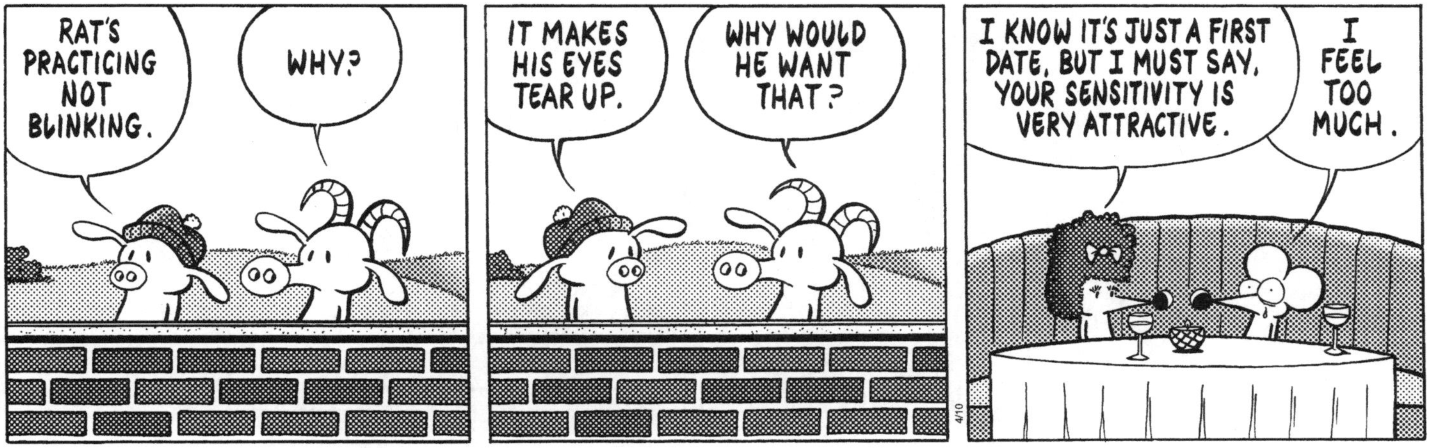
RAT'S PRACTICING NOT BLINKING.
WHY?
IT MAKES HIS EYES TEAR UP.
WHY WOULD HE WANT THAT?
4/10
I KNOW IT'S JUST A FIRST DATE, BUT I MUST SAY, YOUR SENSITIVITY IS VERY ATTRACTIVE.
I FEEL TOO MUCH.

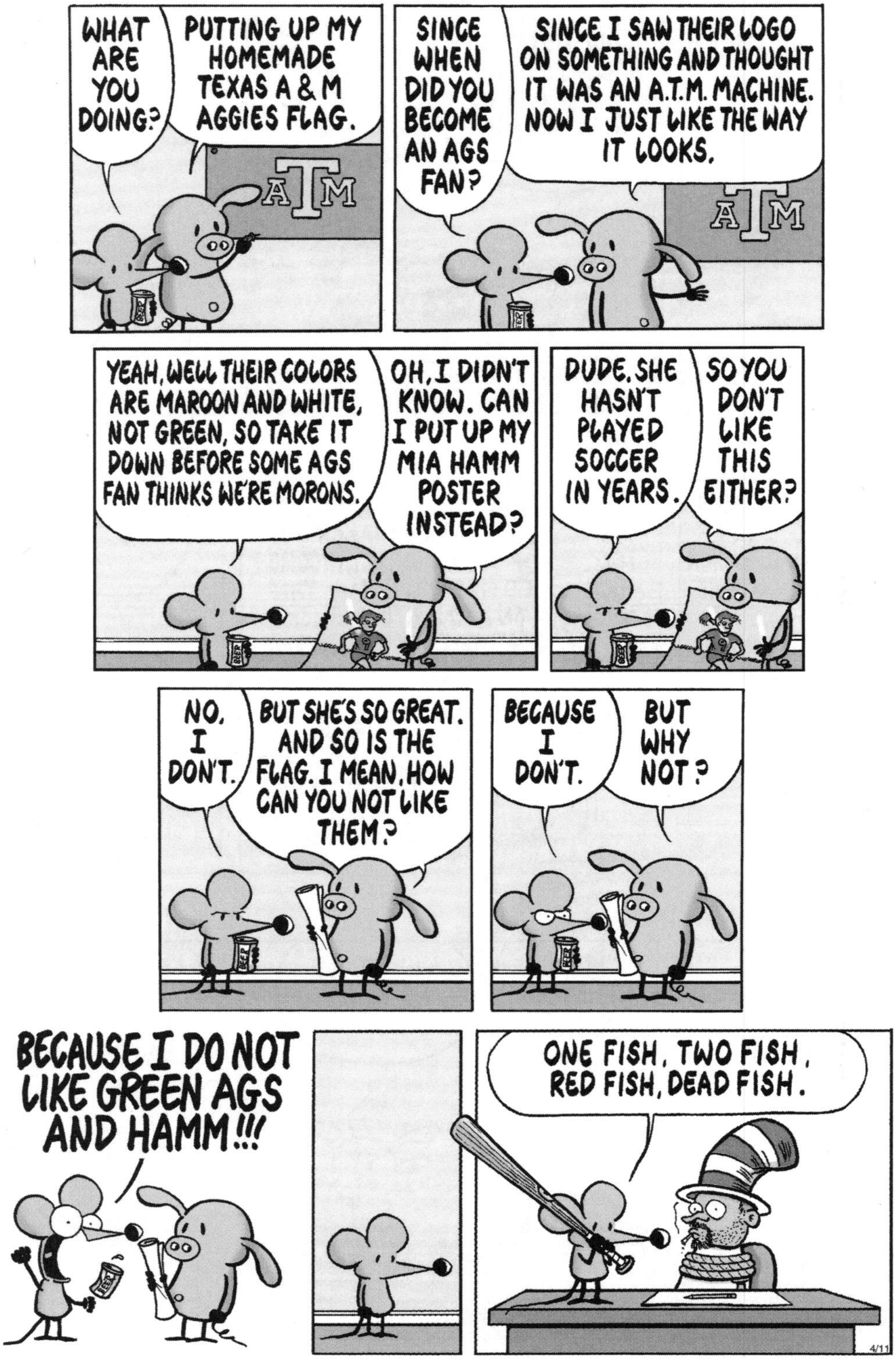
WHAT ARE YOU DOING?
PUTTING UP MY HOMEMADE TEXAS A & M AGGIES FLAG.
A&M
SINCE WHEN DID YOU BECOME AN AGS FAN?
SINCE I SAW THEIR LOGO ON SOMETHING AND THOUGHT IT WAS AN A.T.M. MACHINE. NOW I JUST LIKE THE WAY IT LOOKS.
YEAH, WELL THEIR COLORS ARE MAROON AND WHITE, NOT GREEN, SO TAKE IT DOWN BEFORE SOME AGS FAN THINKS WE'RE MORONS.
OH, I DIDN'T KNOW. CAN I PUT UP MY MIA HAMM POSTER INSTEAD?
DUDE, SHE HASN'T PLAYED SOCCER IN YEARS.
SO YOU DON'T LIKE THIS EITHER?
NO. I DON'T.
BUT SHE'S SO GREAT. AND SO IS THE FLAG. I MEAN, HOW CAN YOU NOT LIKE THEM?
BECAUSE I DON'T.
BUT WHY NOT?
BECAUSE I DO NOT LIKE GREEN AGS AND HAMM!!!
ONE FISH, TWO FISH, RED FISH, DEAD FISH.
4/11

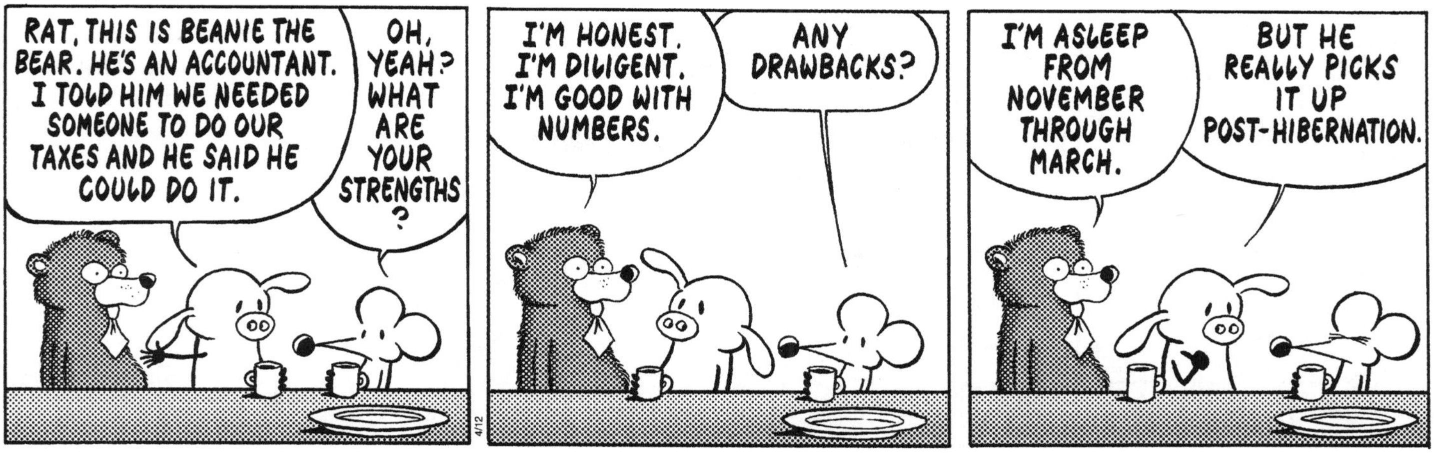
RAT, THIS IS BEANIE THE BEAR. HE'S AN ACCOUNTANT. I TOLD HIM WE NEEDED SOMEONE TO DO OUR TAXES AND HE SAID HE COULD DO IT.
OH, YEAH? WHAT ARE YOUR STRENGTHS?
4/12
I'M HONEST. I'M DILIGENT. I'M GOOD WITH NUMBERS.
ANY DRAWBACKS?
I'M ASLEEP FROM NOVEMBER THROUGH MARCH.
BUT HE REALLY PICKS IT UP POST-HIBERNATION.

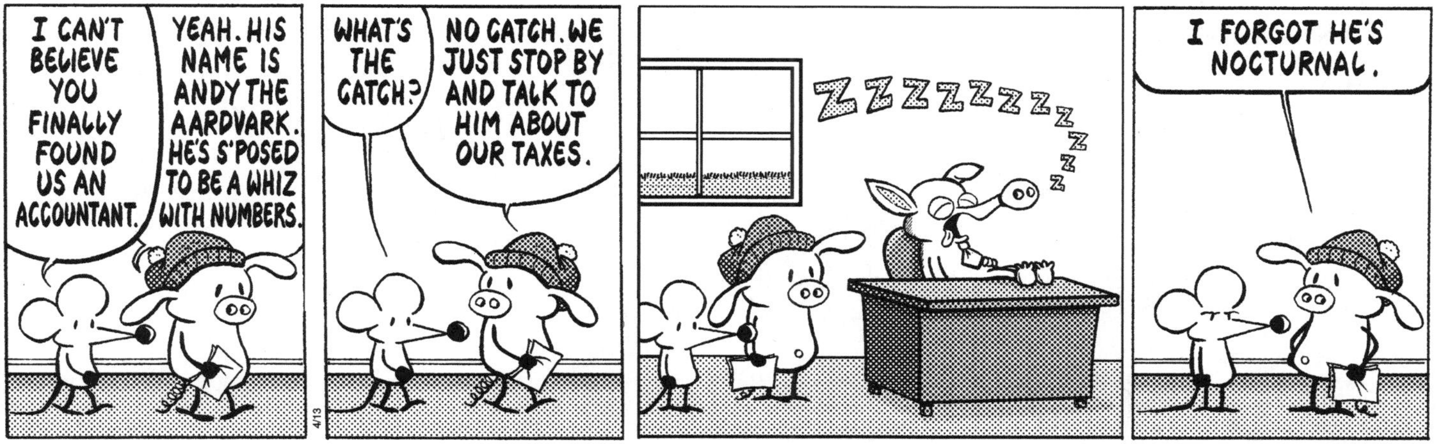
I CAN'T BELIEVE YOU FINALLY FOUND US AN ACCOUNTANT.
YEAH. HIS NAME IS ANDY THE AARDVARK. HE'S S'POSED TO BE A WHIZ WITH NUMBERS.
4/13
WHAT'S THE CATCH?
NO CATCH. WE JUST STOP BY AND TALK TO HIM ABOUT OUR TAXES.
ZZZZZZZzzZZZZ
I FORGOT HE'S NOCTURNAL.

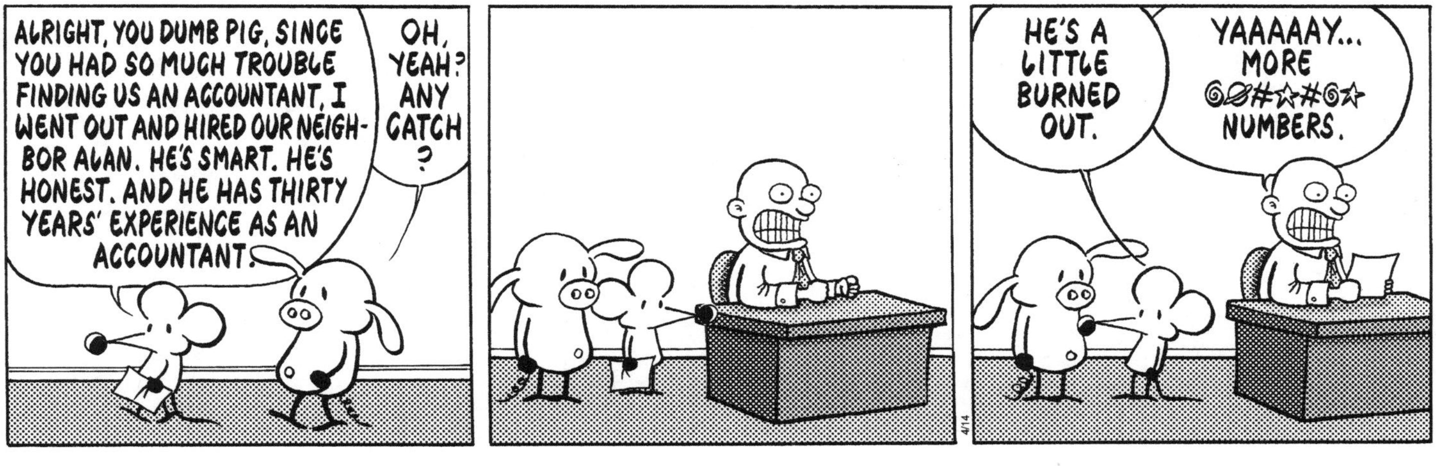
ALRIGHT, YOU DUMB PIG, SINCE YOU HAD SO MUCH TROUBLE FINDING US AN ACCOUNTANT, I WENT OUT AND HIRED OUR NEIGHBOR ALAN. HE'S SMART. HE'S HONEST. AND HE HAS THIRTY YEARS' EXPERIENCE AS AN ACCOUNTANT.
OH, YEAH? ANY CATCH?
4/14
HE'S A LITTLE BURNED OUT.
YAAAAAY... MORE @@#☆#@☆ NUMBERS.

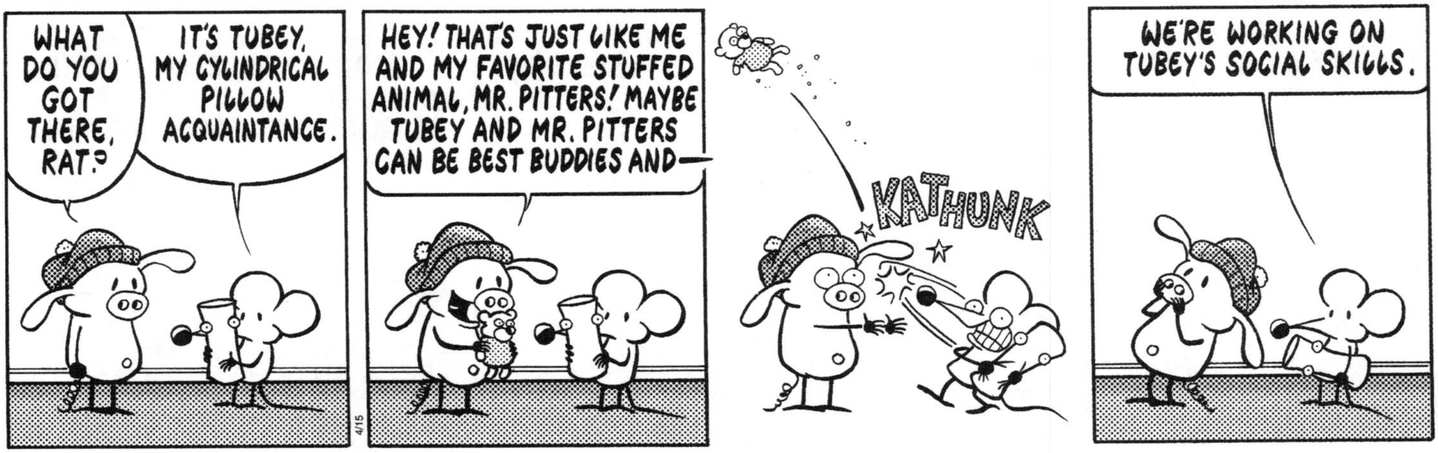
WHAT DO YOU GOT THERE, RAT?
IT'S TUBEY, MY CYLINDRICAL PILLOW ACQUAINTANCE.
4/15
HEY! THAT'S JUST LIKE ME AND MY FAVORITE STUFFED ANIMAL, MR. PITTERS! MAYBE TUBEY AND MR. PITTERS CAN BE BEST BUDDIES AND—
KATHUNK
WE'RE WORKING ON TUBEY'S SOCIAL SKILLS.

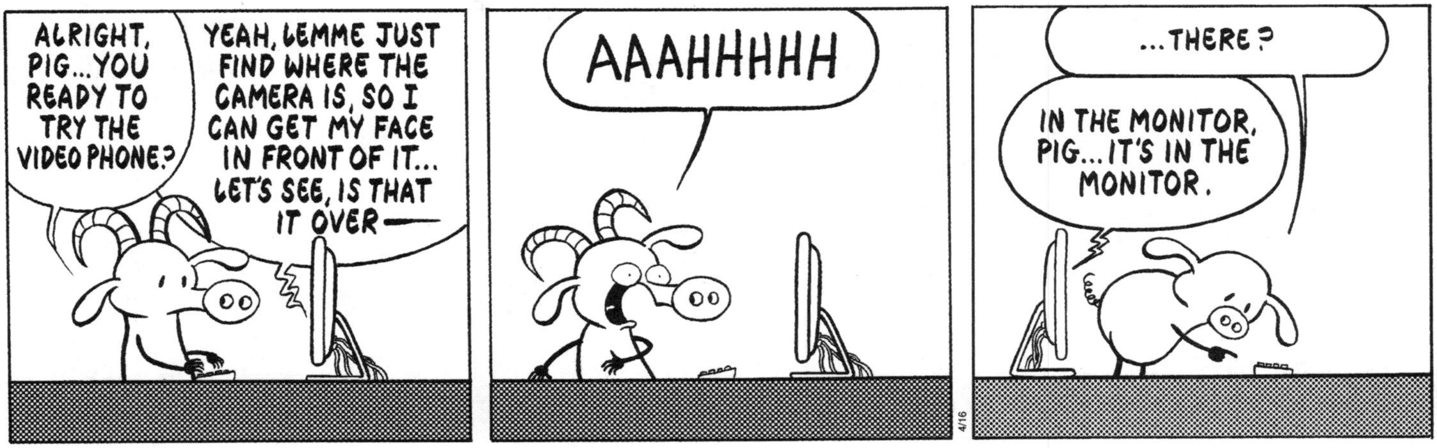
ALRIGHT, PIG... YOU READY TO TRY THE VIDEO PHONE?
YEAH, LEMME JUST FIND WHERE THE CAMERA IS, SO I CAN GET MY FACE IN FRONT OF IT... LET'S SEE, IS THAT IT OVER—
AAAHHHHH
4/16
...THERE?
IN THE MONITOR, PIG... IT'S IN THE MONITOR.

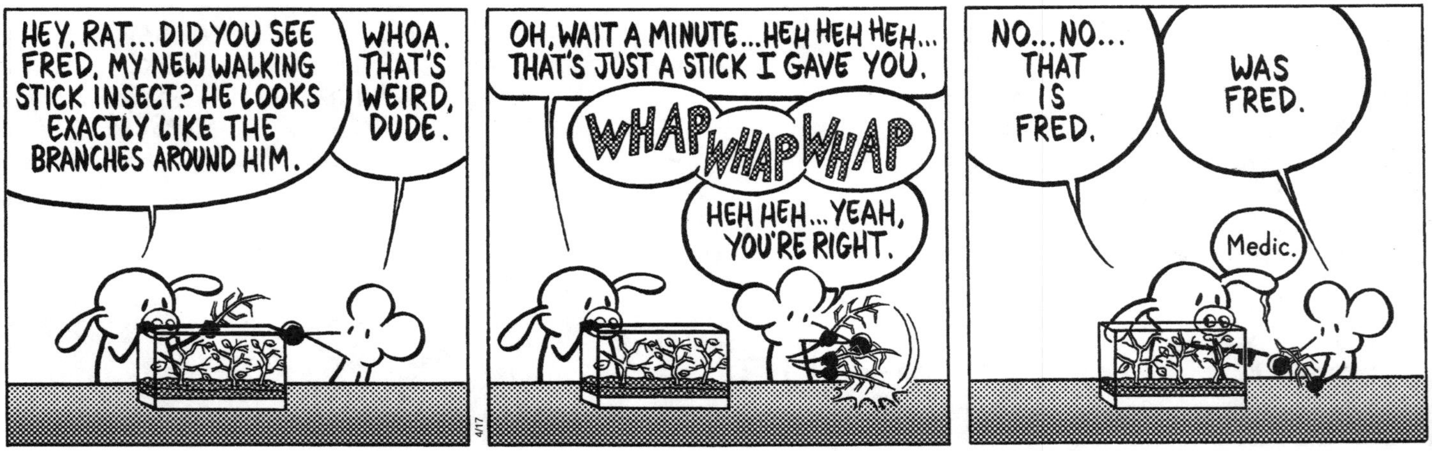
HEY, RAT... DID YOU SEE FRED, MY NEW WALKING STICK INSECT? HE LOOKS EXACTLY LIKE THE BRANCHES AROUND HIM.
WHOA. THAT'S WEIRD, DUDE.
4/17
OH, WAIT A MINUTE... HEH HEH HEH... THAT'S JUST A STICK I GAVE YOU.
WHAP WHAP WHAP
HEH HEH... YEAH, YOU'RE RIGHT.
NO... NO... THAT IS FRED.
WAS FRED.
Medic.

HEY, RAT, IT'S ME, GOAT.
AHHHH...WHAT'S YOUR STUPID FACE DOING ON PIG'S NEW COMPUTER?!
BEER
IT'S 'iCHAT.' IT'S A VIDEO-PHONE.
WHY WOULD I WANT TO SEE YOUR DUMB FACE WHEN WE TALK? I DON'T EVEN WANT TO HEAR YOUR VOICE.
AWW, DON'T BE SUCH A MISANTHROPE... HEY, WHAT KIND OF BEER IS THAT?
WHAT KIND OF— ...YOU CAN SEE ME?!?
BEER
OF COURSE I CAN... IT'S A VIDEOPHONE.
AAAUGHHHHH GET OUT OF MY @#☆!@☆# HOUSE!!
BEER
HEY HEY HEY... CALM DOWN. JUST TERMINATE THE CALL IF YOU DON'T—
KSSHH
IT BROKE.
4/18

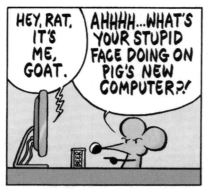

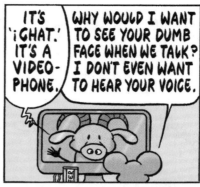

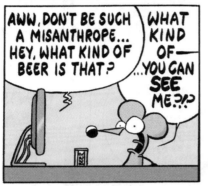

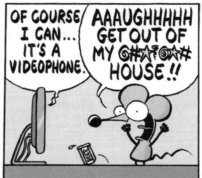

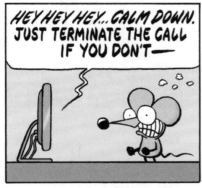

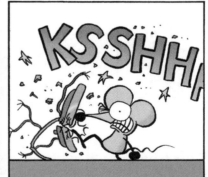

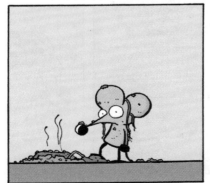

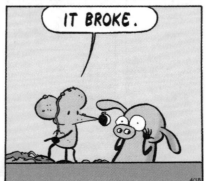

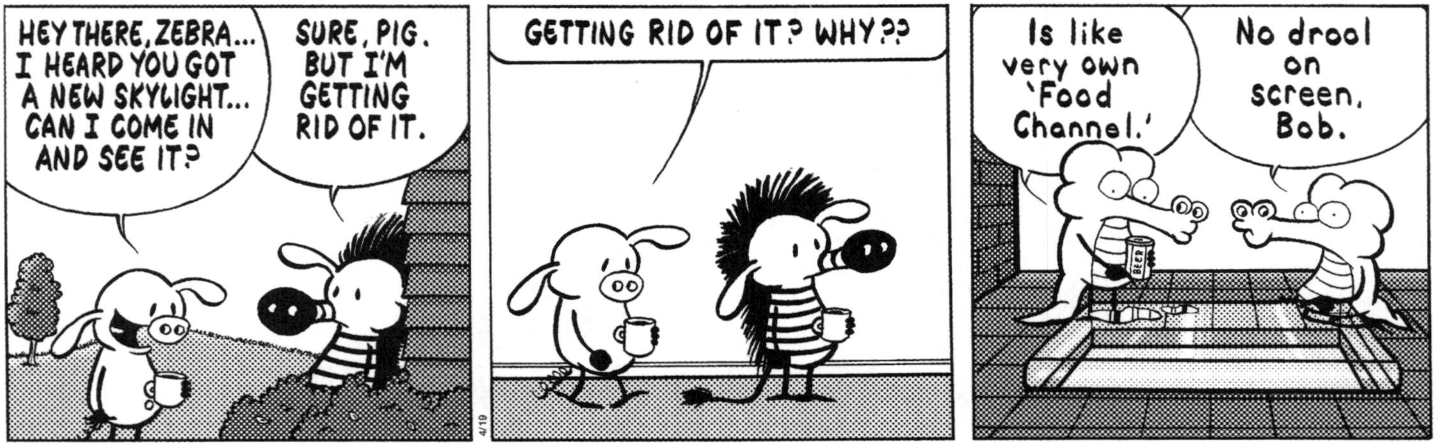
HEY THERE, ZEBRA... I HEARD YOU GOT A NEW SKYLIGHT... CAN I COME IN AND SEE IT?
SURE, PIG. BUT I'M GETTING RID OF IT.
4/19
GETTING RID OF IT? WHY??
Is like very own 'Food Channel.'
BEER
No drool on screen, Bob.

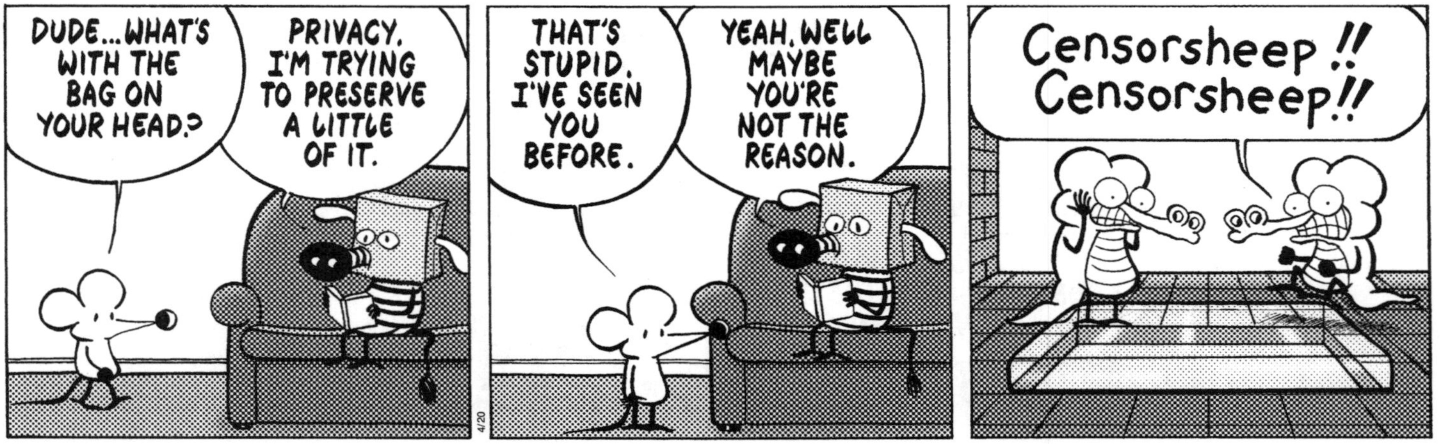
DUDE...WHAT'S WITH THE BAG ON YOUR HEAD?
PRIVACY. I'M TRYING TO PRESERVE A LITTLE OF IT.
4/20
THAT'S STUPID. I'VE SEEN YOU BEFORE.
YEAH, WELL MAYBE YOU'RE NOT THE REASON.
Censorsheep!! Censorsheep!!

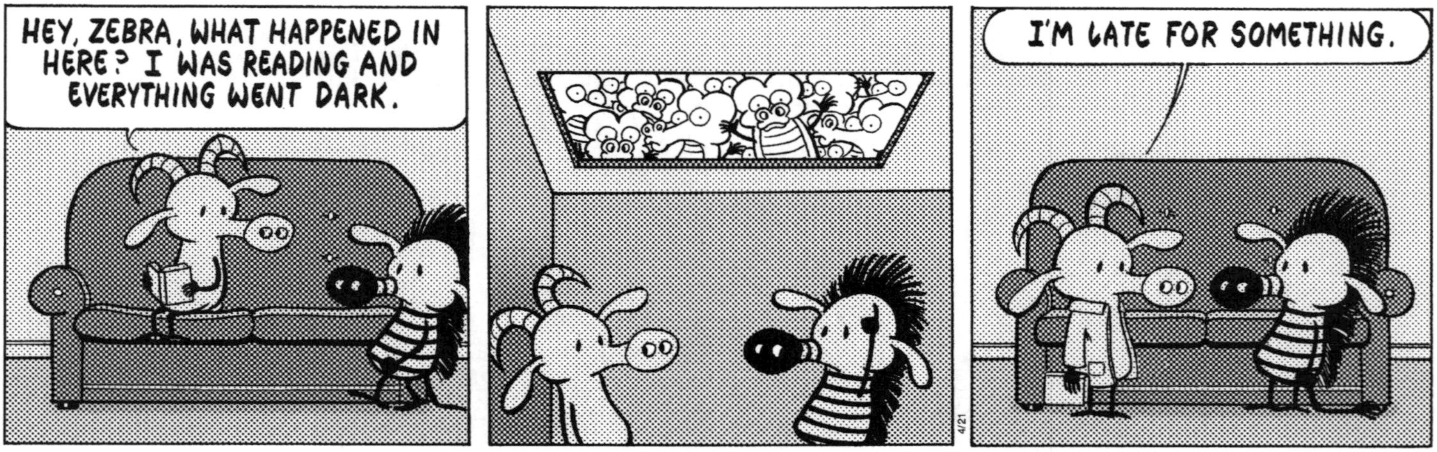
HEY, ZEBRA, WHAT HAPPENED IN HERE? I WAS READING AND EVERYTHING WENT DARK.
4/21
I'M LATE FOR SOMETHING.

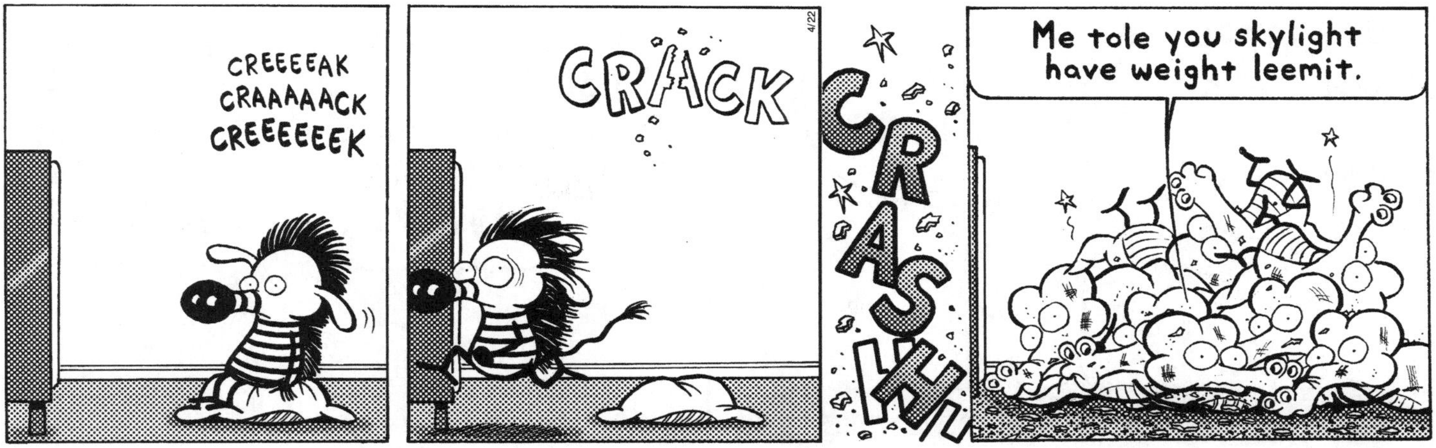
CREEEEAK
CRAAAAACK
CREEEEEEK
CRACK
4/22
CRASH
Me tole you skylight have weight leemit.

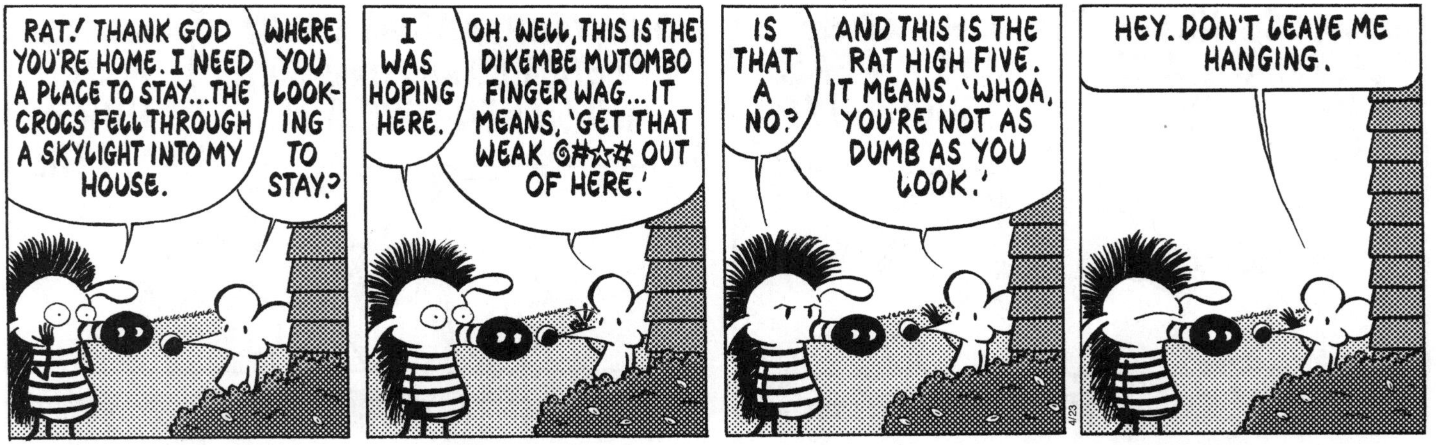
RAT! THANK GOD YOU'RE HOME. I NEED A PLACE TO STAY...THE CROCS FELL THROUGH A SKYLIGHT INTO MY HOUSE.
WHERE YOU LOOK-ING TO STAY?
I WAS HOPING HERE.
OH. WELL, THIS IS THE DIKEMBE MUTOMBO FINGER WAG...IT MEANS, 'GET THAT WEAK @#☆# OUT OF HERE.'
IS THAT A NO?
AND THIS IS THE RAT HIGH FIVE. IT MEANS, 'WHOA, YOU'RE NOT AS DUMB AS YOU LOOK.'
4/23
HEY. DON'T LEAVE ME HANGING.

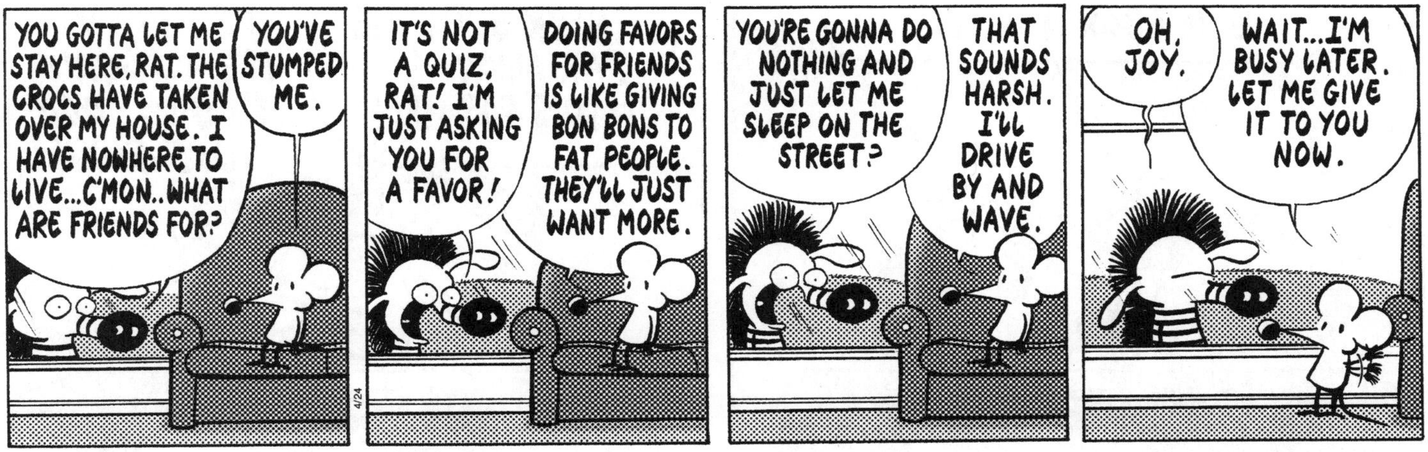
YOU GOTTA LET ME STAY HERE, RAT. THE CROCS HAVE TAKEN OVER MY HOUSE. I HAVE NOWHERE TO LIVE...C'MON..WHAT ARE FRIENDS FOR?
YOU'VE STUMPED ME.
4/24
IT'S NOT A QUIZ, RAT! I'M JUST ASKING YOU FOR A FAVOR!
DOING FAVORS FOR FRIENDS IS LIKE GIVING BON BONS TO FAT PEOPLE. THEY'LL JUST WANT MORE.
YOU'RE GONNA DO NOTHING AND JUST LET ME SLEEP ON THE STREET?
THAT SOUNDS HARSH. I'LL DRIVE BY AND WAVE.
OH, JOY.
WAIT...I'M BUSY LATER. LET ME GIVE IT TO YOU NOW.

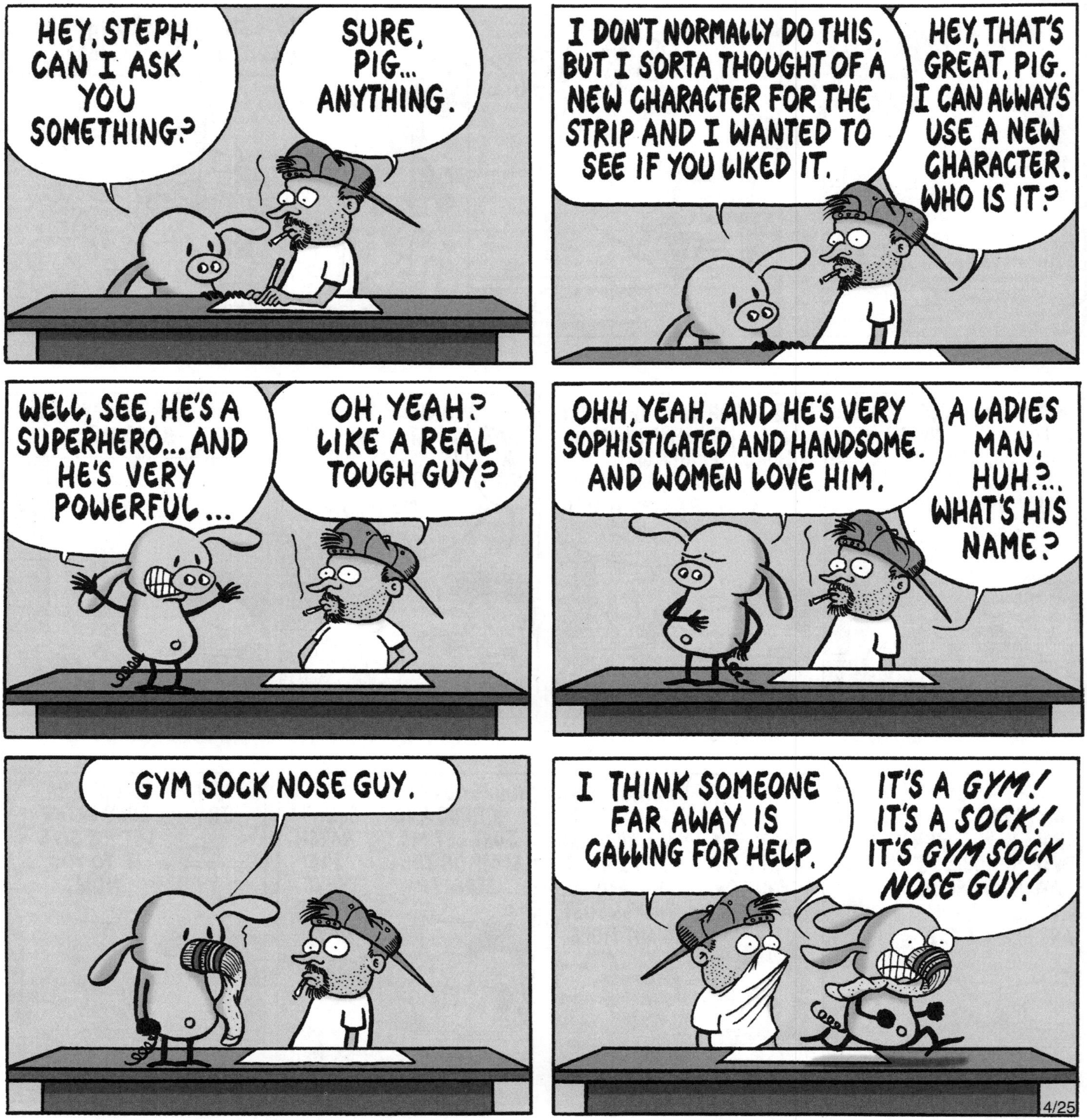
HEY, STEPH, CAN I ASK YOU SOMETHING?
SURE, PIG... ANYTHING.
I DON'T NORMALLY DO THIS, BUT I SORTA THOUGHT OF A NEW CHARACTER FOR THE STRIP AND I WANTED TO SEE IF YOU LIKED IT.
HEY, THAT'S GREAT, PIG. I CAN ALWAYS USE A NEW CHARACTER. WHO IS IT?
WELL, SEE, HE'S A SUPERHERO... AND HE'S VERY POWERFUL...
OH, YEAH? LIKE A REAL TOUGH GUY?
OHH, YEAH. AND HE'S VERY SOPHISTICATED AND HANDSOME. AND WOMEN LOVE HIM.
A LADIES MAN, HUH?... WHAT'S HIS NAME?
GYM SOCK NOSE GUY.
I THINK SOMEONE FAR AWAY IS CALLING FOR HELP.
IT'S A *GYM!* IT'S A *SOCK!* IT'S *GYM SOCK NOSE GUY!*
4/25

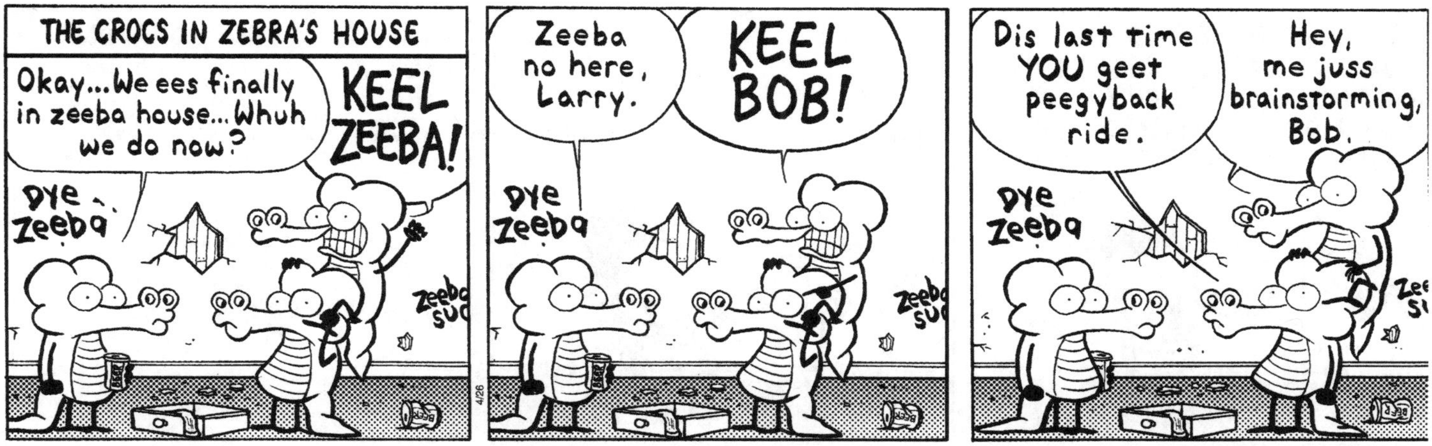
THE CROCS IN ZEBRA'S HOUSE
Okay...We ees finally in zeeba house...Whuh we do now?
KEEL ZEEBA!
Dye Zeeba
Zeeba no here, Larry.
KEEL BOB!
Dye Zeeba
Dis last time YOU geet peegyback ride.
Hey, me juss brainstorming, Bob.
Dye Zeeba

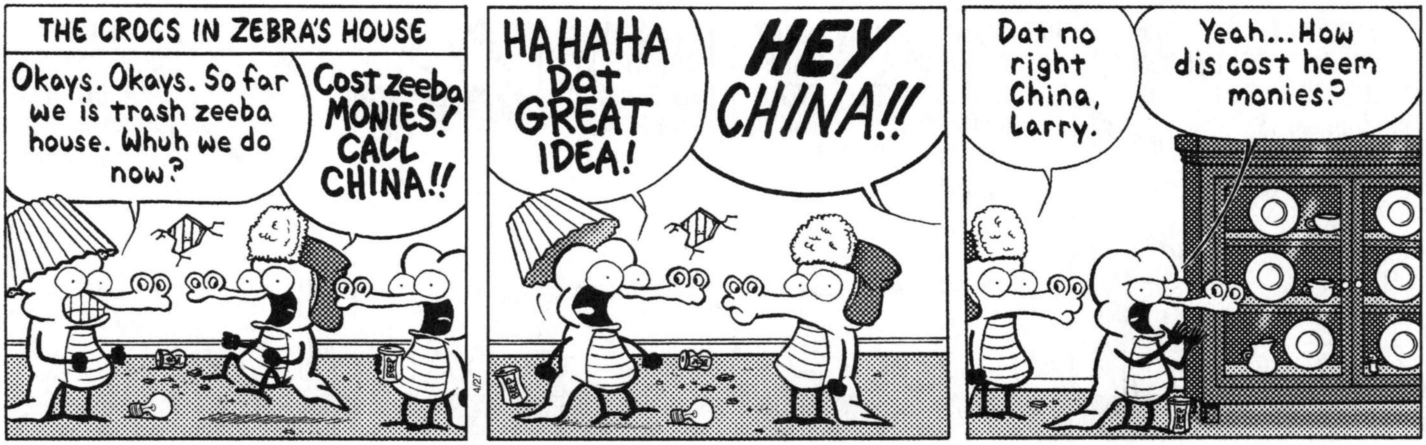
THE CROCS IN ZEBRA'S HOUSE
Okays. Okays. So far we is trash zeeba house. Whuh we do now?
Cost zeeba MONIES! CALL CHINA!!
HAHAHA Dat GREAT IDEA!
HEY CHINA!!
Dat no right China, Larry.
Yeah...How dis cost heem monies?

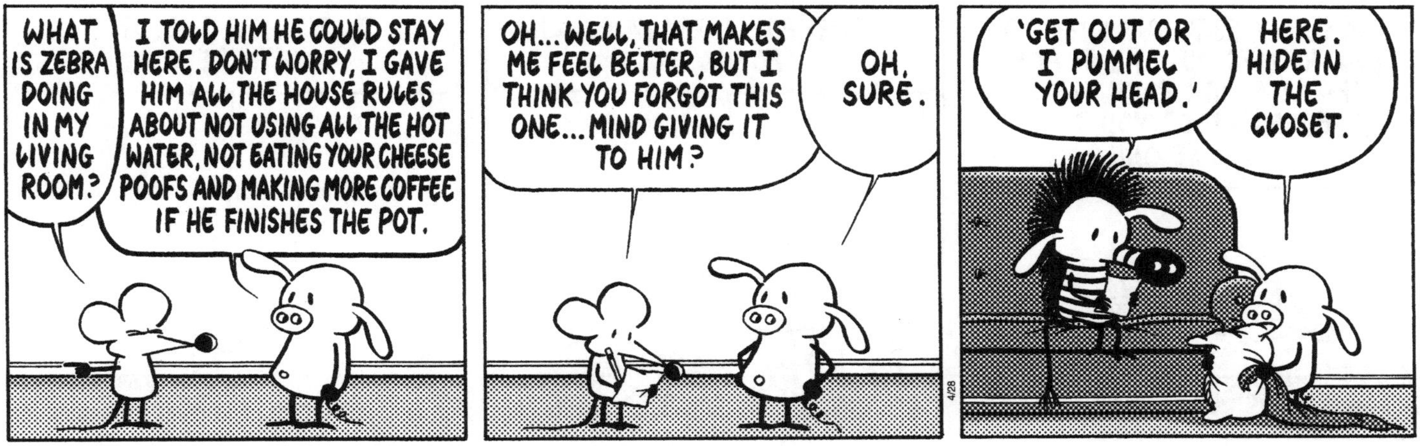
WHAT IS ZEBRA DOING IN MY LIVING ROOM?
I TOLD HIM HE COULD STAY HERE. DON'T WORRY, I GAVE HIM ALL THE HOUSE RULES ABOUT NOT USING ALL THE HOT WATER, NOT EATING YOUR CHEESE POOFS AND MAKING MORE COFFEE IF HE FINISHES THE POT.
OH...WELL, THAT MAKES ME FEEL BETTER, BUT I THINK YOU FORGOT THIS ONE...MIND GIVING IT TO HIM?
OH, SURE.
'GET OUT OR I PUMMEL YOUR HEAD.'
HERE. HIDE IN THE CLOSET.

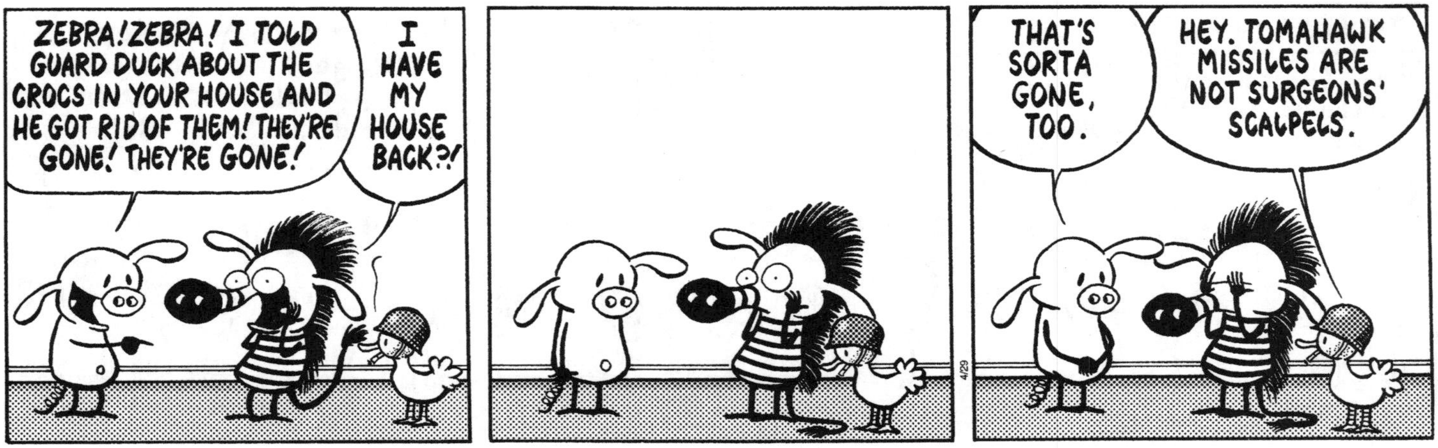
ZEBRA! ZEBRA! I TOLD GUARD DUCK ABOUT THE CROCS IN YOUR HOUSE AND HE GOT RID OF THEM! THEY'RE GONE! THEY'RE GONE!
I HAVE MY HOUSE BACK?!
THAT'S SORTA GONE, TOO.
HEY. TOMAHAWK MISSILES ARE NOT SURGEONS' SCALPELS.
4/29

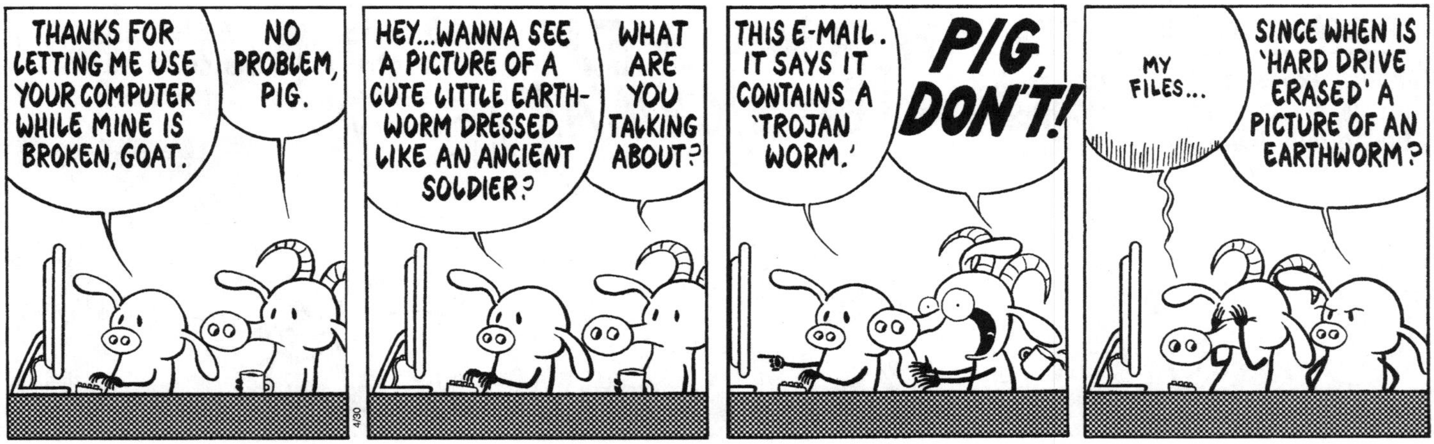
THANKS FOR LETTING ME USE YOUR COMPUTER WHILE MINE IS BROKEN, GOAT.
NO PROBLEM, PIG.
4/30
HEY...WANNA SEE A PICTURE OF A CUTE LITTLE EARTHWORM DRESSED LIKE AN ANCIENT SOLDIER?
WHAT ARE YOU TALKING ABOUT?
THIS E-MAIL. IT SAYS IT CONTAINS A 'TROJAN WORM.'
PIG, DON'T!
MY FILES...
SINCE WHEN IS 'HARD DRIVE ERASED' A PICTURE OF AN EARTHWORM?

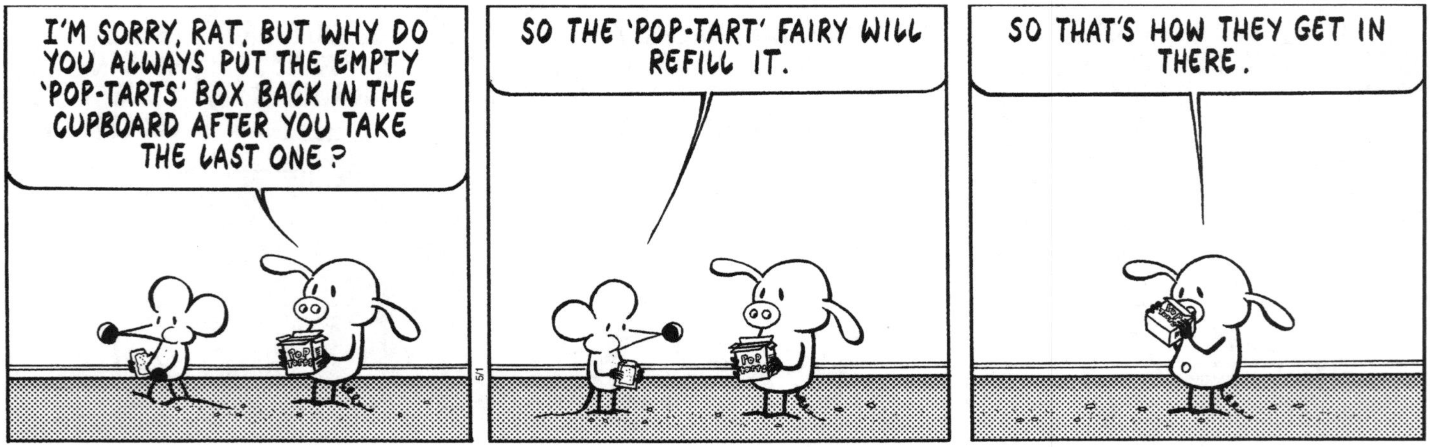
I'M SORRY, RAT, BUT WHY DO YOU ALWAYS PUT THE EMPTY 'POP-TARTS' BOX BACK IN THE CUPBOARD AFTER YOU TAKE THE LAST ONE?
5/1
SO THE 'POP-TART' FAIRY WILL REFILL IT.
SO THAT'S HOW THEY GET IN THERE.

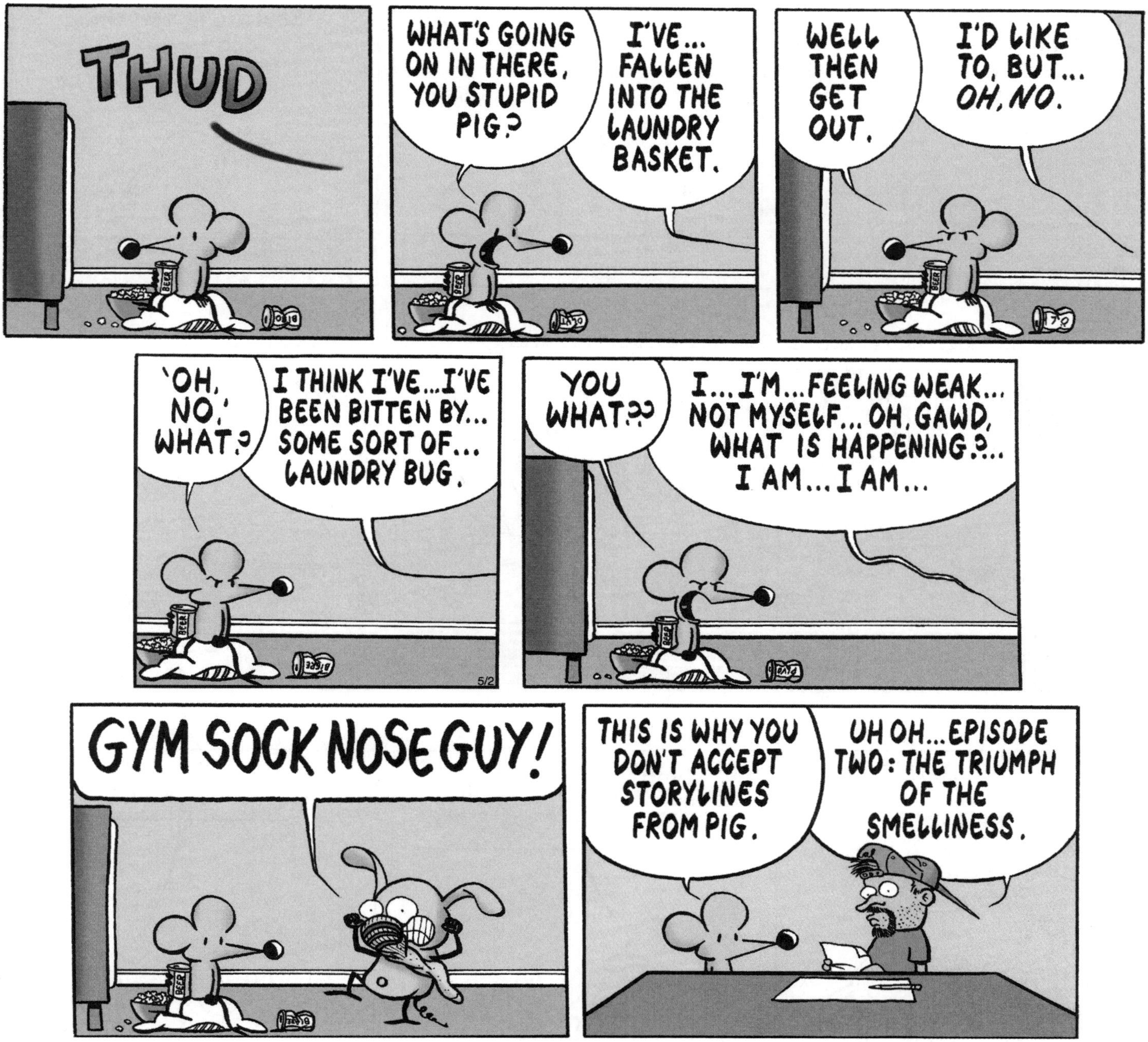
THUD
WHAT'S GOING ON IN THERE, YOU STUPID PIG?
I'VE... FALLEN INTO THE LAUNDRY BASKET.
WELL THEN GET OUT.
I'D LIKE TO, BUT... *OH, NO.*
'OH, NO,' WHAT?
I THINK I'VE...I'VE BEEN BITTEN BY... SOME SORT OF... LAUNDRY BUG.
YOU WHAT??
I...I'M...FEELING WEAK... NOT MYSELF... OH, GAWD, WHAT IS HAPPENING?... I AM...I AM...
GYM SOCK NOSE GUY!
THIS IS WHY YOU DON'T ACCEPT STORYLINES FROM PIG.
UH OH...EPISODE TWO: THE TRIUMPH OF THE SMELLINESS.

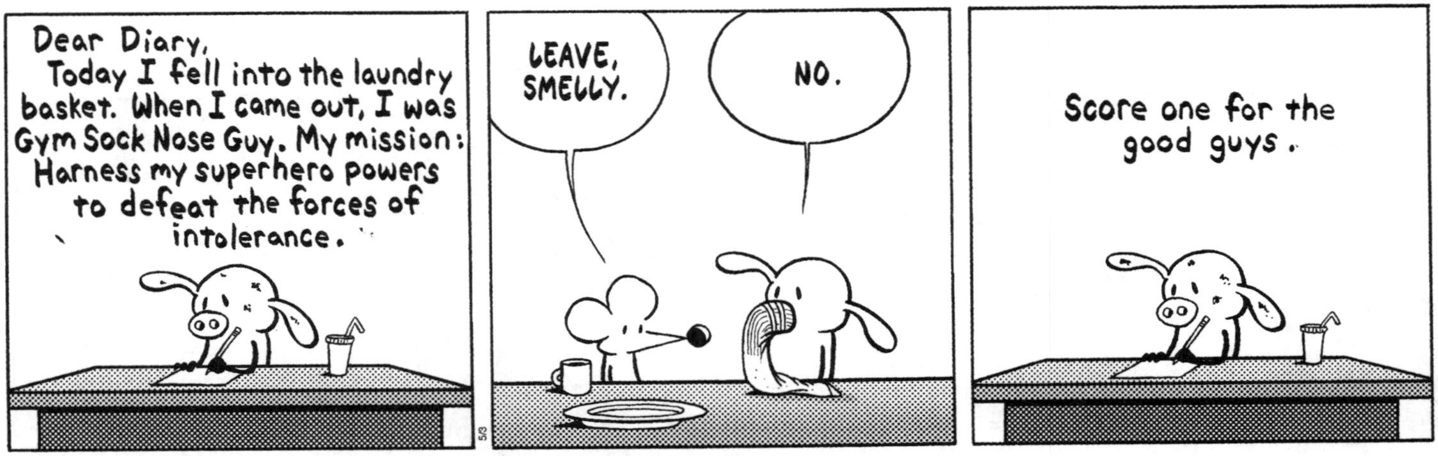
Dear Diary,
Today I fell into the laundry basket. When I came out, I was Gym Sock Nose Guy. My mission: Harness my superhero powers to defeat the forces of intolerance.
5/3
LEAVE, SMELLY.
NO.
Score one for the good guys.

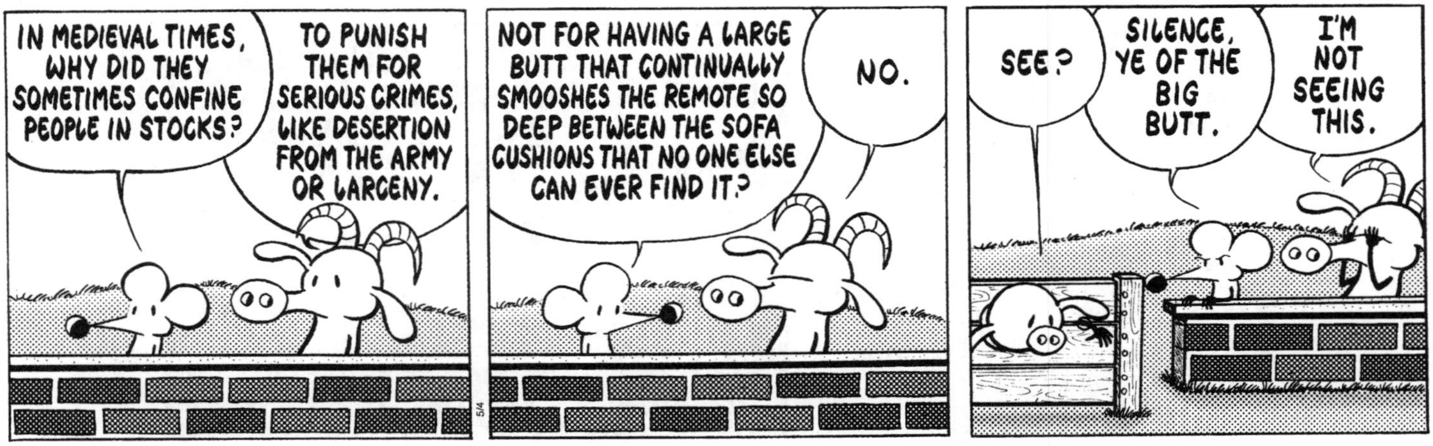
IN MEDIEVAL TIMES, WHY DID THEY SOMETIMES CONFINE PEOPLE IN STOCKS?
TO PUNISH THEM FOR SERIOUS CRIMES, LIKE DESERTION FROM THE ARMY OR LARCENY.
5/4
NOT FOR HAVING A LARGE BUTT THAT CONTINUALLY SMOOSHES THE REMOTE SO DEEP BETWEEN THE SOFA CUSHIONS THAT NO ONE ELSE CAN EVER FIND IT?
NO.
SEE?
SILENCE, YE OF THE BIG BUTT.
I'M NOT SEEING THIS.

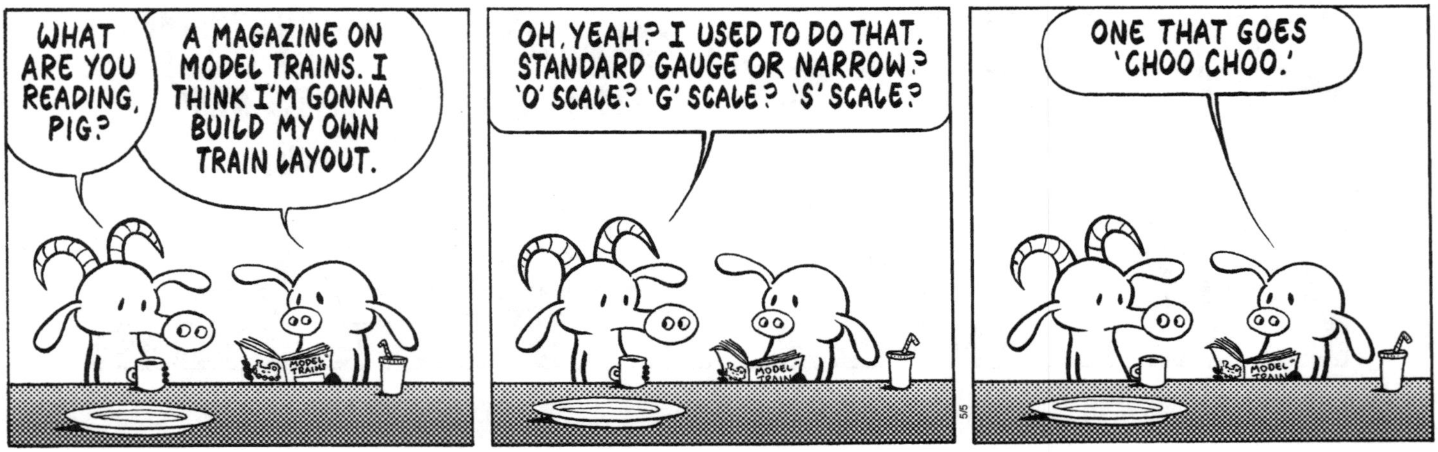
WHAT ARE YOU READING, PIG?
A MAGAZINE ON MODEL TRAINS. I THINK I'M GONNA BUILD MY OWN TRAIN LAYOUT.
MODEL TRAINS
OH, YEAH? I USED TO DO THAT. STANDARD GAUGE OR NARROW? 'O' SCALE? 'G' SCALE? 'S' SCALE?
5/5
ONE THAT GOES 'CHOO CHOO.'

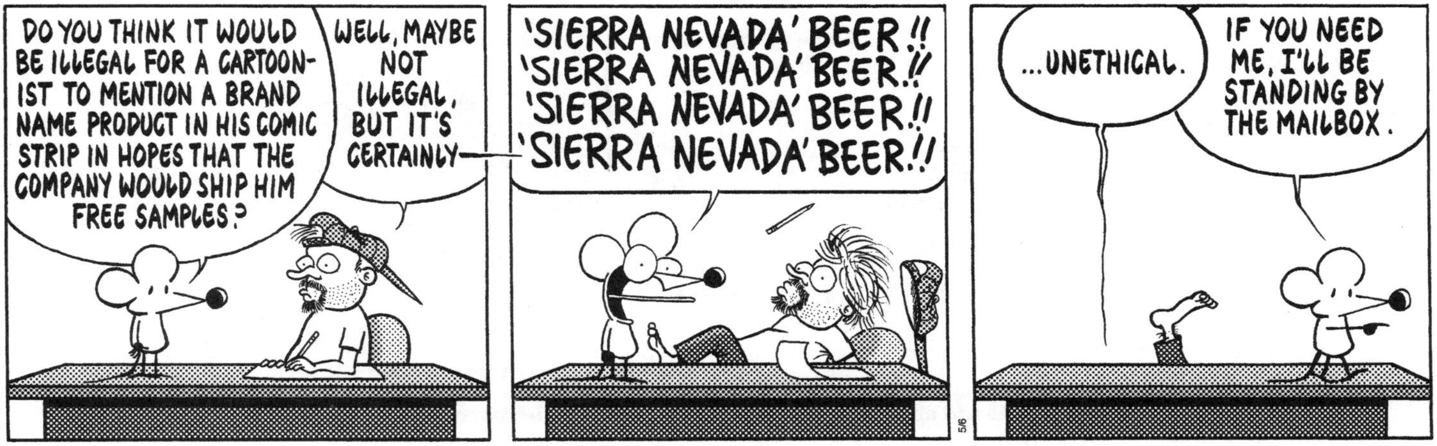
DO YOU THINK IT WOULD BE ILLEGAL FOR A CARTOONIST TO MENTION A BRAND NAME PRODUCT IN HIS COMIC STRIP IN HOPES THAT THE COMPANY WOULD SHIP HIM FREE SAMPLES?
WELL, MAYBE NOT ILLEGAL, BUT IT'S CERTAINLY—
'SIERRA NEVADA' BEER!! 'SIERRA NEVADA' BEER!! 'SIERRA NEVADA' BEER!! 'SIERRA NEVADA' BEER!!
...UNETHICAL.
IF YOU NEED ME, I'LL BE STANDING BY THE MAILBOX.
5/6

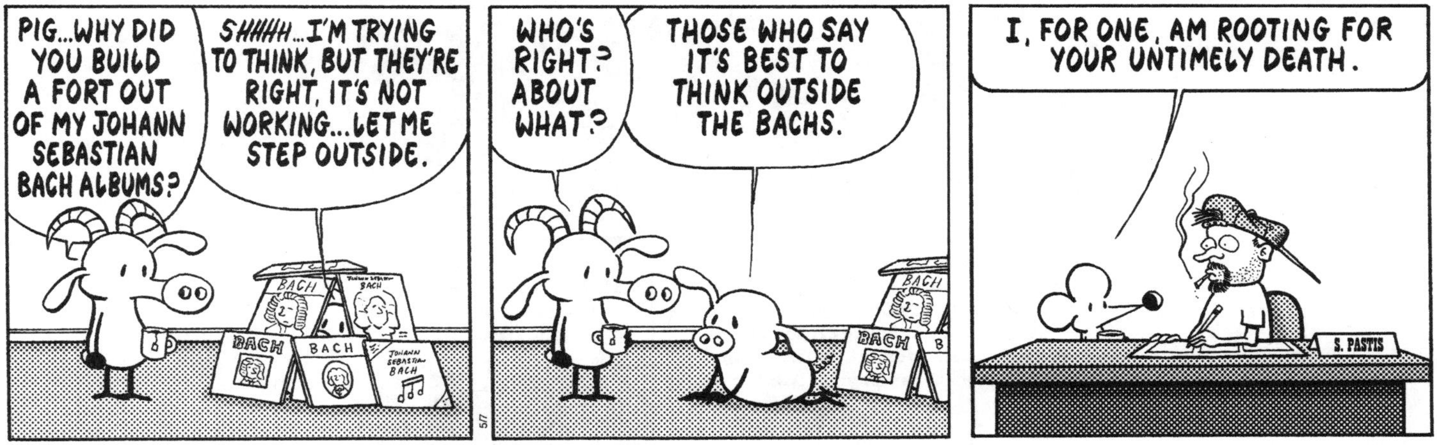
PIG...WHY DID YOU BUILD A FORT OUT OF MY JOHANN SEBASTIAN BACH ALBUMS?
SHHHH...I'M TRYING TO THINK, BUT THEY'RE RIGHT, IT'S NOT WORKING...LET ME STEP OUTSIDE.
BACH
BACH
BACH
JOHANN SEBASTIAN BACH
5/7
WHO'S RIGHT? ABOUT WHAT?
THOSE WHO SAY IT'S BEST TO THINK OUTSIDE THE BACHS.
BACH
I, FOR ONE, AM ROOTING FOR YOUR UNTIMELY DEATH.
S. PASTIS

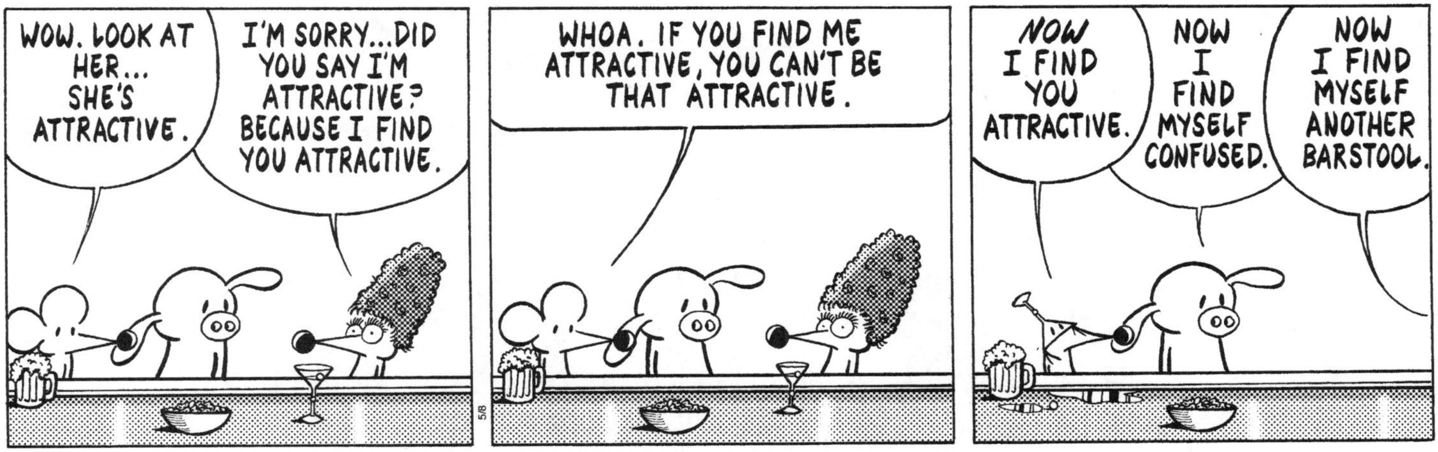
WOW. LOOK AT HER... SHE'S ATTRACTIVE.
I'M SORRY...DID YOU SAY I'M ATTRACTIVE? BECAUSE I FIND YOU ATTRACTIVE.
5/8
WHOA. IF YOU FIND ME ATTRACTIVE, YOU CAN'T BE THAT ATTRACTIVE.
NOW I FIND YOU ATTRACTIVE.
NOW I FIND MYSELF CONFUSED.
NOW I FIND MYSELF ANOTHER BARSTOOL.

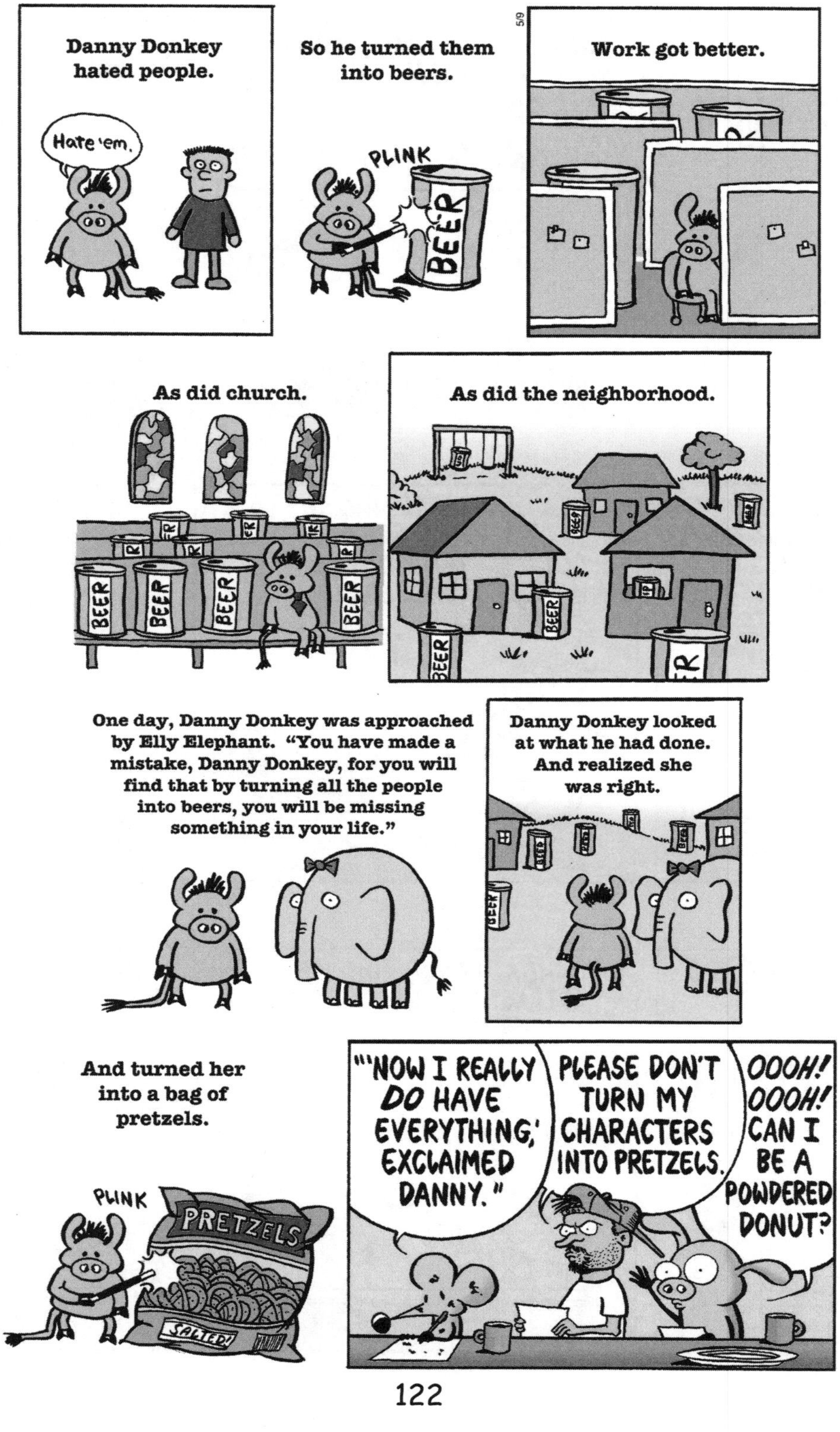
Danny Donkey hated people.
Hate 'em.
So he turned them into beers.
PLINK
BEER
5/9
Work got better.
As did church.
BEER
BEER
BEER
BEER
As did the neighborhood.
BEER
BEER
One day, Danny Donkey was approached by Elly Elephant. "You have made a mistake, Danny Donkey, for you will find that by turning all the people into beers, you will be missing something in your life."
Danny Donkey looked at what he had done. And realized she was right.
And turned her into a bag of pretzels.
PLINK
PRETZELS
SALTED!
"'NOW I REALLY DO HAVE EVERYTHING,' EXCLAIMED DANNY."
PLEASE DON'T TURN MY CHARACTERS INTO PRETZELS.
OOOH! OOOH! CAN I BE A POWDERED DONUT?

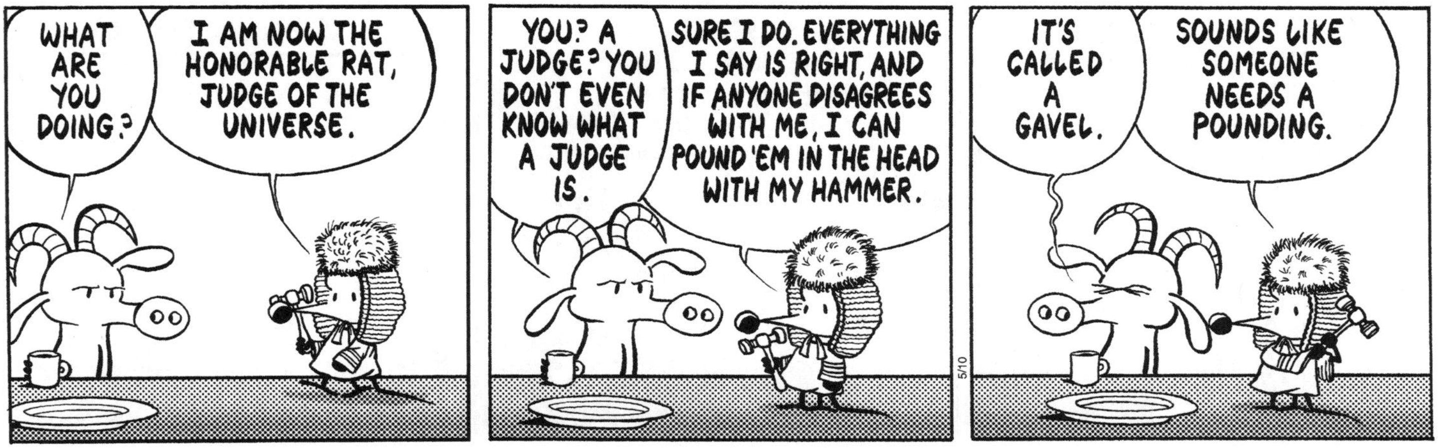
WHAT ARE YOU DOING?
I AM NOW THE HONORABLE RAT, JUDGE OF THE UNIVERSE.
YOU? A JUDGE? YOU DON'T EVEN KNOW WHAT A JUDGE IS.
SURE I DO. EVERYTHING I SAY IS RIGHT, AND IF ANYONE DISAGREES WITH ME, I CAN POUND 'EM IN THE HEAD WITH MY HAMMER.
5/10
IT'S CALLED A GAVEL.
SOUNDS LIKE SOMEONE NEEDS A POUNDING.

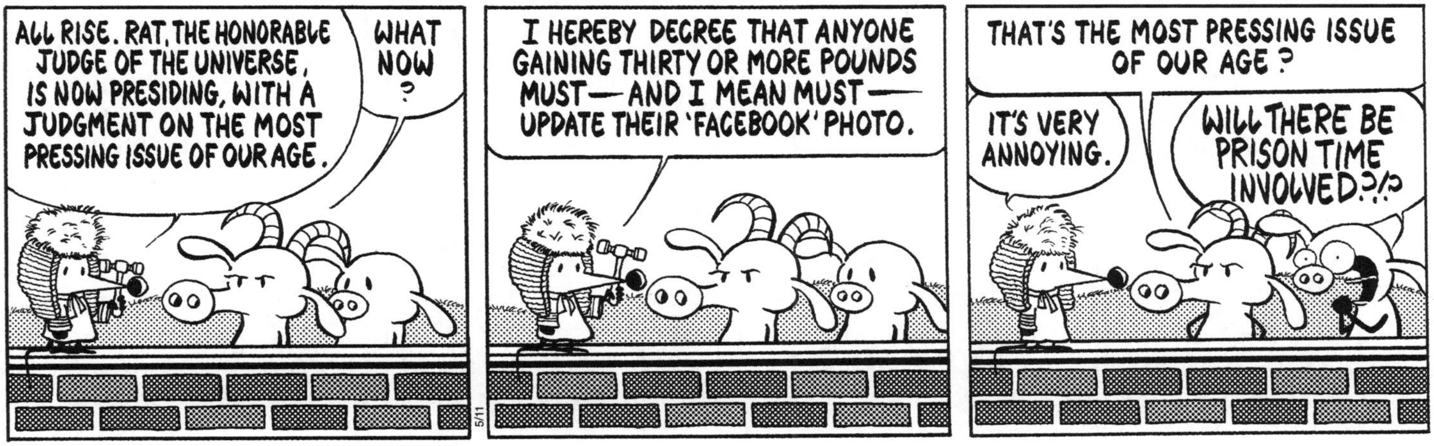
ALL RISE. RAT, THE HONORABLE JUDGE OF THE UNIVERSE, IS NOW PRESIDING, WITH A JUDGMENT ON THE MOST PRESSING ISSUE OF OUR AGE.
WHAT NOW?
5/11
I HEREBY DECREE THAT ANYONE GAINING THIRTY OR MORE POUNDS MUST—AND I MEAN MUST—UPDATE THEIR 'FACEBOOK' PHOTO.
THAT'S THE MOST PRESSING ISSUE OF OUR AGE?
IT'S VERY ANNOYING.
WILL THERE BE PRISON TIME INVOLVED?!?

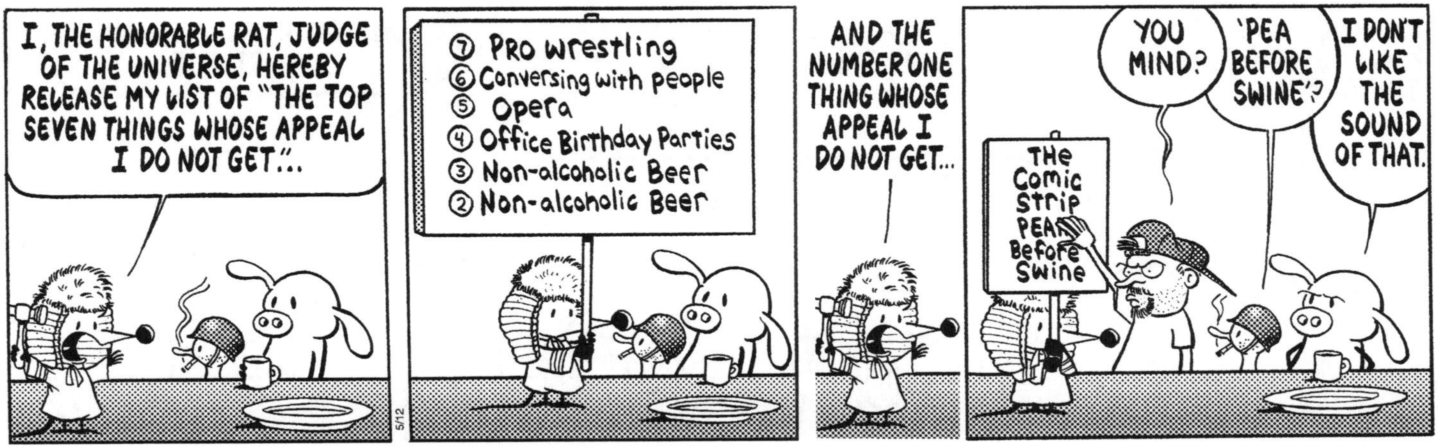
I, THE HONORABLE RAT, JUDGE OF THE UNIVERSE, HEREBY RELEASE MY LIST OF "THE TOP SEVEN THINGS WHOSE APPEAL I DO NOT GET."...
5/12
⑦ Pro wrestling
⑥ Conversing with people
⑤ Opera
④ Office Birthday Parties
③ Non-alcoholic Beer
② Non-alcoholic Beer
AND THE NUMBER ONE THING WHOSE APPEAL I DO NOT GET...
The Comic Strip PEA Before Swine
YOU MIND?
'PEA BEFORE SWINE'?
I DON'T LIKE THE SOUND OF THAT.

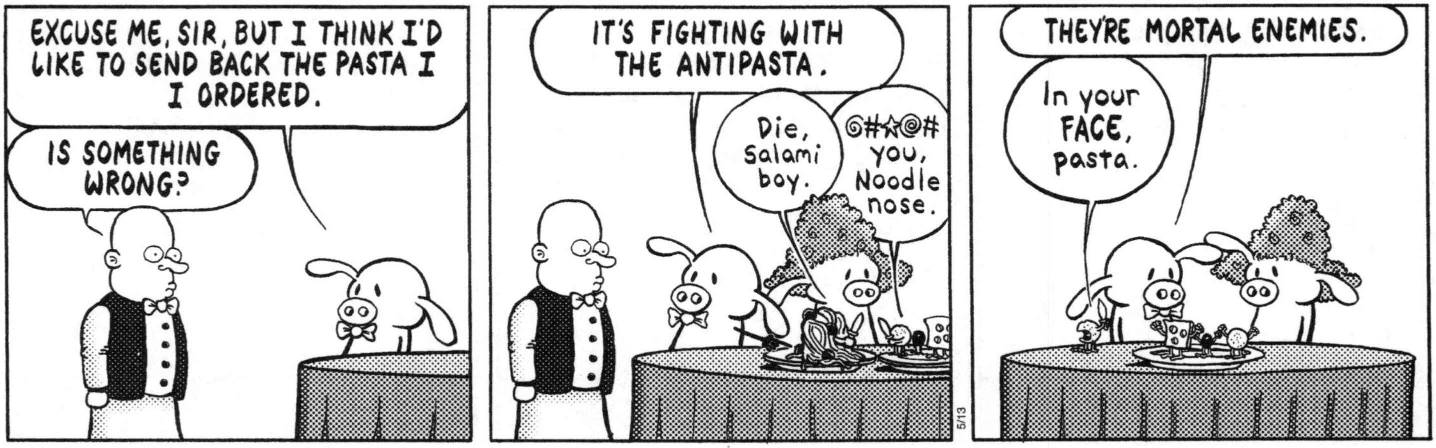
IS SOMETHING WRONG?
EXCUSE ME, SIR, BUT I THINK I'D LIKE TO SEND BACK THE PASTA I I ORDERED.
IT'S FIGHTING WITH THE ANTIPASTA.
Die, Salami boy.
@#☆@# you, Noodle nose.
THEY'RE MORTAL ENEMIES.
In your FACE, pasta.
5/13

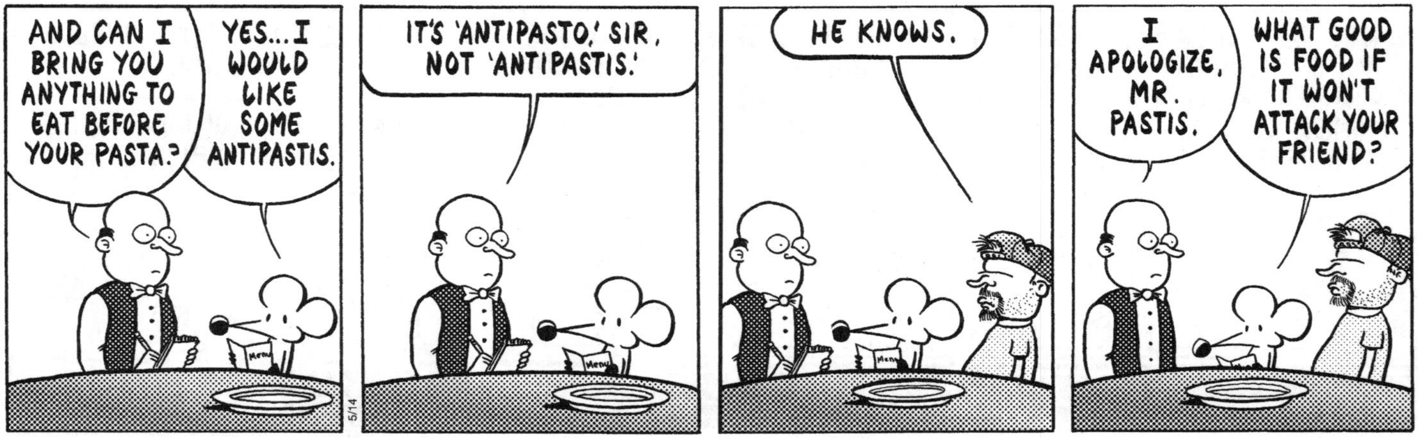
AND CAN I BRING YOU ANYTHING TO EAT BEFORE YOUR PASTA?
YES...I WOULD LIKE SOME ANTIPASTIS.
IT'S 'ANTIPASTO,' SIR, NOT 'ANTIPASTIS.'
HE KNOWS.
I APOLOGIZE, MR. PASTIS.
WHAT GOOD IS FOOD IF IT WON'T ATTACK YOUR FRIEND?
5/14

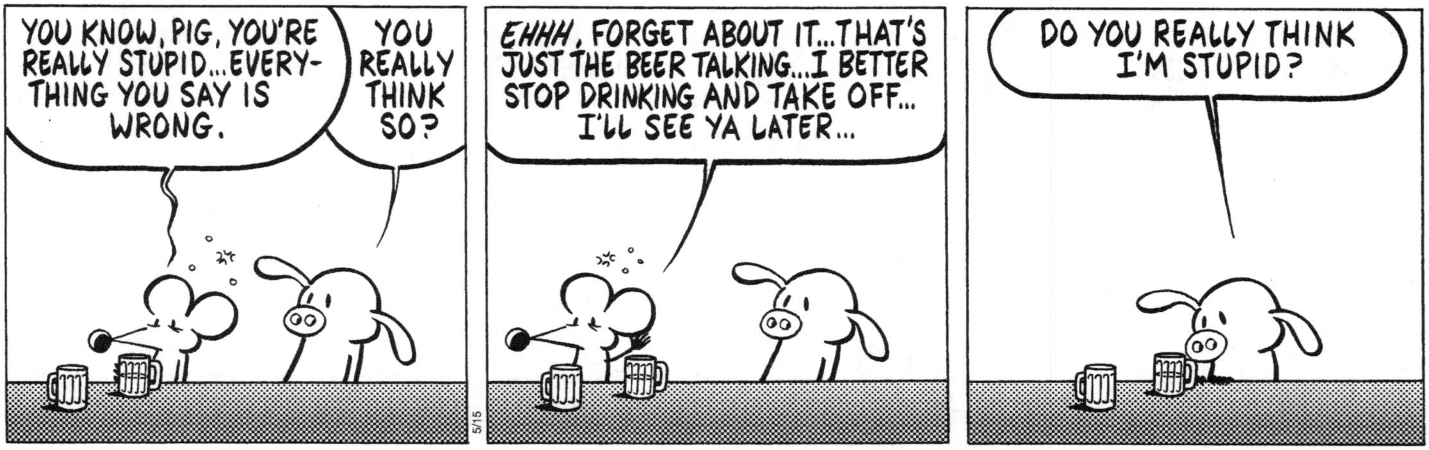
YOU KNOW, PIG, YOU'RE REALLY STUPID...EVERYTHING YOU SAY IS WRONG.
YOU REALLY THINK SO?
EHHH, FORGET ABOUT IT...THAT'S JUST THE BEER TALKING...I BETTER STOP DRINKING AND TAKE OFF... I'LL SEE YA LATER...
DO YOU REALLY THINK I'M STUPID?
5/15

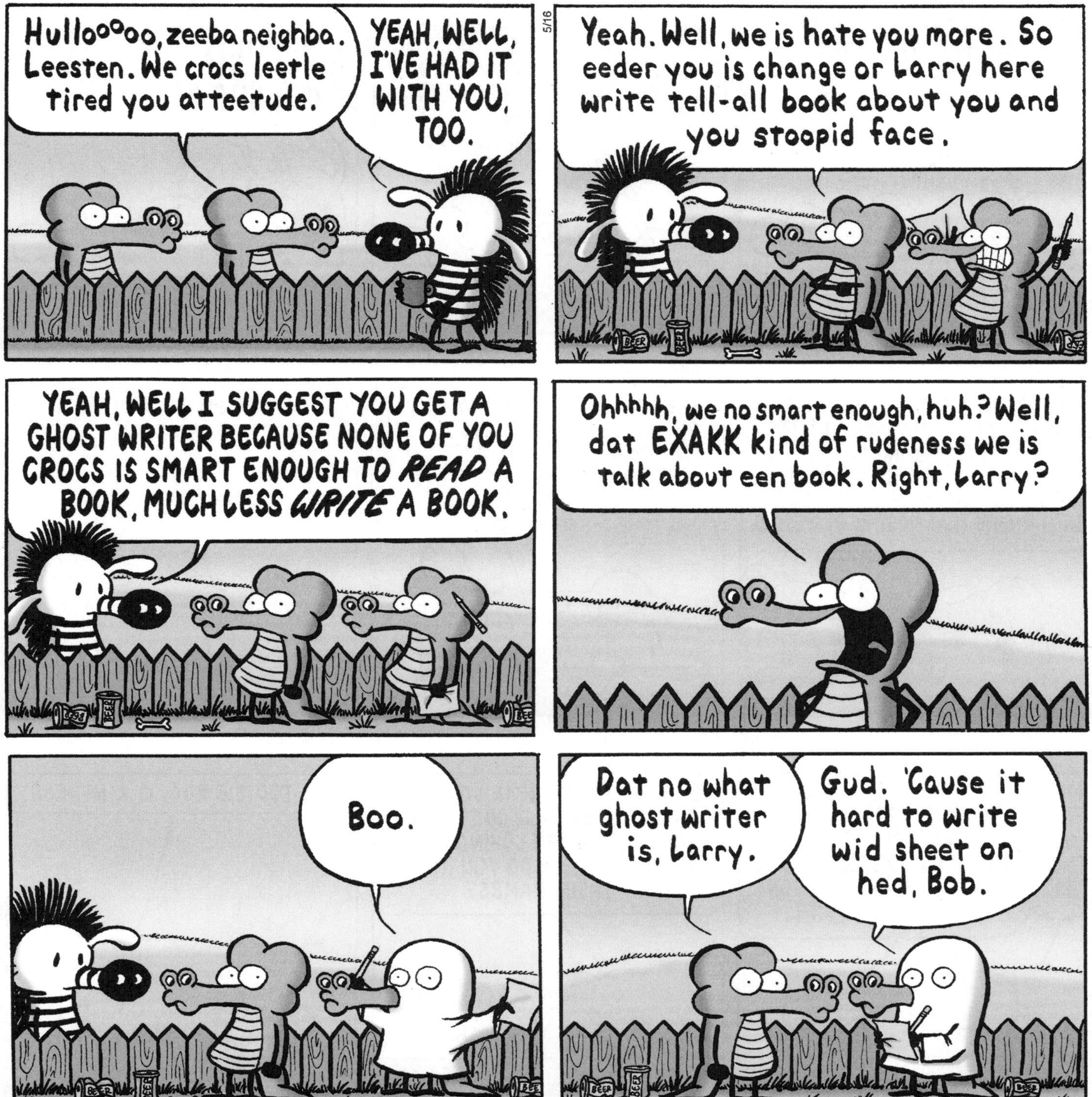

5/16
Hulloooo, zeeba neighba. Leesten. We crocs leetle tired you atteetude.
YEAH, WELL, I'VE HAD IT WITH YOU, TOO.
Yeah. Well, we is hate you more. So eeder you is change or Larry here write tell-all book about you and you stoopid face.
YEAH, WELL I SUGGEST YOU GET A GHOST WRITER BECAUSE NONE OF YOU CROCS IS SMART ENOUGH TO *READ* A BOOK, MUCH LESS *WRITE* A BOOK.
Ohhhhh, we no smart enough, huh? Well, dat EXAKK kind of rudeness we is talk about een book. Right, Larry?
Boo.
Dat no what ghost writer is, Larry.
Gud. 'Cause it hard to write wid sheet on hed, Bob.

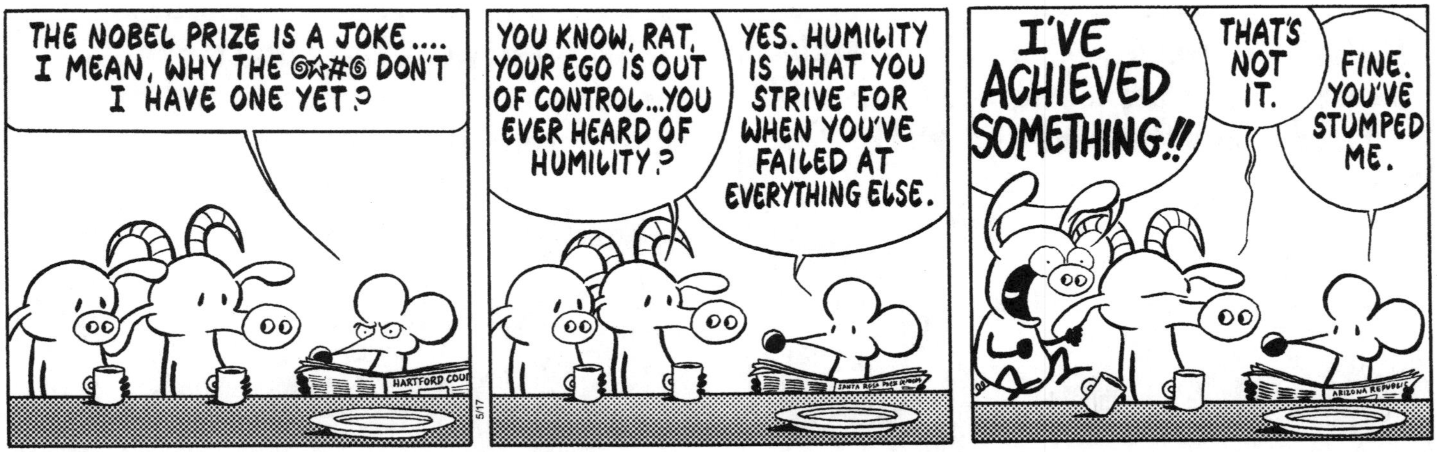
THE NOBEL PRIZE IS A JOKE.... I MEAN, WHY THE @☆#@ DON'T I HAVE ONE YET?
HARTFORD COU
5/17
YOU KNOW, RAT, YOUR EGO IS OUT OF CONTROL...YOU EVER HEARD OF HUMILITY?
YES. HUMILITY IS WHAT YOU STRIVE FOR WHEN YOU'VE FAILED AT EVERYTHING ELSE.
I'VE ACHIEVED SOMETHING!!
THAT'S NOT IT.
FINE. YOU'VE STUMPED ME.
ARIZONA REPUBLIC

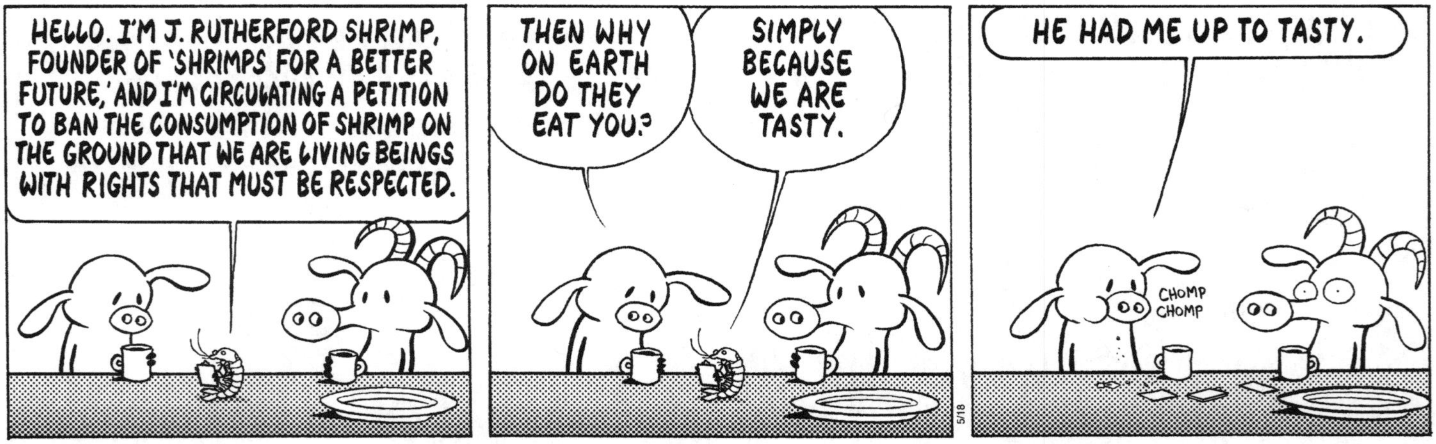
HELLO. I'M J. RUTHERFORD SHRIMP, FOUNDER OF 'SHRIMPS FOR A BETTER FUTURE,' AND I'M CIRCULATING A PETITION TO BAN THE CONSUMPTION OF SHRIMP ON THE GROUND THAT WE ARE LIVING BEINGS WITH RIGHTS THAT MUST BE RESPECTED.
THEN WHY ON EARTH DO THEY EAT YOU?
SIMPLY BECAUSE WE ARE TASTY.
5/18
HE HAD ME UP TO TASTY.
CHOMP CHOMP

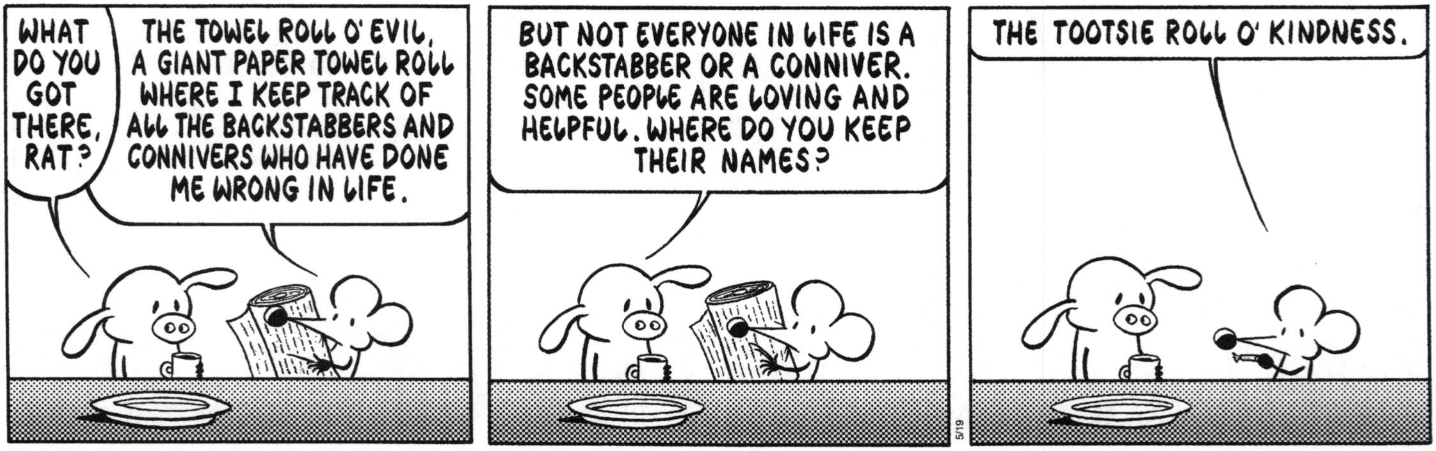
WHAT DO YOU GOT THERE, RAT?
THE TOWEL ROLL O' EVIL, A GIANT PAPER TOWEL ROLL WHERE I KEEP TRACK OF ALL THE BACKSTABBERS AND CONNIVERS WHO HAVE DONE ME WRONG IN LIFE.
BUT NOT EVERYONE IN LIFE IS A BACKSTABBER OR A CONNIVER. SOME PEOPLE ARE LOVING AND HELPFUL. WHERE DO YOU KEEP THEIR NAMES?
5/19
THE TOOTSIE ROLL O' KINDNESS.

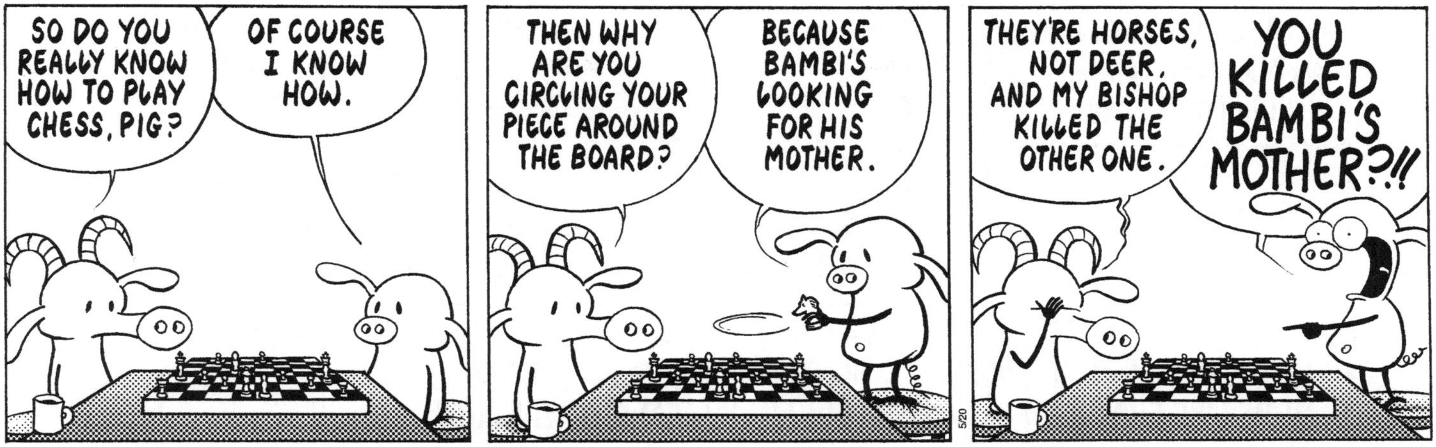
SO DO YOU REALLY KNOW HOW TO PLAY CHESS, PIG?
OF COURSE I KNOW HOW.
THEN WHY ARE YOU CIRCLING YOUR PIECE AROUND THE BOARD?
BECAUSE BAMBI'S LOOKING FOR HIS MOTHER.
THEY'RE HORSES, NOT DEER, AND MY BISHOP KILLED THE OTHER ONE.
YOU KILLED BAMBI'S MOTHER?!!

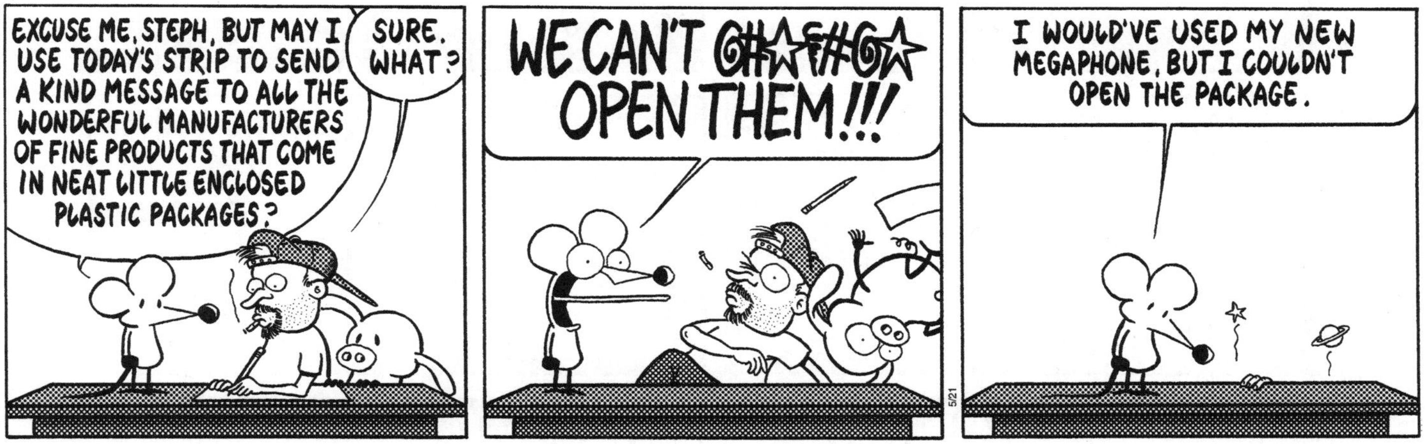
EXCUSE ME, STEPH, BUT MAY I USE TODAY'S STRIP TO SEND A KIND MESSAGE TO ALL THE WONDERFUL MANUFACTURERS OF FINE PRODUCTS THAT COME IN NEAT LITTLE ENCLOSED PLASTIC PACKAGES?
SURE. WHAT?
WE CAN'T @#☆#@☆ OPEN THEM!!!
I WOULD'VE USED MY NEW MEGAPHONE, BUT I COULDN'T OPEN THE PACKAGE.

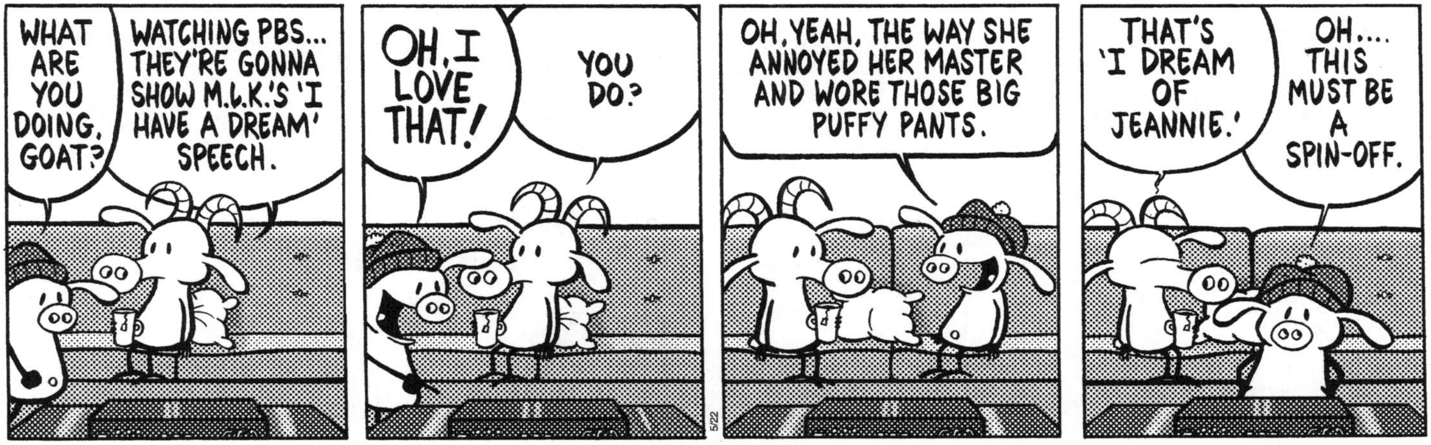
WHAT ARE YOU DOING, GOAT?
WATCHING PBS... THEY'RE GONNA SHOW M.L.K.'S 'I HAVE A DREAM' SPEECH.
OH, I LOVE THAT!
YOU DO?
OH, YEAH, THE WAY SHE ANNOYED HER MASTER AND WORE THOSE BIG PUFFY PANTS.
THAT'S 'I DREAM OF JEANNIE.'
OH.... THIS MUST BE A SPIN-OFF.

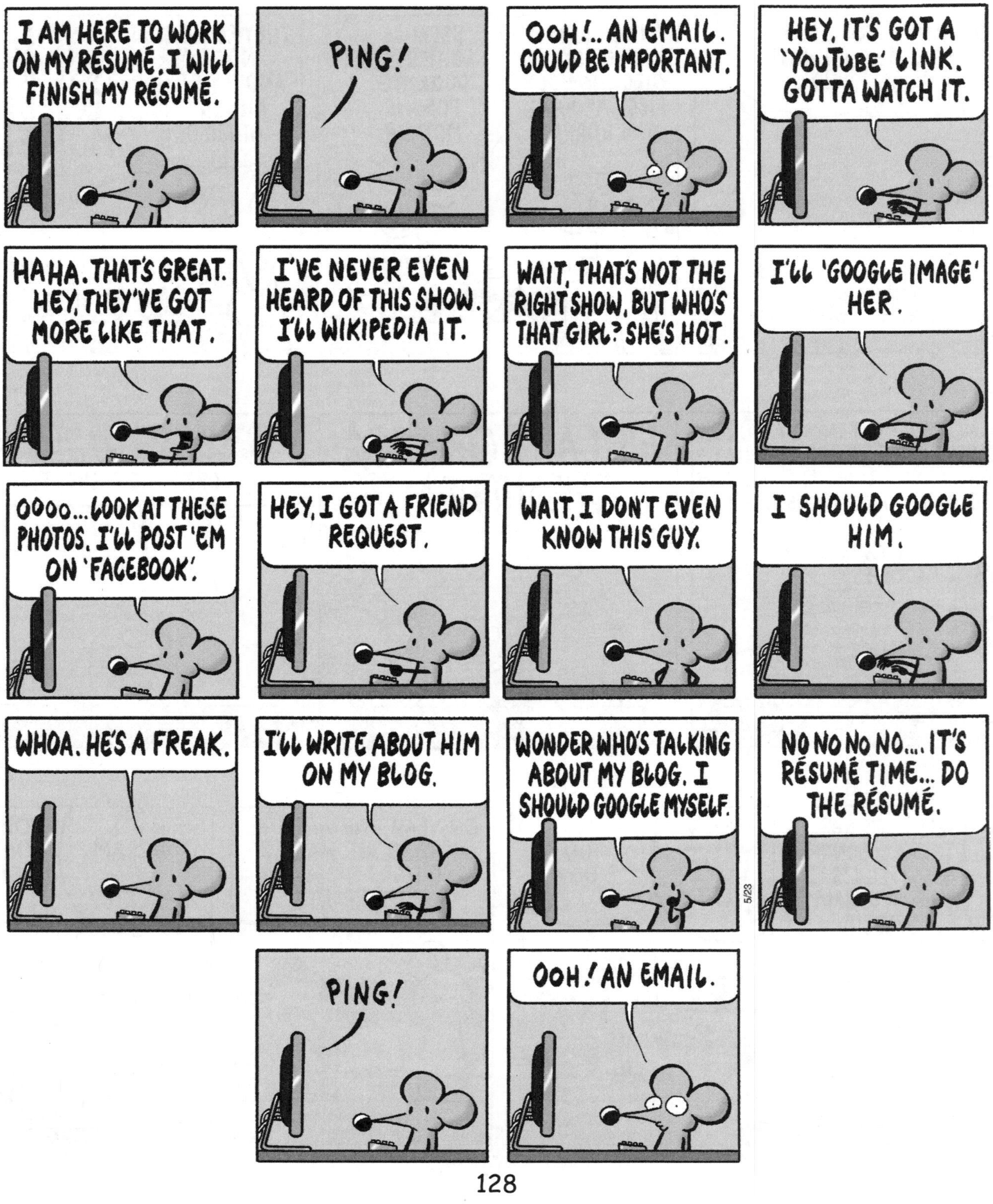
I AM HERE TO WORK ON MY RÉSUMÉ. I WILL FINISH MY RÉSUMÉ.
PING!
OOH!.. AN EMAIL. COULD BE IMPORTANT.
HEY, IT'S GOT A 'YOUTUBE' LINK. GOTTA WATCH IT.
HAHA. THAT'S GREAT. HEY, THEY'VE GOT MORE LIKE THAT.
I'VE NEVER EVEN HEARD OF THIS SHOW. I'LL WIKIPEDIA IT.
WAIT, THAT'S NOT THE RIGHT SHOW, BUT WHO'S THAT GIRL? SHE'S HOT.
I'LL 'GOOGLE IMAGE' HER.
OOOO... LOOK AT THESE PHOTOS. I'LL POST 'EM ON 'FACEBOOK'.
HEY, I GOT A FRIEND REQUEST.
WAIT, I DON'T EVEN KNOW THIS GUY.
I SHOULD GOOGLE HIM.
WHOA. HE'S A FREAK.
I'LL WRITE ABOUT HIM ON MY BLOG.
WONDER WHO'S TALKING ABOUT MY BLOG. I SHOULD GOOGLE MYSELF.
5/23
NO NO NO NO.... IT'S RÉSUMÉ TIME... DO THE RÉSUMÉ.
PING!
OOH! AN EMAIL.